The Culture and Philosophy
of Ridley Scott

The Culture and Philosophy
of Ridley Scott

Edited by Adam Barkman, Ashley Barkman, and Nancy Kang

LEXINGTON BOOKS
Lanham • Boulder • New York • Toronto • Plymouth, UK

Published by Lexington Books
A wholly owned subsidiary of The Rowman & Littlefield Publishing Group, Inc.
4501 Forbes Boulevard, Suite 200, Lanham, Maryland 20706
www.rowman.com

10 Thornbury Road, Plymouth PL6 7PP, United Kingdom

Copyright © 2013 by Lexington Books

British Library Cataloguing in Publication Information Available

Library of Congress Cataloging-in-Publication Data Available

♾ The paper used in this publication meets the minimum requirements of American National Standard for Information Sciences Permanence of Paper for Printed Library Materials, ANSI/NISO Z39.48-1992.

Printed in the United States of America

To Our Parents

Contents

Acknowledgments

Adam Barkman: I would like to thank Ashley and Nancy for their work on this project—Ashley for coming up with the idea and bringing us all together, and Nancy for her competence and skill at all levels throughout this project; it's no exaggeration to say that I could not have done this without you both. I would also like to acknowledge the generous grant I received from Redeemer University College to help fund the typesetting and indexing of this book.

Ashley Barkman: I am thankful to have had the opportunity to collaborate with two brilliant individuals whom I also have the privilege of calling friends: Adam and Nancy, thank you for your hard work and dedication to this project. This volume would not have been possible without either of you!

Nancy Kang: I am grateful to Adam and Ashley Barkman for their invaluable friendship, scholarly enthusiasm, and consummate professionalism; what a gift it was to work with you. I wish to thank my family and my cherished mentors Linda Hutcheon and Silvio Torres-Saillant (among many others) for their unfailing support and true generosity.

The editors would like to thank the contributors for their dedicated work and the editorial team at Lexington Books for their guidance and advice: Lindsey Porambo, Lenore Lautigar, and Johnnie Simpson. Special gratitude is also owed to Caroline Bonarde Ucci for her spectacular image of Ridley Scott for the cover; it is a tribute to an artist by an artist.

Introduction

Nancy Kang, Ashley Barkman, and Adam Barkman

In a room that combines the concrete pallor of a prison with the stifling uniformity of a factory floor, hundreds gaze at a massive screen. The surface vibrates with the words and bespectacled face of a nameless ideologue. The Macintosh computer advertisement of January 1984 offered an evocative play of contrasts between received knowledge and the individual imagination, the power of one versus the power of many. Directed by British-born filmmaker Ridley Scott, the spot aired during the Super Bowl telecast in the United States, its audience a diverse pool of sports fans and soon-to-be global computer enthusiasts. Aside from the voiceover's allusion to George Orwell's iconic novel of industrial-age dystopia, *1984*, the commercial seemed to bring to life the worst fears of the Cold War era; it was a propaganda poster for obedience (or oppression) brought to life. Yet as a commercial for Macintosh, its striking visual rhetoric implied that increasingly powerful forms of technology need not lead to intellectual enslavement but rather new avenues of liberation and enlightenment. This enlightened liberation would be led by a new commercial machine, one that consumers would control, not one that would render them powerless—like the TV ad's captive audience—in front of a screen.

Using increasingly rapid cuts between the robotic minions marching, sitting, and gaping at their leader, the director's eye focuses on riot police in hot pursuit of a strikingly muscular female athlete wielding a hammer. While the male masses are seated, she is in motion; while they connote stagnation and subservience, she symbolizes vitality and verve. Wielding a large hammer—but definitely no sickle—she launches her tool into the face of this Big Brother figure, a face uniquely reminiscent of Eldon Tyrell's, the creator figure from Scott's *Blade Runner* (released just two years earlier). A kind of female Prometheus, her act of rebellion unleashes a blinding spray of light

1

onto the crowd; it is creative destruction, a moment of mass media history written not with lightning but with *lighting*. The revolution, Scott's commercial implies, is not just being televised, it is being computerized, transforming the world through lights, cameras, and more action than the public has ever encountered before. Birthed on screen, the personal computer was touted as a portal to a new world order. Through Scott's stylised lens, the advertisement promised a deliverance from prophecy: the year 1984 would undo the Orwellian legacy of *1984*, allowing consumers to go forth as technological explorers and undertake their own "conquest of [digital] paradise."

All of these themes—the risks of personal initiative versus the pressures of group conformity; oppressive dogmas versus inventive dreams; historical legacy versus the quest for the new—resonate thematically with Scott's larger *oeuvre*. He is part of a cinematic family; his daughter, son, romantic partner as of 2012, and late brother—the respected director Tony Scott—are all affiliated with the entertainment industry. Scott himself has also served in various capacities as producer, executive producer, and production designer, among other roles behind the scenes. Consummately versatile, he straddles the domains of television and film simultaneously. His directorial resume of over thirty feature films (and counting) comprises an ongoing project of grand-scale historical exploration, futuristic experimentation, and artistic mythmaking. All of these achievements offer fertile ground for critical analysis and philosophical discussion, the aim of the eighteen critical essays in this volume. From paradoxical villains in *American Gangster* to the possibility of heavenly marriage in *Gladiator*, these chapters initiate diverse and provocative discussions of Scott's major feature films. While not exhaustive in scope (omitted are sustained discussions of his production projects, short films, and his 2010 adaptation of *Robin Hood*), this collection aims to deliver the broadest—and yet the most in-depth—consideration to date of his cinematic output.

The Culture and Philosophy of Ridley Scott illuminates a nearly comprehensive selection of his films from cutting-edge interdisciplinary perspectives. What makes this collection unique is not merely the diversity of approaches but its timeliness, given the resurgence of interest in his work by ever younger viewers. These include the so-called Millennials, or youth born between the years 1982-2002, who are consuming popular culture with increasingly multidimensional, multimedia-based approaches. The release of Scott's space epic *Prometheus* (2012), although no longer touted by the director to be a prequel to the *Alien* saga that he launched in 1979, sought to come full circle thematically, cementing a reputation for generic experimentation and stunning visual rhetoric forged over the course of four decades of directorial work.

The philosophical questions, arguments, and abstractions posed by these films have produced essays by scholars specializing in such diverse fields as philosophy, media and film studies, popular culture, postcolonial studies, literature, comparative race studies, history, women's and gender studies, and religion. In conceiving of this volume, we were particularly concerned with resonating with interests of undergraduate students as well as seasoned scholars. The audience includes a curious public as well as lifelong fans of Scott's films. The contributors seek to intensify the light shed on such signature works as *The Duellists* (1977), *Blade Runner* (1982)*, Alien* (1979), *Thelma & Louise* (1991), *Gladiator* (2000), *Hannibal* (2001), *Black Hawk Down* (2001), and *American Gangster* (2007). There are also explorations of less profitable—but still conceptually rich—films like *Legend* (1985), *Someone to Watch Over Me* (1987), *Black Rain* (1989), *1492: Conquest of Paradise* (1992), *G. I. Jane* (1997), *Matchstick Men* (2003), *Kingdom of Heaven* (2005), *A Good Year* (2006), and *Body of Lies* (2008). There is also an essay devoted to the television series produced by Scott, *Numb3rs*, which reminds us of the multifaceted nature of his talent.

While these latter works do not always feature prominently in critical discussions of Scott, many of them are highly recognizable. What's more, despite lukewarm profits, critical disdain, or a combination of these, many of the films have asserted themselves as culturally significant in ongoing conversations with contemporary popular culture. For instance, in the wake of 2011's federal repeal of the Don't Ask, Don't Tell (DADT) legislation barring gays and lesbians from the US military, the relevance of *G. I. Jane* reasserts itself with keen irony. Not only did the film reflect upon the "culture wars" of the 1980s and early 1990s, it also demonstrated the complex workings of intersectionality (that is, how race, sex, class, and sexuality combine to varying degrees in the volatile matrix of identity politics). Charges of lesbianism were used as a tool to sustain the tradition of straight white male domination of the highest ranks of military power. Given that issues relating to democratization and gender inclusiveness in institutional spaces are ongoing, Scott's film—however dated—remains a memorable contribution to that highly provocative public discourse.

This volume addresses a gap in analytical conversations about Scott's craft from a multi-disciplinary perspective. Book-length publications devoted to examining his career in the media arts include Laurence Knapp and Andrea Kulas's *Ridley Scott: Interviews*, a chronology and compendium of conversations about his major works[1]; Laurence Raw's ambitious *Ridley Scott Encyclopedia*, which often notes in its summary articles the paucity of critical studies (beyond reviews) of many of the films[2]; and Paul M. Sammon's *Ridley Scott: The Making of His Movies*, which defines itself as "the first book-length study" of the director's work, an intervention into "a period when the most aesthetically threadbare exploitation directors [sic] already have had multiple volumes devoted to their '*oeuvres.*'"[3] The bulk of information, the author states, was derived from two decades of taped interviews with the filmmaker.[4] Given this uniquely personal angle, however, the question arises as to how much beyond informed appreciation this kind of celebratory text can offer. In contrast, *The Films of Ridley Scott* by Richard Alan Schwartz[5] is a scholarly monograph that offers plot summaries and brief explications of twelve films; these range from *The Duellists* through *Hannibal*. Our volume interpolates more recent films into the survey, and instead of compartmentalizing each film as a discrete chapter, aims also to connect them *within* and *across* chapters, depending on the film and the thematic or theoretical frameworks at hand. Above all, these essays do not aim to convey general truths but rather to incite conversations about the films as hermeneutically challenging visual texts; they are platforms for the examination of Scott's artistry and his audience's ongoing negotiation of personal and collective values.

THE PROMETHEAN IMAGINATION

Born on November 30, 1937, in South Shields, Tyne and Wear, England, Scott created an early profile in the arts and public media, primarily through commercials and television shows, before turning to direct and produce films. His interest in the visual arts started with a childhood aptitude for drawing. Despite the possibility of following in his father's military footsteps, Scott's considerable talents gained him admission to West Hartlepool College of Art and the Royal College of Art in London. His first major motion picture was released the year he turned 40, but this was by no means a deviation from his previous career trajectory or achievements. After working as a set designer for companies like the British Broadcasting Corporation (BBC) and producing thousands of advertisements broadcast across Europe, he branched out to large-screen ventures.

Scott's debut *The Duellists* (1977) won the Jury Prize for best first feature at the Cannes Film Festival. It was a Napoleonic-era study of two soldiers in a decades-long duel over the concept of honor. After that initial critical success, Scott embarked on a career-boosting run of science fiction and fantasy films. These were foundational efforts that set the stage for his continuing fame among genre-film enthusiasts. The first was *Alien* (1979), a sci-fi horror film which immersed audiences in palpable terror generated by the implied rather than actual presence of the hissing, gunmetal grey nemesis. Its ensemble cast dwindles down to one, and its gory *peripetia*, or turning points in the plot, remind viewers that human bodies caught in the crushing joints of large-scale ideological machinery can be mindlessly expendable. The capacity of the film to create spin-offs and sequels testified to its longevity and conceptual depth.

Similarly, twenty-first century observers are able to trace the long cultural imprint of *Blade Runner* (1982; re-cut 1992), adapted from Philip K. Dick's novel *Do Androids Dream of Electric Sheep?* (1968). The film's ending, which featured the air-borne escape of protagonist Deckard with Rachel, his replicant lover, into the sunny unknown, caused considerable tension between Scott, the studio, and fans, but the capacity of the work to elicit ongoing discussions about human privilege (even after two decades) is notable. This is in addition to the contribution that the film made to the growing celebrity profile of Harrison Ford as a strong male lead in the adventure and romance genres. *Legend* (1985), starring a young Tom Cruise, did not elicit the same cultish fervor among audiences as the former two films during its initial release. In retrospect, however, the mythic allegory has generated a loyal following for its campy exuberance and the familiarity of its (sometimes hyperbolic) archetypes. Scott derived his vision from the European fairy tale tradition, combining these images and characters with other staples of the fantasy genre: unicorns, goblins, the satanic Dark Lord, a quest motif, royal family members in love with poor commoners, dwarves, fairies, and enchanted forests. Perhaps foreshadowing the cross-generational popularity of texts like J. K. Rowling's Harry Potter series, this film performed the chiasmatic task of making the childish mature and the mature childish, an entertaining if not always intellectually bracing experiment in form and content.

The next two productions, *Someone to Watch Over Me* (1987) and *Black Rain* (1989), were certainly departures from the hallucinogenic realm of princesses and unicorns, but they were standard fare as far as police dramas go. The first depicted a love triangle composed of a refined Manhattan socialite being protected by a newly-promoted detective from the borough of Queens, New York. Her foil is his wife, an unpretentious woman with a loud voice, unadorned demeanor, and vocabulary more urban than urbane. The film doubles as thriller and social class commentary, gesturing to the moral improvisation that surviving as a metropolitan police detective, father, and husband often requires. The plot conformed to the familiar template of upper-class woman meets working-class man; as with James Cameron's 1997 blockbuster *Titanic*, the erotic tensions that ensue are largely a dopamine-fuelled realization of transgressive fantasies more than any realistic premise for long-term romantic compatibility.

In contrast, *Black Rain* (1989) offered a transnational take on the "buddy film" genre, although the "buddy" element is slow to develop. Both ventures—*Someone to Watch Over Me* and this later film—failed to make any major critical waves; neither work was a blockbuster domestically either. The latter film starred Michael Douglas and Andy Garcia as scrappy Manhattan cops sent to Japan in the wake of a *yakuza* gang killing and counterfeiting scandal. Ironically, it was released the same year as another film entitled

Black Rain, a Japanese production based on the nuclear annihilation of Hiroshima in 1945 by the US military. Scott's work mentions the historical origins of its title, updating it as a metaphor for American imperialism in the age of fierce technological competition. The work meditates upon the relatively facile East-meets-West paradigm in a way that reiterates and yet subtly subverts the prevailing stereotypes of the Japanese at that time: as sneaky, opportunistic, emotionally anaesthetized robots bound by feudal traditions. Ironically, these same people were hurtling like a bullet train into the technological age, and many critics of the film highlight the nuances of Yellow Perilism in the depiction of the villains. For comparative observers, the Los Angeles of *Blade Runner*, with its *nouveau* Orientalist imagery (mysteriously cheeky geishas, flashing ideograms, ubiquitous noodle bars, exotic herb shops, and heavily-accented Asian actors) finds an echo in *Black Rain*, only this time back in the motherland, a neon-saturated, smoke-belching Osaka ruled by sword-wielding gangsters. Yipping like hyenas on motorcycles as they circle the American detectives, they demonstrate an admirable (if risible) capacity to transact their business at all hours of the day in dark sunglasses.

Scott claimed his place in popular feminist iconography by directing *Thelma & Louise* in 1991. Although the indeterminate ending was a cause for disagreement among viewers who preferred stark resolutions over cliffhangers (literal or otherwise), the strong performances by the lead and supporting actors, coupled with its original narrative premise, earned Scott his first Oscar nomination for best director. 1992 was less auspicious with the costly endeavor known as *1492: Conquest of Paradise*, a film starring French actor Gerald Depardieu as the Italian-born explorer Cristóbal Colón in Spain. This project celebrated Christopher Columbus's voyage to the New World and narrated the difficulties encountered with contact and transculturation in the West Indies (Hispaniola). The film attempted to recreate Columbus as a family man and visionary (with *Alien*'s Sigourney Weaver playing the role of Queen Isabella, a rather surprising source of romantic tension). After the (ad)venture sunk both critically and commercially, Scott busied himself with miscellaneous production projects, returning in 1996 to the oceanic setting with a film of robust male bonding, *White Squall*.

A *Lord of the Flies* meets *Robinson Crusoe*–type high seas thriller, the film combined the disaster genre with an epic "forces of nature" motif. The teenagers learn the imperative of cooperation for mutual survival, and their hardships eventually translate into ennoblement and a sense of accomplishment and solidarity. A similar venture featuring the vicissitudes of group accountability and theme of human limits was *G. I. Jane* (1997). The catchy/kitschy title has become a popular epithet for women in the military and an extension of *Thelma & Louise*'s meditation on the social, political, and ethical apparatuses meant to regulate women's capacity to enter traditionally male-only spaces and occupations.

The low profits and lack of critical approval stemming from these mid-nineties films propelled Scott again to pursue alternative, smaller-scale projects. The losing streak ended with *Gladiator* (2000), his tribute to the grand scale heroic epic. With its muscular male hero, adrenalized fight sequences, and altogether massive scope, the film was reminiscent of period pieces like Joseph Mankiewicz's *Cleopatra* (1963) or Stanley Kubrick's *Spartacus* (1960). Although he failed to win the Best Director Oscar, Scott's film garnered Best Actor, Best Picture, and three other Academy Awards. Lead actor Russell Crowe would establish a strong rapport with Scott (not unlike Denzel Washington's with Tony Scott), a connection that catalyzed the A-list actor's reappearance in later films.

After that banner year, the director ventured into the serial killer franchise based on novelist Thomas Harris's epicurean cannibal, Dr. Hannibal Lecter. *Hannibal* (2001), a work that connected Italy and the United States through the doctor's elegant penchant for mayhem, was reconfigured through the replacement of Jodie Foster (of *The Silence of the Lambs*) with Julianne Moore. The project managed to be a commercial success, co-existing that year with the more critically well-received *Black Hawk Down* (2001), Scott's gritty drama about the US military pursuit of a Somali warlord in Mogadishu. Four Oscar nominations resulted, with a third nod for best director. In some ways, the sense of a shared mission, and the realization by the United States that a new age of geopolitical strife had emerged after the terrorist attacks of 9/11, rendered the film a poignant rallying point for American solidarity.[6] That a foreign-born director could stand at the helm of such a nationalistically robust project testifies to the adaptability of Scott's craft.

His attention then turned away from the wide historical sweep of the previous films and telescoped back to the United States with the quirky character drama *Matchstick Men* (2003). An obsessive-compulsive, tic-plagued, and fundamentally lonely con man takes the lead in this adult (be)coming-of-age drama. It is a triangulation of "plays" (being played, playing, and extricating oneself as a player from a larger "game") that brings the criminal Roy, his partner Frank, and Amanda (Roy's estranged teenage daughter) together. That appearances prove surprising is among the didactic impressions left by the retro-styled, brightly lit film. Following this effort was *Kingdom of Heaven* (2005), a Crusades-era film as ambitious as its grandiose title implies. Bringing together celebrity actors like Liam Neeson (*Schindler's List*) and Orlando Bloom (*Lord of the Rings*), the quest revisited the complex father-son relationships of *Gladiator* and *Blade Runner*. Despite massive battle scenes, anxiety-inducing portrayals of political brokerage, religious strife, and a landmark depiction of sympathetic Muslim leadership (a notable departure from Islamophobic imagery in the popular media at the time), the film fell flat in terms of profits and garnered only muted critical praise in the mainstream.

The dramatic comedy *A Good Year* (2006) repositioned Crowe as a romantic lead in the lush landscape of Provence, France. The savvy London businessman makes free-wheeling choices about the winery estate of his uncle, finds a vivacious love interest in Marion Cotillard's café owner Fanny, and encounters the trifecta of alternative employment, enjoyment, and escape away from his regular milieu. The film was lightweight as far as most critics were concerned, offering little in comparison to the combined commercial and critical success of the next venture, the biopic of Harlem drug lord Frank Lucas. *American Gangster* (2007) starred Denzel Washington as a gangster, hustler, and family man fuelled by racial hurt and a creative business sense. This version of the self-made man revisited the well-known American myth of entrepreneurial ascent; placing the rags-to-riches businessman in an iconic African American neighborhood and making drugs the currency appropriately complicates the meaning of success. The relationship forged between Lucas and Crowe's New Jersey detective Richie Roberts also exposes wide levels of police corruption, adding considerable ambiguity to the idea of what it means for government agencies—or individuals in their stead—to protect and serve a community. As *Robin Hood* (2010) would later reiterate, the equation of justice and the law is one that cannot be lamely accepted as right.

The following year, Crowe reappeared as a doughy CIA agent directing Leonardo DiCaprio's undercover operative in the Middle East. This film, *Body of Lies* (2008), hearkens back to Scott's treatment of Arab and Muslim characters in *Kingdom of Heaven*, painting them with a more colorful brush than the prevailing Hollywood stereotypes of terrorist/jihadist/militant Islamist. Two years later, Crowe morphed into a rather muddy Robin Hood, opposite feisty if ever-pallid Cate Blanchett, a return by Scott to the world of European folklore that *Legend* first broached. The medieval adventure was no blockbuster in the tradition of *Gladiator*, but it did underscore the director's breadth of interests and his ongoing capacity to create a prismatic understanding of human experience through past, present, *and* future-focused narratives.

MOTIVATED REPRESENTATIONS

The advantage of any readily accessible public medium like film is its capacity to offer a broad range of materials for the development of a critical viewership. In *Outlaw Culture: Resisting Representations* (1994), public intellectual bell hooks (born Gloria Watkins) posits that popular culture is a consummate site for radical pedagogy, or the philosophy and practice of teaching and learning. Aside from their frequent use as a tool of psychological escape, celebrity worship, consumerist fascination, or ideological manipulation, popular films stand at the forefront of a democratizing "classroom-outside-of-a-classroom" model that hooks defines as potentially revolutionary. Critical thinking prompts spectators to realize that what they see on screen is not "natural" so much as a series of *motivated representations.*[7] In her documentary discussion *Cultural Criticism and Transformation* for FORA TV, she deconstructs one pervasive misconception about filmmaking: that movies offer a kind of unadulterated rendition of reality and that their combination of "magic," "pure imagination," and "sheer creativity" instantly legitimizes the medium. Disagreeing with this paradigm, hooks asks the public to consider what kinds of "conscious manipulation[s] of representation" occur on-screen (and by extension, off-screen). With heightened political, social, philosophical, scientific, and artistic sensibilities, viewers will then be equipped to discern the careful choices that make up, like a delicate network of nerves, the body of the film. They will know "what kinds of images will produce a certain kind of impact" on the part of the director, the writers, the actors, the cinematographers, and the rest of the production team.[8]

This theorist's observations gesture to the kind of vigorous intellectual inquiry that Scott's work both elicits and demands. The fact that many of the films have acquired and continue to invite wide viewerships (including some cult followings) does not detract from their presence as texts with untapped, under-examined hermeneutic potential. According to *auteur theory*, a branch of aesthetics and film criticism, it is precisely the director's uniqueness of vision that provides the ballast for hooks's aforementioned theory of motivated representations. With its genesis in the late 1940s, this approach to film evolved through the next decade via publications in André Bazin's periodical *Cahiers du Cinéma* (*Notebooks on Film*), and was popularized internationally by critics like François Truffault (editor and publisher of *Cahiers*) and Columbia University academic Andrew Sarris. What emerged through these manifold discussions over integrity of vision was a sense of the filmmaker's range of accountabilities (to him- or herself, to the studio, to the actors, to the public) as well as his or her prerogative to exercise artistic agency. The director, more so than the screenwriter, the sets, the actors, the editors, the studio, or the rest of the team, charts the course of the film; it is precisely this belief—that Scott is not merely a sort of ambulant machine ushering forth a product through technical expertise alone—justifies the desire to explicate his films from philosophical and cultural studies perspectives.[9]

ALIEN, SELF, OTHER: MAJOR THEMES

Many and diverse are the issues informing Scott's directorial work. Among them are the abstract values enunciated by Maximus, the protagonist of *Gladiator*, whose motto "Strength and honor" emerges in both his personal and martial philosophy. These concepts, alongside others, undergo significant reformulation based on a situational ethics inflected by setting and audience. As *G. I. Jane* demonstrates, what may be defined as strength for a man might not apply to a woman in Navy SEALs training. In *White Squall*, the sheer competition for survival during the storm sweeps away the social codes that usually structure life on land. What is honorable in one environment may thus be impugned or even abandoned in another, especially in conditions of physical or psychological duress. In *Black Rain*, alternatively, detective Nick Conklin finds himself under investigation by the Internal Affairs Bureau for pocketing drug money; hardly unique behavior, this is an act of corruption he justifies with his monetary obligations as ex-husband, absentee father, and working stiff.

Conklin's ethical failings find their match in the impeccable honesty of another civil servant, New Jersey detective Richie Roberts of *American Gangster*, who refuses to filch drug money. Taking this stand leads to scathing ostracism; his precinct colleagues denigrate him as a "fucking boy scout" and abandon their own professional teamwork-based ethics by refusing to help him even when the life of his partner is imperiled. Roberts realizes the paradoxical nature of "honorable" work in this milieu, one which usually lists honor and service to the community among its *raisons d'être*. He learns that loyalty to the system may lead to one's very abandonment by the system, since the latter is not comprised of mere rules and regulations but of morally fallible human beings. As Thelma sardonically reflects in *Thelma & Louise*, "The law is some tricky shit, isn't it?"

Also prominent are the symbolic and moral dialectics of purity and corruption. In *Legend*, we learn that as long as the unicorns (signifiers of virtue) reign, evil will not prevail against those "pure of heart." While the film shows no qualms in exploiting the dualistic aesthetics of good (light) and evil (darkness), it does extend a vision of utopia, something to strive toward in an unstable contemporary world. This kind of stark configuration usually stimulates the moral imagination. Likewise in *Alien*, the android scientist Ash praises the aggressive creature for its superlative purity even though it is unequivocally a killer. Like the alien, Ash is a non-human outsider insinuating himself among humans on the spacecraft. Viewers wonder how the monster's hostility to the human crew, its absent conscience, and naked drive to destroy can be remotely admirable qualities even if ostensibly "pure."

In *1492: Conquest of Paradise*, alternatively, the New World (a *terra incognita* to Columbus but a well-traversed homeland for the indigenous tribes living there) represents a form of ecological and social purity. Notions of noble savagery dwindle into plain savagery through such acts as colonial encroachment, ethnocentrism, linguistic miscommunication, racial stratification, and rebellion against enslavement and dispossession. In *Hannibal*, too, the cannibal aesthete Dr. Lecter punishes those whom he finds guilty of vulgarity and disrespect, since they are affronts to his perversely "pure" codes of social etiquette. Even in the espionage thriller *Body of Lies*, some viewers may discern an unexpected purity in the opening scene's depiction of self-sacrifice through religious martyrdom. Yet, as the film reprises the horror through the Amsterdam marketplace bombing (one which shatters the lives of anonymous camera-toting tourists and bystanders buying flowers), a purity of ideological commitment does not always correspond to constructive, positive, and humane actions.

The effects of symbolic or actual violence, especially sexual violence, reappear in many of Scott's feature films, among them *Alien* (Ash's attempted oral violation of Ripley with a pornographic magazine), *Gladiator* (the implied rape and murder of Maximus's wife), *Blade Runner* (Deckard's alarmingly rough seduction of Rachel), and *G. I. Jane* (Jordan O'Neill's near-public violation during a training exercise). *Thelma & Louise* showcases attempted rape most explicitly, arguing that sometimes an illegal action like murder may be defensible, although emotional and other forms of fallout will result. With the murderer Louise so adamant about avoiding Texas and her memories of the place, we assume she must have experienced some unforgettable, possibly sexual trauma there. This unspoken history is the open secret, the thin connecting threads between actual knowledge and conjecture which snap with accelerating speed and intensity as the women hurtle toward their final act of rebellion. Louise's lukewarm relationship with her supportive yet violent boyfriend incites further suspicion and distrust, not merely of romantic (heterosexual) partnerships but of the state of human relationships generally: why is respect so difficult? Given that it is a road trip movie that traverses state lines, perhaps a larger social commentary is implied, namely the conflicted state of American gender relations. More broadly, with the sheer number of incompatible relationships in this film (more or less all of them, save the liminal friendship/romance of the title characters), Scott offers a scathing critique of human alienation. This is an existential crisis in self-awareness combined with a glaring deficit of empathy, compassion, and ethical responsibility toward others.

This nexus of ignorance and miscommunication gestures to the epistemological depths mined by Scott's films. Just as Thelma and Louise both repudiate former versions of themselves through repeated, violent acts of estrangement from civil (that is, law-abiding) society, Frank Lucas from *American Gangster* struggles with the burden of a racialized past. Unable to forget the brutal Klan murder that first defined his dark skin as a signifier of social inferiority, he pursues a life of crime because it is the only stability that he knows. Bumpy Johnson, his gangster-mentor and father figure, virtually controls him from the grave through the powers of legacy and mutual respect. An ontologically bound man, Lucas is the superlative criminal, impeccably accomplished and ingeniously inventive; he does little, however, to dispel the prevailing stereotypes of black male criminality, a product of the same racial history that prompts him to want more. The problem of negotiating such legacies is that often villains emerge as heroes and vice versa. Lucas is not alone: other walking contradictions include the surgically self-sacrificing cannibal Lecter, the lovingly apologetic cheater Mike Keegan in *Someone to Watch Over Me*, the rakish people's thief Robin Hood, the conscientious con man Roy Waller in *Matchstick Men*, and the humanitarian killers doubling as soldiers in *Black Hawk Down*.

Scott's films tend not to be explicitly political or activist in tone. Much of their appeal lies in their capacity to convey truths through suggestion and nuance (that is, figurative devices like metaphor, antithesis, symbolism, and caricature) rather than pushing forward as heavy-handed morality plays. Some of this careful balancing between ideologically freighted content and aesthetic form may derive from his work as a director and producer of commercials, where the onus is to deliver a concentrated message creatively, emphatically, and yet very quickly. In many of his films, this sense of pressure emerges in relation to a real or imagined cultural menace. The sense of being under surveillance (a part of something and yet apart from it, like the crew of *Alien*'s *Nostromo*) correlates strongly with the irony that constraints may come from the very apparatuses meant to ensure freedom. One of the most crushing instances of this emerges in *Blade Runner*, where the replicants face their "retirement" (a euphemism for extermination) and come to terms with their status as both wanted (in the criminal sense) and unwanted (in the social sense, except perhaps as slave labor on a different planet). Just as the two fighters in *The Duellists* are in a relationship they do not care for—at least to the same degree—they still require one another's participation for ontological consistency. There would be no sense of honor otherwise, making both men character foils with foils, engaged in a compulsive *danse macabre* that reminds them of their obligations to fight for ego gratification and social acceptance concurrently, even though the cost may be their very lives.

LIGHTS, CAMERA, REACTION

Each chapter in this volume recognizes the importance of a film (or set of films) as grounds for critical analysis, but the overarching objective is not to be uniformly celebratory. Its aim is neither hagiography nor premature *Fest-*

schrift that casts Scott as an unparalleled visionary who can do no wrong. Unlike such high-profile Hollywood contemporaries as George Lucas and Steven Spielberg, the mention of Scott's name does not always bring sparks of recognition, although titles of particular works certainly elicit reactions, often in conjunction with the names of celebrities like Russell Crowe and Sigourney Weaver. *The Culture and Philosophy of Ridley Scott* is comprised of essays that, to some degree, examine the philosophical quest for authentic personhood, here mediated by the ideological orientations of the director and production team, their deliberate framing of historical moments, and the resulting performances by actors to create (for the most part) mimetically real characters. The majority of the chapters perform their interpretive work through a meta-critical and meta-historiographical lens: in other words, they understand that each film's constructed cinematic world emerges from a scripted plot and deliberate embeddedness in a narrativized version of history.[10] The audience realizes that the films offer re-created time, not phenomenologically real time; furthermore, the realism is, in fact, artificial and the artifice must then successfully convey a semblance of actuality and coherence (in literary terms, verisimilitude).

Thematic groupings lend internal coherence to the wide spectrum of films amassed here. Chapters in the first section concentrate upon paradoxes of representation, the concept of responsibility, the choices involved in remembering (not always positively) the past, and the necessity of revision as a way of destabilizing the "official" or most accepted versions of events.

To start, "'Good Badmen': Reading Race in *Black Rain*, *American Gangster*, and *Body of Lies*" by Nancy Kang deploys the African American folk archetype of the morally fluid "badman" to assess levels of representational efficacy vis-à-vis white/Euro-American and non-white characters (here, African American, Asian, Arab and Muslim). Kang contends that the films offer an overarching perspective that is largely anti-racist and inclusive in spirit, although with points of friction and contradiction in practice. This is particularly in regard to delineating racialized heroics from stereotypical versions of villainy.

James Edwin Mahon's "A Double-Edged Sword: Honor in *The Duellists*" grapples with the problem of honor as an obsession in this earliest of Scott's feature films. By using military life as one platform and personal relationships as another, the author debates the virtue (or virtue deficit) of valuing one's honor over the emotional and physical well-being of one's associates. Using extensive comparative analysis with Joseph Conrad's original novella, Mahon considers whether narcissistic "satisfaction" can ever be meant for more than one person.

Michael Garcia's "The Trans-Religious Ethics of *Kingdom of Heaven*" interrogates an apparent paradox of the Crusades epic: while it depicts a conflict driven by perceived religious incompatibilities, the work actually subverts the centrality of religion and the necessity of a Higher Power to define morality. Espousing a "naturalistic ethics" of post-religiosity, Garcia offers a mosaic of philosophical perspectives that explain how higher principles *do* exist for people to agree upon that supersede their respective religious allegiances.

Fernando Gabriel Pagnoni Berns grapples with the limits of agency and the role of empathy as they relate to the constant presence (and encroachment) of other people in our lives. His "Levinasian Responsibility in *Someone to Watch Over Me*, *Black Rain*, and *White Squall*" compares and contrasts the actions of police detective protagonists in the first two films, insofar as their choices may jeopardize both their respective careers and the lives of civilians, including their loved ones. Using the philosophy of Emmanuel Levinas, Berns also fleshes out the notion of a responsibility "ethically prior to any community or ontological commitment" in the maritime adventure thriller.

In "Re-Membering Vietnam in Somalia: *Black Hawk Down* and Ethical Militarism in American History Memory," David Zietsma theorizes Scott's recreation of the 1993 US intervention into Mogadishu as an attempt to rehabilitate the image of American troops as ethical humanitarian warriors and soldier-heroes. In light of the representational shadow cast by the devastating effects of the Vietnam War, he critiques how the film "underscore[s] the inherent moral goodness of American military power" and even construes the bodies of the dead as part of a larger, ideologically freighted "civilizing mission."

Silvio Torres-Saillant's "*1492* and the Ethics of Remembering" meditates on Scott's Columbus epic as a narrative of commemoration both burdened and amplified by the mythology of the title character, the so-called founder of the New World. Analyzing the narrative premise (between Columbus and his son) and the ongoing debates about competing versions of the conquest, the author evaluates the film's emphasis on historical veracity in light of its deliberate deviations from that very history.

The second section casts a wide net over the breadth, diversity, and vicissitudes of under-examined lives. These chapters shed much-needed light on the problem of accountability in a mix of hermeneutically dense scenarios, especially as they straddle the human and non-human realms. Many of these are emotionally charged relationships defining what it means to be "normal," accepted, privileged, and understood. Much friction emerges from direct or implied kinships that cross the borders between these realms. Ethical ambiguities abound as well: do creators need to take responsibility for their creations and alternatively, do creations owe any filial obligation to their "parents"? What sorts of genres and forms of visual rhetoric best convey the shades of evil in an already fallen world? Furthermore, if we construe art to be the site where the best of our human capacities emerge, what happens when it is combined with criminal behavior, arguably the realization of our worst moral failings?

Greg Littmann's "What's Wrong with Building Replicants? Artificial Intelligence in *Blade Runner*, *Alien*, and *Prometheus*" makes a case for the comparative validity of replicant lives. With recourse to philosophers like John Stuart Mill and innovators like Alan Turing, the author debates the ethics of conferring agency and life-integrity to artificial life systems. He asks what measures of sameness and difference should be deployed in determining degrees of humanity. If a technologically-mediated life form emerges through human endeavor, should we have special rights over it and to what extent?

Hannibal Lecter's epicureanism takes center stage in Antonio Sanna's "A Villainous Appetite: Erôs, Madness, and the Food Analogy in *Hannibal* and *Legend*." With reference to Dante Alighieri's concepts of spiritual love and Plato's definition of *erôs*, Sanna weighs the excesses of emotional madness and greed (*cupiditas*) against the compassionate, enlightening spirit of charity (*caritas*) in relation to the villains of each film. The usually loving and sustaining language of food takes a sinister if mythically evocative turn for Hannibal Lecter and *Legend*'s deified Darkness.

Janice Shaw's "Detecting Puzzles and Patterns in *Numb3rs*" focuses on Scott's work as a producer of a unique television series that complements his directorial work. With an eye on the conventions of the detective genre, the author juxtaposes the abstract world of quantitative forensic analysis with the qualitative analysis required for piecing together criminal motivations. Focusing on the rapport between the two brothers who drive the problem-solving plots, she explains how Scott's series embeds the solutions in real-world examples of mathematical patterns.

Offering another consideration of form, Carl Sobocinski's "Celebrating Historical Accuracy in *The Duellists*" connects vastly different time periods (our present moment and France during the Napoleonic Wars) with the intention of testing how heightened commitment to historical accuracy proves particularly effective in this film. He reflects with detail upon the historical context behind the fighting pair's actions (for instance, on their military code of ethics in view of larger, European contexts) and evaluates the effects of the score, the costumes, and various scenes as they contrast with other examples of the swashbuckling, action-adventure genre.

Moving between inductive and deductive thinking, Basileios Kroustallis's "Conceptions of Happiness in *Matchstick Men* and *A Good Year*" challenges the viability of a single theory of happiness. Referencing John Kekes's revision of the original Aristotelian concept of *eudaimonia*, the writer argues that enjoyment may be divorced from any cumulative efforts to lead a good life. Instead, he proposes that the greatest enjoyment results from sharing life with others whom we care about, even though doing so may be neither admirable nor rewarding to the self.

Dan Dinello's "Techno-Totalitarianism in *Alien*" debates whether human enslavement is the direct result of technological over-dependency. Weighing the insights of "techno-critics" like Jacques Ellul and Langdon Winner, the author showcases the film's passionate distrust of technology as a corruptor of human values and indeed, human life. He argues that the film's worldview is fundamentally pessimistic, casting humans as prey to "ubiquitous, oppressive technological forces indicative of the moral flaws and authoritarian impulses of its corporate designers."

The final section constellates gender, related questions of identity formation, and the problem of authentic selfhood. Scott's depictions of male and female self-fashioning have continued to provide rich fodder for arguments over traditional versus progressive roles in Western society, especially for women. Aware of how gendered violence and patriarchal privilege (the requisite rule of the father, and by extension, by men) affects each group, chapters in this section meditate on male and female characters as instigators (or harbingers) of larger social shifts. Whether these shifts are ameliorative or destructive is an ongoing point of contention among these writers.

Aviva Dove-Viebahn's "Through Space, Over a Cliff, and Into a Trench: The Shifting Feminist Ideologies of *Alien, Thelma & Louise*, and *G. I. Jane*" grounds its argument in second and third-wave feminist theory; this includes the work of many prominent critics like Judith Butler, Julia Kristeva, Simone de Beauvoir, Judith Halberstam, and Adrienne Rich. Her argument for Ripley's constructive androgyny in *Alien, Thelma & Louise*'s radical counter-attack to the masculinist backlash of the 1980s, and Jordan O'Neil's feminine post-feminism in *G. I. Jane* make for a chiaroscuro of politically super-charged gender perspectives.

Matthew Freeman's "Why Doesn't Hannibal Kill Clarice? The Philosophy of a Monstrous Romantic" casts the iconic Lecter as a "moral monster of the Romantic Age." In a discussion richly informed by the discourse of the nineteenth-century Romantic hero, the author interweaves the themes of innocence and corruption with the trope and actual practice of cannibalism. He also identifies the irony of Lecter's comparative evil in a modern world saturated with even greater monstrosities. The result is an arguably heroic fiend figure.

Lorna Piatti-Farnell's "In the Guise of Character: Costumes, Narrative, and the Reality of Artifice in *Thelma & Louise*" concentrates on the under-examined role of costumes as dynamic repositories of meaning in Scott's film. Using postmodern philosophy and trans-media semiotic theory, the author analyzes Scott's simulacral use of costumes and how they gesture to hyper-representations of identity categories (gender, class, and sexuality). A grounding in genre theory (the popular Western) and regional stereotypes (the South as morally suspect space) also partakes in her study of clothes and costumes as pluralistic artifacts.

Given that appearances may deceive, Elizabeth Abele's "Becoming Authentic in *Matchstick Men* Through the Ultimate Con" identifies the initial mental instability of the protagonist as symptomatic of a larger "sociopathic drive for success in a capitalistic society." Through his journey of recuperative fatherhood, con man Roy Waller is able to move toward a more authentic understanding of his moral compass. Reading the film as part of the mid-life crisis genre, Abele illustrates a shift away from "classic American masculinity" to a more fluid vision of "American manhood."

Sydney Palmer's "Virginity in *Alien:* The Essence of Ripley's Survival" grapples with critic Stephen Mulhall's contention that this exceptional crew-member's drive for self-preservation "alienat[es]" her from real life. The author challenges Mulhall's equation of integrity, celibacy, and virginity, arguing instead that the protagonist's will to protect and defend is rather an *affirmation* of life. The chapter uses Catholic theology and biblical allusion to contrast virginity as embodied by Ripley and ostensible purity of the creature whose very corporeal presence conveys sexual monstrosity and a rejection of life.

Oscillating between the human and more-than-human realm, "*Gladiator*, Gender, and Marriage in Heaven: A Christian Exploration" by Adam Barkman questions whether gender and gendered relationships like marriage are able to endure after death. In conjunction with pivotal scenes in *Gladiator*, a series of provocative questions, philosophical anecdotes, and hypothetical scenarios coalesce into a Christian perspective of how spirit, bodies, gender, and sex collide. Barkman propels readers into a provocative interpretive matrix that supersedes the brief on-screen romantic interludes between Maximus, his late wife, and his fleeting love interest, Lucilla.

MOUNTAINS UPON MOUNTAINS

Our hope is that this volume, like the most effective pieces of creative writing or memorable feature films, will elicit strong reader response. We know that the experience of film is highly varied; the diversity of audience members notwithstanding, even the sites of enjoyment defy uniformity: multiplexes with stadium seating, heritage theatres with unpredictable projectors and sticky floors, local screens with discount double features and striped popcorn boxes, online streaming and pay-per-view options, even nostalgic drive-in joints with the trill of summer crickets accompanying the distant boom of the soundtrack. Broadly conceived, these essays are interpretive acts; like the films they discuss, they strive to reach across time, space, historical and theoretical contexts, languages, and sensory experiences. They are only able to offer possible *avenues* of understanding, not authoritative "last words."

Perhaps for a veteran director, the craft of filmmaking is not unlike climbing a mountain range; one scales crests, peaks, and summits (the popular and lucrative projects that have yielded credibility, major deals, awards, and fame) before stumbling on crags, sliding down flanks, and plummeting through dead air (the creative missteps, suspended or foreclosed projects, box-office flops, and depths of personal conflict). Above all, the director depends on resilience. Ridley Scott owes his longevity to the capacity to use his tools well, a breadth of experiences, the support of those beneath and above, and a keen taste for risk, all necessary to continue the perilous ascent.

NOTES

1. Laurence Knapp and Andrea F. Kulas, *Ridley Scott: Interviews* (Jackson: University Press of Mississippi, 2005). The annotated chronology (xvii-xix), alongside other source material from critical studies and online sites, has informed the biographical section of this introduction.

2. Laurence Raw, *The Ridley Scott Encyclopedia* (Lanham, MD: Scarecrow Press, 2009).

3. Paul M. Sammon, *Ridley Scott: The Making of His Movies* (New York: Thunder's Mouth Press, 1999), 2.

4. Sammon, *Ridley Scott*, 3.

5. Richard Alan Schwartz, *The Films of Ridley Scott* (Westport, CT: Praeger, 2001).

6. Rebecca Flint Marx reflects, "Still bruised from the tragic events of 9/11, however, the American public lined up in droves for the flag-waving Jerry Bruckheimer production." Rebecca Flint Marx, "Ridley Scott Biography," Moviefone, accessed November 9, 2011, http://www.moviefone.com/celebrity/ridley-scott/1134845/biography.

7. bell hooks, *Outlaw Culture: Resisting Representations* (New York: Routledge, 1994).

8. "Challenging Media: bell hooks on Cultural Criticism and Transformation, Pt. 2," Youtube video, 8:41, posted by Challenging Media, November 10, 2011, http://www.youtube.com/watch?v=OQ-XVTzBMvQ&feature=related.

9. See François Truffaut, "A Certain Tendency of the French Cinema," in *Movies and Methods: An Anthology*, ed. Bill Nichols (Berkeley: University of California Press, 1976), 224-37. See also Andrew Sarris, "Notes on the Auteur Theory in 1962," in *Film Theory and Criticism: Introductory Readings*, ed. Gerald Mast and Marshall Cohen (New York: Oxford University Press, 1979), 650-65.

10. This idea derives from the postmodern literary theory of Linda Hutcheon, in particular her idea of "historiographic metafiction." The paradox of the term, she explains, is that literary practitioners may be highly self-aware and deliberate in their aesthetic choices, but in turn integrate real events and historical figures to heighten the reality of what are necessarily unreal situations. See Linda Hutcheon, *A Poetics of Postmodernism: History, Theory, Fiction* (New York: Routledge, 1988).

REFERENCES

"Challenging Media: bell hooks on Cultural Criticism and Transformation, Pt. 2." Youtube video, 8:41. Posted by Challenging Media. November 10, 2011. http://www.youtube.com/watch?v=OQ-XVTzBMvQ&feature=related.
hooks, bell. *Outlaw Culture: Resisting Representations.* New York: Routledge, 1994.

Hutcheon, Linda. *A Poetics of Postmodernism: History, Theory, Fiction.* New York: Routledge, 1988.

Knapp, Laurence F., and Andrea F. Kulas. "Chronology." In *Ridley Scott: Interviews*, edited by Laurence F. Knapp and Andrea F. Kulas, xvii-xix. Jackson, MS: University Press of Mississippi, 2005.

Marx, Rebecca Flint. "Ridley Scott Biography." Moviefone. Accessed November 9, 2011. http://www.moviefone.com/celebrity/ridley-scott/1134845/biography.

Raw, Laurence. *The Ridley Scott Encyclopedia* . Lanham, MD: Scarecrow Press, 2009.

Sammon, Paul M. *Ridley Scott: The Making of His Movies.* New York: Thunder's Mouth Press, 1999.

Sarris, Andrew. "Notes on the Auteur Theory in 1962." In *Film Theory and Criticism: Introductory Readings*, edited by Gerald Mast and Marshall Cohen, 650-65. New York: Oxford University Press, 1979.

Schwartz, Richard Alan. *The Films of Ridley Scott.* Westport, CT: Praeger, 2001.

Truffaut, François. "A Certain Tendency of the French Cinema." In *Movies and Methods: An Anthology*, edited by Bill Nichols, 224-37. Berkeley: University of California Press, 1976.

Part I

Responsibility, Remembering, Revision

Chapter One

"Good Badmen": Reading Race in *American Gangster, Black Rain,* and *Body of Lies*

Nancy Kang

Commenting on Ridley Scott's capacity to integrate artistry and business savvy into his work, Laurence Knapp and Andrea Kulas observe, "As a longstanding commercial artist, [Scott] avoids making overt statements about race or sexuality, but he has been willing to explore gender."[1] This distinction fails to account for the complex politics of visual representation, and how it is difficult to view these identity categories (race, sexuality, and gender) discretely. One only has to think, for instance, of the metamorphosis of American pancake mascot Aunt Jemima from a handkerchief-headed Mammy to a pearl-earringed housewife. Her graphic trajectory reveals how commercial art is an ample platform for covert and overt statements about normative social roles (e.g. the African American woman as former slave, cook, dependable domestic worker, and subsequent symbol of America's ongoing love affair with "ready to serve" foods). Just as art can be a lucrative business and businesses often find themselves enhanced through innovative artistic practices, the ties between race, gender, and sexuality are virtually inextricable. For Scott and other big-budget filmmakers, the cinematic screen is a profit-making industrial apparatus that presents singularly artistic as well as strategically public opportunities for meaning-making. Yet "publicly available" and "publicly minded" are epithets that while similar in spirit and sound, can be drastically different in practice.

Commercial artistry tends to downplay overt social messaging to avoid charges of didacticism or simply boring advertising; after all, so much of what attracts us to products and experiences (like the movies) tends to be subliminal. Yet concepts like ideal audiences and target demographics (e.g.

the "gay dollar" or the "millennial consumer") make it clear that turning a profit requires aesthetic and social strategizing. Market considerations may include the gender, race, and sexuality of the audience, but they may also account for social class, age and generational group, nationality, regional affiliation, levels of education and cultural literacy, and even degree of able-bodiedness. The extent to which a director and production team focuses on these factors may vary, but race is one category that remains under-examined in Scott's *oeuvre*. Going "grand-scale" in terms of themes or plots for the sake of the dollar does not mean that an elision or complication of differences like race or sexuality should be blindly accepted or otherwise ignored.

"Race" here is a cultural category—a lattice-work of discourses and discursive practices—held up by historical specificities and connected through supposedly scientific markers of difference. Films situate "raced" bodies within visual texts in order to convey both shared and specific truths about the lived experiences of these groups of people. But the categories are mutable, the markers often flawed or indeterminate. The reason for the apparent lack of focus on race in Scott's work may be because it is so divisive and personal a concept that it may render a project too commercially "risky." This situation is even more pronounced in the United States given its particularly checkered racial past with slavery and its aftermath. Yet the British-born director concedes that his aesthetics tend to shy away from the typical American optimism of his peers, which for some observers may translate into a convenient amnesia about the sins of the past. He confesses, "I . . . tend to be a bit darker. To look at the dark side. Not because I'm a manic-depressive, but because I find darkness interesting."[2] We would assume, thus, that he might be more willing than most to plunge into the hermeneutic dangers that racial discourses offer, not unlike the fateful leap at the start of his sci-fi epic *Prometheus* (2012) which (re)combines—like a strand of mutant DNA—scientific marvels with a morbid lyricism that tests the very definition of the human.[3]

Most of Scott's *oeuvre*, according to Richard A. Schwartz, espouses liberal values marbled through with neo-classically conservative ideals: balancing passion with reason, believing in personal honor and responsible living, wielding authority in a non-exploitative way, understanding creative individuality while appreciating the merits of teamwork, and expressing concern for collective welfare.[4] Taken alongside these humanistic themes, the politics of race seem to be secondary or even tertiary concerns, competing as they are with plot, action, and visual effects. Yet to ignore race, a fraught social arena that adds starkly *specific* truths to the constructed nature of the cinematic world, would be naïve if not intellectually negligent. There must be a reason that Asian-descent character Ravel (Benedict Wong) in *Prometheus* not only has a European name, he always stays in the ship and follows orders while other characters actively survey, fight, and meet death head-on. While perhaps not intentionally, he reinforces stereotypes of Asians as passive (if diligent) workers who lack leadership and initiative. Similarly, the black captain, Janek (Idris Elba), who also has a European name, plays music on a mini accordion (sans minstrel grin), seeks casual sex from an attractive blonde coworker, and looks suspiciously like a DJ at a turntable (with cocky baseball cap no less) as he prepares for his suicide mission. Clearly, the film predicts that racial stereotypes of Asian passivity and black levity will obtain well past the mid-twenty-first century mark. "Back to the past in the future" is a disheartening prospect indeed for those sensitive to these representations, however well-intentioned or seemingly innocuous.

I argue that Scott engages racial difference in three films (*American Gangster, Black Rain,* and *Body of Lies*) through the paradoxical "good badman" motif that is embodied by the non-white protagonists.[5] In *American Gangster* (2007), it is Harlem drug kingpin Frank Lucas (Denzel Washington); in *Black Rain* (1989), Japanese detective Masahiro Matsumoto (Ken Takakura); in *Body of Lies* (2008), head of the Jordanian General Intelligence Service Hani Salaam (Mark Strong). Of these three films, *American Gangster* (which perhaps deserves the subtitle *Black Reign*), is the most racially progressive of the good badmen configurations because the ontological division between white and non-white protagonist is most ambiguous. His race is precisely why Frank Lucas represents "progress" after amassing his $50 million-dollar fortune through heroin trafficking. This is the opinion of his sometime nemesis and later collaborator, detective Richie Roberts (Russell Crowe). Yet given Lucas's deep involvement in the devastating narcotics trade and culpability in major crimes like murder and grand theft, the question remains as to how groundbreaking his characterization really is in terms of racial uplift. Does Scott effectively re-inscribe or lamely reinforce extant representations of African American males as criminals, hustlers, and social deviants? His approach is more palimpsestic than revolutionary (offering minor changes), but it provides an alternative form of hero worship that does not dispose of caution or realism while understanding that a hero to one community may be a menace to another.

The black gangster film is not new, even sprouting notable sub-genres like the "hood" film and the hip-hop story. Popular examples of the former stretch back to the blaxploitation era with films like *Superfly* (1972), *Black Caesar* (1973), and newer works like *New Jack City* (1991), *Menace II Society* (1993), and *Hoodlum* (1997).[6] As Richard Corliss explains, *American Gangster* celebrates the sea change that occurred in crime circles when the Mafia realized that African Americans like Lucas and Nicky Barnes (Cuba Gooding, Jr.) were no longer mere customers; they were fearsome rivals. What's more, Lucas, passing through the filter of Scott's cinematic process, brings forth such an unexpected combination of choreographed propriety, conservatism, and elitist greed that he perhaps stands as a prototype for today's most successful white-collar criminals.[7]

"Badman" is a neologism originally derived from African American folklore, but the application will be broadened in this discussion beyond that single ethnic and national framework. The simplicity of the word belies its layers of signification and the vast depth of historical consciousness that informs it. In the black folk tradition of the United States, one which stretches back to before slavery and continues today with hip-hop/urban culture, "badness" has often been a site of artistic agency and political resistance.[8] The badman archetype encompasses a spectrum of stylized masculinities constructed through gossip and oral tales (traditionally called "lies" in the South) and other popular genres (jokes and riddles, toasts, songs, rhymes, and more contemporary media like television, film, blogs, streamed videos, and related social media). It is truly a product of a living, evolving vernacular tradition.

Older examples of badmen include the clever tricksters Brer Rabbit and Slave John, both of whom outwit a stronger opponent who is literally or metaphorically white. A more politically extreme variant is the "bad nigger," a name sanitized to "bad brother man"[9] by James Braxton Peterson. In contemporary times, the character type has particular credence in hip-hop culture and comic books. This figure's genealogy includes outlaws like the nineteenth-century slave rebel Nat Turner (1800-1831), shape-shifter Railroad Bill, and legendary brawler Stagolee/Stagger Lee. All embody the racist stereotypes of black criminality, moral bankruptcy, and/or hypersexuality with a gleeful vengeance. Daryl Cumber Dance explains: "*ba-a-ad* is, of course, in the Black community a term of commendation rather than condemnation."[10] The badman thus "kills without blinking an eye. He courts death constantly and doesn't fear dying, probably because he is willing to do battle with the Devil as well as with his human enemies (and he frequently defeats even the Devil)."[11]

Badmen imagine they can amplify their masculinity by diminishing other men through violence or trickery and by abusing women, emotionally and often sexually.[12] Contemporary urban fiction usually makes them out to be rank materialists, craving fine clothes, flashy cars, chunky jewelry, and all the other trappings of capitalist abundance. These spoils have likely been acquired through illegal means (i.e. the drug trade) or some clever manipulation of the justice system. We see this clearly in *American Gangster* with Frank's lavish gifts to his family, all bought with drug money. With characters like corrupt Detective Trupo (Josh Brolin), the film does add that figures in authority are also complicit in games for cash, power, and influence. The badman is courageous for his capacity to embody and exploit a full range of social taboos, but his appeal is mediated by a sense of fear and ambivalence on the part of readers/viewers who may not know how to digest a deeply flawed (and non-white) outlaw hero. The archetype, by being inflected through the freighted adjective "good," challenges such prevailing ideologies as white supremacy and moral absolutism, but his actions are rarely easy to judge because of a penchant in American popular culture for favoring the underdog and rewarding those who "sin boldly." We see evidence of this fascination in the ongoing popularity of criminal justice-related television shows and plotlines centered upon serial killers and other deviants.

Scott's three films present a pattern of interracial competition and eventual cooperation between two protagonists. The usually non-white badman engages in transformative contact with the white protagonist, catalyzing a shift in the latter's self-understanding. The "good" in the badman then emerges for the viewers, who tend to identify normatively with the white lead/white gaze in their initial distrust of this "other." In contrast, the protagonist of color is not always—if even—changed by his counterpart, nor do the two characters necessarily forge any friendship that makes the rapport deserving of the term "buddy film." The search for social justice is less important in these films than using racial difference as a metaphor for the need to cooperate in the service of some broader imperative. In all three films, this need takes the form of the apprehension of major criminals. The "good badman," a figure straddling moral crossroads, invites the audience to reassess aggregate readings of race, reformulate typical understandings of especially African American men vis-à-vis the criminal justice system, and absorb a more variegated worldview from the screen.

AMERICAN GANGSTER

Denzel Washington's depiction of Frank Lucas is self-controlled and regal in a way that recalls his turn as Malcolm X in Spike Lee's 1992 biopic of the black nationalist leader. It is also a subdued shadow of his hyperkinetic, Academy Award–winning role as Alonso in Antoine Fuqua's *Training Day* (2001), a film that illuminated the badman archetype through a nearly grotesque exaggeration of the "dirty cop" figure. Frank follows in the gangster tradition of his mentor, Ellsworth "Bumpy" Johnson, who passes the mantle on by dying in the younger man's arms. He does so while delivering a jeremiad against the decline of American consumer practices. The setting (what Johnson disparages as a "super fucking discount store") adeptly symbolizes the spread of a new, modernized, readily available commodity culture. The older man's complaints about Asia's lean production tactics and threats to American economic hegemony ("Pushing out all the middlemen. Buying direct from the manufacturer. Sony this. Toshiba that. All them Chinks putting Americans out of work") is ironically the global supply chain management strategy that his protégé later uses to dominate the Harlem drug circuit. Of course, Frank's product is imported heroin, not portable electronics; he does, however, sell at discounted prices, making his mentor's tirade heavily ironical in retrospect.

Frank realizes the bourgeois ideals of upward mobility, familial respect, and entrepreneurial empowerment through the very "Chinks" that Bumpy curses for destroying "pride of ownership . . . [and] personal service."[13] Both men are criminals who have capitalized off of a product that exploits the poor, the vulnerable, and socially underserved in their own community, and yet they are revered as benefactors. Their success provides employment, visible markers of public participation (e.g. Bumpy's famous Thanksgiving turkey giveaways, a tradition which Frank continues) and inspiration for disaffected young people of Harlem. Even Frank's young nephew, an aspiring baseball player, forgoes his athletic talents for the seemingly easy fix of the drug dealer's life; in doing so, he immerses himself in the very pattern of criminal inheritance that gave rise to his uncle's success (that is, badman begets badmen). When we observe Frank's unease about being a poor role model, an African proverb comes to mind: "If a father plays the drum, how can he criticize his son for dancing?"

Creative iterations of the badman character are tied to specific socioeconomic circumstances and historical developments. A difference also exists between constructed "badness" (that is, fetishistic or heroic myth-making out of notorious events or individuals) and actual lived experiences of bad behavior (for instance, the testimony of crime victims). A combination of both exists in *American Gangster*. Scott's project enacts the contradiction of the good badman by bringing this character into conversation with other gangster heroes, most of whom are not African American, and then confronting audiences with the question, "At what cost inclusion?" Frank's inheritance is a subtle parody of the family legacy tradition associated with America's white Establishment as well as the Italian American Mafia crime family. Mafiosi like Dominic Cattano (Armand Assante), despite also being the victims of historical prejudice and discrimination in the United States,[14] do not see blacks as equals. By dismissing the intelligence of their African American competitors, they are more in line with the incredulous and racist FBI—as well as their own past victimizers—than they might think.

Although Frank's Latina wife Eva (Lymari Nadal) senses the Cattanos' racism, Frank uses his business acumen and force of personality to provide a dream deal for the consumer: good product at great prices. This is a nightmare scenario for competing drug barons. If he must be "bad," he does so superlatively, as suggested in the symbolic naming of his best-selling "Blue Magic" packets. Out of the blues spirit stirred up by Southern racism comes the "magic" of American entrepreneurship. Neither his lust nor greed motivates his success; rather, his narrative of ascent[15] pivots on intellectual qualities like innovation, chutzpah, and commitment to the pursuit of middle-class values. He states, "The most important thing in business is honesty, integrity, hard work, [and] family." Contrary to Richie Roberts, his Jewish foil who is an ethical cop but a pathetic father and companion, Lucas personifies the dedicated family man. Indeed, his generosity toward Eva, whose own ostentatious gift of a chinchilla coat contradicts his personal philosophy of understated abundance, initiates his public fall. It is ironical that a soft grey coat reminiscent of another badman figure, the well-heeled pimp, symbolically evokes the "grey areas" between morality and immorality, fame and infamy.

American Gangster, like *Black Rain* and *Body of Lies*, qualifies as a "double protagonist film," a genre where both the idea of manhood and "the burden of male representation" are split between two major characters.[16] The interracial angle complicates their assumed equality, however. According to David Greven, the protagonists have comparable importance plot-wise so neither monopolizes the audience's attention. While competitive with one another (not friendly, as would be found in a buddy film), they are "always complementary halves of a dyad . . . two warring halves of one consciousness."[17] This phrasing echoes black intellectual W. E. B. Du Bois's seminal concept of double consciousness, enunciated back in 1903: "One ever feels his two-ness—an American, a Negro; two souls, two thoughts, two unreconciled strivings; two warring ideals in one dark body whose dogged strength alone keeps it from being torn asunder."[18] The description captures the paradox of being a loyal American yet a second-class citizen in the country of one's birth. Scott's film reconfigures the citizenship paradox by presenting Frank as "an American, a Negro," and a criminal—but a superlative and elegant one at that.

The film's titular epithet—"American gangster"—works to reclaim an African American identity from the gutters of racism and other forms of historical exclusion, but ironically valorizes criminality as a form of legitimate national praxis. So much of the plot and symbolism, from the film's title to the smuggling of drugs in the caskets of Vietnam veterans, is invested in domestic mythmaking. America is, after all, the land of opportunistic individualism as much as opportunity-seeking individuals. Some critics might call the film a perverse hagiography for the way it appears to elevate a criminal through the influential medium of popular cinema, but the ongoing presence of police procedural dramas alone should underscore the ambivalence of a society deeply attracted to (yet repelled by) its villains. The romance of Frank Lucas—which includes his fall—comes at a price; he reaches the pantheon of New York's crime society but his family and associates undergo fracture, death, and dissolution; he is incarcerated and separated from his wife, his mother, and his wealth. Even now, as an octogenarian, he continues to be associated with hustling and breaking the law.[19]

At the conclusion when Frank starts collaborating with Richie to collar other criminals (including numerous members of the police force, whom we might characterize as "bad goodmen"), a tentative reconciliation emerges between the two male "halves." Outsider and insider meet but it is not a seamless fusion, the effacement of one or both individuals for a new one. Only Frank qualifies as the "American gangster," brought to that point through Horatio Alger–type self-enterprise (a very national type of triumph) and yet propelled by memories of racial terror in the South (also particular to US experience). Greven offers a series of other readings, including a queer allegory of seduction that casts one protagonist in pursuit of the other as a lover might pursue his beloved,[20] but more relevant to *American Gangster* is the idea that one protagonist functions in the capacity of the masochist who seeks to emulate—or if not that, capture and crush—the dominant masculinity of the narcissistic male counterpart.[21] Given Richie's role as a white law enforcement officer chasing a self-important, highly disciplined, and ruthless black felon, this interpretation has considerably more credence than does the queer reading.[22]

To segue into the next film, I want to offer a variation on Greven's double-protagonist model using literary rather than psychoanalytical terms. In *Aspects of the Novel* (1927), British writer E. M. Forster delineated two types of characters: round ("capable of surprising in a convincing way"[23]) and flat (premised on "a single idea or quality"[24]). This binary can be combined with the adjectives "active" (round characters as unpredictable and mutating) and "passive" (flat characters as generally static types that can be summed up in a sentence). The most successful pairing of the three films ("round/active" with "round/active") is *American Gangster*. As John Powers comments, Richie and Frank "could almost be mirror images of each other,"[25] perhaps reflecting the arbitrariness of their respective sides of the law. Similar to the black vernacular practice of signifyin(g), these characters are "repetitions with a difference."[26] This configuration is visible on the movie posters that juxtapose the men as shadow selves of one another. With Frank clad in black and Richie in white, the chiaroscuro effect belies the moral ambiguity emerging from their close professional rapport, including the epilogue's explanation that Richie eventually serves as Frank's attorney. Neither character is looking at the other head-on (implying a difference of perspectives), but their bodies are clearly paired and explicitly raced, especially Frank's hands. The symbolism suggests that he is invested in a different kind of labor, far from the manual toil associated with black men historically (and in particular, those from the rural South like Frank's family). Each man's lack of corporeal completion (heads being half-severed at the top) suggests that the relationship between their bodies and minds requires further "fleshing out" to better understand the complexities of their respective motivations and similar—but different—worldviews.

BLACK RAIN

The crime thriller *Black Rain* poses an interpretive challenge because the identity of the badman figure is far less obvious than in *American Gangster*. Both protagonists could fall under the aegis of being good *and* bad, one for reasons of flawed character, the other for the accident of nationality. Before discussing the double-protagonist dynamics of Nick Conklin (Michael Douglas) and Masahiro Matsumoto (Ken Takakura), some cultural history is in order. Although the film is set transnationally, bridging New York and Osaka, Japan, the viewership is meant to be primarily Western and white/Euro-American; as such, the discourse of American domestic identity exists in constant conversation with what is perceived to be alien and un-"home"-like. In the popular novel *Her Father's Daughter* (1921) by Gene Stratton Porter, the white Californian narrator argues with anti-Japanese venom in a way that captures much of the nativist sentiment of the time: "[T]he great body of [the Japanese] are mechanical. They are imitative. They are not developing anything great of their own in their own country. . . . They are not missing imitating every thing [sic] that the white man can do anywhere else on earth."[27] She then describes the alarmist scenario of Eastern invaders toting off everything from sewing machines to cars to submarines back to their small island home. Almost seven decades later, these ideas still have credence as *Black Rain* situates the *yakuza*'s crime of counterfeiting American cash as its central source of conflict.

The rapport between the two detectives emerges as a counter-metaphor for the joining of the two counterfeiting plates. While the latter union creates something phony and criminal, Nick and Masahiro's union creates something genuine and law-abiding, cemented through the bond of police fraternity. Yet the characters are hardly carbon copies of one another. While flawed, American cop Nick embodies a renegade independence and robust physicality differing sharply from his Japanese foil's muted (a)sexuality, dogmatic adherence to rules and conventions, and almost child-like belief in collective good. Scott postulates that through their exchange, Masahiro "loses his rigidity" and Nick retrieves lost traditions that still exist—at least in the director's mind—in the East. Among these are love of family and a sense of personal and professional honor.[28] Their relationship, like an elastic band, entails a tightening up of the morally lax Westerner and a reciprocal loosening up of the anal-retentive Easterner. This comparison's simplicity is deceiving.

This film both allegorizes and challenges America's perception of its uncontestable place in the world. The film does have a more expansive worldview than Scott's *1492: Conquest of Paradise* (1992), which casts cultural contact zones[29] as little more than danger zones for the European settler-invaders. The "clash of cultures" motif carries over from *Black Rain* to the later film, and while both works traverse national and international borders, *Black Rain*'s representative American couple—white male and white female, both in Japan against their wishes—reinforces the idea that anything Japanese has little place in the United States. Vast cultural differences are the *sine qua non* of the film's "East meets West" premise. Repatriating the gangster Sato (Yusaku Matsuda) to Japan exemplifies—however subtly—the inclination to send foreigners "back where they came from," especially when they violate American laws. Interestingly enough, Douglas's character also returns to his home country upon completion of his work in Japan (and yes, after violating Japanese laws), but the audience understands that this is not an expulsion but a voluntary and triumphant return.

Black Rain plays out rather obliviously against a real backdrop of Asian-descent individuals and groups living in the United States as supposed "foreigners" despite having been citizens or legal residents for decades, if not generations. While the story of black teenager Emmett Louis Till, murdered in 1955 by Mississippi racists for his whistling at a white woman, has become a recognizable national shame, the same degree of historical solicitude has been denied the 1982 bludgeoning death of Vincent Chin, a 27-year-old Chinese American killed in Detroit. At a bar to celebrate his forthcoming nuptials, Chin was the victim of mistaken ethnic identification and racial scapegoating. Like Till's murderers, his working-class killers (similar to Till's, these individuals were white and related to one another) escaped major punishment because state hate crimes legislation was not yet in place. This galvanizing moment in Asian American history reminds the nation that civil rights victories for one group do not diminish the need for constant vigilance on the part of others.

Assuming that he was of Japanese descent and not even considering that he might be an American with similar opinions about foreign competition, Chin's murderers attacked him as revenge for Japan's success in the domestic and international automobile markets.[30] A contributing factor to their misidentification was the equation of any trace of Asian identity with being "un-American," "foreign," and by extension, "the enemy." These prejudices have deep roots in the WWII experience which surfaces in the film, especially in light of the internment of Japanese Americans (two thirds of whom were US-born), and the timing of the redress package (signed by then-president Ronald Reagan in 1988), one year before the film's release. The title *Black Rain* refers to radioactive fallout from the 1945 bombings of Hiroshima and Nagasaki. The dehydrated victims of the bombing would eagerly open their mouths to drink the rain, but the contaminated liquid only accelerated their deaths, burning them from the inside out. Sugai (Tomisaburo Wakayama), a head gangster, explains that American imperialism and materialist amnesia have corrupted the contemporary Japanese in the same way. Yet the genesis of the anti-Asian bias in the United States began even earlier with two centuries of specifically race-targeted legislation, including denial of basic citizenship rights (e.g. the Chinese Exclusion Acts, beginning in 1882); alien land laws; massacres and attempted "driving outs" of entire populations from cities like Tacoma, Seattle, San Bernadino, and Portland; Asiatic Exclusion Leagues; and related Yellow Perilist groups that surged again during the twentieth century's economic ascendancy of China, Japan, and the Asian Tigers (Hong Kong, Singapore, South Korea, and Taiwan). Distrust of Japan and Japanese-descent people, like growing Sinophobia, is an ongoing problem in the United States today.

Heir to this historical legacy because of its clash-of-cultures premise, *Black Rain* does not deal directly with the complications of Asian American identity in a country that still too often assumes "real" Americans are of European descent and that US global hegemony is both a necessity and a given. Scott tackles the traditional East/West divide, using this motif to endorse a larger premise for human cooperation: eradicating crime. The film is not assimilationist at heart because neither the American nor the Japanese protagonist integrates completely to the other side ("going native"), and the film ends with their parting at an airport, that most recognizable and non-committal of transnational spaces. Their exchange includes both a Japanese bow and a modified American handshake, alongside an exchange of gifts, a custom shared by both cultures. Policing protocols, the English language, and habits like using chopsticks are both resisted and later shared, but the basis of the men's eventual friendship is a dialogic exchange about workplace ethics: to steal or not to steal; to toe the line or take the initiative; to privilege the self or the group, and so on. The premise for Masahiro's "badness" is his disadvantage of being non-American and non-white. He also displays a stubborn insistence on following rules and being deferential to authority. Yet these traits render him "good" once Nick begins to alter his perception about the Japanese. Once they morph from being the "enemies" of his previous perception, they are resourceful partners in the pursuit of *truly* bad men. Of course, this usefulness is predicated on their being second in command rather than the leaders.

Nick's partner and intercultural buffer, Charlie Vincent (Andy Garcia), displays a playful openness to cultural exchange that makes him vulnerable and eventually, expendable. From a jingoistic perspective, he is almost *too* susceptible to influence, too ready to "make friends" with a potential enemy. It is no wonder that he leaves his passport in his jacket, which is then snatched away by the gangsters. This theft symbolizes a xenophobic American fear of Japan's supposed cultural rapacity. Charlie has carelessly forgotten to guard the sanctity of his American identity; he loses his head in the nightclub by letting loose with Masahiro then loses it literally in a moment that shines a Klieg light on a seemingly barbaric national practice. The beheading, hardly a Japanese assault *per se*, is supposed to be an archaic moment in a hyper-charged, futuristic space. The *yakuza*'s deployment of this ancient and yet very contemporary gesture (which recurs in *Body of Lies* as a terrorist trademark) is meant to allegorize the trans-historical presence of international gangsters, ones as ruthless as Sato and as unforgiving as Sugai. Of course, the assumption here is that these gangster-terrorists come from "elsewhere," definitely not from American shores.

Historically, Japan, like the United States, has been no stranger to imperialist designs. Nick's task of escorting trickster badman Sato back to the gangster's homeland, being duped by the sneering younger man, and then feeling out of his element in frenetic Osaka give him the impression he is serving the country that should be serving *him*. Three empires converge and merge in *Black Rain*: the *yakuza* as criminal empire (connecting the United States and Japan through migration of drugs, weapons, grudges, and gang members), the United States as unscrupulous military and cultural empire (to the Japanese), and Japan as unscrupulous commercial empire (to the United States). David Ansen remarks, "Now that the Japanese are beating us at our own industrial games, Hollywood feels free to indulge in a little Asia-bashing again."[31] Nick is supposed to be a red-blooded American male, a renegade detective with disdain for authority ("suits") and an attitude of self-possessed—if at times egotistical—individuality. This brashness fuels his justification for workplace theft, an ethical dilemma revisited by *American Gangster* when Richie refuses to steal any of the drug money he uncovers even though it makes him a pariah among his colleagues. Transported to foreign soil, Nick's insecurities erupt like an irritated pimple as he lacks the assurance that he will "win" when it comes to asserting himself among these non-English-speaking, non-white colleagues. This fear is what casts Masahiro as the "badman": he is stiff and territorial, believes wholeheartedly in hierarchies, and even informs his superior about Nick's having disturbed the crime scene instead of first approaching the visitor with his doubts. Masahiro works through subtlety rather than through direct confrontation and the verbal assertiveness characteristic of his American counterpart. The older detective acquires the epithet "good" by seemingly becoming the "timid Tonto to Nick's Lone Ranger,"[32] although his core values remain relatively static compared to his American partner's eventual attitude adjustment.

If pronounced in the stereotypically Japanese way (conflating the "l"s and "r"s), Nick's surname "Conklin" morphs into "conquerin'," an apt commentary upon his John Wayne–like attitude of cultural superiority over the "little Nips." Even at the final exchange of goodbyes, he calls Masahiro a "cowboy" because the man has proven himself by saving the life of a *gaijin* (foreigner). Like Joyce, the blonde American bar hostess played by Kate Capshaw, he is being rewarded for "picking a side," and that happens to be Nick's. By giving the straight-laced detective the counterfeiting plates, Nick also redeems himself by eschewing greed for honesty. However, he does confer the burden of choice onto his colleague (whether or not to steal), thereby literally passing the buck and keeping the forgeries safely in Japan. Masahiro, we note, has had his name truncated to "Mas" to suit his American partner's preference, an essentially colonial act of renaming, even though it doubles as a gesture of acceptance and comradeship.

Nick's insistence on winning emerges in the initial motorcycle challenge in New York that starts the film, and is later reiterated in the final chase scene where he reprises the wipe-out maneuver to subdue Sato.[33] Instead of impaling the gangster on a sharp stick (planned in the original script[34]), he decides to share the recognition of collaring the criminal with Masahiro, thereby emerging not only as generous but also restrained like his Japanese hosts. But this is a strategic choice on the filmmaker's part: viewers recently witnessed Sato slice off part of his body as ritual punishment; recalling Charlie's death, to see Nick perpetrate bodily harm would make him the same kind of brute as the gangster. His choice actually elevates him above the masochistic savagery of the Japanese. What's more, the impaling would have been a kind of symbolic rape, a feminizing punishment of the misbehaving Asian male coupled with the re-masculinization of the Western male (cowboy-style) as revenge for having had his phallic gun confiscated by Japanese authorities. Such an ending would likely have been too heavy-handed, if not grotesque.

Paul Baumann criticizes the Japanese characters as being "ethnocentric and inscrutable,"[35] always "bowing and scraping" while Masahiro "waxes obsequious and pious."[36] This description sounds like Osaka is peopled with yellow Stepin Fetchits and glib Charlie Chans. Would a Japanese film critic complain about American characters clownishly smiling and shaking hands, since that is the Western equivalent to bowing? Probably not, because the expectation tends to be that the non-West should know about the West's customs and, if possible, try to emulate them (but, given the imitation motif, not too closely). Baumann's impressions parallel the ignorance and haughtiness exemplified by Joyce who has lived in Japan for *seven* years and yet is unable to read the headlines. Surprisingly, she blames her host country for being too finely nuanced in its social customs and declares herself ever ostracized as a foreigner even though viewers may wonder why she stays if she detests the place so much ("Yes means no and maybe means never. . . . No one's going to help a *gaijin*").[37]

As a foreigner who benefits from white male privilege as well as a sense of national entitlement, Nick does not endure the domestic xenophobia of a Vincent Chin; even in Japan, he shrugs off the censure of his hosts (including a deportation order), interferes with what is not his professional jurisdiction (the meetings of the gangsters), and breaks elementary rules of police conduct (taking and destroying evidence from a crime scene). Even if they might view him as the prototypical "ugly American" at the start, audience members come to identify with him as inexorable, his victories inevitable, and his cause righteous. Nick thus manages to belong in an environment that does not even want him. One movie poster trumpets his exceptionalism, making him sound more like a would-be dictator than what Timothy P. Hofmeister calls a "modern warrior."[38] The caption reads, "An American Cop in Japan. Their country. Their laws. Their game. His rules."[39] Such a scenario in the United States with a Japanese cop would be fodder for comedy or political satire, unless the Asian protagonist was a visiting martial arts master or a likeable, non-threatening action comedian like Jackie Chan.

The racist stereotype that informs the entire plot does not undergo much—if any—contestation. Asians remain clever badmen; they are good imitators but lack originality, a fault for which they compensate by appropriating, through sharp practice (in business terms but also literally, given the prevalence of knife and swordplay in this film), the supposed US birthright of world domination. Japan is cast as bound-up in feudal honor codes while its Western counterparts celebrate innovative, self-made men. The former is past-oriented, as if swaying on quaint wooden *getas*, while the latter sprints forward on Nike sneakers (probably manufactured somewhere in Asia). Even Scott, while praising his Japanese cast's lack of ego, reveals his susceptibility to these assumptions: "I thought I was going to get Kabuki Theater, and I didn't get that at all. I got very good, very balanced, *very contemporary,* very real performances."[40] If a contemporary Asian director like Japanese Takashi Miike or Korean Bong Joon-Ho were to declare his surprise that British actors can excel at more than Shakespeare or that American thespians can have a range that exceeds the minstrel show, significant critical fallout would result. Like the long-lasting radioactive residue of black rain, the eponymous film signals the need for more long-term representational variety and accountability, both politically as well as culturally. Where black rain meets the dawn's early light, nationalist storms are sure to follow.

BODY OF LIES

The events of 9-11 detonated waves of negative press across Europe and North America about Arab, Middle Eastern, and Muslim peoples. Many commentators awkwardly conflated religious identities like Sikhs, Hindus, and Muslims, homogenized types of Muslims, and branded all Middle Easterners would-be terrorists. Documentaries like *Reel Bad Arabs* (2006) dissected films that either circumscribe or variegate the identities of this globally diverse group of people. Hollywood's Arabs, depicted in such works as *True Lies* (1994), *Courage Under Fire* (1996), *The Siege* (1998), and *Rules of Engagement* (2000), have paved the way for a perpetuation of anti-Arab and Islamophobic stereotypes.[41] *Body of Lies* partially critiques these with the fatal case of identity theft central to the plot, and yet reinforces them with the terrorist jihadists coming across as swarthy, unshaven, sweating, and ruthlessly violent. The vulnerability of CIA agent Roger Ferris's naked white torso twisting beneath the Islamist's blade symbolizes the US fear of losing control in the Middle East, as well as the sense that alien cultural values would carve the heart out of American freedom-fighters and other "just" men and women.

Scott's *Kingdom of Heaven* (2005) was among those works praised by *Reel Bad Arabs* for bringing forth a startlingly contemporary humanism despite the film's twelfth-century setting.[42] Middle Eastern men in particular have borne the brunt of the negative stereotypes: wealthy sheiks with a yen for dark sunglasses and gold braid; hook-nosed merchants who swindle barter-bashful tourists; hookah-smoking buffoons; and imperious kings with nymphs belly-dancing their way through perfumed harems. Women tend to be viewed as powerless, silenced, cloaked, or else sexually exotic. As Toufic El Rassi states in his graphic novel *Arab in America* (2007), the most identifiable Arab is the brown caricature: "Most of the actors that play the Arabs look like stereotypes, they are dark-skinned and most are in need of a shave or are wearing Islamic or traditional dress."[43] The "violent barbarian" or "sand nigger" stereotype (to recall a racist epithet popularized in the wake of US military deployment in the Middle East) continues to have high currency in American film and television. Reflects El Rassi, "Whenever the Middle East is covered in the news we invariably see the images of crazed Muslim mobs wielding machine guns or marching with scary masks."[44] For any director seeking to contest such views, the challenge is to circumvent the force of racism in popular media (including cable news and radio shows, commercial advertising, and print journalism, including popular magazines that publish controversial cover images like *Newsweek*'s "Muslim Rage" issue of September 2012).[45] These venues often underscore how "they" are not like "us"/the US.

In *Body of Lies*, the good badman is Jordanian intelligence head Hani Salaam. He embodies the most "Westernized" Arab. Mark Strong, a British actor of Austrian and Italian descent, plays him in a race-bending, brownface role.[46] Clean-shaven, articulate, and well-dressed, he is neither the foppish puppet nor the messianic maniac. For viewers most hardened by the barbarian stereotype, he appears an unseemly mimic man, *almost* white but not quite. In that sense, he is a foil to Ferris (Leonardo DiCaprio) who pretends to be a member of the crowd, speaking Arabic, dyeing his hair, and growing a sparse beard, hoping to pass for a local. For other viewers, Hani is a parody of Valentino, a musky sexual enigma who handily combines "menace and attar-of-roses in his tailored Savile Row suits—with incredible delicacy."[47] He contrasts the quotidian menace (another "bad goodman") embodied by Ed Hoffman, Ferris's mild-mannered CIA supervisor (Russell Crowe) who successfully—if at times, absurdly—intertwines his work life with his comfort-ably suburban home life.

Hani's fastidious demeanor, insistence on trustworthiness (which is tied to his aversion to lies, hence the film's title), and reputation as a master torturer render him a kind of queer nobleman, simultaneously masculine and feminine, imperious yet excruciatingly polite. Like a jealous lover, he insists on transparency from Ferris but once crossed, withdraws his assistance until the very last possible moment. His maneuvers result in Ferris's loss of fin-gers (a mini-castration perhaps and echo of Sato's self-punishment), psycho-logical trauma, and eventual detachment from the profession. Hani's use of the greasy epithet "my dear" to address the American oscillates between being oddly humorous and cleverly subversive; it subtly feminizes Ferris, destabilizing him as a typical alpha male reminiscent of Nick Conklin. This robust masculinity the agent must then recuperate by pursuing his native love interest, Aisha, who has the traditionally feminine occupation of nurse and must be "saved" from the terrorist kidnappers. These heroic motions have been carefully and subtly choreographed by Hani; while he lacks the high-tech surveillance equipment of Hoffman's team, he is a skillful infiltrator and does not negotiate with individuals who break his rules.

In *Terrorism and American Cinema*, Robert Cettl observes that even though he needs their help, "[Hani] demands to be treated as an equal, with due respect from the American intelligence community."[48] In many ways, the Jordanian appears to be the least trustworthy, yet emerges as the deliver-er—the good badman—after Ferris falls into the hands of the Islamist mas-termind, Al-Saleem. Of course, the fact that he orchestrated the entire kid-napping (a parallel to Ferris's identity theft of architect Omar Sadiki) emerges later as a warning to the American "war on terror" community about abusing the trust of their foreign colleagues. A flippant attitude toward cultu-ral cooperation, like that of Hoffman, "jeopardizes the success of needed field work rather than ideally complement it as it should. Lies have conse-quences."[49] Ironically, "Salaam" and "Saleem" sound similar; while the for-mer, Hani's surname, means "peace" in Arabic, the latter character's purpose is to destroy this very peace. The line between the two people, Scott reminds us thus, can be very fine indeed; not only do we have to listen carefully to discern the difference, we also have to see carefully. The film is an extended exercise in de- and re-familiarization with the Middle East that the US intelli-gence community feels it knows so well.

A cynical reading of this similarity might suggest that "salaam" would prevail if more Arabs resembled Hani than Al-Saleem, who is, after all, a religious extremist. Yet Hani is no moral pillar; like Hoffman who has "little interest or sympathy . . . when civilians are killed or informants tortured,"[50] Hani has foibles that humanize, not lionize him. While Crowe's Hoffman is an active father, Hani seems to overlook his wife and children while spending time with attractive female colleagues. Both Americans and Jordanians abuse and exploit prisoners through state-sanctioned torture. With a plot dependent on camouflage and split-second judgments, the film lines up Hani and Al-Saleem as a dyadic pairing with Ferris and Hoffman; neither "couple" is very similar other than their shared nationality, religion, or geographical proximity. Yet war brings all of them together with harrowing consequences. It is, thus, the body that "lies" as far as being a reliable index for judging a person's capacities, motivations, or strategic worth.

All three of Scott's aforementioned films—*American Gangster, Black Rain*, and *Body of Lies*—seek to dispel the equation of biology with destiny. As broadly successful artistic ventures featuring interracial partnerships as well as rivalries, they demonstrate how films such as these can be as entertaining and provocative as they are artistically rendered and profitable. The balance just has to be right.

NOTES

1. The author wishes to acknowledge a National Endowment for the Humanities Summer Institute Grant in contemporary African American literature (Pennsylvania State University, 2012) for support for research on this chapter. Laurence F. Knapp and Andrea F. Kulas, introduction to *Ridley Scott: Interviews*, eds. Laurence F. Knapp and Andrea F. Kulas (Jackson: University Press of Mississippi, 2005), xii.

2. Paul M. Sammon, *Ridley Scott: The Making of His Movies* (New York: Thunder's Mouth Press, 1999), 101.

3. *Prometheus*, directed by Ridley Scott (Los Angeles, CA: Twentieth Century Fox, 2012), film.

4. Richard A. Schwartz, *The Films of Ridley Scott* (Westport, CT: Praeger, 2001), viii.

5. *American Gangster*, directed by Ridley Scott (2007; Universal City, CA: Universal Studios Home Entertainment, 2008), DVD; *Black Rain*, directed by Ridley Scott (1989; Hollywood, CA: Paramount Studios, 2006), DVD; *Body of Lies*, directed by Ridley Scott (2008; Burbank, CA: Warner Home Video, 2009), DVD.

6. *American Gangster*'s screenplay is based on Mark Jacobson, "The Return of Superfly," *New York Magazine*, August 14, 2000, accessed July 27, 2012, http://nymag.com/nymag/features/3649/.

7. Richard Corliss, "Biggest Buzz—Review of *American Gangster* and *No Country for Old Men*," *Time*, September 3, 2007, 60.

8. See John Roberts, *From Trickster to Badman: The Black Folk Hero from Slavery to Freedom* (Philadelphia: University of Pennsylvania Press, 1989) and Jerry H. Bryant, *Born in a Mighty Bad Land: The Violent Man in African American Folklore and Fiction* (Bloomington: University of Indiana Press, 2003). For more recent scholarship, see Imani Perry, *Prophets of the Hood: Politics and Poetics in Hip Hop* (Durham, NC: Duke University Press, 2004); William Jelani Cobb, *To the Break of Dawn: A Freestyle on the Hip Hop Aesthetic* (New York: New York University Press, 2004); and Jabari Asim, *The N Word: Who Can Say It, Who Shouldn't, and Why* (New York: Houghton Mifflin, 2007).

9. James Braxton Peterson, "Bad Brother Man: Black Folk Figure Narratives in Comics" (paper presented at the National Endowment for the Humanities Summer Institute in Contemporary African American Literature, Pennsylvania State University, State College, Pennsylvania, July 8-27, 2012).

10. Daryl Cumber Dance, ed., *From My People: 400 Years of African American Folklore* (New York: W.W. Norton, 2002), 3.

11. Daryl Cumber Dance, *Shuckin' and Jivin': Folklore from Contemporary Black Americans* (Bloomington: Indiana University Press, 1978), 224-225.

12. Ibid., 225.

13. Bumpy's epithet conflates Japanese electronics manufacturers with Chinese producers. Frank's contacts, on the other hand, are Southeast Asian heroin traffickers in countries like Vietnam, Myanmar, and Thailand. This kind of minority-minority racism is not always highlighted in films that focus on the reductive black-white racial dichotomy.

14. J. Madison Davis asserts that "Italians were often as discriminated against as African Americans," which in the long view of history (including transatlantic slavery, Jim Crow, and continuing socio-economic disparities) seems inaccurate. Davis does make a valid point about gangster movies: "that the worst of societies' enemies can be motivated by traditional middle-class values." J. Madison Davis, "Living Black, Living White: Cultural Choices in Crime Films," *World Literature Today* 82, no. 3 (May-June 2008): 10, accessed July 14, 2012.

15. A term borrowed from black literary critic Robert Stepto, "narrative of ascent" refers to the literal migration of over 1.5 million African Americans during the early twentieth century (approximately 1910-1930), primarily from rural areas in the South to the industrial North. "Ascent" also denotes elevation and betterment (economically, socially, culturally, and spiritually) that was associated with the escape from Southern racism. Lucas was originally from North Carolina and relocated to New York City where he made his fortune. For the theoretical framework, see Stepto, *From Behind the Veil: A Study of Afro-American Narrative* (Urbana: University of Illinois Press, 1991).

16. David Greven, "Contemporary Hollywood Masculinity and the Double Protagonist Film," *Cinema Journal* 48, no. 4 (2009): 23.

17. Ibid., 24.

18. W. E. B. Du Bois, *The Souls of Black Folk* (Rockville, MD: Arc Manor, 2008).

19. See The Associated Press, "Real-life 'American Gangster' sentenced in $17K Theft," NBCNewYork.com, July 27, 2012, accessed July 27, 2012, http://www.nbcnewyork.com/news/local/Frank-Lucas-American-Gangster-Sentenced-Stealing-Government-Check-164055646.html.

20. Greven, "Contemporary Hollywood," 27.

21. Ibid., 33.

22. Ibid., 43.

23. E. M. Forster, *Aspects of the Novel, and Related Works*, ed. Oliver Stallybrass (London: Edward Arnold, 1974).

24. Ibid., 47.

25. John Powers, "Patriot Games; All in the Family; Big Shots," *Vogue* 197, no. 11 (November 2007): 262.

26. Henry Louis Gates, Jr., ed. *Black Literature and Literary Theory* (New York: Methuen, 1984), 3.

27. Gene Stratton Porter, *Her Father's Daughter* (New York: Doubleday, 1921), 117.

28. Donald Chase, "In *Black Rain*, East Meets West with a Bang! Bang!" in *Ridley Scott: Interviews*, eds. Laurence F. Knapp and Andrea F. Kulas (Jackson: University Press of Mississippi, 2005), 66.

29. For more on the epithet "the contact zone," see Mary Louise Pratt, *Imperial Eyes: Travel Writing and Transculturation* (New York: Routledge, 1992).

30. See Frank H. Wu, "Why Vincent Chin Matters," *New York Times*, June 22, 2012, accessed July 27, 2012, http://www.nytimes.com/2012/06/23/opinion/why-vincent-chin-matters.html.

31. David Ansen, "Rambo Mike Runs Amok," *Newsweek* (October 2, 1989): 70.

32. Brian D. Johnson, "Clichés in Conflict; *Black Rain*," *Maclean's*, October 2, 1989, 65.

33. With brands like Honda, Kawasaki, Mitsubishi, Suzuki, and Yamaha, the Japanese virtuosity in motorcycle manufacturing proves to be an ironical reminder of Nick's hypocritical insularity. The products are used, but the acknowledgment is not given, as if the ends efface the means. Brian D. Johnson suggests that the final racing showdown on the sake farm "repatriates an American symbol of rebellion that has been lost to Japanese technology." While convincing, this suggestion does not account for the fact that Nick would not have been able to beat Sato on

foot (being heavier) and his maneuver is not patently "American." He merely used Japanese technology to beat a Japanese person, and the least desirable type at that. See Johnson, "Clichés in Conflict," 65.

34. Sammon, *Ridley Scott*, 93.

35. Paul Baumann, "Take Your Galoshes: 'Sea of Love' and 'Black Rain,'" *Commonweal* (October 20, 1989): 566.

36. Ibid., 566.

37. Paul Sammon goes further, casting contemporary Japan as "a society seething with corruption and mob violence, with prostitution and the repression of the individual." See Sammon, *Ridley Scott*, 96. Viewers may be confused about what prostitution he is referring to here, since the only major female character is the blonde Joyce who kisses Nick and "chooses [his] side" based on little more than a few conversations and exchanges of glances. While Sato's girlfriend is mentioned (and followed), there is no evidence that she is a prostitute. One wonders whether there is not some tired Western stereotyping of Asian women as prostitutes (the "geisha-girl") going on in this instance.

38. Timothy P. Hofmeister, "Achillean Love and Honor in Ridley Scott's *Black Rain*," *Classical and Modern Literature* 13, no. 1 (Fall 1992): 45.

39. "*Black Rain* Slideshow," Internet Movie Database, accessed August 8, 2012, http://www.imdb.com/media/rm1744280064/tt0096933.

40. Chase, "East Meets West," 68. Emphasis added.

41. *Reel Bad Arabs: How Hollywood Vilifies a People*, directed by Jeremy Earp and Sut Jhally (Northampton, MA: Media Education Foundation, 2006), DVD.

42. See James M. Wall, "Double Vision," *Christian Century* (June 14, 2005): 45.

43. Toufic El Rassi, *Arab in America* (San Francisco: Last Gasp, 2008), 43.

44. Ibid., 48.

45. Alexander Hotz, September 17, 2012 (18:26 pm), comment on *Newsweek* cover, "*Newsweek* 'Muslim rage' cover invokes a rage of its own," *The Guardian US News Blog*, September 17, 2012, http://www.guardian.co.uk/media/us-news-blog/2012/sep/17/muslim-rage-newsweek-magazine-twitter.

46. By "brownface," I allude to the US historical phenomenon of "blackface" and the more recent neologism "yellowface," all expressions referring to an actor's attempt to adopt another racial or ethnic group's "look." This imitation tends to be through cosmetics or a combination of cosmetics with mannerisms and stereotypical speech, often for entertainment purposes.

47. Roger Clarke, "Body of Lies," *Sight and Sound,* December 2008, 55.

48. Robert Cettl, *Terrorism in American Cinema: An Analytical Filmography, 1960-2008* (Jefferson, NC: McFarland, 2008), 52.

49. Ibid., 52.

50. Stuart Levine, "World Helmers Take Dark View," *Variety* 413, no. 1 (November 17-23, 2008): A4.

REFERENCES

American Gangster. DVD. Directed by Ridley Scott. 2007; Universal City, CA: Universal Studios Home Entertainment, 2008.

Ansen, David. "Rambo Mike Runs Amok." *Newsweek* (October 2, 1989): 70.

Asim, Jabari. *The N Word: Who Can Say It, Who Shouldn't, and Why*. New York: Houghton Mifflin, 2007.

The Associated Press. "Real-life 'American Gangster' sentenced in $17K theft." *NBCNewYork.com*, July 27, 2012, accessed July 27, 2012. http://www.nbcnewyork.com/news/local/Frank-Lucas-American-Gangster-Sentenced-Stealing-Government-Check-164055646.html.

Baumann, Paul. "Take Your Galoshes: 'Sea of Love' and 'Black Rain.'" *Commonweal*, October 20, 1989, 116-118; 565-566.

Black Rain. DVD. Directed by Ridley Scott. 1989; Hollywood, CA: Paramount Studios, 2006.

Body of Lies. DVD. Directed by Ridley Scott. 2008; Burbank, CA: Warner Home Video, 2009.

Bryant, Jerry H. *Born in a Mighty Bad Land: The Violent Man in African American Folklore and Fiction*. Bloomington: University of Indiana Press, 2003.

Cettl, Robert. *Terrorism in American Cinema, 1960-2008*. Jefferson, NC: McFarland, 2009.

Chase, Donald. "In *Black Rain*, East Meets West with a Bang! Bang!" In *Ridley Scott: Interviews*, edited by Laurence F. Knapp and Andrea F. Kulas, 64-69. Jackson: University of Mississippi Press, 2005.

Clarke, Roger. "Body of Lies." *Sight and Sound* (December 2008): 55.

Cobb, William Jelani. *To the Break of Dawn: A Freestyle on the Hip Hop Aesthetic*. New York: New York University Press, 2004.

Corliss, Richard. "Biggest Buzz—Review of *American Gangster* and *No Country for Old Men*." *Time*, Sept. 3, 2007.

Dance, Daryl Cumber, ed. *From My People: 400 Years of African American Folklore: An Anthology*. New York: W. W. Norton, 2002.

———. *Shuckin' and Jivin': Folklore from Contemporary African Americans*. Bloomington: University of Indiana Press, 1978.

Davis, J. Madison. "Living Black, Living White: Cultural Choices in Crime Films." *World Literature Today* 82, no. 3 (May-June 2008): 9-11. Accessed July 14, 2012.

Du Bois, W. E. B. *The Souls of Black Folk*. Rockville, MD: Arc Manor, 2008.

El Rassi, Toufic. *Arab in America*. San Francisco: Last Gasp, 2008.

Forster, E. M. *Aspects of the Novel, and Related Works*, edited by Oliver Stallybrass. London: Edward Arnold, 1974.

Gates, Henry Louis, Jr., ed. *Black Literature and Literary Theory*. New York: Methuen, 1984.

Greven, David. "Contemporary Hollywood Masculinity and the Double-Protagonist Film." *Cinema Journal* 48, no. 4 (2009): 22-43.

Guardian US News Blog, The. http://www.guardian.co.uk/world/us-news-blog.

Hofmeister, Timothy P. "Achillean Love and Honor in Ridley Scott's *Black Rain*." *Classical and Modern Literature* 13, no. 1 (Fall 1992): 45-51.

Internet Movie Database. "*Black Rain* Slideshow." Accessed August 8, 2012. http://www.imdb.com/media/rm1744280064/tt0096933.

Jacobson, Mark. "The Return of Superfly." *New York Magazine,* August 14, 2000. Accessed July 27, 2012. http://nymag.com/nymag/features/3649/.

Johnson, Brian D. "Clichés in Conflict; *Black Rain*." *Maclean's*, October 2, 1989, 65.

Knapp, Laurence F., and Andrea F. Kulas. "Introduction." In *Ridley Scott: Interviews*, edited by Laurence F. Knapp and Andrea F. Kulas, vii-xvi. Jackson: University Press of Mississippi, 2005.

Levine, Stuart. "World Helmers Take Dark View." *Variety* 413, no. 1 (November 17-23, 2008): A1, A4.

Perry, Imani. *Prophets of the Hood: Politics and Poetics in Hip Hop*. Durham, NC: Duke University Press, 2004.

Peterson, James Braxton. "Bad Brother Man: Black Folk Figure Narratives in Comics." Paper presented at the National Endowment for the Humanities Summer Institute in Contemporary African American Literature, Penn State University, State College, Pennsylvania, July 8-27, 2012.

Porter, Jean Stratton. *Her Father's Daughter*. New York: Doubleday, 1921.

Powers, John. "Patriot Games; All in the Family; Big Shots." *Vogue* 197, no. 11 (November 2007): 262.

Pratt, Mary Louise. *Imperial Eyes: Travel Writing and Transculturation*. New York: Routledge, 1992.

Prometheus. Directed by Ridley Scott. Los Angeles, CA: Twentieth Century Fox, 2012.

Reel Bad Arabs: How Hollywood Vilifies a People. Directed by Jeremy Earp and Sut Jhally. Northampton, MA: Media Education Foundation, 2006.

Roberts, John. *From Trickster to Badman: The Black Folk Hero from Slavery to Freedom*. Philadelphia: University of Pennsylvania Press, 1989.

Sammon, Paul M. *Ridley Scott: The Making of His Movies*. New York: Thunder's Mouth Press, 1999.

Schwartz, Richard A. *The Films of Ridley Scott*. Westport, CT: Praeger, 2001.

————. Introduction to *The Films of Ridley Scott*, by Schwartz, vii-xii. Westport, CT: Praeger, 2001.

Stepto, Robert. *From Behind the Veil: A Study of Afro-American Narrative*. Urbana: University of Illinois Press, 1991.

Wall, James M. "Double Vision." *Christian Century*, June 14, 2005: 45.

Wu, Frank H. "Why Vincent Chin Matters." *New York Times*, June 22, 2012. Accessed July 27, 2012. http://www.nytimes.com/2012/06/23/opinion/why-vincent-chin-matters.html.

Chapter Two

A Double-Edged Sword: Honor in *The Duellists*

James Edwin Mahon

The Duellists (1977), released on Blu-ray disc in the United States on November 20, 2012, nearly ten days before his 75th birthday, was Sir Ridley Scott's first feature-length film.[1] As one writer has pointed out, "*The Duellists* is a remarkably assured debut, technically dazzling, thematically mature."[2] In competition for the Palme d'Or at the Cannes Film Festival that same year, it won the prize "*avec unanimité*" (unanimously) for best first film by a director.[3] It also won the neophyte filmmaker[4] the prize for Best Foreign Director at the David di Donatello Awards in Italy in 1978, an honor previously bestowed on some of Scott's favorite directors, among them Ingmar Bergman and Akira Kurosawa. These two awards, together with the other nominations that the film received in Britain[5] and the generally positive reviews it earned worldwide (Pauline Kael, for example, called it "consistently entertaining and eerily beautiful"[6]) makes the "relative obscurity into which *The Duellists* soon fell all the more puzzling."[7] Sadly, as Paul Sammon laments, "Once available on Paramount Home Video, virtually forgotten today [1999], only occasionally revived on American cable TV channels like American Movie Classics and Bravo, *The Duellists* has slipped through the pop culture cracks." He adds that it has become Scott's "least-seen, least-appreciated work. One wonders how long this distressing state of affairs will continue, however, since this is definitely a film ripe for rediscovery."[8]

This chapter aims to demonstrate that *The Duellists*, which is "one of the most satisfying cinemations of a Joseph Conrad story yet made"[9] and emblematic of "[o]ne of Ridley Scott's finest hours,"[10] contains the director's deepest meditation thus far on the nature of honor. Honor is a theme in many of his films, including the police thriller *Black Rain* (1989), the historical epics *Gladiator* (2000), *Kingdom of Heaven* (2005), and *Robin Hood* (2010), and the military films *G. I. Jane* (1997) and *Black Hawk Down* (2002).[11] Nevertheless, it is in *The Duellists* that Scott presents us with the most effective treatment yet of the subject, implying that honor is a double-edged sword—a notion capable of being wielded effectively or poorly.

THE TWO HUSSARS

The Duellists—note the English spelling—is an adaptation of the novella *The Duel*[12] by Polish-born Joseph Conrad, one of Scott's favorite authors.[13] It first appeared in serial form in *The Pall Mall Magazine* from January through May 1908.[14] That same year, it was published as a separate text in the United States under the title *The Point of Honor: A Military Tale*.[15] It is a story about two hussar officers in Napoleon Bonaparte's army, Armand D'Hubert and Gabriel Feraud, who fight a duel in Strasbourg in 1800 during a lull in the Napoleonic Wars. D'Hubert, on orders from General Treillard, comes looking for Feraud to tell him that he is confined to barracks for severely wounding the mayor of Strasbourg's nephew in a duel earlier that morning. Feraud is outraged that D'Hubert would hunt him down in the salon of Madame de Lionne, a woman he has an interest in, and publicly embarrass him. Consequently, Feraud challenges him to a duel. Injured in this first encounter, Feraud afterwards insists upon dueling again. They proceed to have a series of duels in various cities over the next fifteen years. These transpire on foot and on horseback, using cavalry sabers, épées (dueling swords), and pistols, ostensibly in order for Feraud to gain "satisfaction." Finally, D'Hubert disarms his challenger in a pistol exchange. Instead of killing his man, he claims that Feraud's life now belongs to him and sends him on his way. The story is based upon the true tale of two French hussar officers, Pierre Dupont de l'Étang[16] and François Fourier-Sarlovèze,[17] who fought a series of duels over nineteen years, beginning in 1794, on foot and on horseback, as a result of the former having delivered a disagreeable message to the latter.[18]

Hussars were light cavalrymen notorious for being impetuous and flamboyant. Napoleon once said that he would be surprised if a hussar lived beyond thirty, and Conrad remarks of his two characters, "they were officers of the cavalry, and their connection with the high-spirited but fanciful animal which carries men into battle seems particularly appropriate."[19] Conrad presents the officers as opposites in almost everything—appearance, regional background, class, and temperament. D'Hubert, who is in the 4th Hussars, is "tall, with an interesting face and moustache the colour of ripe corn."[20] Feraud, who is in the 7th Hussars, is "short and sturdy, with a hooked nose and a thick crop of black curly hair."[21] D'Hubert is a "Northman . . . born sober under the watery skies of Picardy."[22] Feraud is a "Southerner," a "Gascon . . . who . . . was as though born intoxicated with the sunshine of his vine-ripening country."[23] These differences in appearance and regional background are captured in the film by the casting of the tall, blonde, lanky, and relaxed-appearing Californian actor Keith Carradine as D'Hubert, and the shorter, brunette, more muscular and intense New York actor Harvey Keitel as Feraud.[24]

In the novella, one duelist is "a D'Hubert," a member of an aristocratic family, and is considered something of a "dandy."[25] Feraud, on the other hand, has "no connections" and is the son of "an illiterate blacksmith."[26] D'Hubert is thought by his colonel to have a "cool head" (with the exception of when dueling with Feraud), and is judged by his comrades to have "a frank and equable temper." Even to his sister, he has the potential "to prove eventually a sensible fellow."[27] His comrades nickname him "The Strategist."[28] His rival Feraud is "pugnacious," considered by his comrades to have "exuberance" and "simplicity."[29] D'Hubert repeatedly exclaims that Feraud is "mad," a "lunatic" and "impracticable," whereas Feraud considers the other soldier to be "that pretty staff officer" and one of the "general's pets."[30] In the film, the difference in temperament between the two characters is evident from their very first encounter, with D'Hubert continuing to plead for calm as Feraud becomes more and more enraged at him, hurling insults and taunting him until at last they duel. The difference in class emerges more gradually as D'Hubert is shown in more luxurious private quarters and eventually in the country estate of his wealthy sister, Léonie, while Feraud appears first in officers' quarters and later, walking alone in the streets.

THE BONAPARTIST AND THE REALIST

The above differences between D'Hubert and Feraud are not the most important contrasts in the story. The most vital differences are their divergent attitudes towards the military, towards Napoleon Bonaparte, and ultimately, towards dueling. D'Hubert is a career officer, a man "[m]ilitary to the very bottom of his soul."[31] Highly observant of discipline and order, he is consistently promoted to special positions in his regiment, including *officier d'ordonnance* to General Treillard (while a lieutenant) and *aide-de-camp* to the Prince of Ponte Corvo (while a captain). He is also attached to the Major-General's staff after being promoted to General. This upward mobility, it seems, derives from his leadership ability and level-headedness. It is only his dueling with Feraud that causes him to lose favor among his superior officers and impedes his career at various points.

In contrast to D'Hubert, Feraud is "more pugnacious than military" and a "fighter by vocation."[32] He "had been content to give and receive blows for sheer love of armed strife, and without much thought of advancement."[33] He likewise advances in rank and eventually earns the title of general, but he does so seemingly on the strength of his fighting and fearlessness. For him, fighting was the essence of military existence: "A mere fighter all his life, a cavalry man, a *sabreur*, he conceived war with the utmost simplicity, as, in the main, a massed lot of personal contests, a sort of gregarious dueling."[34] In this respect, Feraud resembles the Emperor Napoleon, whose career Conrad described as having "had the quality of a duel against the whole of Europe."[35] Feraud only begins to actively consider his career in the military when D'Hubert is promoted from lieutenant to captain because "Now that D'Hubert was an officer of superior rank there could be no question of a duel. Neither of them could send or receive a challenge without rendering himself amenable to court-martial."[36] Feraud is, however, temperamentally unsuited to "seize showy occasions and to court the favorable opinion of his chiefs like a mere worldling." He confides in a friend, "I don't know how to fawn on the right sort of people. It isn't in my character."[37] He looks upon D'Hubert's advancing in rank as "intrigue, a conspiracy, a cowardly manoeuvre"[38] to avoid fighting with him.

In the film, this difference in the attitude of each protagonist towards the military is again made explicit from their very first encounter. Feraud, within minutes of meeting and quarreling with D'Hubert, calls him "a proper general's poodle." Later, after the final defeat of Napoleon, when Feraud is in danger of imprisonment (and possibly execution) for his anti-royalist beliefs and D'Hubert's future military career remains secure, the colonel pointedly says about Feraud, "Now there was a man who would ride straight at anything. He ends up at the mercy of that sewer rat, Fouché." The clear implication is that D'Hubert is not such a straight rider, but bends with the political wind in order to facilitate his advancement.

The men's contrasting attitudes toward the military are closely connected to their differing perspectives of the Emperor. Feraud is a "rabid Bonapartist."[39] He might even be said to be the embodiment of a saying that Conrad attributes to Napoleon: "for a French soldier, the word impossible does not exist."[40] After the second and final defeat of the leader, no attempts are made to recruit Feraud to the king's army. Conrad explains, "The Royalists knew they could never make anything of him. He loved The Other too well."[41] Feraud never considers D'Hubert to be loyal to Bonaparte and proclaims on numerous occasions after their initial duel, "This man does not love the Emperor."[42] Such an assessment seems unfair. When Napoleon escapes from his first banishment to Elba to rule France again for what was called "The Hundred Days," the injured D'Hubert makes an attempt to saddle his horse and join up: "Such were the effects of imperial magic upon a calm temperament and a pondered mind."[43] He is also said to mistrust "profoundly the advances of Royalist society."[44] There is nevertheless some truth to the idea that D'Hubert, as a career soldier, is not so much loyal to Napoleon as loyal to the commander of the army, whoever that commander may be. His sister, with whom he lives after the war, is a royalist, or at least becomes a royalist upon her successful marriage into a Southern family. D'Hubert himself marries the niece of Le Chevalier de Valmassigue, a rabid royalist. More importantly, after Louis XVIII is restored to the throne, D'Hubert accepts a position as commander of the 5th Cavalry Brigade under the king.

In the film, the difference between D'Hubert and Feraud on the matter of loyalty to Napoleon surfaces early on and remains central to their relationship. In doing so, the cinematic narrative diverges from the novella. In their first encounter, Feraud implies that he fought the duel with the mayor's nephew in order to defend the honor of the 7th Hussars and ultimately, Napoleon: "Would you have them spit upon Napoleon Bonaparte?" D'Hubert's response is "Bonaparte? Bonaparte has no more to do with this than Madame de Lionne." Outside, Feraud becomes incensed, asking if D'Hubert thinks "that name is common coin for the street." D'Hubert tactfully replies, "Whichever name you choose to defend, I used it with the utmost respect and solely in the cause of logic." Back at his lodgings he proceeds to challenge D'Hubert to a duel. Later, he rewrites history and tells his fellow officers that he dueled because D'Hubert said, "For all I care they can spit upon Napoleon Bonaparte." He tells them D'Hubert "is a turncoat. That is a fact." When this story is later reported to D'Hubert, he calls it "impertinent trash." It is indeed "trash" to say that he insulted Napoleon. However, in the film, unlike in the novella, D'Hubert refuses to join Napoleon's forces after the fallen leader escapes from Elba. The good soldier is also shown marrying into a royalist family. It is true that when his wife's guardian, Le Chevalier, proclaims D'Hubert "a royalist now," his noncommittal response is, "In the king's army we'll have more realists than royalists." Nevertheless, in the film, even more so than in the novella, Feraud emerges as the devoted Bonapartist and D'Hubert as the career soldier who has no special loyalty to the Emperor. The irony is that it is the latter's perceived independence that enables him to intercede on Feraud's behalf and save him by appealing to Joseph Fouché, Duke of Otranto and Senator of the Empire. This occurs when Feraud lands on a list of people who are to be executed as enemies of the new order.

By far the most powerful dramatization of the difference in attitude towards Napoleon between Feraud and D'Hubert occurs in costume. For the entire second half of the film, Feraud wears a black bicorn hat—the hat that is most closely associated with Napoleon. With his black hat and his squat figure, Feraud gradually comes to look more and more like Napoleon himself. The final image of the film is of Feraud standing alone on a hillside in that bicorn hat, looking out over an expanse of water. The image is obviously modeled on paintings of Napoleon in exile on the island of Saint Helena. As

D'Hubert (freed of Feraud forever) joyfully rejoins his wife and royalist in-laws at their country mansion, the disgraced duelist effectively becomes a copy of his beloved Emperor. As Charles Shiro Tashiro observes, "The hat evokes Napoleon, of course, still standing on a hillside imagining a battle for future *metteurs-en-scène*."[45]

THE DUELIST AND THE ANTI-DUELIST

The most notable difference between D'Hubert and Feraud is neither their attitude towards the military nor is it their attitude towards Napoleon; it is their approach to dueling. D'Hubert, by his own insistence, "is not a duel-ist"[46] whereas Feraud is an inveterate duelist. This difference is crucial to explaining the nature of their relationship. Properly speaking, there is only *one* duelist.[47] The novella makes it clear that when D'Hubert first notifies Feraud that he is confined to barracks for skewering the mayor's nephew, the latter sees nothing remiss in having fought the duel:

> "What is it you want with me?" he asked, with astonishing indifference. Lieut. D'Hubert could not imagine that in the innocence of his heart and simplicity of his conscience Lieut. Feraud took a view of his duel in which neither remorse nor yet a rational apprehension of consequences had any place. Though he had no clear recollection how the quarrel had originated (it was begun in an estab-lishment where beer and wine are drunk late at night), he had not the slightest doubt of being himself the outraged party. He had had two experienced friends for his seconds. Everything had been done according to the rules governing that sort of adventure. And a duel is obviously fought for the purpose of someone being at least hurt, if not killed outright. The civilian got hurt. That was also in order.[48]

Feraud believes that he is innocent of any misconduct. Being publicly embar-rassed by D'Hubert, he challenges his perceived insulter to a duel: "I mean to cut off your ears to teach you to disturb me with the general's orders when I am talking to a lady!"[49] D'Hubert may not be a duelist, but he is not the sort of man who will back down from a challenge. He later says to Le Chevalier about Feraud, "How is one to refuse to be bitten by a dog that means to bite?"[50] The question implies that there was nothing that he could do except fight Feraud. However, what D'Hubert really means is revealed in what he divulges to the Colonel: "I was put into a damnable position where I had no option; I had no choice whatsoever, consistent with my dignity as a man and an officer."[51]

Honor requires that once D'Hubert accepts Feraud's first challenge to a duel, he must fight; honor also demands that he continue to fight Feraud over the years. Indeed, these encounters appear to be one long, drawn-out duel; after all, the novella is simply called *The Duel*. D'Hubert shares his bitterness with Feraud after years of their dangerous interaction: "You've forced me on a point of honour to keep my life at your disposal, as it were, for fifteen years."[52] Essentially, honor is the leverage that Feraud has over his sparring partner. When his seconds come to challenge D'Hubert on Feraud's behalf for the final duel, they appeal to honor in order to get him to fight, although the duel is illegal: "The General has broken the ministerial order to obtain from you the satisfaction he's entitled to by the laws of honour. . . . It's a risk. But honor before everything."[53] Honor alone compels D'Hubert to do what is against his desire and nature.

The film underscores this difference in attitude towards dueling more explicitly. The opening voice-over explains, "The duelist demands satisfaction. Honor for him is an appetite. This story is about an eccentric kind of hunger." But what is obvious from the beginning is that only Feraud has the "appetite" and "eccentric hunger" for satisfaction. Hence, it is only Feraud who is the duelist by this definition. The opening scene of the film features him expertly dueling with the mayor's nephew and wounding him traumatically, an act not described in Conrad's novella. His dueling even before his meeting with D'Hubert is the reason why D'Hubert is sent to him in the first place. When both men meet, the milder D'Hubert is genuinely shocked to find Feraud so blasé about having fought a duel. When asked whether he did so in the morning, the fiery soldier replies, "Of course." This cavalier attitude earns him the rebuke from his interlocutor, "You make dueling sound like a pastime."

As D'Hubert tries to calm Feraud down, the irate man attempts to bait the officer sent to arrest him. It becomes clear that Feraud will duel on any pretext, pouncing on the former with excitement:

"Can you fight?"

"I see no reason whatever for us to fight."

"What reason would you like? Shall I spit in your face?"

After his duel with Feraud, D'Hubert sends his friend Jacquin, the army surgeon, to attend to Feraud's wounds. Jacquin remarks, "A tomcat would never dream of sending a surgeon to another tomcat." Similarly, Feraud the duelist would never dream of sending a surgeon to another duelist. D'Hubert, the anti-duelist, does.

It is true that at various points in the film, D'Hubert's friends make the point of telling him that he now has a great reputation as a duelist. Nevertheless, they know him well enough to understand that he does not wish for such fame. As his friend Lecourbe observes, "Like it or not, you are a man of reputation. A famous fire-eater. It brings you responsibilities. You must think of yourself as fighting on parade." Here Lecourbe is attempting to get D'Hubert to agree to fight with Feraud again, this time on horseback, "as a compliment to the cavalry. The regiment expects it." D'Hubert must again be talked into dueling (this time with a public mission), and it is honor once again that makes him agree. This is also true of the final duel with pistols at the conclusion of the film. When one of Feraud's two seconds reflects, "Honor before everything," the other chimes in, "Honor first." D'Hubert replies that he could have them all arrested. To this threat, one of them responds, "We have proceeded on the assumption that you were a gentleman." D'Hubert replies, "Yes, damn you! Damn you, I am!" The anti-duelist is made to duel once again by means of an appeal to honor, swept up by the pressure of unwelcome social expectations.

A PRISONER OF HONOR

In the film's production notes, Scott provides his own interpretation of the plot:

> It is the story of two men who fight for no particular reason. Their first encounter becomes a detonator for a duel which leads to other duels that mark their careers. The one man, played by Harvey Keitel, is a prisoner of his own hatred. He must kill or be killed. Keith Carradine plays the other man who is honor bound to fight. It is a fascinating story of man's violence within himself.[54]

One way to understand Scott's interpretation of the story is that while Feraud is a prisoner of an emotion—hatred or rage—which makes him fight with D'Hubert, D'Hubert is a prisoner of honor, and it is honor that makes him fight. It is surely an undesirable thing to be held hostage by an emotion. The negative connotation of being a prisoner notwithstanding, is it always a bad thing to be a "prisoner of honor"—to be "honor-bound"? Furthermore, if Feraud is ostensibly at war with himself because this emotion makes him do something—namely, fight duels—which *in some sense* he does not want to do because it puts him in constant danger, then D'Hubert must be at war with himself as well because honor makes him do something—again, fight duels—which he also does not want to do. But is it always a good thing to be free of honor and do, in an absolute, unqualified sense, whatever one wants to do?

We cannot say Feraud is always a prisoner of his emotions. For much of the story he is, but at the very end he, too, is a prisoner of honor. When D'Hubert finally disarms him in the last pistol exchange, he wants nothing more than for d'Hubert to kill him with his remaining shot. In the film, Feraud shouts, "Go, kill me!" This will give him satisfaction now that he has lost. Scott is quite right that Feraud believes that he "must kill or be killed." D'Hubert, however, refuses to do so. Instead, in a speech that is repeated almost verbatim in the film (in a flashback after he has returned to his pregnant wife, Adèle), D'Hubert explains to Feraud that the defeated man's life now belongs to his vanquisher. He is honor-bound never to duel again and must live or die as D'Hubert sees fit:

> You will fight no more duels now. . . . By every rule of single combat your life belongs to me. That does not mean that I want to take it now. . . . You've forced me on a point of honour to keep my life at your disposal, as it were, for fifteen years. Very well. Now that the matter is decided to my advantage, I am going to do what I like with your life on the same principle. You shall keep it at my disposal as long as I choose. Neither more nor less. You are on your honour till I say the word.[55]

Feraud is finally in the same predicament that D'Hubert has been during all the years of their contact. As he complains in the novella, "It amounts to sitting all the rest of my life with a loaded pistol in a drawer waiting for your word. It's—it's idiotic."

Far from it being a bad thing that Feraud is a prisoner of honor, it is a good thing that he is. He may no longer do whatever he wants to do, in particular, challenge D'Hubert and innocents like him to possibly lethal duels on a mere pretense. It is indeed beneficial to be a prisoner of honor when what the baser aspect of that person desires to do is wrong. This is Scott's answer to the first question that was posed above: it is *not* always a bad thing to be a prisoner of honor because it ensures a measure of self-control.

Reflecting on his role in this film, Keitel has commented, "I still play the villain."[56] However, Feraud is not a true villain because his willingness to be bound by honor and to do as D'Hubert wishes when he loses the pistol match negates—or at least mitigates—his purported villainy. Such willingness to be bound is lacking in a true villain who, at the earliest opportunity, would simply kill the other and do whatever he liked, regardless of what the code of honor dictated. It is indeed the case that a true villain "must kill or be killed." The *yakuza* gangster Sato in Scott's *Black Rain* (1989), the mobster Joey Venza in *Someone to Watch Over Me* (1987), the Emperor Commodus in *Gladiator* (2000), and King John in *Robin Hood* (2010), to name just four of Scott's true villains, "must kill or be killed" (or at least be jailed), since they wish to annihilate or enslave others. They also lack any willingness to be bound by honor, morality, or the force of criminal law. It is precisely because the Muslim leader Saladin in *Kingdom of Heaven* (2005) has the willingness to be bound by honor not to kill or enslave others that he is not a true villain either.

If the case of Feraud suggests being a prisoner of honor is positive, the case of D'Hubert demonstrates the opposite. In the novella, D'Hubert chafes against the bonds of honor and resists dueling even as he duels. What is not fully clear, because it is not clear to D'Hubert himself, is *why* he does not wish to do what honor requires, even as he does it. At first it seems that it is his "worldly" ambition, that is, his desire for self-advancement, that makes him averse to what honor requires: "This absurd affair would ruin his reputation of a sensible, well-behaved, promising young officer. It would damage, at any rate, his immediate prospects, and lose him the goodwill of his general. These worldly preoccupations were no doubt misplaced in view of the solemnity of the moment."[57] However, this explanation seems wrong. As much as D'Hubert is ambitious, he is not like "self-seeking" Fouché, Senator of the Empire, who is "traitor to every man, to every principle and motive of human conduct."[58]

At another point it seems that it is the fear of losing his good name and being the subject of scandal that makes him reluctant to do what honor requires:

> Ridicule would be added to the scandal of the story. He imagined the adorned tale making its way through the garrison of the town, through the whole army on the frontier, with every possible distortion of motive and sentiment and circumstance, spreading doubt upon the sanity of his conduct and the distinction of his taste even to the very ears of his honourable family.[59]

It has indeed been argued that "D'Hubert's obsession with protecting his reputation"[60] compels him to continue to duel. Again this seems insufficient to explain his reluctance to do what honor requires. The one clue to the reason underlying his reluctance to do what honor requires can be found in his colonel's response to D'Hubert's statement that he cannot talk about the duel and its origin because "[i]t will be said that a lieutenant of the 4th Hussars, afraid of meeting his adversary, is hiding behind his colonel."[61] Conrad explains, "But the colonel was well aware that the duelling courage, the single combat courage, is rightly or wrongly supposed to be courage of a special sort. And it was eminently necessary that an officer of his regiment should possess every kind of courage—and prove it, too."[62] Although D'Hubert does not realize it, it is in fact his lack of "duelling courage" that makes him reluctant to duel. This is made clear in the description of his motivation before the final duel with Feraud, when d'Hubert is convinced that he will die: "But if true courage consists in going out to meet an odious danger from which our body, soul, and heart recoil together, General D'Hubert had the opportunity to practice it for the first time in his life."[63] In fighting his last duel, D'Hubert finally experiences true courage, or "duelling courage." It was fear rather than self-interest (or the desire to avoid a scandal) which made him reluctant to do what honor required prior to this moment. The novella's conclusion about honor would appear to be that throughout his life, D'Hubert was motivated by honor to continue to fight with Feraud because he lacked the necessary "single combat courage" to fight. Only in their final encounter is he motivated by that kind of courage. Only then does D'Hubert do what honor requires without experiencing the usual internal strife.

What the novella does not address is the possibility that what honor requires D'Hubert to do, namely fight with Feraud, might be *wrong*, and hence that he might be doing the wrong thing from this kind of courage. Fear points in the direction of not fighting with Feraud. Since he does not succumb to fear, D'Hubert fights. Worldly ambition and self-interest also point in the direction of not fighting. But these motives are no better than fear, and so he fights. What Conrad's text does not consider is the possibility that not fighting could be motivated by a better motive. If this is correct, then it helps to show that what honor requires may be wrong as well.

THE TWO SIDES OF HONOR

While it appears that Gerard Vaughan-Hughes, the author of the screenplay, "attempts a direct adaptation of Conrad's narrative,"[64] the single greatest departure from the novella is in the creation of Laura, D'Hubert's lover in the first half of the film. This is where Scott's picture comes into its own. Vaughan-Hughes said that in the Conrad story, D'Hubert "doesn't have a private life, particularly" and that "Laura is produced to give him a private life."[65] However, this woman is the character who offers the only criticism of honor to be found in the entire film. It is not a coincidence that Scott's own interpretation of his work (quoted above) seems to be a summary of Laura's best lines. It is true that the "Laura subplot also introduces the feminist thread that runs throughout Scott's work."[66] When she confronts Feraud in his army tent, surrounded by assorted officers and women, she shouts at him, "Nobody understands why you fight with Armand. It's supposed to be a secret between the pair of you. I believe it's a secret of your very own. I believe you feed your spite on him with no more sense than a blood-sucking louse." Clearly she believes that it is not honor that motivates Feraud to fight, but spite—a synonym for Scott's "hatred." Feraud is consumed by his spite for D'Hubert and this is why he fights with him. But he keeps his motive secret from everyone else, including D'Hubert. Only Laura has figured it out.

Her visit to Feraud comes after an important scene between Laura and D'Hubert. Laura is giving D'Hubert a bath after his wound has been dressed following the second duel. She asks him why he did not just get up and shake hands with Feraud. He responds:

"I wasn't well. Besides, he would only have stuck me again. He was waiting for the chance."

"Do you mean you would have gone on fighting?"

"No question."

(Sigh of exasperation)

"It would have been the only honorable thing to do."

Next Laura tries to stop D'Hubert from sneezing by getting him to talk about something, such as honor:

"Describe honor."

"Honor?"

"Honor."

"Honor is . . ."

"Go on, you must."

". . . indescribable . . . unchallengeable . . ."

These exchanges reveal that Laura looks upon what the two officers are doing—in the name of honor—as wrong. Not only are they treating life as cheap, they are attempting to kill each other for what she views as an insufficient reason. When she asks D'Hubert to explain what honor is, such that it can motivate him to fight when he clearly does not wish to do so, he is unable to give her an articulate answer. To say that honor is "indescribable" and "unchallengeable" is simply to be unable (or to refuse) to provide an explanation. Although she does not put it in so many words, Laura clearly believes that D'Hubert is a prisoner of honor just as she holds that Feraud is a prisoner of spite. The former does that which he does not want to do—fight duels with his tormenter—because of honor and he cannot even explain why.

Laura realizes that she cannot stop D'Hubert and decides, after a remarkably insightful tarot card reading about "a quarrel pursued for its own sake," that she will give up the man and marry another. She writes "Goodbye" in red lipstick on his sabre and leaves. However, later in the film, she tracks him down. She is now a destitute widow who begs for sustenance and even prostitutes herself. She wants D'Hubert to take her back. He tells her to go back to France and that "There's only grief to be got from following soldiers." She realizes that she has no chance of being taken in by him. Crying, she hollers a last warning, "This time he'll kill you!" and leaves.

Although veiled, what this final exchange reveals is that Laura thinks that the problem with honor is that it is, or can be, destructive. Honor is deleterious when it supersedes more important considerations such as a person's caring for a loved one. On the one hand, in the case of Feraud at the very end of the film, honor makes him stop dueling with D'Hubert. Morally, Feraud should refrain from dueling with D'Hubert because his nemesis is innocent and has done nothing to cause offense. *Therefore, in this case, it is a good thing that honor requires him do something that he does not want to do.* Thus it is a good thing, in this case at least, to be a prisoner of honor.

On the other hand, in the case of D'Hubert, until the very end of the film, honor makes him duel obsessively with Feraud. Dueling is, however, not what he wants to do. It can be agreed that, morally, D'Hubert should not duel with Feraud because it endangers his life without a sufficiently serious reason, which is both bad for him and bad for those who love him. It jeopardizes his military career, drives Laura away, risks making his pregnant young wife a widow, and may render his future child fatherless. Constant dueling feeds Feraud's rage, which is bad for him psychologically as well. *Therefore, in this case, it is a bad thing that honor makes him do something that he does not want to do.* Thus it is a bad thing, in this case at least, to be a prisoner of honor.

From the above parallel discourses, the double-edged sword of honor is unsheathed in *The Duellists*. Being bound by honor can be a good or bad state of affairs depending on whether moral obligations are present or not. As Immanuel Kant theorized about "the inclination to honor," it may light "upon what is in fact in the common interest and in conformity with duty," which then "deserves praise and encouragement"[67]; it may also light upon what is contrary to moral duty, in which case it deserves blame and moral censure.

NOTES

1. Work on this essay was supported by a Lenfest Grant from Washington & Lee University in the summer of 2012. I would like to thank H. F. (Gerry) Lenfest as well as the university for their generosity. Research was conducted at Yale University using materials from the Sterling Memorial Library and the Bass Library, as well as the Whitney Humanities Center. I would like to thank all of the staff for their assistance. Finally, the Leyburn Library at Washington & Lee provided further interlibrary loan materials through the help of the staff, especially Elizabeth Teaffe. I thank the staff for procuring these materials, as well as my father, Joseph Mahon, for reading an earlier draft of this essay and for providing insightful comments. This essay is dedicated to the late Tony Scott.

2. Paul M. Sammon, *Ridley Scott* (London: Orion, 1999), 46.

3. "Awards 1977," Festival de Cannes, accessed August 11, 2012, http://www.festival-cannes.fr/en/archives/1977/awardCompetition.html.

4. I refer to feature films specifically. Scott had written and directed his first film, *Boy and Bicycle* (1962, 1965), a 26-minute black and white film, while still a post-graduate art student at the Royal College of Art in London, using a 16-mm Bolex cine-camera that he borrowed from the college and taught himself how to operate. With funding from the British Film Institute, he re-did the sound three years later, persuading John Barry to record a new version of the track "Onward Christian Spacemen" for the film.

5. In 1978, the film's cinematographer Frank Tidy was nominated for the Best Cinematography Award by the British Society of Cinematographers, and in the same year he was also nominated for a BAFTA for Best Cinematography. At the same awards ceremony, the costume designer, Tom Rand, was nominated for a BAFTA for Best Costume Design.

6. Pauline Kael, "The Current Cinema: "The Duellists"/"The Battle of Chile," *The New Yorker*, January 23, 1978.

7. Sammon, *Ridley Scott*, 46.

8. Ibid. Part of the problem was that Paramount only made seven prints of *The Duellists* in 1977 and marketed it as an art house film. Indeed, as of its release on DVD in a Special Collector's Edition in 2002, it had yet to make back its $900,000 budget. This makes it all the more puzzling why Paramount Pictures Corporation released a tie-in novelization of the film by Gordon Williams.

9. Roderick Davis, "Conrad Cinematized: *The Duellists*," *Literature/Film Quarterly* 8, no. 2 (1980): 125.

10. James Clarke, *Ridley Scott* (London: Virgin Film, 2002), 28.

11. See the entry entitled "HONOR" in Lawrence Raw, *The Ridley Scott Encyclopedia* (Lanham, MD: Scarecrow Press, 2009), 166-167.

12. Joseph Conrad, *The Duel* (Brooklyn, NY: Melville House Publishing, 2011).

13. Conrad's influence upon Scott extends beyond *The Duellists*. In his second feature film, *Alien* (1979), the commercial towing spaceship is called the *Nostromo* after Conrad's novel *Nostromo: A Tale of the Seaboard* (1904), which is about a conflict between big business and workers in a South American mine. The correlation reflects the theme of the conflict between the spaceship's owners, the Weyland Yutani Corporation, and the civilian crew on the spaceship. The *Nostromo*'s shuttle is also called the *Narcissus* after Conrad's 1897 novel *The Nigger of the 'Narcissus'* (published in the United States with the title *The Children of the Sea*) which is about a ship's crewman who becomes infected with a deadly disease. The parallel with the plot of *Alien* is almost too obvious to mention.

14. The original title was *The Duel: A Military Tale*. It was published later in the year as a story in the collection *A Set of Six* (London: Methuen, 1908). The book's cover bore the lines: "A Romantic Tale / An Ironic Tale / An Indignant Tale / A Desperate Tale / A Military Tale / A Pathetic Tale," with "A Military Tale" referring to *The Duel*.

15. *The Point of Honor: A Military Tale* (New York: McClure Company, 1908).

16. The full name is Pierre-Antoine, Comte Dupont de l'Étang (1765-1840).

17. The full name is François Louis Fourier-Sarlovèze (1773-1827).

18. According to the story about the two duelists in *Harper's Magazine* in September 1858, Dupont was ordered by his general to tell Fournier that he was not welcome at a large ball being held on the night of the burial of one of Fournier's victims, a popular young man named Blumm whom Fournier had provoked into dueling. Fournier then replied to Dupont, "I can not fight the general, for his rank; you will, perhaps, have no objection?—you who commit impertinence at second-hand." Quoted in DeLauncey J. Ferguson, "The Plot of Conrad's 'The Duel,'" *Modern Language Notes* 50 (1935): 386.

19. Joseph Conrad, *The Duel* (Brooklyn, NY: Melville House Publishing, 2011), 3.

20. Ibid., 11.

21. Ibid.

22. Ibid., 15.

23. Ibid.

24. Scott had originally intended to cast Oliver Reed as Feraud and Michael York as D'Hubert. Paramount Pictures, however, required him to choose from a list of four up-and-coming American actors.

25. Conrad, *The Duel*, 92, 69, 101.

26. Ibid., 22, 61.

27. Ibid., 42, 35, 61.

28. Ibid., 100.

29. Ibid., 46, 35.

30. Ibid., 15, 13, 15, 35.

31. Ibid., 66.

32. Ibid., 46.

33. Ibid.

34. Ibid., 79.

35. Ibid., 3.

36. Ibid., 45.

37. Ibid., 46.

38. Ibid., 45.

39. Ibid., 71.

40. Ibid., 102.

41. Ibid., 68.

42. Ibid., 62.

43. Ibid., 65.

44. Ibid., 67.

45. Charles Shiro Tashiro, "The Bourgeois Gentleman and the Hussar," *The Spectator: University of Southern California Journal of Film and Television Criticism* 13 (1993): 43.

46. Conrad, *The Duel*, 52.

47. Richard Collins comes closest to making this point when he says about D'Hubert's claim to his sister that he is "not a duelist" that "His identity, in other words, is not completely determined by his actions." Richard Collins, "Truth in Adversaries: Ridley Scott's *The Duellists* and Joseph Conrad's 'The Duel,'" *Studies in the Humanities* 27 (2000): 6.
48. Conrad, *The Duel*, 11.
49. Ibid., 14.
50. Ibid., 93.
51. Ibid., 42.
52. Ibid., 106-107.
53. Ibid., 86.
54. *Paramount Pictures Press Book: The Duellists* (London: Paramount Pictures Corporation, 1977).
55. Conrad, *The Duel*, 106-107.
56. *Paramount Pictures Press Book: The Duellists.*
57. Conrad, *The Duel*, 19.
58. Ibid., 70.
59. Ibid., 22-23.
60. Richard A Schwartz, *The Films of Ridley Scott* (Westport, CT: Praeger, 2001), 4.
61. Conrad, *The Duel*, 40.
62. Ibid., 41.
63. Ibid., 96-97.
64. Allan Simmons, "Cinematic Fidelities in *The Rover* and *The Duellists*," in *Conrad on Film*, ed. Gene M. Moore (Cambridge: Cambridge University Press, 1997), 121.
65. *Duelling Directors: Ridley Scott and Kevin Reynolds*, DVD, directed by Charles de Lauzirika (Los Angeles: Paramount Pictures Corporation, 2002).
66. Schwartz, *The Films of Ridley Scott*, 11.
67. Immanuel Kant, *Groundwork of the Metaphysics of Morals*, ed. and trans. Mary Gregor (Cambridge: Cambridge University Press, 1998), 11.

REFERENCES

Boy and Bicycle. DVD. Directed by Ridley Scott. 1962; London: British Film Institute, 2002.
Clarke, James. *Ridley Scott*. London: Virgin Film, 2002.
Collins, Richard. "Truth in Adversaries: Ridley Scott's *The Duellists* and Joseph Conrad's 'The Duel.'" *Studies in the Humanities* 27 (2000): 1–19.
Conrad, Joseph. *The Children of the Sea. A Tale of the Forecastle*. New York: Dodd, Mead and Company, 1897.
———. *The Duel*. Brooklyn, NY: Melville House Publishing, 2011.
———. *Nostromo. A Tale of the Seaboard*. New York: Harper & Brothers, 1904.
———. *The Point of Honor: A Military Tale*. New York: McClure Company, 1908.
———. *A Set of Six*. London: Methuen, 1908.
Davis, Roderick. "Conrad Cinematized: *The Duellists*." *Literature/Film Quarterly* 8 (1980): 125–132.
Duelling Directors: Ridley Scott and Kevin Reynolds. DVD. Directed by Charles de Lauzirika. Los Angeles: Paramount Pictures, 2002.
The Duellists. DVD. Directed by Ridley Scott. 1977; Los Angeles: Paramount Pictures, 2002.
Ferguson, DeLauncey J. "The Plot of Conrad's 'The Duel.'" *Modern Language Notes* 50 (1935): 385–390.
Festival de Cannes. "Awards 1977." Accessed August 11, 2012. http://www.festivalcannes.fr/en/archives/1977/awardCompetition.html.
Kael, Pauline. "The Current Cinema: 'The Duellists'/'The Battle of Chile.'" *The New Yorker*, January 23, 1978.
Kant, Immanuel. *Groundwork of the Metaphysics of Morals*. Edited and translated by Mary Gregor, with an introduction by Christine Korsgaard. Cambridge: Cambridge University Press, 1998.

Paramount Pictures Press Book: The Duellists. London: Paramount Pictures Corporation, 1977.

Parrill, William B. *Ridley Scott: A Critical Filmography*. Jefferson, NC: McFarland, 2011.

Raw, Lawrence. *The Ridley Scott Encyclopedia*. Lanham, MD: Scarecrow Press, 2009.

Robb, Brian J. *Ridley Scott*. Harpenden, Hertfordshire: Pocket Essentials, 2001.

Sammon, Paul M. *Ridley Scott*. London: Orion, 1999.

Schwartz, Richard A. *The Films of Ridley Scott*. Westport, CT: Praeger, 2001.

Simmons, Allan. "Cinematic Fidelities in *The Rover* and *The Duellists*." In *Conrad on Film*, edited by Gene M. Moore, 120–134. Cambridge: Cambridge University Press, 1997.

Tashiro, Charles Shiro. "The Bourgeois Gentleman and the Hussar." *The Spectator: University of Southern California Journal of Film and Television Criticism* 13 (1993): 33–45.

Williams, Gordon. *The Duellists*. New York: Fontana Books, 1977.

Chapter Three

The Trans-Religious Ethics of *Kingdom of Heaven*

Michael Garcia

Ridley Scott's *Kingdom of Heaven* (2005) immerses the viewer in the philosophical and cultural worldview of the Crusades by taking the point of view of the true believers, both Christian and Muslim, who fought for possession of Jerusalem. That worldview is a thoroughly religious one, with religion touching every aspect of life, and virtually all human experience mediated through the filter of religious beliefs. But while taking a religious point of view, *Kingdom of Heaven* can also be seen as subversive of any conception of ethics as wholly religion-based. In place of this conventional religious view, the film suggests that morality falls within the domain of natural law rather than revealed law; in other words, there are some higher principles that people can agree on despite their religious differences, rather than assuming that ethics are divine commandments revealed, either directly or indirectly, only through one's God.

As is dramatized on an epic scale in *Kingdom of Heaven*, a dangerous consequence of the belief that ethics are revealed is that such a view can lead to intolerance and cultural conflict between religious communities, since different religions have different value systems—contrasting beliefs about what God has ordained as right and wrong—while also often believing in the absolutism of their own values. If ethics are mandated by God, then our ethics cannot be wrong, nor can they be adapted when encountering peoples with ethical beliefs that are contrary to our own. *Kingdom of Heaven* rejects this view by privileging universal ethical principles (such as mercy, tolerance, compassion, benevolence, and generosity, as well as love, fairness, self-control, and reasonableness) over ethical principles exclusive to either Muslims or Christians. The characters that we most identify with in the film, including noble figures of the opposing religions, all embody these higher principles. As such, Saladin (Ghassan Massoud) can be cast as the "good Muslim" to Christians because he adheres to ethical principles that transcend those of his religious faith. Likewise, from the Muslim point of view, Balian (Orlando Bloom) is the "good Christian" despite his heretical religious views.

ETHICS REVEALED

Standing in contrast to the "good" characters in *Kingdom of Heaven* are antagonists such as Guy de Lusignan (Marton Csokas) and Reynald de Cha-tillon (Brendan Gleeson), who together break the peaceful truce through such actions as raiding and pillaging Saracen caravans. Our sense that Guy and Reynald are bad guys, while King Baldwin (Edward Norton) and Saladin are good guys, turns the ethical spotlight on ourselves by raising the following question: how do we know what is good and what is bad? This, it turns out, is a deeply philosophical question, one that can be distilled down by dividing it into two separate questions: What determines right and wrong? and, How do we come to know the difference? These are the fundamental questions of ethics, questions which *Kingdom of Heaven* leads us to reflect on. The first question has a simple answer for twelfth-century Muslims and Christians alike in *Kingdom of Heaven*: divine authority determines what is good and bad. Among theologians, the view that divine authority is known directly is often referred to as the Divine Command Theory, which, as eloquently summed up by philosopher James Rachel, "says that 'morally right' means [arbitrarily] 'commanded by God,' and 'morally wrong' means [arbitrarily] 'forbidden by God.'"[1] Put another way, God's arbitrary will is good, and all else is bad.

If the first of our questions about ethics (What determines right and wrong?) was easy to answer for twelfth-century Jews, Muslims, and Chris-tians, the second question (How do we come to *know* what is right and what is wrong?) was much more difficult. Not all ethical precepts come to us from above, written on tablets of stone as did The Ten Commandments. How does one learn right from wrong for everything else that falls within the moral sphere? More poignantly, how do we know to be skeptical when—echoing Reynald's battle charge of "God wills it!" before attacking a Saracen cara-van—Guy de Lusignan and the Knights Templar chant, "There must be war. God wills it!"[2] The virtuous characters Balian and Saladin may doubt the veracity of claims about God's will such as these, but not even they are told directly by God what is the right thing to do. "God does not speak to me," laments Balian, who has come to Jerusalem seeking forgiveness. Though believing that their God is the source of ethical principles, neither man receives special moral instruction from God, and so must acquire their knowledge of right and wrong in other ways. Knowing right from wrong, then, is also an epistemological question, a question of how we know what we know.

An ongoing debate in both Christian and Muslim societies throughout the time of the Crusades was whether ultimate truth was reasoned, discovered, intuited, or revealed. Is reason the superior path to truth, or is practical experience the better guide? Or are higher truths (such as God's will, or right and wrong) things a person just knows, either by intuition or divine revelation? In developing a natural law theory of morality, the virtually unrivaled medieval theologian Thomas Aquinas (1224-1274) emphasized a rational approach. We know what is right and wrong—even though God does not speak to us in a special way—by appealing to reason, because "human morals are spoken of in relation to reason" and ethical matters "belong to the natural law inasmuch as they are regulated by reason."[3] Aquinas is making the case here for what theologians would call "general revelation," in which truth and ethical principles are discovered, reasoned, and known through natural means. In contrast to this way of knowing is "special revelation" through supernatural means, a way of knowing splendidly presented by influential Islamic philosopher and Aristotelian, Al-Ghazali (1058-1111).

Al-Ghazali argued that since the senses can be easily deceived and our reasoning is often fallacious, that the most reliable source of truth is through revelation. Empirical methods are unreliable since our eyes are not even capable of detecting the movement of a gnomon's shadow on a sundial—and yet it moves! Likewise, reason is not an infallible guide, since syllogistic sophistry is commonplace and arguments based on pure reason are riddled with paradoxes. Zeno's paradoxes, for example, seemed to prove by syllogistic reasoning and against common sense that motion was impossible. Revealed truth is surely a more reliable guide than proofs and arguments such as these, concluded Al-Ghazali, and truth is revealed either through mystical insight or through the Qur'an, an infallible source of revealed truth.[4]

Aquinas agreed with Al-Ghazali's argument that written revelation is a source of revealed truth though—in addition to regarding as infallible a different, substantially discrepant collection of scripture—privileging reason over mystical insight. Though explaining how Christians can come to know ethical truth in the absence of direct revelation, Aquinas's reason-privileging approach shares with Divine Command Theory and Al-Ghazali's mysticism the assumption that our knowledge of good and evil must come, *ultimately*, from God Himself. In the absence of continuous and direct revelation, however, the lingering question for the religiously faithful is (as suggested by Aquinas's naturalistic line of inquiry): what are the more reliable *indirect* means of knowing good and evil? If through religious authorities (mediated revelation) or scripture (written revelation), then how can Balian and Saladin both come to similar conclusions about higher ethical principles when consulting, as with Aquinas and Al-Ghazali, clergy and scriptures that are not only distinct but often contradictory? "You cannot say," King Baldwin instructs Balian on the matters of moral responsibility and moral authority, "But I was told by others to do thus." For believers of either faith, ethical precepts ultimately come from God, but just as important is the belief that, as moral agents, our ethical behavior must ultimately come down to personal responsibility.

Believers of all three Holy Land faiths might seek divine guidance on a specific ethical dilemma through prayer—often itself conceptualized as happening through the intercession of an intermediary, such as the Virgin Mary—but knowledge of more general ethical principles is garnered primarily in other ways. Among these is another, often unexamined, means by which we come to distinguish good from bad. Mainly, we are born into it. That is, we are born into an ethical worldview that we become acculturated to from an early age. Just as none of the people raised by Christian parents in Balian's home village in France would likely come to adopt Islamic religious beliefs and practices, so none of them would likely adopt an ethical worldview in which killing Christians (for whatever religiously-motivated reason) was the will of God. Yet Crusaders from that same village would likely share the belief of the pilgrim stationed outside of Messina who proclaims to those on the road to Jerusalem, "To kill an infidel is not murder." This is the great ethical dilemma for which the Crusades stand as a metaphor in *Kingdom of Heaven*. If ethical principles are universal, and revealed truth the most reliable means of knowing what is right and what is wrong, then why do different faiths so often come to opposite conclusions about what is ethical? How, that is, can religion conceived as the sole source of universal values lead us into a clash-of-values with anyone? Such vexing questions need not necessarily lead us to reject the notion that some values can be considered universal, but they do lead us to question how it is that we know which values are universal and which are not. What, we might ask, is the basis of the shared ethical principles that people of both faiths are agreeing on, when, in *Kingdom of Heaven*, Christians come to accept that a Muslim character can be good despite his faith—and vice versa? And if at least some ethical principles are trans-religious rather than specific to a particular religion, then how do we know what those universal principles are?

WHAT OUGHT WE TO DO?

The question of whether there are higher ethical principles that are shared by those with opposing religious beliefs is part of a long-standing philosophical inquiry about the nature and very existence of universals: ethical principles that are true for all people everywhere. Immanuel Kant (1724-1804) thought that such universals existed, and that they could be reasoned out as "categorical imperatives." Simply stated, Kant's categorical imperative is the idea that the ethical maxim motivating an action should be considered universalizable—a universal law of nature—only if it would still hold if everyone did it.[5] By this reasoning, killing people of other faiths in the name of a holy war would not be a universal ethical principle because we would not want everyone else to do it too—and we certainly would not want people of other faiths killing *us* in the name of a holy war.

Against Kant's claim that there can be any moral universals at all, ethical relativists argue that ethics are different for every culture and, as such, there can be no universals. This would explain why Christians could believe that it is ethical and right to kill any Muslims who stand in the way of their retaking and holding the holy city of Jerusalem while, conversely, Muslims would understandably see such beliefs as unethical and wrong. What is right for Balian is wrong for Saladin because each obeys ethical principles specific to his own culture.

The ethical relativist position fails to explain the existence of higher ethical principles shared by Balian and Saladin, while Kant's categorical imperative fails to account for the all-too-routine conflict between different cultures adhering to competing value systems. Surely there must be what Aristotle (384-322 BC) would call a "golden mean" somewhere between these two positions. Indeed, as paragons of the virtuous person, Balian and Saladin serve as exemplars of Aristotle's "virtue ethics." In showing mercy and compassion to his Muslim captive, Balian will come to be seen as a noble and good person among his Muslim foes despite belonging to a culture whose religiously-specific values clash with theirs. This exceptionalism is foretold by the Saracen knight (Alexander Siddig) when Balian frees him: "Your quality will be known among your enemies before ever you meet them, my friend."

Character traits, however, cannot be separated from deeds. Nor is it enough simply to have virtuous thoughts, an insight summed up in the familiar adage that "the road to hell is paved with good intentions." When translating ethical principles into actual acts, however, what is most ethical often depends on the context of the situation. *Kingdom of Heaven* presents us with a situational ethics dilemma by leading the viewer to sympathize with Balian even though he is a murderer. In trying to justify our sympathy for the character with the wrongfulness of the deed, we may ask ourselves if Balian's murder of the priest might be justified, or at least deserving of consideration due to mitigating circumstances. After all, the priest provoked him by stealing and then wearing his dead wife's necklace, ordering her corpse decapitated, and then telling Balian that his wife was surely in hell. We might also note that it was an emotional response—our identification with and empathy for the person committing the deed—that led us to ask this ethical question, underscoring the extent to which, as put forth by David Hume (1711-1776) and Anthony Ashley Cooper (1671-1713), emotions and moral sentiments guide our value judgments rather than pure reason, as Kant proposed.[6]

Consequentialist philosophers such as Jeremy Bentham (1748-1832) and John Stuart Mill (1806-1873) would later combine the emotional basis of value judgments—stressing "pleasure" or "happiness" as the teleological goal of ethics—with a logic-driven moral calculus.[7] Their "utilitarianism" focuses on the outcomes or consequences of an action, such as striving to attain "the greatest good for the greatest number" of people. We see this concept as one of Balian's noble virtues when he chooses to stay and defend the people of Jerusalem rather than escape and save himself when he has the chance to do so. The German philosopher Friedrich Nietzsche (1844-1900), however, might object here, arguing that Balian is motivated exclusively by the "slave morality" thinking of Christianity: the young Frenchman does not risk his life to save others because he is altruistic or thinks like a utilitarian, but because he believes that God will punish him for abandoning Jerusalem (the kingdom of heaven on earth), and reward him (with an everlasting kingdom of heaven in the afterlife) for sacrificing his own life to defend the holy city and the people within its walls.[8]

Nietzsche's genealogy of how it is that we come to believe what we believe about moral principles raises a provocative ethical question: do only Balian's actions matter, or do his beliefs as well? Kant elicits a similar question by focusing on our *reasons* for doing "the right thing" or not. If beliefs and reasons are less important than deeds, then one's religious faith is much less important, from an ethical point of view, than what one actually does. As such, carrying out a suicide bombing among innocent civilians is immoral whether the attacker is a Christian ideologue in Oklahoma or an Islamic fundamentalist from Nigeria. "The quality of mercy is not strain'd," as Portia pleads in *The Merchant of Venice*, regardless of an individual's religious beliefs.[9]

ETHICS NATURALIZED

The themes of religious tolerance, the possibility of interfaith harmony, and the existence of trans-religious ethical values as depicted in *Kingdom of Heaven* remain relevant to us today. The Crusades have ended, but religious conflict remains and continues to revolve primarily around the periodically resurgent conviction that not only are one's own religious beliefs coextensive with absolutist ethical mandates but that other cultures and religions must necessarily agree with those values. And though organized religion is often enough a source or channel of shared universal values—as seen in the apparent universality in all major religions of some version of the Golden Rule—any such ethical convergence is counterbalanced by a long history of religion as a source of value-based conflict, as epitomized by the Crusades of an earlier millennium and the religious fundamentalism of Al-Qaeda in the modern age. Nevertheless, the customary association of ethics with religious belief has led many to conclude that without religion there would be no morality.

The privileging of trans-religious ethical values in *Kingdom of Heaven* suggests just the opposite: that some higher values exist and are apprehended by people in spite of the particular beliefs of their religious community. The characters in the film, even more so than most people today, are thoroughly immersed in a theistic point-of-view and see their respective faiths as the ultimate source of moral understanding. Many of them would agree with the dictum that "without God and the future life," as Fyodor Dostoevsky famously put it, "everything is permitted."[10] At the same time, these characters also practice a kind of moral reasoning that leads them to arrive at ethical principles that would seem to exceed a purely faith-based transmission of moral values. Time and again these universal values are elevated above religiously-conveyed ethical beliefs that put them in conflict with the rival faith. Balian, for example, clearly gives greater weight to natural methods of inquiry than to what is held up as revealed ethical truth when his moral reasoning leads him to burn the bodies of the dead so as to protect the living from disease. When told by the bishop that burning the bodies of the dead would cause God to delay their resurrection until Judgment Day, Balian reflects before concluding that God would understand and that "if he does not, then he is not God." The statement is not a rejection of God—Balian is a true believer, and his belief in an afterlife is part of the ethical dilemma for him—but it *is* an affirmation that universal ethical principles can be known outside of revealed truth, and that moral agents regardless of religious orientation are most ethical when giving precedence to rational inquiry through natural means over claims based on religious authority alone.

As suggested by Balian's principled rejection of religious orthodoxy while yet retaining his religious faith, the moral philosophy that should most appeal to religious believers might also, initially, be the least intuitive one from the theistic point of view: a naturalistic model of ethics that treats morality as independent of God. Indeed, this is precisely the path that Aquinas's natural law theory of morality puts us on by suggesting that any universal "laws" that are true for all of humankind are also knowable through rational inquiry regardless of one's faith. Aquinas, it should be noted, does not take naturalism that far. Rather, he follows St. Augustine (354-430) in assuming the unity of truth—that natural knowledge and revealed knowledge are not only compatible but also work together—and argues that if still in doubt after consulting the book of nature, that we should then turn to the revelations of a particular sacred text (the Bible) and the interpretations of religious authorities ("wise men") for moral clarification.[11] Contemporary versions of ethics naturalized, in contrast, are more likely to turn to a wholly biological and cultural understanding of ethics than to an account that is, ultimately, dependent on religious faith.

While studying "the biological origins of moral reasoning," E. O. Wilson concludes that "outside the clearest ethical precepts, such as the condemnation of slavery, child abuse, and genocide, which all will agree should be opposed everywhere without exception, there is a large gray domain inherently difficult to navigate."[12] Human nature, in other words, is not programmed with clear and absolute values across the entire ethical spectrum, in part because of competing drives and instincts. Indeed, absolutism of any kind can be dangerous, as Queen Sibylla (Eva Green) reminds us by rebuking Balian for his refusal to "do a little evil to do a greater good."

Further complicating any understanding of human morality is that it is also a cultural phenomenon, and any naturalistic approach must also explain how it is possible to get an "ought" from an "is," an apparent conflation of values with facts that G. E. Moore (1873-1958) called the "naturalistic fallacy."[13] As if in response to Moore, Michael Shermer articulates a well-accepted conception of how the biological origins of an incipient moral sense merge and overlap with strictly cultural dimensions (the domain of "ought") of morality when he writes, "Our moral sentiments . . . evolved out of premoral feelings of our hominid, primate, and mammalian ancestors. . . . I consider these sentiments to be premoral because morality involves *right and wrong thoughts and behaviors in the context of a social group*."[14] Understanding ethics as having a "natural" biological component would partially explain the universality, across religions and cultures, of the Golden Rule. It cannot be forgotten, however, that biology is inextricably linked with culture, and that the two interact to shape our moral sense. This interplay between nature and culture is seen in the shared chivalric code of honor—a set of values that gives a specific cultural form to premoral sentiments, and that also transcends religious differences—by which Saladin promises safe conduct to the defeated Christians and Balian upholds his oath to "safeguard the helpless."

MORAL SENTIMENTS

Kingdom of Heaven guides us to be more sympathetic toward some characters than to others—namely, those who embody admirable qualities and live according to universal ethical principles such as mercy, tolerance, compassion, benevolence, and generosity. The logic of the film's "argument" is emotional, persuading viewers through filmic rhetoric such as imagery, dialogue, and non-diegetic sound primarily at the level of affect. It is not by cold reasoning and a rigid moral calculus that we come to see the Saracen knight who returns the favor of sparing Balian's life as a good man. Rather, we are emotionally persuaded that he is a good man, despite his being cast as the enemy from a Western viewer's perspective. Our identification with the "good Muslim"—or the "good badman," as Nancy Kang poetically dubs the basis of her chapter that starts this volume—subverts any notion that ethics exist exclusively within the domain of religious belief. Rather, the higher ethical principles embodied by all of these characters are trans-religious in nature, communally derived and culturally specific yet (for reasons inherent to the premoral stamp of human nature and the capacity to reason) universally agreed upon—in varying degrees—by people of all faiths.

A twenty-first century "good Muslim" character appears in a subsequent Ridley Scott film, *Body of Lies* (2008), which, as with *Kingdom of Heaven*, features William Monahan as screenwriter. Hani (Mark Strong) is the Jordanian intelligence director who manages to bring down a terrorist cell of jihadist fundamentalists when the heavy-handed American techniques of invasion, torture, and interrogation fail. Though we might question his willingness to take whatever measures he deems necessary to accomplish what he sees as the greater good, Hani's character comes across as more trustworthy and reliable than that of his American counterpart, Ed Hoffman (Russell Crowe), whose cultural disengagement with the Middle East leads him to act as if operating in a moral vacuum. Caught between Hani and Hoffman is CIA operative Roger Ferris (Leonardo DiCaprio) who, unlike Hoffman, his stateside-based controller, feels morally responsible and conscience-stricken when American actions cause harm and death to local civilians and collaborators.

Body of Lies can be thought of as the sequel to Scott's *Black Hawk Down* (2002) in that it, too, is a story of modern warfare, but it doubles as a sequel to *Kingdom of Heaven* in its continued exploration of cross-cultural awareness and shared ethical principles. The film tests the limits of ethical reasoning by examining questions of right and wrong deep inside E. O. Wilson's "large gray domain": the highly ambiguous moral context of espionage and international politics. In the absence of clear moral guidelines, and in a murky, extra-judicial context in which the justification of murder and torture is routine, the characters are often left to make their own judgments on complex moral issues. Even more so than in clear-cut ethical situations, moral "reasoning" and determinations of right and wrong in this ambiguous context are as much a matter of moral sentiments as of logical inference. Hoffman, for instance, maintains a deliberate emotional detachment so as not to allow himself to get close enough to care about the foreign peoples and cultures who are the casualties of Bush-era American involvement in the Middle East. In doing so, he seems to think of some of the more questionable actions committed on behalf of his agency and his country as amoral rather than moral—or immoral, for that matter. Ferris, in contrast, partly relies on his emotions as a moral compass, and in a climactic moment, makes an emotionally-motivated ethical decision to trade himself as a prisoner in order to secure the freedom of Aisha, a local nurse who has been kidnapped by an organization aware of his romantic interest in her, and whom he has put in danger by being seen with in public.

The central metaphor of *Body of Lies*, as signaled by the title, is lying. In a world of lies and mistrust, Hani's most sacrosanct ethical principle is "Never lie to me," a precept soon breached by both Hoffman and Ferris. For Hani, the violation of this ethical principle is about more than simply having accurate information; it is about who a person can trust, and trust is primarily an emotional state, a sentiment, even when solidly based on a rational reckoning of past experiences with the trusted individual. The same logic of trust plays out in the hearts and minds of Western viewers of the film as they move from Islamophobic suspicion and distrust of this Muslim character (and the vast majority of "good Muslims" that he represents) to the realization that shared recognition of and aspiration to higher ethical principles affirm—despite our cultural differences—our common humanity.

A KINGDOM OF HEAVEN ON EARTH

However we explain the existence of the higher principles embodied by the characters that we most identify and sympathize with in *Kingdom of Heaven* and *Body of Lies*, these films lead us to conclude that there are ethical principles that transcend those justified by any particular culture or religion. This insight inclines us to believe that not only can morality exist without religion but also, as presented through the eyes of the religiously faithful in *Kingdom of Heaven*, that higher ethical principles often prevail despite religious authority. If even the most fervent of religionists—those prepared to wage a holy war in the name of their beliefs—can come to such ethical conclusions, the film suggests, then surely the rest of us can too. Viewers of all religious faiths leave the film inspired to be more tolerant, compassionate, and benevolent. Through religious tolerance and interfaith harmony, Jerusalem can, as the metaphorical title urges, indeed become not only the "kingdom of conscience" that Balian and his father, Godfrey (Liam Neeson), fight for, but also a "kingdom of heaven" on earth. Implied in this vision is that through greater cross-cultural understanding and trans-religious ethics such as tolerance, compassion, and benevolence, we can make a heaven on earth of the rest of the world too. That is the real crusade of this film.

NOTES

1. James Rachel, *The Elements of Moral Philosophy*, 2nd ed. (New York: McGraw-Hill, 1993), 47.

2. *Kingdom of Heaven*, DVD, directed by Ridley Scott (Los Angeles, CA: 20th Century Fox, 2005); *Body of Lies*, DVD, directed by Ridley Scott (Burbank, CA: Warner Home Videos, 2008).

3. Thomas Aquinas, *Summa Theologica*, quoted in Michael Peterson et al., eds., *Philosophy of Religion: Selected Readings*, 3rd ed. (New York: Oxford University Press, 2007), 641.

4. See Al-Ghazali, *Deliverance from Error*.

5. See Immanuel Kant, *Groundwork of the Metaphysics of Morals*.

6. See David Hume, *An Enquiry Concerning the Principles of Morals*. See Cooper, Anthony Ashley, *Inquiry Concerning Virtue* and *Characteristicks of Men, Manners, Opinions, Times*.

7. See John Stuart Mill, *Utilitarianism*.

8. See Friedrich Nietzsche, *Beyond Good and Evil, Toward a Genealogy of Morals*, and *The Will to Power* in *Basic Writings*.

9. William Shakespeare, *The Merchant of Venice* 4.1.184.

10. Fyodor Dostoevsky, *The Brothers Karamazov*, trans. Richard Pevear and Larissa Volokhonsky (New York: Farrar, Straus and Giroux, 2002), 589. The quotation appears in ellipsis form and was also popularized by Existentialist philosopher Jean-Paul Sartre (1905-1980), who, in his essay "Existentialism is a Humanism" (1946), saw the "without God" premise not as the end of ethics but as its beginning—the point at which people become full moral agents.

11. See Augustine, *Confessions*.

12. Edward O. Wilson, *The Social Conquest of Earth* (New York: Norton, 2012), 254.

13. G. E. Moore, *Principia Ethica* (New York: Cambridge University Press, 1948), quoted in Ethel Albert, et al., eds., *Great Traditions in Ethics,* 6th ed. (Belmont, CA: Wadsworth: 1988), 288.

14. Michael Shermer, *The Science of Good and Evil: Why People Cheat, Gossip, Care, Share, and Follow the Golden Rule* (New York: Owl Books, 2004), 26-27.

REFERENCES

Albert, Ethel, Theodore C. Denise, and Sheldon P. Peterfreund, eds. *Great Traditions in Ethics*. 6th ed. Belmont, CA: Wadsworth: 1988.

Al-Ghazali, Abu Hamid Muhammad. *Deliverance from Error: Five Key Texts Including His Spiritual Autobiography, al-Munqidh min al-Dalal*. 2nd ed. Translated by Ilse Lichtenstadter and R. J. McCarthy. Louisville, KY: Fons Vitae, 2004.

Aquinas, Thomas. *Selected Writings*, edited by Thomas McInerny. New York: Penguin Classics, 1999.

Aristotle, *Nicomachean Ethics*. 2nd ed. Translated by Terence Irwin. Indianapolis, IN: Hackett Publishing, 1999.

Augustine. *Confessions*. Translated by Garry Wills. New York: Penguin Classics, 2008.

Body of Lies. DVD. Directed by Ridley Scott. 2008; Burbank, CA: Warner Home Video, 2009.

Cooper, Anthony Ashley. *Characteristicks of Men, Manners, Opinions, Times*. Indianapolis, IN: Liberty Fund, 2001.

Dostoevsky, Fyodor. *The Brothers Karamazov*. Translated by Richard Pevear and Larissa Volokhonsky. New York: Farrar, Straus and Giroux, 2002.

Hume, David. *An Enquiry Concerning the Principles of Morals*, edited by J. B. Schneewind. Indianapolis, IN: Hackett Publishing, 1983.

Kant, Immanuel. *Groundwork of the Metaphysics of Morals*, edited by Mary Gregor. Cambridge: Cambridge University Press, 1998.

Kingdom of Heaven. DVD. Directed by Ridley Scott. Los Angeles, CA: 20th Century Fox, 2005.

Mill, John Stuart. *Utilitarianism*. 2nd ed. Edited by George Sher. Indianapolis, IN: Hackett Publishing, 2002.

Moore, G. E. *Principia Ethica*. 2nd ed. Edited by Thomas Baldwin. New York: Cambridge University Press, 1993.

Nietzsche, Friedrich. *Basic Writings of Nietzsche*. Translated by Walter Kaufmann. New York: Modern Library, 2000.

Peterson, Michael, William Hasker, Bruce Reichenbach, and David Basinger, eds. *Philosophy of Religion: Selected Readings*. 3rd ed. New York: Oxford University Press, 2007.

Rachel, James. *The Elements of Moral Philosophy*. 2nd ed. New York: McGraw-Hill, 1993.

Sartre, Jean-Paul. *Existentialism Is a Humanism*. Translated by Carol Macomber. New Haven, CT: Yale University Press, 2007.

Shakespeare, William. *The Comical History of the Merchant of Venice, or Otherwise Called the Jew of Venice*. In *The Norton Shakespeare: Based on the Oxford Edition*. 2nd ed., edited by Stephen Greenblatt, Walter Cohen, Jean E. Howard, and Katharine Eisaman Maus, 1111-1176. New York: Norton, 2008.

Shermer, Michael. *The Science of Good and Evil: Why People Cheat, Gossip, Care, Share, and Follow the Golden Rule*. New York: Owl Books, 2004.

Wilson, Edward O. *The Social Conquest of Earth*. New York: Norton, 2012.

Chapter Four

Levinasian Responsibility in *Someone to Watch Over Me, Black Rain,* and *White Squall*

Fernando Gabriel Pagnoni Berns

Since *The Duellists* (1977), Ridley Scott has made a series of films in which such philosophical concepts as strength of will and responsibility are the foundations of character development. In this first work, set during the Napoleonic era, the honorable soldier D'Hubert (Keith Carradine) unintentionally offends Feraud (Harvey Keitel) and from that moment on, the two men cross paths over the years in what appears to be a never-ending duel. The story can be read as a kind of psychological horror film: the rational humanist D'Hubert is pursued for life by the obsessive and unstoppable Feraud. This first feature film bore traces of Scott's larger ideological vision of responsibility which has since been fleshed out in subsequent projects. D'Hubert does not do anything to merit the fury of Feraud, yet the innocent man must bear the weight[1] of the latter's almost inexplicable hatred. D'Hubert, whether he likes it or not, is responsible[2] for the attitudes and actions of others because his dueling partner, "through a series of senseless misunderstandings," chooses him as an enemy. Now, the two men are bound almost inextricably by honor and its obligations.

These ideas about responsibility resonate with Emmanuel Levinas's reasoning that the constitution of a subject is its capacity to be "for-the-other" in an encounter "face-to-face" with that other. Fundamental to this analysis is the idea that the individual and his or her ego[3] is "hostage"[4] to the demands of the other (as D'Hubert is to Feraud's demands), an idea that is strongly present in three other films by Scott: *Someone to Watch Over Me* (1987), *Black Rain* (1989), and *White Squall* (1996). I argue that these films clearly demonstrate a Levinasian sense of responsibility.

Contrary to the idea of causal determinacy, Levinas presents a radical notion of human empathy, one understood as taking responsibility for the other. This is a responsibility ethically prior to any community[5] or ontological commitment. The freely made decisions of the individual are vulnerable to the call of the other and therefore he or she is capable of taking the other's place. But this means, too, that the other and his or her respective needs are now a burden on the individual subject's life.

CAUSAL DETERMINACY AND ITS DECONSTRUCTION

Causal determinacy is substantiated by a person's free will, namely the ability to choose between two or more possible courses of action. Individuals are really free when empowered to act as they wish, which in turn entails an *absence of constraints* that prevent them from doing what they want.[6] Freedom of action will thus depend on freedom of will[7] and the lack of any kind of causal determinism.

However, many philosophers in the Western tradition have argued for "compatibilism," the theory that says determinism is compatible with free will.[8] Human subjects can be predestined to a certain situation, but once in that situation, are free to choose the options that they consider best for themselves and their lives. What would make the subjects really free is the fact that they can choose between two or more options in what is called the Principle of Alternate Possibilities.[9] This principle states that individuals are morally responsible for their choices and actions only if they could have acted otherwise.

Friedrich Nietzsche reformulated the compatibilist's position to accommodate his own unique idea of responsibility. In *On the Genealogy of Morals* (1967), he critiques the authority of religion in creating concepts such as morality and ethics to reveal the material and historical origins of human values. In this text and in the "Critique of Morality" present in *The Will to Power* (1968), he refers to the inability to find truly natural and universal concepts (that is, ideological devices that are not historically constructed and based on cultural and societal specificities). This idea is not an invitation to fall into nihilistic relativism. What Nietzsche seeks is actually a genealogical deconstruction of concepts such as morality and responsibility which would no longer be based on ideas like accountability. Nietzsche's genealogy is not just a dismissal of ethics as such, but is rather an attack on a certain way of understanding ethics. The criticism focuses on the equation of responsibility with accountability, which, for Nietzsche, is at the heart of Christianity and its emphasis on sin and guilt.[10]

Nietzsche believed that the concept of accountability is artificially created in view of finding a culprit. This concept rests on the temporary paradigm of cause and effect: an individual commits an action which leads to a present effect and he (or she) is thus guilty of the harmful effect of that action if it was done freely. What is of juridical consequence is the relation between the action and free agency. As Rosalyn Diprose argues, this idea demands "continuity between past and future."[11] Also, for this kind of liability to work, one should accept notions such as good and evil as non-historical: "There are *no eternal facts,* just as there are no absolute truths."[12] Nietzsche denounced such ideas, not to mention the idea of free will, as fictions. These concepts are "imposed" by tradition and reinforced by means of universalized philosophies. Both Levinas and Nietzsche wanted to return to the subject as an individual, away from homogenizing ideas. Accountability is a juridical term, not a "natural" one. An agent-cause is required in case punishment needs to be doled out. Moreover, as François Raffoul explains, the notion that an action is equivalent to the intent of the individual who performs it is untrustworthy; he inquires, "how do we know for certain that intention exhausts the act?"[13]

Levinas builds upon Nietzsche's rejection of the essentialist ideas of responsibility and temporal continuity. He thinks responsibility does not come from free will but from positioning ourselves "for-the-other." A person is responsible by only having been chosen by another, as is the case in *The Duellists.* Ethics exist in the intersubjective relationship with the other, in a meeting "face-to-face" with the other, and this relationship exists "beyond the grasp of ontology."[14] Levinas argues that responsibility is not some aspect of subjectivity, but rather its very core. Responsibility is not the consequence of the faculty of free will, nor is it even based on the pre-given self. It does not even supplement an existential foundation. Subjects are ethical beings and their ethical nature precedes their ontological constitution; the responsibility exists prior to these beings. Levinas thus deconstructs the traditional relation between responsibility and the self. The individuals are now responsible for everything other than themselves, as in the statement, "I am concerned for what does not matter to me because as such, as a matter of the other, it matters to me."[15]

For Levinas, non-indifference is a constitutive part of human relationships. It is therefore not possible to *be* indifferent to the other. A person can choose to be indifferent, but that indifference is already an answer to the other. There is always a concern for the other, an asymmetrical concern which is oblivious to reciprocity; herein lies the asymmetry of responsibility of which Levinas speaks.

SCOTT AND LEVINAS: RESPONSIBILITY IS FOR-THE-OTHER

Someone to Watch Over Me, *Black Rain*, and *White Squall* illustrate notions of responsibility on par with Levinas's concepts of being for-the-other. *Someone to Watch Over Me* and *Black Rain* can be considered thematically twin films. Both present a similar plot: a policeman protagonist placed in foreign circumstances has to make life-and-death decisions. These decisions threaten the lives of innocents, and the officer must take an ethical position in which the other is the one who will matter most. The other must supersede the family, work, even the self. In *Someone to Watch Over Me*, the police detective is Mike Keegan (Tom Berenger), who lives a quiet suburban life with his wife, Ellie (Lorraine Bracco) and their son, Tommy (Harley Cross). Mike is commissioned to protect Claire Gregory (Mimi Rogers), a wealthy socialite who witnessed a murder committed by a thug named Joey Venza (Andreas Katsulas). Similarly, in *Black Rain*, Nick Conklin is a proficient if corrupt cop who, with his partner Charlie Vincent (Andy Garcia), must escort a Japanese criminal, Sato (Yusaku Matsuda), whom they captured after a gangland slaughter in a bar, to his native country where he is to be handed over to the local authorities.

When the two policemen (Keegan and Conklin) agree to perform their respective tasks, they leave behind safe worlds for ones where circumstances seem very difficult to handle: Keegan immerses himself in a world of luxury apartments and high-class Manhattan society, and Conklin plunges headlong into a country whose language and customs are foreign to him. Prior to this, both men deal with their well-defined responsibilities; Keegan has a stable family (a wife and child) to handle, while Conklin must deal with a sour divorce and supporting his son on a limited salary.

The opening credits for *Someone to Watch Over Me* feature scenes of New York with the song that gives the film its name. Already, this title speaks of responsibility; a "someone" needs another person to take care of him or her. The scene involves an aerial shot of the city where all kinds of buildings can be seen at night. These buildings symbolize lonely people who cannot find "someone" (even anyone) to be their guardians. This shot emphasizes the alienation of the metropolis. Amid this lack of connection, Levinas describes "holiness" in "watching over someone other, in responding to someone other."[16] In our busy lives, the figure and presence of the others as individuals are typically "occluded, hidden, or forgotten"[17] and only the "face-to-face" encounter can change this situation.

The initial credit sequence segues into Mike and Ellie's evening at a casual party among lower middle-class friends and colleagues, all celebrating Mike's promotion and reassignment in a better area of the city. The film contrasts with another party, this one taking place among the upper classes, where Claire and her friend Neil Steinhart (John Rubinstein) share a friendly moment. Claire is questioned about whether her relationship with Neil is getting serious and her answer cannot be clearer: "It's nice to have somebody you can count on." Before that, Claire described Steinhart as "solid," an adjective associated with dependability. This woman, while not "needy" in the economic sense, obviously has a need for someone to take care of her emotionally and physically, and this is what she prioritizes in a man. Claire, after witnessing a murder at the party, will come to see how her life is intermingled, from that point on, with the life of Keegan. This encounter finally allows her to find someone who will take care of her literally (as in, professionally), not in the figurative sense that Venza plans (that is, killing her to resolve the problem of her having witnessed the crime).

In *Black Rain*, Conklin appears in the initial scenes as a sleazy police officer who does not fulfill his ethical role in society based on his job description. The film opens with him getting ready to appear before Internal Affairs personnel for possible theft, a sin he later confesses to while in Japan. Conklin is clearly not doing his duty: he neither complies with society (he is accused of corruption) nor supports his family (he is late with alimony). This irresponsibility can also be observed in his handling of his motorcycle, which he dangerously uses to win bets. But Conklin handles that world very well. If things are not perfect, it is because Conklin is amoral, selfish, and apparently does not care for anyone more than himself. How can we solve this problem about ego and superficiality in relationships? As Catherine Chalier points out, "Levinas does not think that egoism can disappear by means of a respect for moral principles," but "only the encounter with the fragility of the other, in driving that egoism to find the resources to help him, forces it—for a little while, in any case—to lay down its weapons."[18] Only when Conklin is interested in something or someone else will he put aside his amoral attitude and take on the responsibility of caring for others. Only in environments different from everyday life will he bear a responsibility that may not appear fitting to his usual existence, and in the process, become subject, since that happens "in acting out on the concern for the welfare of others."[19]

Because both Conklin and Keegan obey the law as if it were a superior being, their actions are far from being their own: they respond to the norms of their professions, such as protecting witnesses or transferring criminals. Claire, at the beginning, has doubts about denouncing Venza for fear of possible reprisals. It is Keegan who convinces her to do "the right thing." He assures her that the killer will spend the rest of his days in prison. But on a legal technicality, Venza is released and Claire is now in mortal danger because of Keegan's ethical naiveté. He did not convince Claire based on his own personal ethics, but rather based on the conviction that justice will prevail and Venza will suffer the appropriate punishment. Keegan is only responsible to a higher power than himself, which illustrates the reciprocity of responsibility in what Levinas would call a totalizing and universalistic way.[20] But now Claire is in danger and he must take charge of her care. Justice fails and now Keegan must take responsibility not for his personal faults, but for the system's. By this token, we must take care of things that are not really our fault, since Levinas understands responsibility as responsibility for the other, even when we have not done anything to or for that person.[21] The responsibility for the other is "incumbent on [us]."[22] It is not really Mike's fault, but he must make himself responsible for the other anyway. The chain of causal determinacy is broken.

Conklin is also not guilty of having delivered a dangerous man to the wrong people (Sato's accomplices) since the new circumstances prevent him from properly assessing his actions. He simply assumes that these people dressed as police officers are really police officers and that the Japanese document presented to him to sign is legal. In any language that is not understood, the form loses all its semantic value to the other and becomes only gibberish. In both films, the classical chain of liability based on cause and effect is blurred. Keegan is not completely responsible for his actions; he only complies with the actions that society, as an abstract entity, has instituted for such situations. As an agent of duty, he must convince the witness to testify, under the idea that the law will be responsible for her and later, Venza's incarceration. The law dictates generalities; only when it fails does the other appear as a victim.

Keegan will assume his role as the agent responsible for the care of strangers while he is still responsible for the safety of his own family. He is a hostage to this situation, to the endless demands of being a good father, a good cop, and a good husband, while Claire is such a weak person that he must sacrifice his own life (including his marriage and job) to protect her. This sacrifice seems to be based in the guilt that he feels about the dangers that are now stalking the woman. She is his responsibility not just because he is a cop but because he convinced her to testify. But doing that is part of Keegan's job, not an action taken just by him. For Levinas, he is a "hostage" because this responsibility for the other is non-reciprocal, infinite, and nonvoluntary. The subject only can represent *non-indifference* to the other.[23]

Viewers may wonder whether Claire and Mike are really even in love given that when they start the affair, it is based more on the need for protection (to be given and taken) than erotic attraction. In fact, near the end of the film, Keegan returns to his wife, a person with whom he has a history. Keegan cannot even protect Claire properly. When Venza sends a hit man to her home, the detective encounters serious difficulties in stopping the intruder simply because he does not understand the architecture of Claire's labyrinthine mansion. He will not know for sure if he is really aiming at the killer or at his image reflected in one of the many mirrors of the house, the same space where he does not find the right doors at the film's start. The foreign surroundings put him in a weak position where he also needs someone to care for him. Ellie puts herself on guard when she notices that someone is "taking care" of her husband (that is, pampering him, buying him ties, showing him a more refined world, as well as satisfying him sexually). Both Claire and Keegan will discover themselves as dependents of one another, knowing that the feeling of safety emanates from the mere presence of the other. This can be mistaken as love.

As lost as Keegan is in Claire's house, Conklin struggles in Japan, failing to arrive on time to save Charlie from a bunch of gangster motorcyclists. He is pained not only by the loss of his friend, but also by the absolute lack of protection that he feels in that alien country. This loss will force him to be open to both the Japanese detective Masahiro (Ken Takakura), with whom he maintains a strained relationship from the beginning, as well as a suspicious bar hostess (and possible prostitute) to whom he relates simply because she is an American and speaks English. With the death of Charlie, Conklin accepts the weight of the world on his shoulders, deciding not to withdraw from Japan until he finds the murderers of his partner and liberates the Japanese society from the threat he himself released. If Levinas insists that "the face is infinity, the Other, the Foreigner,"[24] where the beholder recognizes the otherness hidden in the flow of everyday life, the foreigner's social and geographical contexts exacerbate this discovery of him or her as a person that should be under someone's care.

When Masahiro questions him about his corruption, an embarrassed Conklin avoids the detective's gaze. Keegan also avoids looking at his wife when she asks bluntly if he is having an affair. Levinas argues that the concern for the other starts with a face-to-face encounter, where the mortality and the fragility of the other's face is a reflection of the self's own naked face.[25] The recognition of the other's death is prior to the recognition of one's own death; only in the fragility of the other can we recognize our own fragility and status as humans. Both detectives take on the death of another being as their burden to bear: Conklin owns up to the death of his partner and Keegan confronts the death threats which his family receives. This situation not only endangers Claire, but also Ellie and their son, increasing the weight that Keegan takes on as professional and personal protector. Now he must answer to both women without hurting either of them, an almost impossible feat.

While the shift in perceptions about responsibility is clear in the two films, the new social and geographical contexts are depicted as "negative"[26] frames that allow the frailty of both policemen to surface. The lack of confidence in their actions is what permits them to open up some of their more vulnerable areas to other individuals' needs, which now both men find as their own responsibilities. It is in *White Squall* where Levinasian responsibility is concretized in a more positive way, even when a tragedy strikes at the end. Here, when individuals very different from one another come together, they discover that taking care of another's problems is the real core of human relationships and a possible way to a true community of ethical beings.

WHITE SQUALL AND A NEW ETHICS OF HUMAN RELATIONSHIPS

In this film, a group of boys from different socio-economic backgrounds meet in a survivalist context; they will need to help each other to minimize damage and loss of life. This new environment is the *Albatross*, a training ship commanded by Captain Christopher Sheldon (Jeff Bridges) and his wife Alice (Caroline Goodall). Except for those who run the boat, the environment is disconcertingly alien and the new rules very stringent. The captain makes it clear by announcing to the boys, "[E]ach one of you is responsible for the rest." In another moment, he reminds them, "[W]here we go one, we go all."

In terms of personality, the students are as different as their backgrounds. Each is there for his own reasons: "Some of us are here for discipline, some for escape, and the rest don't even know why." Everyone must necessarily set aside differences and consider the safety and well-being of others. This is illustrated especially in the main character, Charles Gieg (Scott Wolf), who since his arrival, privileges the interests of his companions over his own. When the film approaches its climax, Charles emerges as the one who "keeps everyone together." Of course, he is not the only leader, and after months of travel, interest in others will become central for each of the crew. For example, when Frank Beaumont (Jeremy Sisto) is cast out of the ship for killing an innocent dolphin, Gil Martin (Ryan Phillippe) will strive to overcome his fear of heights to say goodbye to his friend from the height of the sails as a risky demonstration of affection. The boys come together with "love and concern that seeks the creation of genuine community," not in a homogeneous way that blurs identities but in a "plural community of singularities"[27] where everyone matters.

When the end comes and a terrible storm sinks the boat, the media will fall on the captain to determine his level of responsibility. But what the media wants is the responsibility denounced by Nietzsche, one sourced in cause and effect that seeks the easy solution: one or two guilty subjects to imprison and punish. The media cannot understand that the unfortunate events simply do not correspond to anyone's wrongdoing: the captain loses his wife and Charles has to leave his friend Gil to die. What stands out is the total absence of real culprits. Frank, ejected from the boat, is now present at the trial as a reminder of the captain's flaws; he finally gives up. Betraying his father who is eager to profit from the trial, he rings the bell that he kept from the sunken ship, accepting as a priority other people's interests over the profit motive. The film ends with the boys around their captain, each of them having managed to be for-the-other, and that is where the captain and the theories of Levinas eventually win out.

Scott seems, through many of his films, to be increasingly convinced of the need to understand responsibility as it was explained by Levinas. Yet the recurrence of the use of alien contexts to catalyze changes in understanding is constant. Apparently, as a global society, we are still immersed in the negative idea that responsibility is a term for legal liability, something for which a person must be blamed or receive punishment. But Levinas's proposal to place the concern for the other as one's own priority (which he acknowledges as a "crazy demand"[28]) seems only realizable under contexts in which human frailty can show up without being identified as a weakness. Those alien contexts help us to be open to others. A new ethics of community integration will allow a person to see him- or herself reflected in the other. As Charles Gieg reflects in *White Squall*, thinking of his friends aboard the ship, "I'm not sure where I fit in, but I can see a small piece of myself in each of them." The story in which everyone gives up their own needs in favor of the other's needs still remains to be told. Perhaps we, as a human society, are not ready yet for such a phenomenon, but the anticipation of more in-depth philosophizing on the subject—namely in future Ridley Scott films—is worth the wait.

NOTES

1. William Parrill, *Ridley Scott: A Critical Filmography* (Jefferson, NC: McFarland, 2011), 32.

2. He caused the hatred of his opponent with an action (the true nature of the offense is ambiguous: apparently, Feraud is upset because D'Hubert is a messenger of bad news), so the classical chain of cause-effect remains. But Feraud's hate seems excessive compared to the (non-)action committed by D'Hubert.

3. Emmanuel Levinas, *Collected Philosophical Papers*, trans. Alphonso Lingis (Boston: Martinus Nijhoff Publishers, 1987), 149.

4. Ibid., 123.

5. Ibid., 41.

6. Robert Kane, *A Contemporary Introduction to Free Will* (New York: Oxford University Press, 2005), 13.

7. Thomas Pink, *Free Will: A Very Short Introduction* (New York: Oxford University Press, 2004), 5.

8. Ibid., 18; Joseph Keim Campbell, *Free Will* (Malden, MA: Polity Press, 2011), 86; Bob Doyle, *Free Will: The Scandal in Philosophy* (Cambridge, MA: Phi Press, 2011), 64.

9. Ibid., 393; Harry Frankfurt, "Alternate Possibilities and Moral Responsibility," *The Journal of Philosophy* 66, no. 23 (1969): 829.

10. Daniel Conway, "Genealogy and Critical Method," in *Nietzsche, Genealogy, Morality: Essays on Nietzsche's Genealogy of Morals*, ed. Richard Schacht (Berkeley: University of California Press, 1994), 326.

11. Rosalyn Diprose, "Nietzsche, Levinas, and the Meaning of Responsibility," in *Nietzsche and Levinas: After the Death of a Certain God*, ed. Jill Stauffer and Bettina Bergo (New York: Columbia University Press, 2009), 116.

12. Friedrich Nietzsche, *Human, All Too Human: A Book for Free Spirits*, trans. R. J. Hollingdale (New York: Cambridge University Press, 1996), 13.

13. François Raffoul, *The Origins of Responsibility* (Bloomington: Indiana University Press, 2010), 97.

14. Williams Paul Simmons, "The Third Levinas' Theoretical Move from An-Archical Ethics to the Realm of Justice and Politics," *Philosophy & Social Criticism* 25, no. 6 (1999): 85.

15. Raffoul, *The Origins of Responsibility*, 197.

16. Levinas, *Is It Righteous to Be*, ed. Jill Robbins (Stanford, CA: Stanford University Press, 2001), 54-55.

17. Michael Morgan, *Discovering Levinas* (Cambridge: Cambridge University Press, 2007), 61.

18. Catherine Chalier, *What Ought I To Do? Morality in Kant and Levinas*, trans. Jane Marie Todd (Ithaca, NY: Cornell University Press, 2002), 53.

19. A. T. Nuyen, "Altruism as the Condition of Subjectivity," in *Altruistic Reveries: Perspectives from the Humanities and Social Sciences*, ed. Basant Kapur and Kim-Chong Chong (Norwell, MA: Kluwer Academic Publishers, 2002), 37.

20. John Llewelyn, *Emmanuel Levinas: The Genealogy of Ethics* (New York: Routledge, 1995), 171.

21. Emmanuel Levinas, *Ethics and Infinity* (Pittsburgh, PA: Duquesne University Press, 1985), 95.

22. Ibid., 96.

23. Levinas, *Is It Righteous to Be?* 55.

24. Gideon Baker, *Politicizing Ethics in International Relations: Cosmopolitanism and Hospitality* (New York: Routledge, 2011), 75.

25. Emmanuel Levinas, *Time and the Other*, trans. Richard Cohen (Pittsburgh, PA: Duquesne University Press, 1987), 78.

26. "Negative" works in the sense that these new contexts are alienating and loaded with terrible, de-centering situations such as murders.

27. Howard Caygill, *Levinas and the Political* (New York: Routledge, 2002), 101.

28. Emmanuel Levinas, *Is It Righteous to Be?* 54.

REFERENCES

Baker, Gideon. *Politicizing Ethics in International Relations: Cosmopolitanism and Hospitality*. New York: Routledge, 2011.

Black Rain. DVD. Directed by Ridley Scott. 1989; Hollywood, CA: Paramount Studios, 2006.

Caygill, Howard. *Levinas and the Political*. New York: Routledge, 2002.

Chalier, Catherine. *What Ought I to Do? Morality in Kant and Levinas*. Translated by Jane Marie Todd. Ithaca, NY: Cornell University Press, 2002.

Conway, Daniel. "Genealogy and Critical Method." In *Nietzsche, Genealogy, Morality: Essays on Nietzsche's Genealogy of Morals*, edited by Richard Schacht, 318-333. Berkeley: University of California Press, 1994.

Diprose, Rosalyn. "Nietzsche, Levinas, and the Meaning of Responsibility." In *Nietzsche and Levinas: After the Death of a Certain God*, edited by Jill Stauffer and Bettina Bergo, 116-133. New York: Columbia University Press, 2009.

Doyle, Bob. *Free Will: The Scandal in Philosophy*. Cambridge, MA: Phi Press, 2011.

Frankfurt, Harry. "Alternate Possibilities and Moral Responsibility." *The Journal of Philosophy* 66, no. 23 (1969): 829-839.

Kane, Robert. *A Contemporary Introduction to Free Will*. New York: Oxford University Press, 2005.

Keim Campbell, Joseph. *Free Will*. Malden, MA: Polity Press, 2011.

Levinas, Emmanuel. *Collected Philosophical Papers*. Translated by Alphonso Lingis. Boston, MA: Martinus Nijhoff Publishers, 1987.

———. *Is It Righteous to Be?* edited by Jill Robbins. Stanford, CA: Stanford University Press, 2001.

———. "Language and Proximity." In *Collected Philosophical Papers*. Translated by Alphonso Lingis, 109-127. Boston, MA: Martinus Nijhoff Publishers, 1987.

———. *Time and the Other*. Translated by Richard Cohen. Pittsburgh, PA: Duquesne University Press, 1987.

———. *Ethics and Infinity*. Pittsburgh, PA: Duquesne University Press, 1985.

Llewelyn, John. *Emmanuel Levinas: The Genealogy of Ethics*. New York: Routledge, 1995.

Morgan, Michael. *Discovering Levinas*. Cambridge: Cambridge University Press, 2007.

Nahmias, Eddy, et al. "Is Incompatibilism Intuitive?" In *Experimental Philosophy*, edited by Joshua Knobe and Shaun Nichols, 81-104. New York: Oxford University Press, 2008.

Nietzsche, Friedrich. *Human, All Too Human: A Book for Free Spirits*. Translated by R. J. Hollingdale. Cambridge: Cambridge University Press, 1996.

———. *The Will to Power*. Translated by Walter Kaufmann and R. J. Hollingdale. New York: Vintage-Random House, 1968.

———. *On the Genealogy of Morals and Ecce Homo*. Translated by Walter Kauffman. New York: Vintage, 1967.

Nuyen, A. T. "Altruism as the Condition of Subjectivity," in *Altruistic Reveries: Perspectives from the Humanities and Social Sciences*, edited by Basant Kapur and Kim-Chong Chong, 35-47. Norwell, MA: Kluwer Academic Publishers, 2002.

Parrill, William. *Ridley Scott: A Critical Filmography*. Jefferson, NC: McFarland, 2011.

Pink, Thomas. *Free Will: A Very Short Introduction*. New York: Oxford University Press, 2004.

Raffoul, François. *The Origins of Responsibility*. Bloomington, IN: Indiana University Press, 2010.

Simmons, Williams P. "The Third Levinas' Theoretical Move from An-Archical Ethics to the Realm of Justice and Politics." *Philosophy & Social Criticism* 25, no. 6 (1999): 83–104.

Someone to Watch Over Me. DVD. Directed by Ridley Scott. 1987; Culver City, CA: Sony Pictures Home Entertainment, 1999.

White Squall. DVD. Directed by Ridley Scott. 1996; Burbank, CA: Walt Disney Studios Home Entertainment, 1999.

Williams, Clifford. *Free Will and Determinism: A Dialogue*. Indianapolis, IN: Hackett, 1980.

Chapter Five

Re-Membering Vietnam in Somalia: *Black Hawk Down* and Ethical Militarism in American Historical Memory

David Zietsma

Since the end of the 1970s, American culture has attempted to integrate the historical memory of the Vietnam War into a larger national narrative centered on spreading freedom and democracy around the globe. The Vietnam War problematized America's sense of divine purpose by suggesting imperial motivations on the part of the United States, revealing the fact that American soldiers committed atrocities, and ending in an ignoble retreat as Saigon fell to North Vietnamese forces. As a result, in the late 1970s, the United States experienced cultural anxiety over the righteousness of its role in the world, particularly its projection of military power. The image of the average soldier as a "hero," a representation stemming from the wartime culture of World War II (namely through government propaganda, films, comic books, novels, and other media depicting American soldiers as morally upstanding men who risked their lives to defeat evil), gradually began to unravel. Post–Vietnam War malaise submerged the heroic image of the returning soldiers in a counter-narrative of an army composed of racists, drug addicts, disloyal fraggers, opportunists, human rights violators, and naïve (often feminized) idealists.[1]

Ridley Scott's *Black Hawk Down* (2001) may be interpreted as partaking in the soldier-hero's cultural rehabilitation in recent United States history. Despite the film's surface disavowal of war as a terrifying and hellish experience, it uses a costly 1993 intervention in Somalia to underscore the inherent moral goodness of American military power. It casts average American soldiers as ethical humanitarians who avoid unnecessary violence and willingly die for each other while upholding their commitment to duty. Their dead bodies function as a site of transformation in the film; they are a means by which the generically ethical warrior is written into a larger narrative of individual soldier-heroes who act in service of a greater civilizing mission.

While *Black Hawk Down* is ostensibly about a US intervention in Somalia, it is deeply enmeshed in the re-membering of the Vietnam War through soldier-heroes and the cultural erasure of that war's legacy of imperialism. Consequently, motifs and imagery from the culture of Vietnam War memory, particularly from films based on the conflict, emerge in Scott's retelling of the Somalia tragedy.[2] Re-membering Vietnam in *Black Hawk Down* reflects a discourse celebrating militarism through the tropes of ethical violence, courage, and self-sacrifice. As part of the ongoing (re)integration of military violence into American national identity, this discourse empowers the projection of United States power abroad by engendering strong popular support for "the troops," imaged in *Black Hawk Down* as virtuous warriors engaged in a "humanitarian" effort to bring democracy and material progress to a backward people.

HUMANITARIAN MISSIONS AND ETHICAL VIOLENCE

Black Hawk Down frames the 1993 incident within a larger story of humanitarian aid meant to offset the regime of an inhumane Somali warlord, Mohamed Farrah Aidid. Scott accomplishes this contrast through a series of epigraphs juxtaposing the cruel Aidid and the humanitarian efforts led by the American soldiers. With the camera tracking over emaciated Somali corpses, text on the screen informs the viewer that the eruption of civil war in 1992 caused "famine on a biblical scale," resulting in the death of 300,000 Somalis. Aidid stands at the center of it all, a warlord general whose seizure of the food aid has presumably caused a good many of these deaths. "Hunger is his weapon," the film states, but "Behind a force of 20,000 US Marines, food is delivered and order is restored." After the Marines leave, however, Aidid's inhumanity resurfaces as he attacks UN peacekeepers, including American personnel, and kills twenty-four Pakistanis. According to the screen text, the United States finally sends in their elite Rangers, the Delta Force, and the 160th SOAR (Special Operations Aviation Regiment) to "remove Aidid and restore order" to Somalia.

After depicting a long but fruitless effort on the part of the global community working in the area, the film cuts to October 2, 1993, one day before the US raid of Mogadishu, to establish the humanitarian imperative of the Special Forces sent to "restore order." Instead of corpses, the screen shows Somalis desperately trying to retrieve food from a recently arrived aid shipment while a US helicopter circles nearby. Soon Aidid's militia appears and sprays the crowd with bullets, declaring that the food belongs to Aidid. The circling Americans display shock and righteous anger as the militia mows down hungry civilians. Despite their ethical impulse to fire on the gun-toting aggressors, a request for "permission to engage" is quickly denied by some faceless voice speaking bureaucratic jargon about "UN jurisdiction."

Black Hawk Down thus foreshadows the army's violence in a narrative of ethical intervention whose violence is already justified by the inhumanity of the enemy. Consequently, the film depicts the Americans engaging in violence only as a last and necessary resort. Scott depicts the capture of Aidid ally and Somali businessman Osman Ali Atto (George Harris), as a surgical operation that results in no loss of life: elite forces in helicopters surround Atto's three-car motorcade, expertly shooting engines and tires to prevent harm to anyone. Atto himself later claimed that the film's depiction was completely false, that "people were hurt, people were killed."[3] While captured, the man is able to smoke Cuban cigars and is even offered warm tea by his even-tempered American interrogator, General Garrison (Sam Shephard).

To establish the inherently ethical character of American soldiers, Scott emphasizes their efforts to avoid unnecessary violence during the raid of Mogadishu. In the briefing, Garrison specifically reminds the assault leaders that they will be traveling through friendly neighborhoods and so are to avoid shooting as much as possible. As US forces enter the target area by air and through the streets, Scott not once but *twice* portrays soldiers waiting until they are absolutely sure that they are being fired at before opening fire themselves. It is as if the director wants to ensure that the viewer will not miss the ethical impulse to refrain from violence until the last possible moment. For instance, members of Staff Sergeant Eversmann's chalk wait until they hear the hissing of the bullets before they return fire; it is patently obvious that the Somali militia is already shooting at them. In another case, a Humvee gunner withholds fire while being fired upon until Lieutenant Colonel Danny McKnight (Tom Sizemore) orders him to return fire. Both examples illustrate that violence is a last resort, taking place only when the enemy shoots first and there is no other way but to defend oneself and one's team.

Once the Americans engage Aidid's militia in force, the film accompanies the former's expert dispatching of enemy Somalis with a clear concern for women and children. After the first Black Hawk helicopter crashes down, overhead shots show US forces and Somalis racing on foot down parallel streets toward the fiery site. The Americans are alerted through headsets to "be advised: women and children among them." A few scenes later, an American soldier loses his way and attempts to escape pursuing militia by ducking into a building in which he finds a poorly outfitted schoolroom and a Somali woman huddling several children together even as enemy bullets pierce the door. Rather than use the civilians as human shields or as hostages, the soldier smiles, beckons at them to keep quiet, and waves a friendly good-bye when he leaves the building. As he exits, he narrowly escapes a burst of gunfire from a Somali child-soldier; instead of firing at the gun-toting young-ster, he runs onward toward the crash site. A final instance of ethical concern for women and children occurs at the end of the raid as the American forces leave the hostile zone: a thin woman hiding a rifle in her clothes suddenly uncovers it, but the Americans refuse to fire at her until she attacks first, after which they reluctantly shoot her dead.

Black Hawk Down thus positions the enemies of America's humanitarian intervention as choosing their own demise by the very act of shooting at those whose impulses are so excessively moral that they can barely bring themselves to return fire. Throughout the film, the mission to bring aid in the face of inhumane opposition, the reluctance to begin firing, and the constant awareness of (and concern for) women and children portrays the violence of American soldiers as inherently ethical. This brand of violence is a last resort, used only when all other humanitarian efforts or diplomacy have failed and the enemy has left them no choice.

COURAGEOUS SELF-SACRIFICE

The film also images the soldier-hero as a skilled warrior willing to die in order to save others and complete the mission. Scott foreshadows such sacri-ficial commitment through a conversation between communications operator Mike Kurth (Gabriel Casseus) and Sergeant Eversmann (Josh Hartnett) that takes place before the raid. Eversmann indicates that he wants to help the Somali people and that he believes in the mission's larger ideals. Kurth responds that they are trained to fight and asks whether Eversmann was trained to fight as well. The young Eversmann responds that he was "trained to make a difference." The film thus invites the viewer into a journey of realizing the importance of martial values not for their own sake but for the sake of making "a difference."

The film first establishes the American soldiers as skilled warriors before imbuing them with the spirit of courageous self-sacrifice, the latter being the ethical direction of martial competence. In the opening scenes of the raid, the operation proceeds with machine-like precision as each soldier carries out his duties expertly, securing the target buildings and capturing Somali leaders. This is what the soldiers were trained to do. The raid only begins to go badly when a new recruit from one of the Ranger security squads misses a drop rope and falls out of a helicopter. The situation worsens when a Black Hawk helicopter is shot and crashes within the hostile area of the city. Under heavy enemy fire from rooftops, windows, and "technicals" (pickup trucks with mounted machine guns), the Rangers make their way to the first crash site.

While the film shows the Somalis fighting wildly and inaccurately (proving true a pre-raid comment made by one soldier that Somalis "can't shoot worth shit"), the Americans repeatedly hit their targets or lob grenades with remarkable precision and effect.

As the American forces become mired in the violence of the city, the film transforms the skilled warriors into heroes through their willingness to lay their lives on the line for the group and for the cause; it is as if self-sacrifice exists as part of the American soldier's very DNA. For example, the efforts of Corporal Jamie Smith (Charlie Hofheimer) to save Lance Twombly (Tom Hardy) cast self-sacrifice as a reflexive moral response that rigorous training has simply worked to optimize. The action takes place after Eversmann's troops have secured a corner of the first crash site and three lost members of his chalk have found their way there. Twombly is the last of the three soldiers to dash for safety but trips and falls when he is caught in the open by enemy militia. Without thinking and without regard for himself, Smith instantly jumps up to grab Twombly in order to drag him to safety. Smith's deed is seemingly instinctual and unstoppable. To make this point, the films depicts Eversmann futilely yelling, "Smith, NO!" as the man is already on his way. Smith is hit but manages to return Twombly to safety. As the savior Smith lies dying, Eversmann tells him that he "did what he was trained to do. [He] should be proud of that." The viewer thus understands Eversmann to have been correct in his earlier debate with Kurth: American soldiers are trained as warriors to make a difference and to save lives, not just to fight for fighting's sake.

The film also depicts the soldier-hero's self-sacrifice as a function of volition. For instance, when the Humvees that had returned to base are about to go out again to help with the crash site rescue, Thomas (Tac Fitzgerald) is scared and says he cannot go back into the fighting. His officer tells him kindly but firmly that others feel the same way, but that "it's what you do right now that makes a difference." Thomas, duly motivated, then demonstrates his heroism by jumping in one of the vehicles at that last minute; his courage has trumped his fears.

In an even more poignant exaltation of self-sacrifice, *Black Hawk Down* details the story of two Delta force snipers, Gary Gordon (Nicolaj Coster-Waldau) and Randy Shughart (Johnny Strong), who voluntarily attempt to secure the second crash site against all odds. Their effort emerges as being doomed from the beginning as overhead shots show Somali crowds converging, pack-like, on the downed helicopter from all sides. Gordon and Shughart, flying in a helicopter above, volunteer to be dropped in to secure the site just in case there are survivors. Their initial request is denied before the action cuts back to the base camp to pick up the humvee column storyline, leaving the viewer to wonder at the increasing danger facing Michael Durant (Ron Eldard), the lone survivor of the second downed helicopter. When the camera returns to the second crash site, more crowds descend on the chopper and the action flips back to Gordon and Shughart in the helicopter. Scott now belabours the choice of the snipers to potentially sacrifice themselves in a drawn-out scene, beginning with a radio communication that bursts out, "Shughart and Gordon *again* request permission to secure." Another voice informs the distant General Garrison that "crowds are in the hundreds now" and the two snipers "know what they are asking."

Scott punctuates Gordon and Shughart's heroic self-sacrifice by focusing in on an exchange between them and General Garrison. The superior officer announces, "This is Garrison. I want to make sure that you understand what you're asking, so say it out loud and clear." Shughart immediately responds with what amounts to a third request to be placed directly into danger: "We're asking to go in and set up a perimeter until ground support arrives." Garrison responds that there is no way of knowing when support will arrive. Gordon acknowledges the danger with a simple "Roger that." Garrison once more inquires, "You still want to go?" and this time Shughart answers with a resolute, "Yes, sir." After five instances that make it clear that the snipers desire to place themselves in extreme danger, the film cuts to the helicopter putting them on the ground and the tragic scenes of them killing countless Somalis before they themselves are killed. In the end, their efforts manage to save the downed pilot Durant by buying enough time for the Somali militia leaders to arrive and take him hostage.

THE LIVING DEAD

Black Hawk Down portrays the American soldiers first and foremost as ordinary, good-hearted men whose deaths reveal their true heroism. The film's plot thus deliberately avoids the kind of deeper character development found in other war films such as *Saving Private Ryan* (1998), *Casualties of War* (1989), and *Born on the Fourth of July* (1989). Several early scenes take place in and around the American base, showing pilots light-heartedly arguing over Scrabble words and troops easily chatting and sharing laughs. The US force is composed of artists, chess players, lovers of food, husbands, fathers, and nervous new arrivals, but no intimate personal stories emerge about any one of them. They are flat characters meant to be recognizable as Everymen.

The transformation of such average men into heroes occurs by means of death, the point at which the soldier emerges from the "army of one" and becomes a unique individual to be commemorated and remembered. Death as the "ultimate sacrifice" confirms the courage of that particular soldier and thereby testifies to the courage and ethical character of all the soldiers, sanitizing the violent acts in which they have been engaged. In other words, in death, a collective American identity centered on an ethical humanitarian mission is reaffirmed. Concrete celebrations of the dead individuals who "sacrificed" for that mission are actually rituals of national identity.[4] As a result, *Black Hawk Down* "forgets" the US intervention's most poignant media images, namely, those of celebrating Somalis dragging a dead US soldier through the streets, the corpse bloated, naked, and filthy. The initial photographs, taken by *Toronto Star* reporter Paul Watson (who won a Pulitzer Prize for them), made the American military action in Somalia front-page news in many parts of the world. But the only image of Somalis with a dead US soldier in *Black Hawk Down* are those of Somalis raising the clean, pants-clad body of one of the dead snipers into the air before the film cuts away.

Scott's film inverts the unheroic—indeed, dehumanized—reality of the soldier's corpse by articulating the living heroism of dead American servicemen. The emphasis that *Black Hawk Down* makes on the motto "no one is left behind" consequently includes corpses as "no ones," even at the cost of more American lives. For example, the final convoy rescue scenes show the Americans attempting to remove a pilot's dead body from the first downed helicopter. When the task proves impossible to accomplish by hand, large industrial tools cut open the entire cock-pit. All this takes place in an open square with Somali militia firing relentlessly from the windows and rooftops of surrounding buildings. Even though the convoy arrives at 2:00 am and might have left for safety shortly thereafter, the dead pilot cannot be left behind. General Garrison emphasizes this point to McKnight when the problem of the trapped body is reported back to base: "Danny, no one gets left behind. You understand me, son?" The film finally cuts to the corpse being lifted to "safety" as the sun rises in the background. The night has passed, but the dead body has been "saved," and no one has thus been left behind.

The film's final scenes highlight the message that ethical American warriors live on as heroes in death. The action begins with Eversmann talking to the body of Smith, the corporal who died saving Twombly's life. The staff sergeant confesses that he, Eversmann, has been changed, and that a new understanding of what has happened has dawned on him. He then recounts a story of someone back home asking him prior to the arrival in Somalia whether the troops "think [they're] heroes." He was unable to respond then, he explains, but his answer is clear now: "I'd say no. I'd say there's no way in hell. Nobody asks to be a hero. It just sometimes turns out that way." He then puts his hand reassuringly on the body and adds, "I'm gonna talk to your ma and pa when I get home, okay?" Eversmann's intimate conversation with Smith's corpse removes Smith from death by elevating him above the generic "army of one" and acknowledging that it "turns out" that Smith is a hero with a history, a family, and a personal story of courageous self-sacrifice that his family needs to hear. Eversmann will be replicating what the entire film aims to accomplish: to tell a living story, even of the dead. The camera then pans out to take in a large room, empty save for numerous gurneys on which dead bodies rest, organized in perfectly ordered fashion with personal space around each. To emphasize each body's individuality, two medical technicians focus each on a particular gurney, giving the dead highly personalized attention. On this side of the conflict, it appears, no one is a mere statistic. Like Smith, each of these dead bodies must have a history that has culminated in the ultimate heroic act of losing a life.

The living dead thus convey heroism from beyond the grave. From these gurneys, the film cuts to the final scene where caskets sit in the back of a cargo plane, again a personal space perimeter secured around each. The cargo door closes behind them, indicating that the dead bodies of the living heroes are about to travel home; as the dictum goes, no one is left behind. The screen turns black and the voice of Sergeant First Class Shughart is heard reading a letter to his wife, emphasizing their mutual love and their children. Like Smith, Shughart becomes an individual in death, a hero whose memory will live on through his sacrifice for others, whose sacrifice becomes ever clearer as his personal story emerges. Title screens follow, indicating that one thousand Somalis and nineteen Americans died, and then the dead Americans are listed by full name and rank. For the first time in the film, the viewer has privileged access to the deceased's full names. These are signifiers of identity widely and publicly available only after the men's deaths.

Black Hawk Down thus suggests that America's military heroes will not be left behind by their comrades in arms or by American society writ large. The film's content and form coalesce to convey a message to the living dead: we (Scott's team) make this film and viewers watch it as a demonstration of the way you (the soldier) and your heroism can thus be immortalized and remembered. In contrast, of course, nameless Somali bodies are ripped apart by lethal American artillery without pause and without the equal contextualization of grief or tragedy. Lives worthy or capable of grief are limited to America's humanitarian warriors.[5] In sum, the dead soldier, formerly part of a generic mass of similarly trained living bodies, becomes an individual hero whose name and life we can intimately know and celebrate, whose sacrifice becomes clear only in death.

RE-MEMBERING VIETNAM IN SOMALIA

Although directly concerned with US intervention in Somalia, *Black Hawk Down* reflects the broader discourse celebrating American militarism through the image of the soldier-hero, a discourse that emerged earlier in the 1980s as part of the historical memory of the Vietnam War. Mark Bowden, the author of a book on which the screenplay was based, said that researching and writing about the East African country helped him rethink the view he had of the US military, namely impressions rooted in his understanding of the Vietnam War.[6] Scott's film reflects this cultural reimaging since the late 1970s. By the end of the 1980s, the cultural memory of the Vietnam War in film and other cultural forms blamed the US defeat on a non-committal national government, incompetent military leadership from those not involved in field combat, an unreliable ally, and an unsupportive public on the home front.[7] Each of these motifs is also evident in Scott's retelling of the Mogadishu incident.

Early in the film, the viewer is treated to a conspicuous contrasting of non-committal "Washington" (the national government) and the American soldier (US Marines). While the soldiers are agents who restore order, Washington (just as in *Rambo: First Blood*, for instance) is the monolithic, distant, directing voice that does not fully commit to the operation even while growing "impatient." When General Garrison tells an aide that Somalia is complex, he is informed that "most of Washington might disagree" and that "they've been calling for these daily situation reports every morning this week." Despite Washington's demand for action, however, the federal government has not properly outfitted the US forces for the task assigned. As Garrison informs his commanders in the pre-raid briefing, "I have requested light armor and AC-130 Specter gunships, but Washington, in all its wisdom, decided against this."

Incompetent military leadership, another motif of Vietnam War–based cultural memory, emerges in the film's portrayal of General Garrison. The scenes centered on the Somali intelligence "source" cast him as placing faith in an unknown person. During his briefing, Garrison describes the intelligence as being "as good as it gets" and the scene ends with two veteran soldiers, Hoot (Eric Bana) and McKnight, commenting on the target area's impossibly hostile nature and the difficulty of daylight operations without adequate air cover. Nevertheless, as good soldiers, they carry on with their duties. But Garrison's questionable decision-making is immediately brought to light when the general, now in the command center with his inner circle, comments that he is unsure about the reliability of the Somali intelligence source because "it's [the source's] first time out." Scott emphasizes Garrison's dubious intelligence decision when the source, a cab driver who is supposed to park a car in front of the target building, stops his car elsewhere and claims he is in front of the target building. He then confesses that he is just scared and will now drive to the correct site. Just as in other fictional representations of Vietnam like *Platoon* (1986) or the novel *Matterhorn* by Karl Marlantes, American soldiers are being placed into dangerously hostile territory by generals who have inadequate intelligence but lack the capacity—whether professionally or personally—to be forthcoming about any doubts.[8]

Black Hawk Down also engages the motif of American soldiers serving amid the dual problem of questionable public support on the domestic front and unreliable military allies. When Hoot is asked by Eversmann why he keeps going back out again to the field, Hoot explains that those at home "won't understand. They won't understand why we do it." But more than just understanding, the film imagines that Americans are skeptical about the larger humanitarian need to restore order in places like Somalia; this is not unlike the scepticism evinced about the Vietnam conflict as depicted in *Born on the Fourth of July*. As Eversmann notes, people back home ask, "Why are you going to fight somebody else's war?" The absence of competent allies on the ground, in turn, aggravates this lack of domestic support. In place of the South Vietnamese Army in Somalia, the Pakistani 10th Mountain Division serves as the unreliable ally. Not only does the Pakistani force take an unbearable amount of time to get ready, the American soldiers on the ground do not trust the forces to adequately cover their retreat from the hostile territory, an interpretation later disputed by the Pakistanis themselves.[9]

Several scenes are also reminiscent of Vietnam War films. For example, the images of the American helicopters taking off to music from the 1960s could fit just as well into Francis Ford Coppola's *Apocalypse Now* (1979), the television series *Tour of Duty* (1987-1990), and a host of other productions in which the American Air Cavalry serves as a central image of the Vietnam experience. The music featured in *Black Hawk Down* is Elvis Presley's "Suspicious Minds," a number one song in 1969, the year of Woodstock and the height of the anti–Vietnam War protest movements. In another instance, the presence of the battle-hardened veteran combat officer reflects an archetype that emerged alongside the historical memory of the Vietnam War. On multiple occasions, Colonel McKnight stands tall, seemingly oblivious to the bullets hissing by him and ricocheting all around his body as everyone else ducks for cover. Like Sergeant Barnes (Tom Berenger) in *Platoon* or Zeke Anderson (Terence Knox) in *Tour of Duty*, McKnight is fearless and virtually indestructible. Of any Vietnam War memory that stands out, however, the most conspicuous parallel is when a sergeant attempts to take a look at the foot of Specialist John Grimes (Ewan McGregor). Films celebrating the camaraderie developed despite an unwinnable war used the image of officers checking their men's feet, since this often happened while in Vietnam. Frequent rains and long walks through swamps and muddy trails could lead to gangrene and other podiatric problems if soldiers were not vigilant. Thus, officers would have to check out their troops to ensure the men's feet were dry and healthy. The insertion of such a scene into the arid, dusty, and hostile city streets of Mogadishu is a testimony to the contextualization of the Somali intervention in the ongoing cultural construction of the Vietnam War.

In addition to motifs and imagery, historical references to the US intervention in Vietnam play a subtle but important role in the film. Scott uses the exchanges between Garrison and Atto to remind the viewer of the troubled history of US global military interventions. Shortly after Atto is captured, he points out to Garrison that the Americans are new to the country and do not understand the context of the war. For Garrison, the mission is to capture Aidid; he wants Atto's help. But Atto declines, stating, "I do know something about history." He sees the intervention and Somali civil war as part of "shaping tomorrow. . . . A tomorrow without a lot of Arkansas white boys' ideas in it." What history is Atto referring to, wherein the United States intervened only to leave the civil war intact? Garrison's conversation with a top aide immediately after leaving the captive provides a clue. When he is told they are running out of time, Garrison responds, "This isn't Iraq, you know. Much more complicated than that." The aide remarks that Washington might disagree. The reference to Iraq, the complicated nature of Somalia's internal conflict, and the reference to military history all take place within the same scene. Collectively, they make reference to the government's lack of knowledge about the situation in the besieged nation. The intervention into the African country is thus contrasted with the ostensibly clean-cut Gulf War, which then-President George H. W. Bush claimed in 1991 had helped Americans kick the Vietnam Syndrome once and for all. For both Garrison and Atto, Somalia is much more like Vietnam than the more recent experiences in Iraq.

The film, with its ethical warrior-heroes returning from combat both dead and alive, re-members the Vietnam War by situating the heroic exploits of the American force in Somalia within a broader narrative of the US failure in Vietnam. It begs the question of what might have happened in Somalia had Washington properly supplied the mission, had General Garrison chosen a better time and location, had the American public understood and supported the effort, and had more reliable allies provided aid when necessary. But just like in Vietnam, the skill, courage, and heroism of the troops on the ground could not make up for the larger political and organizational problems they faced. And so immediately after listing the full names and ranks of the dead heroes, the film's final screens inform the audience that "Delta Sgts. Gary Gordon and Randy Shughart were the first soldiers to receive the Medal of Honor posthumously since the Vietnam War." The heroes of Somalia are thus transposed onto those of the earlier conflict.

ETHICAL MILITARISM, HISTORY, AND THE ERASURE OF
VIOLENCE

Since the early 1980s, a re-vitalization of American militarism has occurred
through the reconstruction of the soldier-hero image. Initially, the filmic reimagining of the Vietnam War through works like *Apocalypse Now* and
Platoon depicted US soldiers as generally good men caught in the hell of a
war they could not understand. This disjuncture often corrupted them. Other
films such as *Rambo: First Blood* (1983) and *Missing in Action* (1984) revi-
talized the manly warrior persona of the American soldier by depicting muscular heroes fighting evil against all odds, including opposition from within
America itself.[10] Scott's *Black Hawk Down* is part of a wave of films since
the early 1990s set in war zones other than Vietnam that also imagined the
military to be peopled by soldier-heroes and thus worked to complete the
erasure of the often negative image that had emerged of the military during
the Vietnam War.[11]

The reimagining of American militarism in the wake of the Vietnam War
is a crucial part of ongoing popular support for the military and military
values in American culture. For example, in May 2002, several months after
the opening of *Black Hawk Down*, NFL star safety Pat Tillman joined the
United States Army. The athlete hoped to succeed a long line of soldier-
heroes who had risked their lives for a greater good. "My great grandfather
was at Pearl Harbor, and a lot of my family has . . . gone and fought in wars,
and I really haven't done a damn thing as far as laying myself on the line like
that," he told NBC after 9/11. Tillman could have signed a new contract and
made millions of dollars playing a sport he loved, but instead he went to
Afghanistan where he was killed in April of 2004.[12] Speaking at the White
House Correspondents' dinner a few days later, President George W. Bush
projected the soldier-hero image onto Tillman's dead body: "The loss of
Army Corporal Pat Tillman . . . reminds us of the character of the men and
women who serve on our behalf." He added, "[Tillman] knew there were
many like him, making their own sacrifices. They fill the ranks of the Armed
Forces. Every day, somewhere, they do brave and good things without notice. . . . They're willing to give up their lives." A national funeral was held
on ESPN for Tillman, whose dead body paradoxically reflected the living
goodness of the American soldier. "He is a hero. . . . He was a brave man,"
pronounced the vice-president of Tillman's former team, the Arizona Cardi-
nals. He continued, "There are very few people who have the courage to do
what he did, the courage to . . . make the ultimate sacrifice." That Tillman's
death was ruled by the Pentagon to be the result of friendly fire leaves a bitter
irony in the wake of these celebrations of life and legacy.

Black Hawk Down suggests that any US soldier's ultimate sacrifice reflects America's role as supporter of a universal humanitarianism. The film

thus elides national interest in the current projection of military power by re-membering the imperialism of the Vietnam War by means of ethical soldier-heroes. "In a global universe which legitimates itself with a global morality, sovereign states are no longer exempt from moral judgements," Slavoj Žižek points out in an analysis of worldwide violence. [13] Hence we witness the film's sharp differentiation between the ethical American soldier and the politically compromised, self-interested national government in Washington. The military's intervention is part of a global humanitarian agenda, not the push for national aggrandizement. In other words, re-membering Vietnam in Somalia is part of the erasure of unethical militarism in American historical memory, an erasure that occurs by splitting the agents of military power (the soldiers) from the directors of military power (the national government), and imagining the former as agents of a universal morality. As the film's preface states, after news spread of rampant starvation in Somalia, "The world re-sponds. Behind a force of 20,000 US Marines, food is delivered and order is restored." What "world" is this but the civilized, humanitarian world, the world that stands opposed to Aidid and disorder, the world that has embraced American progress and freedom?

The US intervention's humanitarian framework thus works to erase the military violence that resulted in more than 1000 dead Somalis. The Somali casualties function as the "other" of the humanitarian world and are imaged throughout the film as an indistinguishable mass of backward people who, in Eversmann's words, "have no jobs, no food, no education, no future." The Americans "can either help, or [they] can sit back and watch the country destroy itself on CNN." Just as Vietnam War films often imagine a chaotic, uncivilized Vietnam awaiting the benefits of American civilization, *Black Hawk Down* elides the culture and history of the Somali people and imagines them as unaware of their own desperate need for the so-called civilizing mission rooted in American social, political, and economic models.

The character of Eversmann encapsulates *Black Hawk Down*'s rehabilita-tion of American militarism through the ethical humanitarianism embodied by the soldier-hero. It is a rehabilitation that takes the film's message beyond an exaltation of warrior brotherhood. [14] Consequently, the end of the film moves from Hoot's belief that he is fighting only for the men next to him to Eversmann enunciating the living heroism of Smith's corpse. Hoot's limited view is trumped by the humanitarian mission verbalized by Eversmann and immortalized in Smith's dead body. Like those before them in Vietnam, Smith, Eversmann, Gordon, Shughart, and all the American soldiers in So-malia have proven themselves heroes despite the government in Washington, the intractable generals, and the indifferent or unsupportive public. In *Black Hawk Down*, these soldier-heroes represent the latent moral potential of American military power, which, when marshalled in the name of global humanitarianism, might bring (among other possibilities) food, jobs, education, and a future to the rest of the world.

NOTES

1. Andrew J. Huebner, *The Warrior Image: Soldiers in American Culture from the Second World War to the Vietnam Era* (Chapel Hill: University of North Carolina Press, 2008); Carl Boggs and Tom Pollard, *The Hollywood War Machine: US Militarism and Popular Culture* (Boulder, CO: Paradigm, 2007), 88-101. Some of the images of American soldiers in Vietnam were only slowly rewritten. See Jeremy Kuzmarov, *The Myth of the Addicted Army: Vietnam and the Modern War on Drugs* (Amherst: University of Massachusetts Press, 2009). On the rise of the righteous nation narrative, see David Zietsma, "'Sin Has No History': Religion, National Identity, and US Intervention, 1937-1941," *Diplomatic History* 31 (June 2007): 531-565.

2. On the historical memory of the Vietnam War in American culture see Jeremy M. Devine, *Vietnam at 24 Frames a Second: A Critical and Thematic Analysis of Over 400 Films about the Vietnam War* (Austin: University of Texas Press, 1999); Linda Dittmar and Gene Michaud, ed., *From Hanoi to Hollywood: The Vietnam War in American Film* (New Brunswick, NJ: Rutgers University Press, 2000); Michael Anderegg, ed., *Inventing Vietnam: The War in Film and Television* (Philadelphia, PA: Temple University Press, 1991).

3. "Warlord Thumbs Down for Somalia Film," BBC News, January 29, 2002, accessed September 9, 2012, http://news.bbc.co.uk/2/hi/africa/1789170.stm.

4. On the cultural politics of memorializing the war dead, see Lisa M. Boudreau, *Bodies of War: World War I and the Politics of Commemoration in America, 1919-1933* (New York: New York University Press, 2010); Franny Nudelman, *John Brown's Body: Slavery, Violence, and the Culture of War* (Chapel Hill: University of North Carolina Press, 2004).

5. On the connection between grief, commemoration, and violence see Judith Butler, *Precarious Life: The Powers of Mourning and Violence* (New York: Verso, 2004), 19-49.

6. "'Hawk' flies into heart of Somalia raid," *USA Today*, February 12, 1999, accessed September 9, 2012, http://www.usatoday.com/life/enter/books/b1064.htm.

7. See H. Bruce Franklin, *Vietnam and Other American Fantasies* (Amherst: University of Massachusetts Press, 2000); Jerry Lembcke, *The Spitting Image: Myth, Memory, and the Legacy of Vietnam* (New York: New York University Press, 1998).

8. Karl Marlantes, *Matterhorn: A Novel of the Vietnam War* (New York: Atlantic Monthly Press, 2010).

9. Pervez Musharraf, *In the Line of Fire: A Memoir* (New York: Free Press, 2006), 76.

10. Susan Jeffords, *Hard Bodies: Hollywood Masculinity in the Reagan Era* (New Brunswick, NJ: Rutgers University Press, 2002); Susan Jeffords, *The Remasculinization of America: Gender and the Vietnam War* (Bloomington: Indiana University Press, 1989).

11. Boggs and Pollard, *Hollywood War Machine*.

12. Ty Hawkins, *Reading Vietnam Amid the War on Terror* (New York: Palgrave Macmillan, 2012), 1-2; "Ex-NFL Star Tillman makes 'ultimate sacrifice': safety, who gave up big salary to join army, killed in Afghanistan," MSNBC, April 26, 2004, accessed on September 9, 2012, http://www.msnbc.msn.com/id/4815441/ns/world_news/t/ex-nfl-star-tillman-makes-ultimate-sacrifice/#.UE1HLZbhd5I.

13. Slavoj Žižek, *Violence: Six Sideways Reflections* (New York: Picador, 2008), 117.

14. While I largely agree with Klien's work on establishing sympathy with the image of the soldier, I am suggesting a larger national narrative of humanitarianism is at stake in the film. See Stephen Klien, "Public Character and the Simulacrum: The Construction of the Soldier Patriot and Citizen Agency in *Black Hawk Down*" in *Critical Studies in Media Communication* 22 (December 2005): 427-449.

REFERENCES

Anderegg, Michael, ed. *Inventing Vietnam: The War in Film and Television*. Philadelphia, PA: Temple University Press, 1991.

Black Hawk Down. DVD. Directed by Ridley Scott. 2001; Culver City, CA: Sony Pictures Home Entertainment, 2002.

Boggs, Carl and Tom Pollard. *The Hollywood War Machine: US Militarism and Popular Culture*. Boulder, CO: Paradigm, 2007.

Boudreau, Lisa M. *Bodies of War: World War I and the Politics of Commemoration in America, 1919-1933*. New York: New York University Press, 2010.

Butler, Judith. *Precarious Life: The Powers of Mourning and Violence*. New York: Verso, 2004.

Devine, Jeremy M. *Vietnam at 24 Frames a Second: A Critical and Thematic Analysis of Over 400 Films about the Vietnam War*. Austin: University of Texas Press, 1999.

Dittmar, Linda and Gene Michaud, eds. *From Hanoi to Hollywood: The Vietnam War in American Film*. New Brunswick, NJ: Rutgers University Press, 2000.

"Ex-NFL Star Tillman makes 'ultimate sacrifice:' safety, who gave up big salary to join army, killed in Afghanistan." MSNBC.com, April 26, 2004. Accessed on September 9, 2012. http://www.msnbc.msn.com/id/4815441/ns/world_news/t/ex-nfl-star-tillman-makes-ultimate-sacrifice/#.UE1HLZbhd5I.

Franklin, H. Bruce. *Vietnam and Other American Fantasies*. Amherst: University of Massachusetts Press, 2000.

"'Hawk' flies into heart of Somalia raid." *USA Today*, February 12, 1999. Accessed on September 9, 2012. http://www.usatoday.com/life/enter/books/b1064.htm.

Hawkins, Ty. *Reading Vietnam Amid the War on Terror*. New York: Palgrave Macmillan, 2012.

Huebner, Andrew J. *The Warrior Image: Soldiers in American Culture from the Second World War to the Vietnam Era*. Chapel Hill: University of North Carolina Press, 2008.

Jeffords, Susan. *Hard Bodies: Hollywood Masculinity in the Reagan Era*. New Brunswick, NJ: Rutgers University Press, 2002.

———. *The Remasculinization of America: Gender and the Vietnam War*. Bloomington: Indiana University Press, 1989.

Klien, Stephen. "Public Character and the Simulacrum: The Construction of the Soldier Patriot and Citizen Agency in *Black Hawk Down*," *Critical Studies in Media Communication* 22 (December 2005): 427-449.

Kuzmarov, Jeremy. *The Myth of the Addicted Army: Vietnam and the Modern War on Drugs*. Amherst: University of Massachusetts Press, 2009.

Lembcke, Jerry. *The Spitting Image: Myth, Memory, and the Legacy of Vietnam*. New York: New York University Press, 1998.

Marlantes, Karl. *Matterhorn: A Novel of the Vietnam War*. New York: Atlantic Monthly Press, 2010.

Musharraf, Pervez. *In the Line of Fire: A Memoir*. New York: Free Press, 2006.

Nudelman, Franny. *John Brown's Body: Slavery, Violence, and the Culture of War*. Chapel Hill: University of North Carolina Press, 2004.

"Warlord Thumbs Down for Somalia Film," BBC News. January 29, 2002. Accessed September 9, 2012. http://news.bbc.co.uk/2/hi/africa/1789170.stm.

Zietsma, David. "'Sin Has No History': Religion, National Identity, and US Intervention, 1937-1941." *Diplomatic History* 31 (2007): 531-565.

Žižek, Slavoj. *Violence: Six Sideways Reflections*. New York: Picador, 2008.

Chapter Six

1492 and the Ethics of Remembering

Silvio Torres-Saillant

A self-identified historical film, *1492: Conquest of Paradise* (1992) sets out to do on the screen what the historians have long done on the page, namely to rememorate the exploits of Christopher Columbus from a particular standpoint. Ridley Scott's venture into historical film illustrates the extent to which the cinematic medium "can offer a method of representation comparable with historiography itself."[1] Commenting on the suitability of the medium to tell the story of the past, Mike Chopra-Gant suggests that film "offers much greater potential for photo-realist representation of events—a chance to see what it was like rather than merely read about it—," thereby engaging us at a more dynamic level in "the experience of history than the conventional written work."[2] Arguably, in this most visual of eras, a film may have a greater impact on collective understandings of past events than the corresponding books or articles. As a result, historical films merit critical scrutiny perhaps more urgently than written renditions of former times. Engaging films critically to celebrate the meritorious ones and challenge any we find taking "excessive liberties with historical fact" seems the most prudent manner of interaction with cinema that repackages history for a mass audience.[3]

Certain schools of philosophy, history, literature, and cultural studies, under the aegis of postmodernism, casually dismiss the practice and truth claims of history, reducing its meaning to "no more than a series of conventions for thinking about the past."[4] That dismissal lies outside the concerns of the present chapter. This text starts with a view of history as a string of past events which, though they may have happened long ago, continue to have a discernible impact on the lives and life-chances of people today. I posit that any public historical exercise involving the colonial transaction has to confront the reality of living and breathing interlocutors who bear on their shoulders the outcomes of the episodes explored therein. The colonial transaction unleashed by the arrival of Columbus in the Caribbean caused the enrichment of some alongside the impoverishment of others; the rise of some alongside the subjection of others. With the legacy of that history so present among us, manifested in chronically unequal levels of empowerment, it would defy the limits of the humane imagination to think of it as an open field for hermeneutic creativity unencumbered by powerful reactions of insulted or gratified sectors of the audience. Therefore, I approach Scott's *1492: Conquest of Paradise* as the vigorous intervention of a "cinematic historian" contending with issues that emanate from the "historical problem" that the filmmaker set out to tackle.[5] As will become clear in the pages that follow, Scott chose to address the problem of Columbus in a manner that gratified those whom we may deem heirs of the Columbian project and mocked those who inherited the long-term effects of its atrocities.

John Glen's film *Christopher Columbus: The Discovery* antedated Scott's by a matter of months. The former was released in August 1992 and the latter in October of the same year, within days of the official date of the much-touted commemoration of the "discovery." Both works set out to chronicle the achievement of Cristoforo Colombo, the Genoese sailor who, under the Spanish flag, braved the unknown seas with the hope of charting a new trade route to India and China. In so doing, he endeavored to circumvent mediation by the Ottoman Turks who, at the time, controlled most maritime trade routes between Europe and Asia. Both films wished to capitalize on the frenzy over the Columbian legacy that was taking hold of America and Europe with the approaching 500th anniversary of Columbus's crossing of the Atlantic, ushering in the conquest of the Americas by European Christians. The Glen film (produced by the well-known father-son duo of Alexander and Ilya Salkind) disappointed audiences and critics alike. Its depiction of Columbus as a witty, fearless, intellectually dexterous, and charming idealist did not make any significant impression, its large budget notwithstanding. A review of the film mordantly noted that by the time the Genoese's three-ship fleet sets sail, "half the movie is over and the audience is ready to jump ship."[6] The script simply repeats many of the better known stereotypes about Columbus, his relationship with Queen Isabel, and his ambiguous rapport with the indigenous peoples he encounters at the end of his transatlantic voyage. According to the aforementioned review, the film was made "for no better reason than the marketing ploy of a 500th anniversary," and it fundamentally lacked "the vision thing."[7]

Scott's *1492: Conquest of Paradise*, on the other hand, abounds with the filmmaker's omnivorous vision of Columbus as creator of a new world of light, freedom, and progress out of the prejudice, oppression, and blindness that pervaded his times. Scott places Columbus among a handful of great men (for instance, Leonardo da Vinci, Michelangelo, and Thomas More), who entered history as "creators of this new movement out of darkness into light toward the renaissance."[8] Lest the audience fail to get the point from the actual plot, *1942* opens with an explanatory epigraph that drives this point home: "500 years ago, Spain was a nation gripped by fear and superstition, ruled by the crown and a ruthless Inquisition that persecuted men for daring to dream. One man challenged this power. Driven by his sense of destiny, he crossed the sea of darkness in search of honor, gold, and the greater glory of God." Columbus sets sail on August 3, 1492, arrives on the island of Guanahani on October 12, and starts a relationship with the native Tainos there with the conscientiousness expressed in the warning he gives his men upon arrival: "They are not savages; and neither will we be." After the first voyage, having taken possession of the land of the Tainos in the name of Almighty God and the Spanish crown and materializing his title of Admiral of the Ocean Sea and Viceroy of the Indies (one that he had negotiated with his sponsors via the Santa Fe Treaty), he comes back to Spain in total triumph. He returns with such spoils as gold, flora, fauna, and enslaved Indians.

Convinced of the wisdom of their investment, the monarchs Ferdinand and Isabel increase their support of the enterprise of the Indies, and the Admiral goes back to the Caribbean in charge of an impressive seventeen-ship fleet. While the original crew consisted of men of lowly station who, by virtue of their impecuniousness, could afford to risk their lives sailing into the vast unknown, the staff for the second voyage included professionals, priests, skilled workers, and nobles sent by the government to engage in the serious work of colonization. In Scott's film, the second voyage marks the beginning of Columbus's troubles. The nobles, represented by the pallid character Moxica, arrogantly flaunt their superior social rank and their contempt for the authority of the Admiral, a born commoner. They refuse to work side by side with plebeians and Indians in building Santo Domingo, inaugural seat of Spanish rule in the hemisphere, and the Admiral must force them to cooperate. At one dramatic moment in the film, an embittered Moxica, upon the Admiral's demand, has to relinquish his fine horse to the collective effort (led by Columbus personally) of lifting a gigantic iron bell to the high dome of the colony's first Christian church. The conflict with the nobles gradually intensifies, causing war with the natives and discontent among the settlers, especially as the island of Santo Domingo did not reveal itself as the fount of inexhaustible precious metals and gems that Columbus had so ardently yearned for since reading the accounts of Marco Polo.

Polo, the Venetian adventurer who spent over twenty years in the service of Kublai Khan in Asia during the latter half of the thirteenth century, left compelling descriptions of the abundance of wealth he had seen in those lands, particularly in Zipangu (Japan), an island not yet under his control. The connotations of the word Zipangu had resonated tantalizingly with those of Cibao, the name given by the Tainos to the northern portions of the island of Santo Domingo. Polo's depiction of the island of wealth, as illustrated by these greed-provoking passages, must have proven unsettling to the ambitious mariner: "They have gold in the greatest abundance, its sources being inexhaustible, but as the king does not allow its export, few merchants visit the country." Polo provides this enticing picture of the ruler's abode: "[the] extraordinary richness of the sovereign's palace, according to what we are told by those who have access to the place, is a wonderful sight. The entire roof is covered with a plating of gold, in the same manner as we cover houses, or more properly churches, with lead. The ceilings of the hall are of the same precious metal; many of the apartments have small tables of pure gold, of considerable thickness, and the windows have also golden ornaments. So vast, indeed, are the riches of the palace, that it is impossible to convey an idea of them." Besides the gilded splendor, Polo refers to the pearls abounding in the island: "round in shape, and of great size equal in value to, or even exceeding that of the white pearls," as well as "a number of precious stones." On account of the great wealth characterizing the magnificent island, Kublai Khan harbored a fervent desire to conquer "and annex it to his dominion." He could not do so because of a strife developing between the two commanders to whom he had entrusted the task.[9]

With the precious metals and gems of Santo Domingo not emerging at a rate commensurate with expectations instilled by Columbus's reading of Polo, the Indians deserting, the nobles conspiring by inciting armed rebellion on the island while also sending defamatory complaints to the authorities in Spain, and violent tropical hurricanes destroying the edifices, the first Spanish city in the Americas was clearly in danger. Columbus has to look defeat straight in the eye. In 1499, a member of the Order of Calatrava named Francisco de Bobadilla lands in Santo Domingo with credentials from the monarchs of Spain appointing him as the new Governor of the Indies. Columbus resignedly accepts the authority of Bobadilla, who not only replaces him on the job but also upholds the accusations of reckless management that the crown had received, finding him guilty and shipping him back to Spain in chains. "I'm afraid," explains Bobadilla to Columbus in a tone of mock sympathy after formally unseating him, "that is not the only bad news." He proceeds to inform the man of the official discovery of the new continent by Florentine navigator Amerigo Vespucci.

At this point, the script of Scott's film privileges dramatic impact over historical accuracy. Vespucci's participation as observer in the Portuguese expeditions that explored the east coast of South America would begin to sail in 1499 and the cartographic descriptions attributed to him identifying the continent as a region not yet known to European geographers, his *Mundus Novus*, did not appear in print until 1502. But the anachronism in *1492: Conquest of Paradise* seems useful to hammer in the film's central emphasis: the obstacles that the visionary mariner had to contend with in a world ruled by superstition and prejudice against those who "dar[ed] to dream." After all, Columbus fought the incredulity of the cosmographers at the University of Salamanca who dismissed his ideas about the shape of the planet, the reticence of patrons who, only after long consideration, hesitantly provided the resources he needed for the enterprise, the near mutiny of his impatient crew on board, the wrath of the sea, the tropical climate, and the recurrence of rebellion on the island. After his obdurate resistance against all those odds, he finds himself the victim of malicious calumny and falls from grace with his patrons. Going to jail, he suffers the ignominy of seeing the result of his great work attributed to someone else.

The film winds down after the Queen, showing still a remnant of her initial identification with his passion, grants Columbus the wish to sail to the new continent one more time before he dies (provided that he stay away from Santo Domingo). He comes out of his audience with the Queen and meets with Sanchez, the fictional character who had first supported him but later turned against him to advance the interests of Bobadilla. Sanchez chides him for so fiercely holding on to a dream. Columbus puts an end to the exchange by asserting that dreamers like him have made "civilization"; looking at Sanchez unblinkingly, he tells him about the one thing that will set the two of them apart forever: "I did it; you didn't." In a next scene, Arojaz, the Salamanca University professor and a priest who had most virulently antagonized the proposal of the first voyage, notices Sanchez's eyes trailing on Columbus as the mariner prepares to set sail on his fourth and final voyage. Columbus has previously witnessed the inimical Arojaz lecturing to a learned audience, with the monarchs in tow, about the great exploits of Americo Vespucci and the University of Salamanca's conviction from the outset that such a voyage was possible. The priest shares a disparaging comment about Columbus: "[W]hat a tragedy! What a waste of a life!" Sanchez fails to echo the priest's sentiment. Instead he didactically tells him that if either of them is ever remembered for anything it will be because of what Columbus has done. The film then cuts to the final scene of an aged Columbus, presumably already back from his fourth voyage, beginning to dictate the story of his life to his son Fernando. We then learn from the textual epilogue that precedes the closing credits that "Fernando's biography restored his father's name to its place in history."

COLUMBUS AND POWER: THE LURE OF HAGIOGRAPHY

As illustrated in the foregoing synopsis, *1492: Conquest of Paradise* privileges the official version of "the discovery" narrative. A testimony of what the official version posited came in the same year of the release of Scott's film from the American historian Howard Zinn, author of the influential *A*

People's History of the United States (1980). Zinn illustrated the narrative that children learned in school by recalling the way Samuel Eliot Morison, the Rear Admiral of the United States Naval Reserve who won a Pulitzer Prize for his biography of Columbus entitled *Admiral of the Ocean Sea* (1942), evoked in amazement "the wonder, the delight of those October days in 1492 when the New World gracefully yielded her virginity to the conquering Castilians."[10] Zinn uses the occasion to confess his former ignorance of the history involved in the matter. Despite having received a Ph.D. in history, for long he remained unaware of the butchery that took place in Hispaniola or the slave raids that the Admiral marshaled to send Tainos for sale in Seville. Only when he began work on *A People's History* did he learn about Columbus beyond what school children knew.[11]

Similarly attesting to the resilience of "the way we were taught about Columbus in school," Hans Koning, the author of two books on the enterprise of the Indies, has emphasized the extent to which the remembrance of the Columbian project without attention to the viewpoint of the victims remains "the final record."[12] Perhaps Scott's decision to cast his dice on the side of the official version may have surprised those fans who regard him as an original filmmaker with a knack for stories that go against the grain of received opinion. The ideological side he ended up favoring could hardly have come by accident. Many historians of the revisionist kind, namely those contesting the official story, had enunciated their views widely during the 1980s. Historically-minded civil and human rights activists had likewise called for revised narratives of the conquest and colonization of the Americas that would interrupt the continuous aggression that the official version had long perpetrated against people of indigenous and African descent. These were groups whose ancestors bore the brunt of European encroachment into their lands. Indeed, the interviews in which Scott has defended the picture of Columbus drawn by his film evince not only an awareness of the debate of the 1980s but a hardline ideological will to participate in it as an antagonist of the "revisionists."

The *Variety* review of *1492* described it as "a lumbering one-dimensional historical fresco" which failed to become "the complex, ambiguous character study" that the filmmaker had strived for, despite the difficulty of dramatizing the story of Columbus.[13] A review by Owen Gleiberman decried the film's presentation of the Admiral as "the same cardboard visionary we learned about in school," which made the viewing experience "as exciting as doing your homework."[14] Critic Chris Hicks declared the movie "the season's biggest disappointment," while Desson Howe regarded it as "not quite as ridiculous as Salkind's Columbus film, but twice as disappointing."[15] Even sympathetic commentators could not praise the film in terms more committal than those of Roger Ebert, who deemed it a "satisfactory" film "in its own way and up to a certain point."[16]

In the spring of 1992, journalist Jack Matthews followed Scott to Costa Rica to cover the shooting of the film. There he observed the director's precision while reproducing the scene of Columbus's landing in Guanahani and his facing "the Indians on the beach that day." Matthews interviewed screenwriter Roselyne Bosch, a 31-year-old French journalist who, at the time, worked as a staff writer for the weekly news magazine *Le Point*. Bosch had discovered Columbus in 1987 while researching an article on Spain's long-range plan for celebrating the 500th anniversary of the first voyage. In the interview, Bosch clearly positions herself as a writer with a hardline interpretation of the history that is reflected in her script. Invested in challenging what she regards as the current tendency to view Columbus through "the cliché of genocide," she noted that while Columbus "imposed his views" once he reached the land of the Tainos, he cannot be blamed "for the massacres that followed" any more than one can blame "Christ for the Inquisition." Bosch contended that with the invention of the printing press half a century earlier, "the formation of a global community" had already taken off. "Knowledge drove people forward whether the church and government liked it or not," she argues, adding that if Columbus had not run ashore in the West Indies, someone else would have done so.[17] Scott also made his historical position known in words that resonated with Bosch's dismissal of "the cliché of genocide." Articulating his "little patience with those who see Columbus as the symbol for all that has gone wrong with the world," he settled for an image of the Genoese navigator as "a visionary" and "a man with a conscience. But, most of all, he was a man of his times, and the times were different."[18] When he read Bosch's script, the depiction of Columbus he found there gave him reason to doubt the largely negative views of the mariner then in circulation. He liked Bosch's approach to Columbus "as a character study." "The bottom line is he defined the age," insists Scott.[19]

The contours of Scott's thoughts from the interview with Matthews emerged more clearly after the release of *1492: Conquest of Paradise* in a conversation with the Brazilian journalist and film critic Ana Maria Bahiana. This interview frames the terms of the exchange along lines suggested by the Matthews article. Evidently identifying with the historical ideology of the filmmaker, Bahiana formulates her questions so as to provide him with discursive opportunities to refute "the recent revisionist wave that has all but revised Christopher Columbus's status as a hero of humankind."[20] She characterizes the script by Bosch as "carefully researched" and asks Scott for his take on "the recent revisionist upsurge that tries to blame Columbus for every single evil that befell America." The filmmaker gladly seizes the opportunity to discredit attempts to criticize Columbus for "his methods and results in the fifteenth century," insisting that today's standards cannot apply to the "normal" behavior of the explorer's time.[21] The filmmaker and the interviewer concur that as "a man of his times," Columbus "should not and cannot be analyzed and judged by today's historical standards."[22] Scott deems it "pointless" to engage in that kind of revisionist effort. What was considered "normal" behavior then, "sociopolitical" or otherwise, cannot be judged by today's standards. The director contends the Admiral had not had the benefit of the following five hundred years of "colonization," with all its brutality, to be the "humanist he may have been by today's standards."[23]

In the pages ahead we will have occasion to discuss whether we may or may not pass judgment on the wrongdoings of the past, should Caligula, Ivan the Terrible, or Adolph Eichmann have committed them. At any rate, nothing in Scott's words would constitute a direct refutation of the claim that the conquest of the Americas unleashed events that, for the centuries that followed, undermined the life chances of indigenous peoples and African-descended populations in the area and beyond. Many organizations prior to 1992 had advocated a reconsideration of the conquest that sought to restore the human dignity that school textbooks and official memorialization of the Columbian legacy had continuously denied such people of indigenous and African origins. That Scott knew about such advocacy seems clear from remarks of his in a July 1991 interview with film critic Amy Taubin. A bit cavalier, he makes the following prediction: "*Columbus* is going to be very unpopular. We're going to have every Indian society after us for racism. But his vision was very extreme—even more extreme than NASA's and more daunting. His crew believed he was going to sail to the edge of the world. The NASA people, at least, have their co-ordinates when they send up a mission."[24] In other words, already more than a year from the completion of his film, not yet called *1492*, Scott knew that his particular historical interpretation had a high likelihood of causing offense to people of indigenous ancestry. But he did not see their offense as reason to reconsider his hermeneutic choice as cinematic historian.

Perhaps Scott could not afford to give much consideration to the sensibilities of "every Indian society" especially given the greater might and political sway of the forces that his interpretation of the Columbus would please. In particular, his narrative would gratify Spain. Since the final blow to its former empire in the Spanish-American War of 1898 when the United States removed the last remnants of an Iberian imperial presence in the hemisphere, Spain has sought to compensate at the level of symbolic politics, investing abundant resources in promoting its heritage of past greatness throughout the world. The shooting of *1492: Conquest of Paradise* occurred precisely as Spain prepared to commemorate the quincentenary of "the discovery." That the cultural commissars of the Spanish government, after reading the script, should have decided to invest generously in Scott's film might provide a clue to his motivations. The filmmaker recalls that "in Spain we had enormous financial aid from the Ministry of Culture, which was planning the celebration three years ago. There was no real problem with the Ministry in terms of accuracy of the story other than minor requests."[25]

The embrace of Scott's film in official circles of the United States could be expected on the basis of the proclamation issued by the then-President on Columbus Day, 1989. As head of state of the country that has played the most vigorous role in promoting the heroic exploits of the Genoese mariner since the eighteenth century to the present, George H. W. Bush identified the Columbian enterprise with American success. He equated honoring "the skilled and courageous navigator who discovered the Americas," bringing "to our ancestors the promise of the New World," with paying tribute to "the generations of brave and bold Americans who, like the Genoese mariner, have overcome great odds in order to chart the unknown."[26] The presidential proclamation looked forward to three years thence, 1992, when "the United States will commemorate the 500th anniversary of the arrival of Columbus on these shores and proudly participate in events honoring the great explorer," announcing also "the educational and commemorative events and programs" then being planned by the Christopher Columbus Quincentenary Jubilee Commission, an entity established by the Congress as early as 1984.[27] Nor would the Vatican have reason to quarrel with the narrative of *1492: Conquest of Paradise*. Within days of the film's release, Pope John Paul VI travelled to Santo Domingo, the city in the Dominican Republic most centrally featured in the story, to celebrate the spread of Christianity for which that first Spanish colony had served as a decisive stepping stone. The pope went there to dedicate the Columbus Lighthouse (*El Faro a Colón*), a monument of pharaonic proportions built by the Dominican government at an incalculable cost (and against the wishes of the population). This landmark paid the same kind of tribute that Scott's film aimed to lavish upon the name of Columbus and assert the country's primacy as a cradle of Christian civilization in the Americas.

With so many powerful forces grouping to salute the Genoese mariner— Spain's Fifth Centennial Commission and Ministry of Culture, the United States government and cultural institutions, the Vatican, and the mainstream film industry, among others—the voices advocating a reconsideration of the narrative of "the discovery" could hardly be heard in 1992. One wonders, then, about the urgency of Bosch and Scott to launch their epistemological warfare against the "revisionists." Why would they want to want to snub the claims of the indigenous and African-descended populations in the United States and Latin America that on a daily basis feel on their flesh and minds the social impact of the dispossession, destitution, and dehumanization perpetrated by Christian Europe against their ancestors beginning in 1492? In taking that position, *1492: Conquest of Paradise* risks being perceived as a conservative and reactionary manifesto against the corrective discourse of minority voices. At a more academic level, with the film viewed as the work of a "cinematic historian," Scott chooses to converse pugnaciously with representatives of the more humane historiography which does not content itself with the wisdom of H. P. Hartley's historical formula ("The past is a foreign country: they do things differently there") which encourages brushing aside the crimes of the past, apparently failing to see their repercussions in the present or the future.

A different engagement with history may find it proper to pass judgment on the wrongdoings of the past as a way of preventing their reoccurrence. Some would contend that conceptually condoning the horrors of the past makes one complicit with them, apart from authorizing their repetition. Some of the most provocative analyses of the Columbian legacy published by non-conservative historians over the last forty years have concerned themselves with the consequences of past horrors. The violence unleashed by "the discovery" throughout the Americas during the period of conquest and colonial domination created paradigms of social relations that have charted a path of destruction that reaches into the present day. These historians came after the concentration camps of the Holocaust and the intra-European wars of the first half of the twentieth century when it dawned on many Western scholars that the violence that earlier generations of intellectuals had tolerated when their people committed it against racial others had now come home to haunt them. Out of that awakening came documents like the "Resolutions and Manifestoes of Scientists," a compilation of statements by social science and biology associations repudiating the use of race to explain historical phenomena.[28] Among men and women of letters, the French literary scholar René Étiemble declared any "humanism" ridiculous "which does not set as its main objective the elimination of racism."[29]

One cannot fault Scott, with his 31-year-old script writer who discovered Columbus in 1987, for not knowing the serious scholarship on Columbus; he makes his living as a talented mainstream filmmaker, not as an erudite historian. Strangely enough, he audaciously enters into the historiographical fray with a film whose name provokingly echoes the title of Kirkpatrick Sale's *The Conquest of Paradise: Christopher Columbus and the Columbian Legacy* (1990), a scholarly study of the conquest and colonization. Sale emphasizes some of the mostly deleterious contemporary effects of the events in question while meticulously chronicling the central role of the United States in constructing the glorious image of the Admiral that Scott's film seeks to rescue from the revisionists.[30] By 1988, Sale notes, some sixty-five geopolitical entities in thirty-seven states paid homage to the name of the Admiral in the United States, surpassing all other eponyms except Washington.[31] The process leading to that proliferation of eponymous designations, which would reflect itself in the name of the District of Columbia, the country's very capital, started some two centuries earlier when patriotic American voices began to disseminate their equation between the Columbian enterprise and the rise of the United States. The first major epic of the newly minted American Republic, Joel Barlow's *The Vision of Columbus* (1787), which the poet would later reissue in an edition entitled *The Columbiad*, opens with a chained Columbus in a dungeon, the queen (his protector) already dead, and without prospect of recognition for the world he has given to Spain. The deity Hesper, the brother of Atlas, appears to him in his dark prison and soothes the pain of his disappointment. The god takes him on an aerial trip across the hemisphere to show him the expansion of his initial work by other conquerors and soldiers, all of which will increase his credit, giving him everlasting fame. Even more important, Hesper shows him the northern portions of the hemisphere, the site of the future United States of America, where a stronger and wiser people, a superior race, will bring his discovery to its greatest outcome.

On October 12, 1792, while travelling and doing itinerant preaching in England, Reverend Elhanan Winchester, one of the founders of the United States General Convention of Universalists, later known as the Universalist Church of America, delivered in London an oration to commemorate "three hundred years from the day on which Columbus landed in the new world." Characteristically for Anglo-American and English pronouncements at the time, Winchester praises Columbus, condemns the Spanish (except for the caring Queen Isabella), and grieves the mariner's fall from grace with the crown, dramatizing his ensuing incarceration and the indignity of having the name of Amerigo Vespucci christen the newfound lands. He expresses the wish that the United States would seek to rectify the wrongs done to Columbus "by altering the name in their jurisdiction, and styling themselves, THE UNITED STATES OF COLUMBIA."[32] Winchester appreciated in particular "the full importance of the discovery of America" as the source of "the greater part of the gold and silver of Europe," the "amazing quantity of wealth which the several nations of Europe possess," and how the region "has enriched the world at large, and especially Europe."[33] Much like Barlow, Winchester saw the 1607 Jamestown settlement and the 1620 establishment of Plymouth as English extensions of the Columbian spirit. By the time of his London oration, Winchester could already attest to the material advancement of his people on this land: "O, America! land of liberty, peace, and plenty! . . . I have lived to behold thee free and independent, rising to glory and extensive empire; blessed with all the good things of this life, and a happy prospect for better things to come."[34] As a result, a spirit of gratitude towards the Genoese mariner whose "discovery" had made it possible already circulated heavily throughout the land.

Columbus has long done well in the cultural mainstream of the United States. The nation's official discourse throughout the nineteenth century drew its data about Columbus from the enormously successful Washington Irving biography *The Life and Voyages of Columbus* (1829), simultaneously published in London (four volumes) and New York (three volumes). It was an international hit.[35] The American ambassador in Spain, Alexander Everett, had learned about the work of Martín Fernández de Navarrete, a scholar who had just completed a Spanish edition of the journal kept by the Admiral during his four voyages. Ambassador Everett thought that the American audience should immediately have access to the text, so he commissioned Irving, then in France, to undertake the translation, for which he received room and board in the house of the Madrid-based American bibliophile Obadiah Rich in addition to regular access to consultations with Fernández de Navarrete.[36] Instead of the translation, Irving produced his *Life and Voyages*, which mixes fact and fiction indiscriminately, and for the sake of dramatic effect, regularly disfigures the research made available to him by Fernández de Navarrete. As a result, his representation of the words, deeds, and situations of Columbus constitutes "a glaring abdication of the responsibility of the historian in favor of the license of the novelist."[37] Irving was not without his philosophy of history. Well acquainted with the more skeptical ideas of Columbus and his "discovery" advanced by authors such as the Abbé Guillaume Raynal and Samuel Johnson, who did not uncritically celebrate the colonial transàction, Irving had a categorical answer for them. He was downright condemnatory of what he saw as the following:

> a certain meddlesome spirit, which, in the garb of learned research, goes prying about the traces of history, casting down its monuments and marring and mutilating its fairest trophies. Care should be taken to vindicate great names from such pernicious erudition. It defeats one of the most salutary purposes of history, that of furnishing examples of what human genius and laudable enterprise may accomplish.[38]

The Irving school of historical remembering—the one liberated from the facts of history—proved triumphant in the end. Witness the advocacy of various groups in Italy and the United States from 1856 through 1918 to have Columbus "recognized as an official saint by the Catholic Church."[39] The Vatican had played a role in promoting a pious image of Columbus through Pope Leo XIII's July 16, 1892 encyclical "proclaiming that Columbus had undertaken his great voyage with the object of preparing and facilitating the way for the diffusion of the Faith, and that all his works conformed to religion and were inspired by piety."[40] However, the Admiral's failure to marry his partner Beatriz Enríquez de Arana, the mother of Fernando, apart from the lack of evidence that he had actually performed miracles, kept the Vatican from even beginning "the beatification process."[41] That drawback aside, the growing popularity of Columbus in the United States rose to nearly religious adoration. Indeed, writing while he headed the 1893 Chicago Columbian Exposition's Bureau of the American Republics, William E. Curtis stated that "the effigy of the Admiral of the Indies" has been "painted and carved more often, perhaps, than [that] of any other except the Savior of Mankind."[42] Similarly, informed by Irving's manner of remembering the past, Columbus became a model disseminated by the schools to instill a sense of courage, resolve, and enterprise in the minds of the next generation, "an example of good character for young readers, distorting history in the interest of inspiring children."[43] In 1892, the 400th anniversary celebration of the first voyage attracted double the audience and quadrupled the cost of the Centennial Exposition seventeen years earlier. The statue of the Genoese mariner on the southeast corner of New York City's Central Park, renamed Columbus Circle, stands as an iconic reminder of the magnitude of the festivities.[44]

Perhaps the ultimate triumph of Irving's cavalier dismissal of historical veracity came in the words of New York Railroad President Chauncey Depew whose address to opera-goers at Carnegie Hall sent daggers into serious students of the past: "If there is anything I detest more than another, it is that spirit of critical historical inquiry which doubts everything; that modern spirit which destroys all the illusions and all the hopes which have been the inspiration of patriotism through all the centuries."[45] As Claudia L. Bushman has shown, by 1892 the glorification of Columbus had become a factor in the discourse of American patriotism. Consequently, advocacy for revisions of the narrativized Columbian legacy could make one suspect of harboring un-American sentiments. Perhaps that explains the fortune of proposals outlining commemorative projects of the 500th anniversary of "the discovery" that presented "revisionist" views of the historical event in question when they reached the decision-making desk at the National Endowment for the Humanities (NEH). At the time, Lynne Cheney, wife of the Bush administration's defense secretary, headed the NEH; a conservative regime prevailed in the organization. As a result, many so-called revisionist ideas for remembering 1492 failed to receive funding approval even when they enjoyed the warm endorsement of peer reviewers.[46]

The narrative nourished by promoters of the heroic, visionary Columbus, creator of a new world of light out of a foreground of darkness, has a large army of powerful advocates in church, government, and big business. Scott's *1492: Conquest of Paradise* may have intended to go against the grain of received opinion. But he aimed his darts in too safe and too conservative a fashion. As his film simply echoed the historical position of the powerful (the Vatican, the governments of Spain and the United States, as well as white supremacist and Eurocentric scholars), he chose non-conservative scholars and minority voices as his antagonists. *1492: Conquest of Paradise* aggressively responds to the Commission for Studies on the History of Church in Latin America, whose October 12, 1989 document "The Santo Domingo Statement" asked official discourse to be "attentive to the clamor of the indigenous and Afro-American peoples."[47] The film operates as a rebuttal to the American Library Association's "Columbus Quincentennial Resolution" which urged libraries to examine the event from "an authentic Native American perspective."[48] In quarrelling with the less conservative and less empowered side of the Columbian debate, Scott's endeavor lost the possibility of contributing some valuable historical insight as far as films go, even something worthy of his talent. *1492* simply became a diminutive player in the centuries-old, multitudinous cadre of entities engaged in conservative, ethnocentric, and morally compromised evocations of the historical events surrounding the conquest and colonization of the Americas. Even Scott's contention that, in fairness to the Admiral, we should judge him in the context of his own times simply borrows from that same centuries-old tradition of Columbian hagiography.

The renowned Spanish scholar Salvador de Madariaga wrote a biography, published in 1939, in which he deemed it inappropriate to condemn the Admiral "for his inability to handle the Indians with the technique of a contemporary anthropologist," asserting further that the Genoese navigator "approached his tasks on the whole with honorable intention and with an amount of freedom from prejudice, of intellectual detachment and of power of observation altogether unusual in his day and possibly also in ours." The Admiral's limitations, continues the author, "were for the most part due to his time and to the novelty and difficulty of his task," a "difficulty" greatly exacerbated by the fact that "the natives would not work."[49] Despite the somewhat casual diction of Madariaga's observation regarding the "difficulty" that Columbus had to face with the workforce on the colony, the Indians were not recalcitrant union members in the course of a labor dispute. Strikingly, Madariaga actually faulted the Tainos for failing to cooperate more enthusiastically with a regime that subjected them to a life of continuous forced labor in a condition of perpetual servitude. The distinguished author wrote his book while living in England, where he had found a place among liberal intellectuals, having chosen exile over the ideological rigidity of the dictatorship of Francisco Franco after the overthrow of the preceding democratic republic. But, despite his liberal affiliations, the insensitivity of his remarks suggests that he probably shared with the authoritarian Falangistas, members of the fascist Spanish party that collaborated with the right-wing Franco dictatorship, a desire to cherish a narrative of Spain's past imperial greatness and the lasting contributions it made to the world. Capturing the former Spanish grandeur within the confines of Christendom and its growing overseas dominions needed a gallant and pious Columbus to be constructed and maintained.

The new world of precious metals, minerals, stones, arable lands, and vast populations available for captive labor alongside imported workers fueled the emerging industries that Columbus opened up. European greed yielded previously unimaginable wealth especially for the Spanish, the English, and the

French. The offspring of those great beneficiaries will likely remember the enterprise of conquest and colonization with approbation just as the descendants of those to whom the same events meant ruin and unspeakable loss will remember them with indignation. Witness the prologue to a 1946 edition of the diaries of Columbus authored by Ignacio Anzoátegui, a conservative Catholic man of letters born in Argentina, where he distinguished himself as a spokesperson for the virtues of *Hispanidad*. This was a sort of metaphysics of Spanish ethnicity, translated often as "Hispanicity," which with him rose to religious ardor. In the prologue he quite categorically explains that "Columbus was born so that Spain could redeem an unrepentant world," adding that "Spain put to sea to convert Asians."[50] "Spain," he continues, "did not set out in a colonizing spirit, but one of selflessness; not to exploit a land, but to pour in it her being and her blood, to throw herself into it with her soul and her life."[51] The French, whose colonial possessions proved significant economically and politically, also did not fail to produce hagiographic evocations of the Admiral. Antoine Roselly de Lorgues, the author, among other related works, of *Christophe Colomb: Histoire de sa vie et de ses voyages* (1856), contended that the mariner had sailed not for the sake of territory for Spain but for the purpose of bringing the true religion to the heathens. Roselly de Lorgues actually began the campaign for the canonization of Columbus "that won powerful support among Catholic clergy and laypeople" on both sides of the Atlantic.[52] An earlier biography by the poet and playwright Alphonse de Lamartine, *Christophe Colomb* (1853), did not reach a similar pinnacle of adoration but did repeat the overall texture of the image embroidered by Washington Irving.[53] Indeed, both Philip Freneau's book-length poem *The Pictures of Columbus, The Genoese* (1788) and Barlow's *Vision of Columbus* (1787) drew largely on the epic poem *La Colombiade, ou, La foi porté au nouveau monde* (1756) by the French aristocrat Anne-Marie du Boccage, a friend of Voltaire, who inaugurates the picture of the despondent, defeated hero, comforted by disclosure of a panorama of things to come as happens through the apparition of Hesper in Barlow's poem.

The English embraced the cult of Columbus with caution, largely because of their interest in competing with Spain for naval supremacy as well as for the enterprise of conquest and colonization. The success of Columbus's first voyage on behalf of Spain motivated King Henry VII's sponsorship of Giovanni Caboto's 1497 expedition. The publications of Richard Hakluyt and Samuel Purchas convey English aspirations to enlarge their dominions along lines similar to those spearheaded by popish Spain. However, as we gather from an anonymous 1776 political pamphlet that chronicles the "Discovery of America by Columbus" and launches an attack on the Ministry for its handling of the strife with the thirteen colonies across the Atlantic, by then the English narrative scheme that celebrates the enterprise of the Genoese while condemning Spain had already taken form. The anonymous author, for instance, describes Columbus's capture and enslavement of the Indians in Guanahani in almost endearing terms. The Admiral "at his departure very prudently took with him some of the natives, that they might learn the Spanish tongue, and be his guides and interpreters in this new scene of affairs."[54] While recounting that as he moved from island to island, the sailor inquired "everywhere for gold, which was the only object of commerce he thought worth his cause," the author proceeds to exculpate him from the apparent greed of this quest. Simply, Columbus saw gold as "the only thing that could give the court of Spain a high opinion of his discoveries."[55] By 1776, with the racist imagination having taken hold of Christian Europe, the anonymous English author does not realize that his manner of chronicling the interethnic encounter in the Caribbean itself draws its logic from events and historical developments unleashed by Columbus's pioneering work of colonization. Evoking the reaction of the Tainos of Haiti or Quisqueya, thenceforward named Española or Santo Domingo, the anonymous writer reports that the natives took the Spaniards "for men come from heaven; and it was no wonder, considering the extreme novelty of their appearance, and the prodigious superiority they had in every respect over a people in all the nakedness of uncultivated nature." Over 280 years after the first voyage, it had become natural for voices of the English public sphere (like the anonymous author) to assume they had the authority to fix peoples and cultures outside of Europe, hence his mild appraisal of the Hispaniola natives as "a humane and hospitable people, in a state of simplicity fit to work upon."[56]

At any rate, the defense of Columbus from the indignities he endured, "his disinterested behavior, his immovable fidelity to the ungrateful crown he served," came with an indictment of Spain.[57] By 1776 also, the British narrative of benign colonialism apparently already held sway. Comparing the incentives that the Spanish had for their colonial adventures to those of their English counterparts, the author says, "Our colonies were settled without any view to these great advantages which we have drawn from them. Virginia was constructed out of the wrecks of an armament designed on a golden adventure, which first tempted us to America. And those who settled New England and Maryland, meant them only as asylums from religious persecution."[58] But undoubtedly, the English as well as the French, who both owe the prosperity and rise of their civilizations to the vast spoils extracted from the Western hemisphere in the profitable colonial enterprises that followed the "discovery," cannot help but regard the Genoese mariner, sailing under the flag of imperial Spain, as a compelling progenitor.

FERNANDO AND MONTESINOS

The decision by the screenwriter, embraced by the director, to tell the story of Columbus in *1492: Conquest of Paradise* as if from the perspective of his son Fernando largely determined the tenor of the film's narrative. In the film, Fernando appears as an innocent, cute, mild-mannered boy who exudes great love and admiration for his father. Perhaps this representation matches the historical profile of Fernando in his childhood. The adult Fernando was a different story. A scholar and entrepreneur, he wrote a biography of his father with an account of the four voyages which appeared in print in Italian translation in 1571, over thirty years after the author's death, the Spanish original now lost. After returning from his first voyage, the Admiral had Fernando appointed a page to Prince Don Juan, heir to the thrones of Castile and Aragon. With the Prince's untimely death, the boy then entered the service of Queen Isabella. At age thirteen, he joined his father on the fourth and last voyage to the Americas. The boy did not develop his father's passion for the sea or for explorations of conquest. His older half-brother Diego, appointed governor of Española in 1509, took Fernando with him to the colony, but within a few months the twenty-one-year-old Fernando secured permission to return to Spain. Apart from an interest in scholarly pursuits and developing a library, Fernando dedicated himself to securing the monies and the titles that the Crown had agreed to extend to Columbus by virtue of the Santa Fe capitulations (10% of all the profits extracted from ventures in the "new world" plus the title of Admiral of the Ocean Sea and Viceroy of the Indies, which his family would inherit in perpetuity). Acknowledging the material gain that informed Columbus in his negotiation with the monarchs, *1492: Conquest of Paradise* showcases a surprised Queen Isabella, after having an audience with him, commenting to Santangel: "I thought you said he was an idealist." As legal adviser to his older brother, Diego, and later to Mariá de Toledo (Diego's widow), Fernando played a key role in the protracted litigation between the Columbus family and the Crown. The legal case continued until 1536, when the Council of the Indies offered the Columbus family a deal: a yearly income of 10,000 ducats in perpetuity and the Duchy of Veragua, an area on the western part of the Isthmus of Panama, in exchange for their renouncing the revenues owed them by virtue of the Santa Fe treaty as well as the titles therein stipulated.[59]

Fernando's foreword describes his father as "a person worthy of eternal glory for his discovery of the West Indies," and he declares himself ideally suited to write about the man.[60] During the nineteenth century, Irving would draw largely on Fernando's account to weave his tale of glory about the Admiral. In a quasi-comical circularity, the Galician historian of the colonial period Ramón Iglesia Parga (1905-1948), during his exile in Mexico following the rise of Franco in Spain, prepared an edition of the *Life of the Admiral* by Fernando (called in the book Hernando) in which he draws on Irving to lend credibility to the story told therein. Quarrelling with some "hypercritical historians of the past century" who had challenged the factual accuracy of particular passages or situations in the story told by the son, Iglesia, in his prologue, quotes a judgment by Irving asserting the reliability of the author. The passage quoted by Iglesia has Irving saying that Fernando "was a man of probity, and writes more dispassionately than could be expected, when treating matters which affected the honor, the interests, and the happiness of his father."[61] Some aspects of Fernando's book do require the friendly eyes with which Irving and Iglesia chose to read it, such as his laborious efforts to concoct noble origins for his father, inventing the story of a high-born family that suffered a reversal of fortune, ending up in poverty. Historians dismiss Fernando's insistence on noble beginnings as stemming purely from the social pressures exerted on him by the circles that he frequented from the time of his arrival in the monarchal court. Connected with the desire to invent an aristocratic pedigree for his father in the *Life*, Fernando commits the filial disgrace of mentioning his father's first wife, who possessed social rank, but not his own mother, a commoner whom his father never married.

The adult Fernando exhibits little compassion for human suffering if the victims fall for the benefit of his father's projects. When narrating the elder's arrival in the Caribbean, he offers this snapshot: "in the presence of the many natives assembled there, he took possession of it in the name of the Catholic Sovereign with appropriate ceremony and words."[62] After taking Guanahani by means of the appropriate ceremonies, Columbus then receives the adulation of the members of his crew who acknowledge his title of Admiral and, in some pertinent cases, effusively apologize for any disrespect they may have shown him during the long journey. Then, perceiving that the Indians who had "assembled to watch this celebration and rejoicing" were "a peaceful, and gentle, and very simple people," the Admiral proceeded to gratify them with "little red caps and glass beads which they hung about their necks, together with other trifles that they cherished as if they were precious stones of great price."[63] The gentleness and peacefulness of the Indians he encountered in the Caribbean did not preclude their drastic subjection, their captivity, and their requirement to pay a tribute. Fernando does not feel the need to justify the action, but simply praises his father for doing so: "He reduced the Indians to such obedience and tranquility that they all promised to pay tribute to the Catholic Sovereigns every three months, as follows: In the Cibao region, where the gold mines were, every person of fourteen years of age or upward was to pay a large hawk's bell (*un cascabel grande*) of gold dust; all others each to pay twenty-five pounds of cotton. Whenever an Indian delivered this tribute, he was to receive a brass or copper token which he must wear about his neck as proof that he had made his payment; any Indian found without such a token was to be punished."[64] During a tribute collection session, Moxica, the nobleman who operates as Columbus's antagonist in *1492: Conquest of Paradise*, unsheathes his sword and cuts off the right hand of an Indian who has failed to produce a satisfactory tribute. Perhaps that scene illustrates the kinds of punishment that an Indian could suffer if found without the required token around his neck that Fernando so dispassionately describes.

Fernando's impious narrative goes as far as to characterize as a blessing massive deaths among the natives even as they and the Spanish settlers lived peacefully. At one point peace reigned in the island after the capture of a rebellious chief named Caonabo. However, the numerical disparity between the Christian invaders and the local population gave the former cause for concern: "two hundred poorly armed men" (Spaniards) vis-à-vis a multitude of natives. The Admiral's son describes the natives as eminently docile, to such a degree that "a Christian could safely go wherever he pleased, and the Indians themselves offered to carry him pick-a-back." But peace and docility apparently did not suffice. Almighty God himself deemed it necessary to intervene with a lethal measure: "the Lord wished to punish the Indians, and so visited them with such shortage of food and such a variety of plagues that he reduced their numbers by two-thirds, that it might be made clear that such wonderful conquests proceeded from his supreme hand and not from our strength or intelligence or the cowardice of the Indians; for even admitting the superiority of our men, it was obvious that the numerical preponderance of the Indian would have nullified this advantage."[65] Perhaps the Lord works in ways more inscrutable than those imagined by the Admiral's son. If the reduction of the size of the Indian population in order to make their domination by the Christians more feasible was in fact the Lord's will, He did not need to participate in the logistics of these earthly affairs directly. With the Indians spending the majority of their waking hours in the laborious task of securing the gold dust or the cotton that the invaders demanded of them, they probably did not have much time left for the cultivation of their soil or for fishing and hunting, hence the shortages of food. Similarly, the toxic presence of the Spaniards with the germs they carried in their bodies, their breaths, their clothes, their horses, and the other animals they introduced starting with the second voyage, could give a terrestrial explanation to the "variety of plagues" that visited the natives. Even though he was a scholar, Fernando probably lacked the necessary knowledge of epidemiology to realize that every Christian who arrived in the Americas functioned as a killing machine even before drawing a sword or aiming a fire-spitting arquebus. Europeans would later become quite knowledgeable of the natural weapons of mass destruction they possessed even to the point of harnessing their military potential, especially after Lord Jeffery Amherst in the eighteenth century deployed smallpox-infected blankets in his onslaught against North American Indians in Pennsylvania. In short, one cannot go to Fernando for

clues to help humanize the image of the Admiral. In his unrestrained commitment to paint in a good light everything that his father did, he would even
have God Almighty appear as a genocidal fiend for the purpose of aiding the
Columbian project.

Scott's insistence on Columbus as a "man of his times" might serve to
contextualize Fernando's attitude toward the indigenous population of Hispaniola and other Caribbean sites explored by his father. However, even in
the *Life of the Admiral* we gain a glimpse of an attitude that might give us
pause regarding the decisive role played by "his times" in determining the
inhumane outlook of the writer. While Fernando spoke of the natives only as
a feature of the landscape, as an ignorant mass worthy only as labor meant to
amass wealth for Christians, he deemed it appropriate to reproduce in his
book the *Relación*, which Fray Ramón Pané, a humble anchorite of the Order
of St. Jerome, had written about the "antiquities of the Indians." However
skeptical Pané may have been about the spiritual value of Taino forms of
worship, it matters nonetheless that he took efforts to study and understand
their belief system and their cosmology. Even if, fervent missionary that he
was, he wished nothing but Christian conversion for the natives, he acknowledged that they had a religion and a sense of the divine. One would also
expect for Fernando to have heard about the sermons that made the Dominican priest Fray Antón de Montesinos famous and infamous on the colony of
Santo Domingo in 1511 during the administration of Diego Colón, the author's older half-brother. With the support of his supervisor in the Santo
Domingo branch of the Order of Friars Preachers, Montesinos used his ser-
mon on the fourth Sunday of Advent to denounce the entire logic of the
colonial regime. He declared Governor Colón, the church patriarchs, the
army, and the plantation owners to have reached a state of mortal sin. He
asserted the essential humanity of the Indians and denied any moral ascen-
dency to the covetous foreigners who had come into these lands, committed
murder and theft against the Indians, and reduced the native population to
debilitating captivity. With the strident rhetorical question "*¿Con qué dere-
cho?*" ("What gives you the right?"), Montesinos indicted the rationale and
the practice of the colonial transaction in a setting that directly involved the
Columbus family.[66] Shall we then say, in keeping with Scott's ideology of
remembering, that Montesinos was not "a man of his times"? Fray Bartolomé
de las Casas, a recruit in the ship that took Fray Nicolás de Ovando as the
new governor to Santo Domingo in 1502, arrived in the colony with the same
disregard for Indian humanity that would later characterize Fernando. He had
an *encomienda* which afforded him arable land and a supply of captive
Indian laborers whose yield would bring him profit. But the moral appeal of
Montesinos's precedent and his own religious piety in the face of the atrocities he witnessed (having previously been a perpetrator of some himself)

resulted in the radical change of heart that accounts for the reputation he has long enjoyed as "protector of the Indians."

Irrespective of the double emphasis that runs through Scott's evocation of Columbus as simultaneously "a man of his times" and "a visionary" (suggesting an image of him as paradoxically "ahead of his time"), the Admiral chose the path of power not of greatness. Similarly, *1492: Conquest of Paradise* chose power over greatness in the matter of which side to align with in the debates over the morality of the conquest that raged in 1992, when the film was released. The Columbian enterprise did create something radically new, a new world of social relations, which changed the dynamics of conquest and domination, spawning ideologies responsible for five centuries of a darkness so dense that the prejudice and narrowness fomented by the Inquisition in medieval Europe pales into morning sun by comparison. The Columbian project bequeathed to us a baleful legacy that has wrought much havoc on the health of human relations ever since, namely racism, among the most contemptible products of human depravity. The racialization of humanity birthed a new kind of evil into the world; the Europeans themselves had no notion of it, as eminent historians like Arnold Toynbee and Basil Davidson argued years ago, even though post-Columbian racists might invoke, among others, Aristotle in their quest for respectable ideological precedents.[67] Before 1492, for instance, it would most likely not have occurred even to Christians that they could go elsewhere in the world to civilize other peoples or to think of the paleness of their skin as constituting a marker of superiority that would guarantee the success and moral legitimacy of their endeavors. Marco Polo could not have possibly harbored any thoughts of colonizing the lands he visited during his travels in Asia nor to think of himself as better than the inhabitants of those parts. There he witnessed displays of wealth, power, and knowledge then unimaginable for the Europe of his time.

MARCO POLO: BEFORE RACISM

Laurence Bergreen misses the mark when describing Polo's "exceptionally harsh and racist portrayal of the Zanzibari," which in his view raises questions about the authenticity of the traveler's description of the island. He suggests that the Venetian may have drawn his descriptions from information about "nearby East Africa."[68] The passage that Bergreen comments on does show Polo's repugnance for the physical features of the Zanzibari, namely the size of their mouths, noses, ears, eyes, and the coarseness of their hair.[69] Polo characterizes Zanzibari women as "the most ill-favored in the world."[70] He passes a very harsh judgment on the physical features of Zanzibari people, which, ironically, Bergreen seems to suggest should apply to East Africans instead, but the Venetian's dislike of the Zanzibari or any other people's phenotype in no way corresponds to racism as we understand it in modern times. Human beings in antiquity could find people from other ethnicities or regions ugly or beautiful. That today such an expression of preference for the looks of some groups over those of others should strike us as racist is itself the result of the racism that the new world of social relations inaugurated starting in 1492. Properly understood, racism consists of an ideology that posits race, the genetic stock of people, to explain human behavior, levels of attainment, intelligence, and the overall worth of persons. Racism does not appear in a person's greater attraction to the looks of Apache women than to Javanese ones, or in a dislike of the typical build of an average Sri Lankan man over an Igbo one. Racism implies a prior knowledge about a person's capabilities, character, intellect, actions, and feelings on the basis of the branch or subdivision of the human family from which he or she comes. Polo had no access to the logic of the Dominican monk Tomás Ortiz, who in 1525 wrote to the Council of the Indies providing an assessment of the native inhabitants Columbus found in the Americas. Given to "sodomy more than any other nation," they lack "justice among them. They go naked. They have no respect for love or for virginity. They are stupid and silly. They have no respect for truth, save when it is to their advantage. They are unstable. They have no knowledge of what foresight means." Ortiz further finds them "ungrateful," "changeable," and "brutal," leading him to conclude that "God has never created a race more full of vice and composed without the least mixture of kindness and culture."[71] With greater academic training to draw on, the philosopher and theologian Juan Ginés de Sepulveda, the principal antagonist of Bartolomé de las Casas in the Valladolid debates convened by Charles V to settle the moral question of the captivity of the Indians, contrasted the quality of Spaniards (possessors of "prudence, genius, magnanimity, temperance, humanity, and religion") with that of the natives, "little men [*hombrecillos*] without letters, monuments to preserve their history, written laws or private property."[72] Endowed with nothing "but barbaric institutions and customs," the natives lacked "even vestige of humanity," according to Sepulveda, who further found them uncivilized and contaminated with obscenities and impieties, lending unquestionable certainty to the justice of their captivity.[73]

The conceptual machinery that would confer credence to the reasoning deployed by the likes of Ortiz and Sepulveda, subsequently taking hold of the imagination of the intelligentsia of the Christian West, would not become available to Europeans for nearly a century and a half after Marco Polo's generation. As a result, the Venetian adventurer could find physical ugliness in the people of Zanzibar, but that unsightly appearance did not tarnish their souls, their intellect, their actions, their abilities, or their heritage. Polo describes their physical strength, such as their capacity to carry a load that would require "four of our people to carry."[74] He praises their talent for producing a delightful wine made "from rice and sugar, with the addition of some spicy drugs" that he found "very pleasant to the taste, having the intoxicating quality of wine from grapevines."[75] They possess extraordinary courage: "their people display much bravery in battle and contempt of death." Their lack of horses they make up with skillful use of elephants and camels, which they deploy in warfare to great effect.[76] Phenotype comes up in the narrative of Polo in connection with the Kingdom of Kollam, where many Jews and Christians reside.[77] He says that "all the people, both male and female, are black, and, with the exception of a small piece of cloth attached to the front of their bodies, they go quite naked: their manners are extremely sensual, and they take as wives their relations by blood, and the widows of their deceased brothers."[78] Polo feels no need to editorialize about the blackness, the nakedness, the sensuality, or the marital practices of people in that part of India.

Polo was not oblivious to complexion, probably a function of not being visually impaired. He describes the people of Ormus as having "a dark color."[79] He attributes an "evil disposition" to the people of Bascia, who have great knowledge and skill in the art of magic, which they study assiduously. They worship idols, invoke demons, and "are of a dark complexion," but the Venetian says nothing that will encourage our making a connection between their actions and their skin hue.[80] Regarding the province of Kesmur (Kashmir), the dwelling of a people "of a dark complexion, but by no means black," he describes the women there as "very beautiful."[81] With no reference to phenotype, Polo comments favorably on the people of Abbascia (Abyssinia): "brave and good warriors constantly engaged in hostility with the Soldan of Aden, the people of Nubia, and many others whose countries border upon theirs."[82] Significantly, Polo encounters a remarkable valorization of blackness among inhabitants of the province of Maabar, where "the natives, although black, are not born of so deep a dye as they afterwards attain by artificial means, esteeming blackness the perfection of beauty. For this purpose, three times every day, they rub the children over with oil of sesame."[83] Blackness plays a meaningful role, in contrast to whiteness, in their religious worship: "The images of their deities they represent black, but the devil they paint white, and assert that all the demons are of that colour."[84] The extent to which paleness of skin did not constitute an inherent marker of superiority to Polo stands out in his scathing appraisal of the inhabitants of an area of the northern region of the Tartars, apparently present-day Siberia, in whom whiteness appears in a rather poor light. He describes the people there as "well made and tall, but of a pallid complexion." He then proceeds to emphasize their lawlessness: "not united under the government of a king or prince," they lack "laws or usages, in the manner of brute creation. Their intellects are also dull, and they have an air of stupidity."[85]

A NEW WORLD OF SOCIAL RELATIONS

Marco Polo's generation lacked the schemes of thought required for despising entire branches of the human species based on race. The Columbian enterprise, with the advent of a new moral climate brought about by the sudden discovery of the dehumanization of differentiated populations as a profit-making operation, provided European Christians with the conceptual tools to construct themselves as superior, their captives as inferior, and the resulting social order as a divinely-condoned, beneficent outcome. Drawing largely on the work of Alfred W. Crosby's *The Columbian Exchange* (1973) and *Ecological Imperialism* (1986), Charles C. Mann's *1493: Uncovering the New World Columbus Created* (2011) reviews the rearrangement of flora, fauna, and agricultural developments that took place across the planet as a result of the voyages of Columbus and the historical dynamics that ensued. The phenomenon ended up taking "corn (maize) to Africa and sweet potatoes to East Asia, horses and apples to the Americas, and rhubarb and eucalyptus to Europe," apart from swapping about "a host of less-familiar organisms like insects, grasses, bacteria, and viruses."[86] Emphasizing its ecological impact on the globe, the Columbian enterprise, Mann maintains, marked not the "discovery" but the "creation" of a new world, making him the only person "of all the members of humankind who ever walked the earth" who has the distinction of having "inaugurated a new era in the history of life."[87]

Focusing on the human history of the conquest spearheaded by the Genoese mariner, Bergreen's *Columbus: The Four Voyages* (2011) also pays tribute to Crosby's original analysis in an interlude entitled "The Columbian Exchange."[88] Bergreen avoids the pitfalls of hagiography, gesturing to the suffering caused by the "discovery," taking note, for instance, of the voracity with which the Admiral appraised the Tainos as potential servants the very moment he set eyes on them.[89] The author nonetheless ends up cheering for Columbus, contending that whatever scorn Columbus may have engendered, the four voyages constitute "one of the greatest adventure stories in history."[90] The Israeli television producer Zvi Dor-Ner told the story of the Genoese mariner on the small screen to great acclaim in 1991, the year before the quincentenary and the release of Scott's film. Dor-Ner focused on human events as well as on ecology, gesturing to Crosby's work in a reference to the way in which tomatoes, originally from Mexico, became a symbol of the Italian cuisine that had existed without it for centuries.[91] He, too, of course, has to genuflect before the symbolic hegemony of the Admiral, who "changed the world. He took his world, the world of the Middle Ages, and set it on its way to becoming the place we inhabit today. . . . He put the known and the unknown parts of the world together, and removed the whole from the realm of myth."[92]

It would probably take a visionary cinematic historian with the imagination, moral rectitude, and intellectual insight necessary to revisit the story of Columbus in order to give us a great film on the Admiral's enterprise and its consequences, one that, without hagiography or conceptual complicity with perpetrators of colonial genocide, can teach something significant about the nature of individual ambition and the good or evil it may thrust upon the world. Such a project would have to overcome a stumbling block that has seemed insurmountable to many chroniclers of the Columbian project in film, television, or on the page. How do we narrate the events of the conquest and colonization of the Americas outside of the logic of human relations to which those events gave currency and which have shaped the structure of our thoughts? That logic takes the form of mental shackles that instill in us as presuppositions the very notions that we should be examining and questioning constantly. When Dor-Ner, Scott, Bosch, or Glen celebrate the fact that the Genoese sailor took the world of the Middle Ages and set it on its road to becoming what we have today, there should be something that reminds them that the "we" is a very partial one. The phrase "the Middle Ages" causes us to think only of Europe. But for the Tainos or the Aztecs or the Mayans, that was the period prior to their conquest, colonization, dispossession, and genocides; that is, before the inaugural stage was set for five centuries of dehumanization and the struggle to survive. The same applies to the sons and daughters of Africa. Can we afford morally to continue gloating over the world that came to be while mocking the concern over the world that the Christian West destroyed? The petulant dismissal of large-scale mass destruction as "the cliché of genocide" cannot help us to create the new world of equality and justice that we all, descendants of the winners no less than descendants of the losers, desperately need. A humane and sensitive approach to the horrors of the past would enable us to see the error of celebrating our liberation from "the realm of myth" as a result of the Columbian enterprise. The conquest and colonization of the Americas gave rise to the most detrimental and most intellectually stultifying of all myths, the one that Christian nations of Europe created in order to reap material benefit from the oppression of other peoples: the myth of inferior races.

NOTES

1. Leger Grendon, *Shadows of the Past: Studies in the Historical Fiction Film* (Philadelphia, PA: Temple University Press, 1994), 223.

2. Mike Chopra-Gant, *Cinema and History: The Telling of Stories* (London: Wallflower Press, 2008), 100.

3. Ibid., 102.

4. Robert A. Rosenstone, *History on Film/Film on History* (Harlow: Pearson-Longman, 2006), 133.

5. Ibid., 113, 123.

6. David Ansen, "Columbus as a Hollywood Hustler," *Daily Beast*, September 6, 1992.

7. Ibid.

8. Ana Maria Bahiana, "1492: Conquest of Paradise," in *Ridley Scott: Interviews*, ed. Laurence F. Knapp and Andrea F. Kulas (Jackson: University Press of Mississippi, 2005), 8.

9. Marco Polo, *The Travels of Marco Polo [The Venetian]*, trans. Manuel Komroff (New York: Garden City Publishing, 1930), 265.

10. Howard Zinn, "1492-1992: A Historian's Perspective," in *Confronting Columbus: An Anthology*, ed. John Yewell, Chris Dodge, and Jan DeSirey (Jefferson, NC: McFarland, 1992), 6.

11. Ibid., 3, 5.

12. Hans Koning, "1492: Fact and Fancy," in *Confronting Columbus: An Anthology*, ed. John Yewell, Chris Dodge, and Jan DeSirey (Jefferson, NC: McFarland, 1992), 202-203.

13. Todd McCarthy, "1492: Conquest of Paradise," in *Ridley Scott* by Paul Sammon (New York: Thunder's Mouth Press, 1992), 145.

14. Owen Gleiberman, "1492: The Conquest of Paradise," *Entertainment Weekly – EW.com*, October 16, 1992, accessed August 1, 2012, http://www.ew.com/ew/article/0,,20164943,00.html.

15. Chris Hicks, "1492: Conquest of Paradise," *Deseret News*, October 13, 1992. Desson Howe, *Washington Post*, October 9, 1992.

16. Roger Ebert, "1492: Conquest of Paradise," *Rogerebert.com: Reviews*, October 9, 1992, accessed August 1, 2012, http://rogerebert.suntimes.com/apps/pbcs.dll/article?AID=/19921009/REVIEWS/210090301/1023.

17. Jack Matthews, "Voyage of Rediscovery," *Los Angeles Times*, May 3, 1992.

18. Matthews, "Voyage of Rediscovery," May 3, 1992.

19. Matthews, "Voyage of Rediscovery," May 3, 1992.

20. Bahiana, "1492," 83.

21. Ibid., 84-85.

22. Ibid., 83.

23. Ibid., 85.

24. Amy Taubin, "Ridley Scott's Road Work," in *Ridley Scott: Interviews*, ed. Laurence F. Knapp and Andrea F. Kulas (Jackson: University Press of Mississippi, 2005), 80.

25. Bahiana, "1492," 87.

26. George H. W. Bush, "Columbus Day, 1989: A Proclamation by the President of the United States," in *Confronting Columbus: An Anthology*, ed. John Yewell, Chris Dodge, and Jan DeSirey (Jefferson, NC: McFarland, 1992), 200.

27. Ibid.

28. Ruth Benedict, *Race: Science and Politics* (New York: Viking Press, 1945), 195-199.

29. Léon-Francois Hoffmann, *Le nègre romantique: personage litteraire et obsession collective* (Paris: Payot, 1973), 7.

30. Kirkpatrick Sale, *The Conquest of Paradise: Christopher Columbus and the Columbian Legacy* (New York: Alfred A. Knopf, 1990), 363-364.

31. Sale, *The Conquest of Paradise*, 360.

32. Elhanan Winchester, *Oration on the Discovery of America* (London: Keeble and Acutts, 1792), 14.

33. Ibid., 25.

34. Ibid., 32.

35. Sale, *The Conquest of Paradise*, 343.

36. Ibid., 342.

37. Ibid., 344.

38. Benjamin Keen, "Introduction—Christopher Columbus in History: Images of the Man and His Work: 1492," in *The Life of the Admiral Christopher Columbus by His Son*, ed. Benjamin Keen (New Brunswick, NJ: Rutgers University Press, 1992), xxxvi.

39. Sale, *The Conquest of Paradise*, 349.

40. Keen, "Introduction—Christopher Columbus," xliii.

41. Sale, *The Conquest of Paradise*, 349.

42. Ibid., 348.

43. Claudia L. Bushman, *America Discovers Columbus: How an Italian Explorer Became an American Hero* (Hanover, NH: University Press of New England, 1992), 98.

44. Sale, *The Conquest of Paradise*, 352.

45. Ibid., 351.

46. Keen, "Introduction—Christopher Columbus," lvi.

47. John Yewell, Chris Dodge, and Jan DeSirey, eds. *Confronting Columbus: An Anthology* (Jefferson, NC: McFarland, 1992), 197-199.

48. Yewell, Dodge, and DeSirey, *Contesting Columbus*, 196.

49. Keen, "Introduction—Christopher Columbus," l.

50. Ignacio B. Anzoátegui, "Prólogo," in *Los cuatro viajes del Almirante y su testamento, por Cristóbal Colón*, ed. Ignacio B. Anzoátegui, 6th edition (Colección Austral, Madrid: Espasa-Calpe, S. A., 1977), 12-13.

51. Ibid., 13.

52. Keen, "Introduction—Christopher Columbus," xxxvi-xxxviii.

53. Ibid., xxxvi.

54. Anon. *The Discovery of America by Columbus* (London: n. p., 1776), 5.

55. Ibid.

56. Ibid.

57. Ibid., 25.

58. Ibid., 19.

59. Keen, "Introduction—Christopher Columbus," xi.

60. Ibid., lxxi.

61. Ramón Iglesia, "Prólogo," in *Vida del Almirante Cristóbal Colón escrita por su hijo*, ed. Ramón Iglesia (Mexico City: Fondo de Cultura Económica, 1947), 12, 14.

62. Fernando Colón, *The Life of the Admiral Christopher Columbus by His Son*, trans. and annotated Benjamin Keen (New Brunswick, NJ: Rutgers University Press, 1992), 59.

63. Ibid., 60.

64. Ibid., 149-150.

65. Ibid., 150.

66. Felix Jay, ed. and trans., *Three Dominican Pioneers in the New World: Antonio de Montesinos, Domingo de Betanzos, Gonzalo Lucero* (Lewiston, NY: Edwin Mellen Press, 2002), 18-38.

67. Arnold J. Toynbee, *A Study of History*, 2nd. ed., vol.1 (London: Oxford University Press, 1935), 223-224. Basil Davidson, *The Story of Africa* (London: Mitchell Beazley Publishers, 1984), 45. The argument here is that slavery in the ancient world was not racial. Aristotle in *The Politics* does report on the belief held by Greeks that they were superior to foreigners, which gave them license to enslave the latter. But Aristotle's idea of the "natural slave" seems to apply to people in general. The contention that Nature distinguishes between the bodies of freemen and slaves, making the former "upright" and the latter "strong," does not presuppose a racial binary, but rather a formula to establish differences of endowment among the population. Aristotle, *The Politics of Aristotle*, trans. Benjamin Jowett (Oxford: Clarendon Press, 1885), 2-12; Aristotle, *Politics: Book I and II*, trans. Trevor J. Saunders (Oxford: Clarendon Press, 1995), 7-8. For Aristotle, slavery is part of the social system and the structure of the household. A slave is someone who occupies a given position in society, not someone identified with a particular ancestry. Susan Lape argues that Athenians developed stories "to describe and explain how birth and blood made them who they were, qualifying them and entitling them for citizenship." But Lape distinguishes that narrative tendency from racial identity or racist thinking. She uses the term "racialism" instead and for the purpose of translating the phenomenon to a modern audience, settling for what she calls "the myth of racial citizenship." Susan Lape, *Race and Citizenship in the Classical Athenian Democracy* (Cambridge: Cambridge University Press, 2010), 32.

68. Laurence Bergreen, *Marco Polo: From Venice to Xanadu* (New York: Viking 2011), 295.

69. Polo, *The Travels*, 315.

70. Ibid.

71. Sale, *The Conquest of Paradise*, 202.

128   *Silvio Torres-Saillant*

72. Ibid.
73. Ibid.
74. Polo, *The Travels*, 315.
75. Ibid.
76. Ibid.
77. Ibid., 302.
78. Ibid., 303.
79. Ibid., 49.
80. Ibid., 63.
81. Ibid., 64.
82. Ibid., 317.
83. Ibid., 296.
84. Ibid.
85. Ibid., 347.
86. Charles C. Mann, *1493: Uncovering the New World Columbus Created* (New York: Alfred A. Knopf, 2011), vi.
87. Ibid., xv, 4.
88. Laurence Bergreen, *Columbus: The Four Voyages* (New York: Viking, 2011), 221-224.
89. Ibid., 14.
90. Ibid., 368.
91. Zvi Dor-Ner (with William G. Scheller), *Columbus and the Age of Discovery* (New York: William Morrow and Company, 1991), 272.
92. Ibid., 1.

REFERENCES

1492: Conquest of Paradise. DVD. Directed by Ridley Scott. 1992; Sao Paulo: Spectra Nova, 1992.
Anon. *The Discovery of America by Columbus*. London: n. p., 1776.
Ansen, David. "Columbus as a Hollywood Hustler." *Daily Beast*, September 6, 1992. Accessed August 1, 2012. http://www.thedailybeast.com/newsweek/1992/09/06/columbus-as-a-holly-wood-hustler.
Anzoátegui, Ignacio B. "Prólogo." Prologue to *Los cuatro viajes del Almirante y su testamento* by Cristóbal Colón. 6th ed. Edited by Ignacio B. Anzoátegui, 11-13. Colección Austral. Madrid: Espasa-Calpe, S. A., 1977.
Aristotle. *Politics: Book I and II*. Translated by Trevor J. Saunders. Oxford: Clarendon Press, 1995.
Aristotle. *The Politics of Aristotle*. Translated by Benjamin Jowett. Oxford: Clarendon Press, 1885.
Bahiana, Ana Maria. "1492: Conquest of Paradise." In *Ridley Scott: Interviews*, edited by Laurence F. Knapp and Andrea F. Kulas, 81-88. Jackson: University Press of Mississippi, 2005.
Benedict, Ruth. *Race: Science and Politics*. New York: Viking Press, 1945.
Bergreen, Laurence. *Columbus: The Four Voyages*. New York: Viking, 2011.
———. *Marco Polo: From Venice to Xanadu*. New York: Alfred A. Knopf, 2007.
Bush, George H. W. "Columbus Day, 1989: A Proclamation by the President of the United States." In *Confronting Columbus: An Anthology*, edited by John Yewell, Chris Dodge, and Jan DeSirey, 200-201. Jefferson, NC: McFarland, 1992.
Bushman, Claudia L. *America Discovers Columbus: How an Italian Explorer Became an American Hero*. Hanover, NH: University Press of New England, 1992.
Chopra-Gant, Mike. *Cinema and History: The Telling of Stories*. London: Wallflower Press, 2008.
Christopher Columbus: The Discovery. VHS. Directed by John Glen. 1992; Burbank, CA: Warner Home Video, 1994.

Colón, Fernando. *The Life of the Admiral Christopher Columbus by His Son*. Translated and annotated by Benjamin Keen. New Brunswick, NJ: Rutgers University Press, 1992.

Colón, Hernando [Fernando]. *Vida del Almirante Don Cristóbal Colón escrita por su hijo*, edited by Ramón Iglesia. Mexico City: Fondo de Cultura Económica, 1947.

Davidson, Basil. *The Story of Africa*. London: Mitchell Beazley Publishers, 1984.

De Montesinos, Antonio, Domingo de Betanzos, and Gonzalo Lucero. *Three Dominican Pioneers in the New World: Antonio de Montesinos, Domingo de Betanzos, Gonzalo Lucero*, edited and translated by Felix Jay. Lewiston, NY: Edwin Mellen Press, 2002.

Dor-Ner, Zvi, and William G. Scheller. *Columbus and the Age of Discovery*. New York: William Morrow, 1991.

Ebert, Roger. "1492: Conquest of Paradise." *Rogerebert.com: Reviews*. Accessed August 1, 2012. http://rogerebert.suntimes.com/apps/pbcs.dll/article?AID=/19921009/REVIEWS/210090301/1023.

Gleiberman, Owen. "1492: The Conquest of Paradise." *Entertainment Weekly -EW.com*. Accessed August 1, 2012. http://www.ew.com/ew/article/0,,20164943,00.html.

Grendon, Leger. *Shadows of the Past: Studies in the Historical Fiction Film*. Philadelphia, PA: Temple University Press, 1994.

Hicks, Chris. "1492: Conquest of Paradise." *Deseret News*. Accessed August 1, 2012. http://www.deseretnews.com/article/700000002/1492-Conquest-of-Paradise.html.

Hoffmann, Léon-François. *Le nègre romantique: personnage littéraire et obsession collective*. Paris: Payot, 1973.

Howe, Desson. "1492: Conquest of Paradise." *Washington Post*, October 9, 1992. Accessed August 1, 2012. http://www.washingtonpost.com/wpsrv/style/longterm/movies/videos/1492conquest.

Iglesia, Ramón. "Prólogo." In *Vida del Almirante Don Cristóbal Colón escrita por su hijo*, edited by Ramón Iglesia, 7-19. Mexico City: Fondo de Cultura Económica, 1947.

Keen, Benjamin. "Introduction—Christopher Columbus in History: Images of the Man and His Work: 1492." In *The Life of the Admiral Christopher Columbus by His Son*. Translated by Benjamin Keen, xxi-lxviii. New Brunswick: Rutgers University Press, 1992.

Koning, Hans. "1492: Fact and Fancy." In *Confronting Columbus: An Anthology*, edited by John Yewell, Chris Dodge, and Jan DeSirey, 202-203. Jefferson, NC: McFarland, 1992.

Lape, Susan. *Race and Citizenship in the Classical Athenian Democracy*. Cambridge: Cambridge University Press, 2010.

Mann, Charles C. *1493: Uncovering the New World Columbus Created*. New York: Alfred A. Knopf, 2011.

Matthews, Jack. "Voyage of Rediscovery." *Los Angeles Times*, May 3, 1992. Accessed August 1, 2012. http://latimes.com/print/1992-05-03.

McCarthy, Todd. "1492: Conquest of Paradise." In *Ridley Scott* by Paul M. Sammon, 145-147. New York: Thunder's Mouth Press, 1992.

Polo, Marco. *The Travels of Marco Polo [The Venetian]*, edited by Manuel Komroff. New York: Garden City Publishing, 1930.

Rosenstone, Robert A. *History on Film/Film on History*. Harlow: Pearson-Longman, 2006.

Sale, Kirkpatrick. *The Conquest of Paradise: Christopher Columbus and the Columbian Legacy*. New York: Alfred A. Knopf, 1990.

Taubin, Amy. "Ridley Scott's Road Work." In *Ridley Scott: Interviews*, edited by Laurence F. Knapp and Andrea F. Kulas, 75-80. Jackson: University Press of Mississippi, 2005.

Toynbee, Arnold J. *A Study of History*. 2nd edition. Vol. 1. London: Oxford University Press, 1935.

Winchester, Elhanan. *Oration on the Discovery of America*. London: Keeble and Acutts, 1792.

Yewell, John, Chris Dodge, and Jan Sirey, eds. *Confronting Columbus: An Anthology*. Jefferson, NC: McFarland, 1992.

Zinn, Howard. "1492-1992: A Historian's Perspective." In *Confronting Columbus: An Anthology*, edited by John Yewell, Chris Dodge, and Jan DeSirey, 1-14. Jefferson, NC: McFarland, 1992.

Part II

Real Lives, Alienated Lives, Ideal Lives

Chapter Seven

What's Wrong with Building Replicants? Artificial Intelligence in *Blade Runner*, *Alien*, and *Prometheus*

Greg Littmann

Amid the chilling smog, rain, and crowded streets of futuristic Los Angeles in *Blade Runner* (1982), a pair of dying artificial humans on the run from a life of off-world slavery hunt for the genius biologist who gave them life. In the empty depths of space, aboard the doomed spaceship *Nostromo* in *Alien* (1979), a synthetic man on a secret mission loyally sacrifices his life in service to the corporation that owns him. On a strange and hostile planet far from Earth in *Prometheus* (2012), an obsessed archaeologist on a quest for the "engineers" who designed humanity joins forces with a bitter android resentful toward his own human designers. More than any other theme, the relationship between the created and the creator binds together the science fiction films of Ridley Scott. What moral duties do creators owe to those that they create? Are the created mere tools to be used or sacrificed at the whim of their originators, or are they deserving of something more—perhaps even recognition as "people" with all of the rights that such status may entail?

How we ought to treat artificial forms of life becomes an increasingly important issue as humans continue to develop sophisticated computer systems and perform wonders with genetic engineering. Philosophically challenging films like the grim science fiction nightmares of Scott are useful when we ask ourselves about our real-world obligations, since these allow us to test our preconceptions against hypothetical situations to see whether our theories are consistent. For example, we might have a moral theory that it is always wrong to lie, but this does not stand up in the face of a hypothetical situation like that of *Blade Runner* in which a professional killer is asking questions to track down and "retire" innocent refugees. In this chapter, I will be focusing on *Blade Runner* in particular, since the theme of human duty to our creations underlies that entire film. Let us begin, then, by asking why we might think that the Nexus-6 Replicants of *Blade Runner* are being mistreated when they are "used off-world as slave labor, in the hazardous exploration and colonization of other planets."

"I THINK, SEBASTIAN, THEREFORE I AM." — PRIS

One reason that we might be concerned about the way that replicants are treated is that they seem to have thoughts and feelings. They act as though they, like humans, have emotions and concerns. Combat model Roy Batty (Rutger Hauer) acts as if he is filled with the desire for life, a desire so strong that he will let nothing stand in his way. He behaves as though he is in love with pleasure model Pris (Daryl Hannah), fighting for her life along with his own. When he learns that she has been killed by the blade runner Rick Deckard (Harrison Ford), his face shows grief. He not only gently kisses her dead lips, but also wipes her blood on his face as he weeps and then howls like a wolf—ostentatious mourning even in Los Angeles. Roy also displays emotional turmoil when he comes face to face with genetic engineer Eldon Tyrell. "It's not an easy thing to meet your maker," he states grimly, and his apparent rage at the old man is so great that he crushes Tyrell's skull with his bare hands.[1] He also reports feelings of guilt over actions he has taken: "I have done . . . questionable things," he confesses, staring at the floor. Similarly, Roy responds to physical harm as if he is in pain. As his body begins to shut down, he drives nails through his hands to allow his fists to unclench, and he cries out and contorts his face as he pushes the nails in, just like a human being would. Scott cuts back and forth between Roy grimacing in pain as he tends to his wounded hand and Deckard reacting similarly as he tends to *his* wounded hand, underscoring their shared experience. Roy even displays a sense of humor, clowning with a pair of fake eyeballs for the toy-loving "genetic designer" J. F. Sebastian.

As Roy chases Deckard through the abandoned apartment building, he taunts him, calling, singing, and laughing maniacally at his former pursuer, like a man driven mad with grief and hatred. When his time comes to die, the replicant shows a terrible sadness, crying like a human being at the thought of all his memories being lost forever. Having fought Deckard to the edge of the roof of Sebastian's towering apartment complex, and now standing over the detective as he dangles over the ledge, Roy shows an appreciation for both revenge and terror. "Quite a thing to live in fear, isn't it? That's what it is to be a slave," he informs his helpless enemy. Roy's final act, that which defines him as a character more than any other, is supremely emotional: having chased Deckard this far to take his revenge, Roy spares the blade runner from death at the last second, preventing him from falling to the street. Roy seems to find life—any life—too valuable to be thrown away.

Pris displays a fierce determination to live and a strong emotional attachment to Roy. She also exhibits a sense of play sophisticated enough to want to dress up and paint her face while waiting in Sebastian's apartment. She smiles at herself in the mirror as she admires her new makeup, exhibiting human behavior even though she has no one other than herself to convince of her attractiveness. When attacking Deckard, she shows signs of physical strain and rage. Similarly, the actions of replicant Zhora (Joanna Cassidy) convey tired resignation when Deckard talks his way into her dressing room; she then sheds tears when he shoots her. Leon (Brion James) expresses confusion when tested by the blade runner Holden (Morgan Paull), murderous fury at Holden and Deckard, and also subtler emotions like loneliness by keeping photographs of strangers in his apartment.

As for love interest Rachel (Sean Young), she displays human emotions so convincingly that she can snag the heart of a blade runner. "I want you," she tells Deckard after some leading from him, just as if her desire were genuine. She acts as though she cares about him and even kills Leon to save Deckard's life at considerable risk to herself. After the killing, she gets the shakes, an involuntary response that ironically shows a level of humanity rarely present in sympathetic characters in popular contemporary films.

In *Alien*, the android Ash (Ian Holm) shows a similar capacity for emotional expression. While he is a reserved fellow, even by the standard set by the chilly crew of the commercial towing spaceship *Nostromo*, he conveys his worries about landing on the unknown planetoid, offers a smile to his colleagues on the surface to assure the explorers that they are in contact with the ship, exhibits frustration with Ripley (Sigourney Weaver) for interfering with his work, and even gasps with fear when the alien bursts out of Executive Officer Kane (John Hurt) at dinner. Once his cover as an android is blown, he still displays smug superiority and reports feelings of respect towards the alien. When Chief Navigator Lambert (Veronica Cartwright) accuses him with a steely "You admire it," Ash's severed head gurgles back, "I admire its purity." His final act is to taunt Ripley by expressing mock empathy, asking her to delay his disconnection just long enough to tell her (with a smile), "I can't lie to you about your chances, but . . . you have my sympathies."

In *Prometheus*, the android David (Michael Fassbender) may be the epitome of cool detachment, but he is not above expressing feelings. He demonstrates a passion for the film *Lawrence of Arabia* (1962), compassion towards vomiting crewmates waking up from stasis, awe at the technology of the engineers, and delight at finding a living specimen. He is even willing to express resentment, like Roy and Pris, against his human oppressors. When archaeologist Charlie Holloway (Logan Marshall-Greene) tells him that humans created androids just because they could, David sadly asks, "Can you imagine how disappointing it would be for you to hear the same thing from your creator?" David sometimes likes to pretend that he has no feelings; he claims that he is not capable of feeling disappointment and that "want" is not a concept that he is familiar with. Yet it is the sense of brooding bitterness that David carries with him that, more than anything else, defines his character. He *acts* as though he is bottling up a tremendous rage behind a veneer of polite subservience. Later, his poisoning of Holloway indicates how lethal those suppressed thoughts can be.

"'MORE HUMAN THAN HUMAN' IS OUR MOTTO." — TYRELL

So the replicants and androids of Scott's cinematic worlds act as though they are sentient beings. But could this not be just a façade, their shows of emotion as fake as the smile on a shop mannequin? Deckard himself justifies his work by claiming, "Replicants are like any other machine," as if dismissing the idea that a replicant really is a thinking, conscious system distinct from a toaster or a washing machine. But how are we to decide whether a system can genuinely *think?* One proposal is that we should accept that a system thinks if it passes a type of test known as the Turing Test. The Turing Test is based on a game first proposed by English computer genius Alan Turing (1912–1954). Turing's contribution to the development of the computer is enormous, his technological legacy easily outstripping that of the fictional Tyrell.

   In Turing's game, a human player must attempt to work out whether he or she is communicating with a human being in another room or with a machine that has been programmed to respond like a human. Turing never intended his work to be applied to the question of whether machines think—a question that he regarded as "too meaningless" to be worth exploring.[2] However, others have proposed that if a human playing Turing's game cannot tell whether the machine s/he is interacting with is a machine or another human being, then the machine can think. Some philosophers have maintained that we should grant that the machine under question thinks because the Turing Test provides excellent evidence of thought. Other philosophers maintain that we should grant that the machine thinks because, given the very meaning of the word "think," it is impossible for a machine to be conversing like a human without thinking. In their view, there is simply no more to thinking than behaving like a creature that thinks.

   Of course, a Turing Test could be set at any level of difficulty. Even very simple computers might pass very simple Turing Tests. When Deckard enters the elevator of his apartment building, he interacts with the machine verbally. "Voice print identification. Your floor number please," the elevator asks him, to which he replies "Deckard, ninety-seven." "Ninety-seven, thank you," responds the machine and it begins to take him to his floor. If Deckard were not familiar with elevator computers, he could easily have taken himself to be speaking to another human. Likewise, Sebastian's toys might well pass simple Turing Tests if they remained out of sight. For example, the diminutive toy soldier and bear greet their creator's return by chanting, "Home again, home again, jiggity jig. Good evening, Dad!" and no doubt produce responses to other stimuli. Even the toy clown, whose only action is to laugh when someone walks by, could pass a Turing Test if the test were basic enough. Obviously, we would not want to accept that such simple devices must be *thinking*, not unless we also want to concede that our toy store shelves are loaded with sentient beings (an idea that children might espouse, but adults less so).

However, the Turing Tests that the Nexus-6 Replicants pass are extremely demanding; if passing a sufficiently demanding Turing Test is an indication of thought, then the replicants of *Blade Runner* are thinking creatures. They pass as humans (among humans) all the time. The team of escaping replicants led by Roy Batty has been hiding on Earth for more than two weeks. Leon has managed to rent a hotel room and land a job as a waste disposal engineer, while Zhora holds down a job dancing in silver paint while wearing a synthetic snake. When Pris approaches the brilliant geneticist Sebastian to talk her way into his apartment and enlist his help, she easily convinces him that she is as human as he is. Perhaps most impressively, Rachel unwittingly fools blade runner Deckard, a specialist in detecting and retiring replicants. Indeed, as above noted, Rachel passes so well for human that Deckard is able to fall in love with her. Presumably, he is not the only one Rachel has been fooling. Unaware that she is a replicant and living obliviously as a human being, she maintains friendships, forms professional relationships, and otherwise relates to human beings on a daily basis. This includes chatting with her coworkers as they wait for the elevator to reach the thousandth floor, or gossiping at the salon as she has her hair done in the latest retro 1940s style. Similarly, in *Alien*, the crew of the *Nostromo* is oblivious to the fact that their science officer, Ash, is an android, even though they work alongside him closely. He, too, passes the Turing Test with flying colors.

In fact, so ineffective are Turing Tests for distinguishing replicants from human beings that the blade runners do not use them at all. Instead, they make use of the fictional Voight-Kampff machine to measure the physical reactions subjects have to emotionally provocative questions. By tracking not only the linguistic responses but also the biological reactions of subjects, the Voight-Kampff Test flies in the face of the Turing Test, intended to allow us to judge whether a system thinks without succumbing to prejudices against systems that are different from us physically. The Voight-Kampff Test is not a test for thought *per se*, but it *is* intended to allow the blade runner to judge (adult) personhood in the legally relevant sense (that is, the one that determines whether a being may wander off through the crazy, smoggy streets of Scott's LA or receive a bullet to the head from the neighborhood blade runner). The Voight-Kampff test determines whether subjects are replicants by observing their physical response to questions, even if the subject's *linguistic* responses are indistinguishable from those of a human being. Deckard has to observe Rachel's physical responses to more than one hundred questions in order to determine that she is a replicant; her verbal responses alone tell him nothing about her humanity. It does not matter, at least from the point of view of the Turing Test, whether the lack of physical response is due to an innate biological difference or an emotional immaturity in replicants caused by their lack of experience. If a machine-like lack of empathy cannot be identified by linguistic responses alone, then such a factor must not be relevant to judging whether a system thinks.

"REPLICANTS ARE LIKE ANY OTHER MACHINE." — DECKARD

While the Turing Test may or may not provide solid evidence that a system thinks, it is impossible to *know* whether a system thinks based solely on its observable behavior. This point was established by twentieth-century American philosopher John Searle (1932–).[3] Searle presents us with a hypothetical situation that has become known as the "Chinese Room Thought Experiment." He asks us to imagine a non-Chinese speaking man hired to sit in a room filled with stacks of paper covered in Chinese characters. There are two slots in the wall: an "in" slot and an "out" slot. More pieces of paper covered in Chinese characters are fed into the room through the "in" slot. The poor sap's job is to look up these incoming characters in his rulebook to find out which piece of paper he should post through the "out" slot in response.

Searle points out that the system just described could function as if it understood Chinese. With a sufficiently complicated rulebook, the man in the room could, in principle, match input to output so well that someone outside the room would be unable to tell if s/he were corresponding with a Chinese speaker in the room or not. Yet despite the fact that the system functions like a Chinese speaker, the man in the room does not *understand* Chinese. He is mechanically matching input to output with no conception of what any of it means. What this demonstrates is that functioning like a thinking being does not require any understanding or awareness of what actions are being taken. All that is required is mechanically matching the right input to the right output. This means that a system's ability to pass the Turing Test cannot guarantee that it thinks, rather that it is just mechanically doing what it is programmed to do. In fact, it means that no possible test could ever guarantee that a system thinks, since the only way to test whether a system thinks is to observe how it functions; any functioning could be performed by a system that has no understanding at all and therefore does no thinking. For this reason, there is no way for Deckard or any other human to know for sure whether the replicants are thinking creatures. There is nothing that these beings could possibly do that could not be done by a machine with no consciousness, and no way that they could possibly act that would distinguish them from a system that simulates human thought and feeling but understands no more than a fridge or a toaster. This is true also, of course, for the androids of *Alien* and *Prometheus*.

However, this uncertainty cuts both ways. If we can never tell for certain whether a system is thinking, then we can never tell for certain that a system is *not* thinking. If androids and replicants are *acting* as though they are thinking, then we might give them the benefit of the doubt. After all, we ourselves can provide no better evidence that we have thoughts and feelings than that we behave as if we have them. We expect other human beings to respect our rights as people and not to treat us as mere objects and tools, but since Searle has shown that a system without thought can exhibit any behavior a system *with* thought can exhibit, the question arises as to why anyone should think that anyone else is a thinking, feeling creature. Someone who believes that he or she is the only one who genuinely has thoughts and feelings is known as a solipsist. While few philosophers have identified themselves as solipsists, many have been concerned that we lack good justification for rejecting solipsism. Direct access to our own thoughts and feelings gives us reason to believe that *we* personally are sentient, but we have no such evidence in the case of other people.

"YOU'RE SO DIFFERENT. YOU'RE SO PERFECT."—SEBASTIAN

Perhaps the best argument for rejecting solipsism was given by nineteenth-century English philosopher John Stuart Mill (1806-1873).[4] Mill offers an argument by analogy between ourselves and other human beings. We know directly that we have thoughts and feelings; we do not know directly that other people have thoughts and feelings, but we know that they behave in the same way that we do. They smile under circumstances that would make us smile with happiness and say "ouch" under circumstances that would cause us to cry out in pain. Furthermore, our bodies are composed of similar material as that of other people, arranged in more or less the same way. Given the similarity of our behaviors and physical structure to other human beings, Mill concluded that other human beings are also likely to have thoughts and feelings. We cannot be *certain* that they do, but it seems at least *probable*.

Mill's standard coincides with the spirit of the Voight-Kampff Test, since he judges other humans to have thoughts and feelings on the grounds that they are physically like him, as well as that they behave like him. This premise would be a problem for replicants since they are not physically human. It is unclear to what extent Nexus-6 Replicants are physically different. The reliance on blade runners to observe physiological responses to questions with the help of a Voight-Kampff machine might suggest that the replicants are so like humans that this test is the only way to tell us apart. However, the abilities demonstrated by replicants rule out such close similarity.

Replicants can withstand extreme cold (as Leon demonstrates by plunging his hand into liquid nitrogen in Hannibal Chew's workshop Eye Works) and also extreme heat (as Pris demonstrates by plunging her hand into boiling water at Sebastian's apartment). Leon is so strong than he can punch a hole in the side of a truck and later overpower Deckard with minimal, if any, exertion. Roy, likewise, is so resistant to injury than he can smash his head right through a wall just to say something snarky to the person on the other side. Pris is so strong and agile that Deckard has no chance against her in hand to hand combat, and only defeats her by shooting her multiple times. When she dies, she expires not as most of us would (gasping on the carpet and clutching our wound), but rather goes into wild spasms, beating her arms and legs against the floor like a broken machine with a short circuit. This is an interpretation of android death also displayed by Ash in *Alien*. So it seems likely that when the prologue in *Blade Runner* tells us that replicants are "virtually identical to a human," this describes their outward appearance rather than the details of their biology. The Voight-Kampff Test is not the only way to tell a replicant from a human being, just the method that is the least invasive and unpleasant. One wonders whether there were complaints from the public about the boiling water and head-through-a-wall tests.

Despite the biological differences between humans and replicants, applying Mill's standard would be to a replicant's advantage. The Voight-Kampff Test hunts for differences between the subject and humans, using these differences as grounds to deny replicants political rights. Mill's standard, on the other hand, also asks us to hunt for *similarities* in biology and behavior alike, treating similarity as evidence that a subject has a thinking, feeling mind like we do. Replicants are almost identical to human beings in their behavior and at least similar to human beings in their biology. Because our best grounds for judging other human beings to have minds is that other human beings are behaviorally and physically similar to us, it would be unjust discrimination to refuse to grant (on the same grounds) that replicants also have minds.

Androids like those from *Alien* and *Prometheus* are more difficult cases. Their milky white "blood," transparent internal tubing, and ability to survive as disembodied heads suggests a physical structure far removed from that of a human. With Mill's model, we have less evidence that the androids really think than that the replicants really think. This seems appropriate: we really do have more evidence that systems that are physically *like us* can think than that systems that are physically *unlike us* can think. However, before allegations of speciesism arise for prejudice against our inorganic sisters and brothers, I still think that androids like Ash and David should be regarded as thinking beings. Their behavior is so much like that of thinking beings that this similarity outweighs all of the physical differences. The evidence that androids think may not be as overwhelming as the evidence that suggests replicants do, but it certainly seems to be enough to give androids the benefit of the doubt.

"QUITE AN EXPERIENCE TO LIVE IN FEAR, ISN'T IT?"—ROY

Allowing that replicants and other artificial beings have thoughts and feelings like ours is not yet to allow that they have the rights that we have. For instance, it violates their rights if we ship them off-world to work as slave laborers who are forced to undertake the most hazardous jobs involved in colonizing other planets. Tyrell, for example, accepts that replicants have thoughts and emotions but has no problem with treating them like slaves. Indeed, the history of slavery has been the history of the abuse of those who are acknowledged to have thoughts and feelings, even if those thoughts and feelings are not always thought to be of the same quality as those of the slave owners. Rather, what we say about our moral duties towards replicants and other artificial beings is going to depend on what characteristics of a creature we think indicate that it has moral rights. This has been the subject of much disagreement among philosophers.

For example, eighteenth-century German philosopher Immanuel Kant (1724–1804) influentially claimed that people have moral rights by virtue of being rational agents. What marks a human out over a dog as having a right to personal freedom and moral consideration is that the human has a capacity to reason. Believing that humans are the only rational beings, Kant expresses our duties in terms of "humanity," instructing us to "act in such a way that you treat humanity, whether in your own person or the person of any other, never simply as a means but always at the same time as an end."[5] In other words, we may not treat other humans as mere tools, exploiting them for our personal benefit without concern for their own desires and best interests. Nexus-6 Replicants are easily as rational as humans; in the words of the film's introduction, they are "at least equal in intelligence, to the genetic engineers who created them." According to the Kantian model, the replicants must also be treated as ends in themselves and must never be used as mere tools for the Tyrell Corporation to make money, or for humanity to colonize space.

On the other hand, Mill proposed a very different view of the justification of human rights. He maintained that the only thing that matters in itself is happiness. An act is morally right if it would best promote the happiness of people in general. Mill wrote that "actions are right in proportion as they tend to promote happiness; wrong as they tend to produce the reverse of happiness. By happiness is intended pleasure and the absence of pain."[6] Mill thought that intellectual and cultural pleasures, those he called "higher pleasures," are more valuable than pleasures that are not intellectually demanding. However, anything that people enjoy is good if they are not doing any harm; even a grown man like Sebastian playing with mechanical dolls is a good thing, simply because he enjoys doing so.

Mill's model does not assign human beings any inalienable rights, since anyone's interests might, in principle, be overridden for the greater happiness. However, while Mill accepted that there are no inalienable rights, he believed that *in practice*, giving people personal rights is the most effective way to promote general happiness. He placed particular emphasis on the need for personal freedom, writing, "The only part of the conduct of anyone for which he is amenable to society is that which concerns others. In the part which merely concerns himself, his independence is, of right, absolute."[7]

While Mill never directly addressed the issue of Nexus-6 Replicants forced to shovel sulfur on Venus or being burned to death in attack ships off the shoulder of Orion, it would be alien to the spirit of his moral philosophy to treat the interests of replicants as less important than those of human beings. Replicants are probably not only as capable of pleasure and suffering as humans are, but just as capable as humans of appreciating the intellectual pleasures that Mill prized. Mill was a passionate advocate of extending political equality to the disenfranchised and powerless. He championed abolishing the African slave trade, giving women the right to vote, and improving conditions for the working classes. It is hard to see him standing idly by as a new form of slavery takes hold, the slavery of replicants. Indeed, Mill reminds us that we must always be on the lookout for social injustices that we have been blind to thus far. He explains: "The entire history of social improvement has been a series of transitions, by which one custom or institution after another, from being a supposed primary necessity of social existence, has passed into the rank of a universally stigmatized injustice and tyranny. So it has been with the distinctions of slaves and freemen, nobles and serfs, patricians and plebians; and so it will be, and in part already is, with the aristocracies of colour, race, and sex."[8] Surely Mill would be on the side of Roy, Pris, Zhora, and Leon in their quest for freedom from the Tyrell Corporation.

The approaches of Kant and Mill toward the question of what makes a creature worthy of moral concern do not exhaust the possible approaches to that question. However, they illustrate just how difficult it would be to draw a line between humans and creatures like replicants and androids that in any way justifies giving them fewer rights than those we have ourselves. To discriminate against them just because *they* are not *us* seems as reprehensible as discriminating against someone just because she or he is of a different race, sex, or ethnicity.

Where does this leave us? We still do not have a clear method for distinguishing between systems that think and systems that do not, or between people and mere things. Nor do we have a clear policy as to how to proceed in the fields of artificial intelligence and genetic engineering in such a way that we respect the rights of artificial beings. That would be too much to hope for even in a volume entirely devoted to those issues, let alone these few pages. However, I hope at the very least that it is clear that the question of how we are to treat artificial beings is an important one, and one that is constantly at the forefront as our technology grows increasingly sophisticated and pervasive.

NOTES

1. The killing of the unloving father-as-creator is a common theme in Scott's films. The Roman emperor Commodus strangles his father Marcus Aurelius in *Gladiator* with the complaint "Father, I would have butchered the whole world if you would have only loved me!" In *Prometheus*, the carnage spans generations. David the android gets to watch as his uncaring creator Peter Weyland (Guy Pearce) is killed by one of the mysterious Engineers, just before the Engineer himself is killed (albeit indirectly) by one of its own abandoned creations, a surviving human.

2. Alan Turing, "Computing Machinery and Intelligence," *Mind* 59, no. 236 (1950): 442.

3. John Searle, "Minds, Brains and Programs," in *Behavioral and Brain Sciences*, vol. 3, ed. Sol Tax, 417-457 (New York: Cambridge University Press, 1980).

4. John Stuart Mill, *An Examination of Sir William Hamilton's Philosophy* (London: Longmans, 2004).

5. Immanuel Kant, *Groundwork of the Metaphysics of Morals*, ed. Mary Gregor (Cambridge: Cambridge University Press, 1998), 38.

6. John Stuart Mill, "Utilitarianism," in *Utilitarianism and Other Essays*, ed. Alan Ryan (London: Penguin Classics, 1987), 278.

7. John Stuart Mill, "On Liberty," in *On Liberty and The Subjection of Women* (London: Penguin Classics, 2007), 16.

8. Mill, *Utilitarianism*, 337.

REFERENCES

Alien. DVD. Directed by Ridley Scott. 1979. Los Angeles, CA: Twentieth Century Fox, 1999.

Blade Runner. DVD. Directed by Ridley Scott. 1982. Burbank, CA: Warner Home Video, 2010.

Kant, Immanuel. *Groundwork of the Metaphysics of Morals*, edited by Mary Gregor. Cambridge: Cambridge University Press, 1998.

Mill, John Stuart. *An Examination of Sir William Hamilton's Philosophy*. London: Longmans, 2004.

———. "On Liberty." In *On Liberty and The Subjection of Women*. London: Penguin Classics, 2007.

———. "Utilitarianism." In *Utilitarianism and Other Essays*, edited by Alan Ryan. London: Penguin Classics, 1987.

Prometheus. Directed by Ridley Scott. Los Angeles, CA: Twentieth Century Fox, 2012.

Searle, John. "Minds, Brains and Programs." In *Behavioral and Brain Sciences*, vol. 3, edited by Sol Tax, 417-457. New York: Cambridge University Press, 1980.

Turing, Alan. "Computing Machinery and Intelligence." *Mind* 59, no. 236, 433-60 (1950).

Chapter Eight

A Villainous Appetite: *Erôs*, Madness, and the Food Analogy in *Hannibal* and *Legend*

Antonio Sanna

This chapter posits that the relationship between Dr. Hannibal Lecter and Clarice Starling in Ridley Scott's film *Hannibal* (2001) is founded on the terms of a courtship, although it is partly (and transgressively) characterized as a relationship between a psychiatrist and his patient. I shall initially examine the love poem of Dante Alighieri repeatedly quoted by the Doctor to establish a parallel between the experience of love defined by the medieval Italian writer and that of Hannibal. This shall evidence the fact that Lecter is divided between his will to elevate himself through a serious relationship with Starling and his cannibalistic interest towards her. Similarly, in the early Ridley Scott film *Legend* (1985), the character of the Dark Lord is divided between the excesses of greed and the generosity of charity. I conclude that these two villains represent both the madness caused by love and love's dual nature as described by the Greek philosopher Plato in both the *Symposium* and the *Phaedrus*.

In Thomas Harris's Gothic novels *Red Dragon* (1981) and *The Silence of the Lambs* (1988), the sexuality of Hannibal Lecter—an elegant, distinguished, and brilliant psychiatrist as much as a sadistic cannibal—is neither specifically identified nor explicitly critiqued. In both novels, Lecter has no physical relationship with or discernable attraction to anyone, man or woman. He is mainly described by the other characters as "a monster" and "a pure sociopath."[1] The first explicit mention of his sexuality occurs in the novel *Hannibal* (1999) when FBI section chief Jack Crawford contemplates the possibility that Lecter might be attracted to Clarice Starling, the agent who is charged with finding the fugitive cannibal. Such a possibility is neither validated nor contradicted by Starling, who affirms, "We don't know anything about his sexual preferences."[2]

Lecter's sexuality is unequivocally confirmed in Scott's cinematic adaptation. Indeed, over the course of the plot, the Doctor (Anthony Hopkins) falls in love with Agent Starling (Julianne Moore). He becomes very interested in Clarice's emotional well-being as much as in her physical appearance. On the one hand, he deeply cares about her psychological condition on the job. This is demonstrated by the fact that, after what he defines as "the course of [Clarice's] disgrace and public shaming" due to the Evelda Drumgo's fish-market killing, Lecter breaks ten years of silence by writing the agent a compassionate letter of support in order to comfort her for the "sorry, petty end of a promising career."

Lecter often explicitly addresses Starling with terms more appropriate to a courtship than the relationship between a fugitive and the agent responsible for capturing him. Indeed, when he and Starling meet in person in Mason Verger's mansion, Lecter expresses his appreciation for her appearance in spite of the immediate danger they are both facing. In this scene, the Doctor finds himself a prisoner of Verger (Gary Oldman): he is tied to a freight elevator in a Christ-like position and offered as a meal to a pack of voracious wild boars expressly trained to eat human flesh. Starling breaks into Verger's mansion and quickly unties Lecter while the wild boars are encroaching upon the two by forcing their way through a wooden gate. At this precise moment, Lecter smiles at the agent and says, "You look well." The prospect of being eaten alive has no priority over his need to offer a compliment. Moreover, Lecter does not merely appreciate Starling's appearance; he even attempts to render her more attractive after her shooting. He lavishly dresses her in a pair of Gucci shoes and a Versace dress before preparing a sumptuous candle-lit dinner for her. In this scene near the conclusion of the film, Lecter and Starling are finally able to talk to each other face to face after the prolonged period of Lecter's disappearance and decade of hiding. He demonstrates his immediate priorities by addressing her with the same type of simple, admiring observation: "You look beautiful."

Lecter's feelings for Starling can also be deduced by interpreting the film's allusions to the love poems by Dante Alighieri, one of the major writers of early Italian literature. Viewers draw a parallel between the ardor evinced by the poet and that of the American doctor towards the FBI agent. After all, the film's plot spends considerable time in Florence, Dante's home town.[3] In such works as the *Vita Nuova* and the *Divina Commedia* (*Divine Comedy*), Dante glorifies and celebrates his love for Beatrice, the girl he met in 1274 when he was nine years old. Beatrice was for Dante a love at first sight that lasted for all of the poet's life. Much of the adoration is fantasy, as they never had any sustained or reciprocal relationship and she died in 1290. Such a love was therefore neither developed nor consummated, but experienced by Dante in a spiritual way. Like Dante and Beatrice, Lecter has seen Clarice only a few times in the past and has only briefly talked to her. For a great part of *Hannibal*, when Lecter is living in Florence as the curator of the Capponi Library, Clarice is only a distant presence reaching him through the titles of the newspapers or through the mobile phone of Inspector Pazzi. Lecter thus addresses her only with his letters and through poetry rather than in person.

We must stress that the Italian poet exalted Beatrice as a sort of living, divine miracle; his encounters with her and her premature death had, to him, a salvific power. He saw her as a sort of "personalized Messiah" who could have guided him to salvation.[4] However, many of the words by Dante quoted throughout the film can easily be interpreted as referring to Lecter's feelings towards Starling. Specifically, during the reception after the opera scene, Pazzi's wife Allegra (Francesca Neri) reads aloud the first sonnet from Dante's *Vita Nuova* in front of Lecter. This thirteenth-century poem, titled "A ciascun'alma presa e gentil core" describes Dante's rapturous vision of his lady while she is sleeping in the arms of Love, who then offers her a lover's heart. Lecter rapturously listens to Allegra reading from Dante's poem (which also constitutes the very libretto of the opera performance they just viewed) and then recites part of it himself: "[H]e woke her then and trembling and obedient, she ate that burning heart out of his hand. Weeping I saw him [Love] then depart from me." Could we not apply these words to Lecter's feelings and inclinations as well? This approach would be corroborated by the fact that after Allegra's comment on the poem ("Do you believe that a man could become so obsessed with a woman from a single encounter?"), Lecter replies, "Could he daily feel a stab of hunger for her and find nourishment in the very sight of her? I think so." Although these words allude to Lecter's unconscionable practice of cannibalism, the Doctor reformulates Dante's image of love through a food analogy (the eating of the lover's heart) that also describes the mere sight of the loved one as a source of nourishment. This passage helps establish a connection between erotic and romantic longing and physical hunger. The language of food that often offers figurative approaches for describing romantic and sexual experiences is here given a further twist by the fact that Hannibal is perhaps literally interested in satisfying his hunger through the body of Clarice. The idea of the amorous quest is therefore wedded to the possibility of Lecter feeding on his victim, including her very symbolic heart, as a form of ritual worship, not necessarily as an act of sadistic carnage.

Lecter's attraction for Starling is thus evident in Scott's film. We could establish another parallel between his love for the agent and the overall function of the Gothic or horror genres as described by Clive Bloom. Bloom argues that Gothic fictions can frequently be interpreted as "disturbing but conservative" because they finally restore "things to the status quo and [are] dedicated to the ultimate return to normalcy."[5] This usually happens when the monster or villain is defeated or the danger is averted at the end of the narrative; as such, the norms of nature or of human society previously violated by the inimical presence are finally re-established. Bloom's argument could be applied to Lecter's behavior as well. Indeed, by developing an attraction for Starling and apparently ignoring (or overriding) his cannibalistic interests towards her, the Doctor seems to be restoring the status quo, the "natural" order he has repeatedly violated by killing numerous people and feeding on them. He seems to be returning to "normalcy" at least as society defines it; his lack of literal appetite for her is a deviation from his own cannibalizing norm, but it now coincides with the norms of civil society, especially in relation to more typical Western courtship practices.

Nevertheless, Lecter's murders of Pazzi and FBI agent Paul Krendler could definitely be seen as a disruption of the legal "norms" of contemporary society. In Harris's novels and their cinematic adaptations, the Doctor is initially presented as a valuable member of society: he is a forensic psychiatrist who helps the FBI to identify and categorize criminals. He is, at first, pictured as a gentleman with flawless manners. After being unmasked and captured by agent Will Graham in *Red Dragon*, Lecter is discovered to have repeatedly committed one of the most serious taboos of Western society: cannibalism. The cultivated, polite host and learned gentleman is indeed a murderer of innocent people and has eaten their organs, even serving them as delicious meals to the acquaintances of his victims. In this respect as well, Hannibal embodies the very function of the Gothic genre itself. Even though his attachment to Starling could demonstrate sincere affection and tenderness, the story is, to quote Bloom, "not recuperative and conservative but radical and subversive, dedicated to excess and marginality."[6] With his murderous practices and alternative appetites, Lecter's behavior is certainly "dedicated to excess" and definitely marginal in respect to the conduct of the majority of law-abiding human beings in the contemporary era.

The figure of the Doctor could also be interpreted as duplicitous if we consider the bond between him and Agent Starling as actually reproducing the relationship between an analyst and his or her patient (counter-transference). Indeed, from her first visit to the Baltimore State Hospital for the Criminally Insane in Jonathan Demme's *The Silence of the Lambs* (1991), Starling affirms: "I'm here to learn from you." She thus voluntarily assigns Lecter the position of learning resource, but this position of trust could also be seen as attributing to him the roles of mentor, surrogate father, teacher, or analyst.[7] Subsequently, during her other visits to the hospital, Starling entrusts her memories to the Doctor in exchange for his help in the identification of "Buffalo Bill," the serial killer Jame Gumb.

Hannibal's role as Starling's personal therapist is further represented in Scott's *Hannibal*. After ten years of silence and hiding, he sends Starling a hand-written letter precisely at a moment of deep crisis. In such a letter, Lecter examines the FBI agent's psychology through a reading of her feelings for her dead parents: "And now do you see [your father] shamed and crushed by your disgrace? . . . Will your failure reflect on [your parents]?" Subsequently, when dining with her at Krendler's house, Lecter attempts to convince Starling to abandon the FBI, insisting on the fact that the Bureau is corrupted and misogynistic. In this sense, the Doctor still offers his professional skills and guidance to her, further validating his role as her counsellor and analyst. This role is confirmed by the fact that Starling accepts and never openly contradicts his observations: with tears filling her eyes, she seems to silently agree with his statements about the FBI, "the institution that doesn't love [her] back. . . . [T]hose people [she] despise[s] almost as much as they despise [her]."

In this respect, assuming Lecter is in love with Starling implies that he is a therapist who has developed a counter-transference love for his "patient," as Stephen M. Fuller has discerned.[8] Instead of remaining emotionally detached from the woman's experiences and emotions, Lecter becomes personally involved with her. His love for Starling is openly demonstrated by means of his kiss during the climactic scene against the refrigerator and is further confirmed by his choice to cut off his own hand instead of Starling's in order to free himself from the handcuffs she has restrained him with to prevent his escape.

Hannibal features the character of a therapist provoking horror in the viewer as well as in his "patient," Clarice. Indeed, the ambivalent relationship between the analysed and analyst, supposedly established on the basis of reciprocal trust and personal non-involvement, is transgressively portrayed as unduly personal. Starling is scared of Lecter: she is nervous in his presence and definitely frightened by the possibility that he could cannibalize her too. These are sensations and feelings which are also (ideally) shared by the viewers of the film. Indeed, *Hannibal* is intended to stimulate the fear of a therapist who dissects not only the mind of the patient, but also the tissues of her very body. Hannibal's threat is that of a trusted individual and professional who can ingest a person's thoughts and emotions as much as the organs which allegedly produce them. Indeed, he can expose people's thoughts, emotions, and fears as readily as he can expose (in Krendler's case) their very brains. Although it is not stated explicitly, Clarice knows that Lecter would have had to disrobe her to remove not only the bullet but also her soiled clothes; her physical vulnerability would have been undeniable, an apt correlation to her psychological "undressing" by Lecter.

We could also argue that by embedding into the Gothic genre the anxieties surrounding the counter-transference experience between therapist and patient, *Hannibal* presents a *positive* characterization of psychoanalysis. Viewers know a priori that they are dealing with a fictitious story which is generally structured to frighten its audience. In this way, they are aware that such facts could hardly occur in their "real" lives in the world (or, at least, they sincerely hope so). In this way as well, *Hannibal* epitomizes the functions of the Gothic genre as both transgressive and conservative in respect to the general norms and practices of contemporary society. On the one hand, the Gothic offers a beneficial escape from the moral, civic, and sexual duties of real life and allows the viewer to fantasize about the possibility of a sexual relationship between an analyst and a patient, or even the possibility of practicing cannibalism with an explicitly erotic charge. In this sense, *Hannibal* exemplifies what Richard Davenport-Hines defines as the "evasive" function of the Gothic genre, which puts "into play what silencing, denial and infantilisation tried to police . . . by the release of repressed affects and by the exploration of foreclosed topics."[9] On the other hand, "real" life offers the viewer and the reader a reassuring confirmation and re-establishment of society's values as well as the expressed prohibition against such unacceptable acts as cannibalism. Therefore, as Jerrold E. Hogle observes in regard to Gothic narratives, the "deviations" from the norm are finally placed "at a definite, though haunting distance from us" and re-affirmed as mere fantasies.[10]

How can viewers be certain that Lecter does not want to cannibalize Starling? It would be logical to assume that she, too, could be a victim of his appetites which, in this case, are both sexual and culinary. We could think of the Doctor as he differentiates between these types of appetites and therefore represents what the Greek philosopher Plato describes as *erôs*. This term indicates passionate sexual desire but is also associated with madness. In the *Phaedrus*, Plato (through the speech of Lysias) argues that love is a form of madness; persons in love are "not sane," but they "cannot help themselves."[11] Similarly, the "sociopath" Lecter appears to be obsessed with Clarice, following her while jogging, violating her home while she is asleep, and killing her rival Krendler as if to earn her approval.

In the *Phaedrus*, Plato also describes the human soul as complex and tortured by conflicting emotions when reacting to the sight of beauty. Indeed, he specifies that every person is ruled by two different principles: an innate "desire for pleasure" and a rational and acquired conviction that "causes us to aim at excellence."[12] The former drags the human being to excess and, in the context of enjoying beauty, this excess is called *erôs*. To illustrate his point, Plato evokes the myth of the winged charioteer who drives a pair of horses. The good horse corresponds to the restraint experienced by the lover when facing beauty, whereas the undisciplined horse represents the instinct to immediately jump at the loved one and declare one's feelings. In particular, he describes the second "lustful horse" as "resist[ing] with all his strength" the rational will of the charioteer, a representation of the intellect.[13] We could think of Lecter as exemplifying the human division between the excesses derived from hedonism (the desire for pleasure) and the aforementioned pursuit of level-headedness and the excellence of restraint. Lecter perfectly embodies the juxtaposition of these attitudes through his behavior; he must balance his desire to consume the female agent as a meal with his ennobling love for her and the need to protect her from that kind of harm from others.

According to Plato, when the person is in front of the love interest, the charioteer is able to restrain the wild horse at the last moment. Subsequently, "after several repetitions of this treatment, the wicked horse abandons his lustful ways; meekly now he executes the wishes of his driver, and when he catches sight of the loved one is ready to die of fear. So at last it comes about that the soul of the lover waits upon his beloved in reverence and awe."[14] This is the description of true love, balanced between the moderating influences of patience and reason and the unruliness of desire, between the generosity of *caritas* (charity) and the excesses of *cupiditas* (greed). Could we not apply this allegory to Lecter's behavior as well? If we interpret his actions as demonstrating a sincere love for Starling, then we could explain his "lustful horse" as finally tamed by his conviction "to aim at excellence" by attempting to initiate a serious (and non-fatal) relationship with her. This reading finds a further parallel in Plato's dialogue in the *Symposium* where the philosopher argues that "desire and love are directed at what you don't have, what isn't there, and what you need."[15] In this sense, love comes from a state of deficiency, but it is also "the desire to have the good forever."[16] Because Starling is a person who firmly believes in moral values and therefore is a representative of both goodness and justice, Lecter's love for her could symbolize an attraction for a "normal" and morally correct life, which he obviously lacks.

This reading could be affirmed as well by the Dark Lord in the fantasy film *Legend*; this deity admits to being attracted to a mortal because of her purity, something he definitely lacks. Among Scott's films, the associations of culinary appetite with sexual desire are indeed not unique to *Hannibal*. In *Legend* there are numerous references to eating, many of them cannibalistic, either literally or figuratively. For instance, Princess Lili (Mia Sara), the personification of innocence, finds herself attracted to the peasant cabin of her friend Nell because of the freely available food there. She enters the abode and helps herself to the bountiful table, declaring that in spite of being "poor folk," the inhabitants enjoy a kind of life that is "very rich." She then gives the food to her admirer, Jack, crossing not only class lines but territorial lines, as Jack lives in the forest.

The goblin Blix, who is following and using Lili and Jack as bait for the capture of the sacred unicorns, compares Lili to flesh to be eaten as a meal: "Maybe innocent, maybe sweet. Ain't half as nice as rotting meat." Blix often associates objects and persons with food; indeed, he affirms that the shot of the poisoned stinger is "as sweet as pie," and later threatens to turn his companion Pox into dainty "pork chops." After the unicorn horn "castration," the goblin's other comrade, Blunder, explicitly mentions how he wishes to eat Lili's brains "like jam," while the porcine Pox delights in the prospect of "suck[ing] her bones." This metaphor, we could say, renders clear his desire to assault her body, presumably sexually as well, since all three of these characters are as animal(istic) as they are human-like.

On the quest to retrieve the stolen horn, Jack faces the possibility of death in the mouth of Meg Mucklebones, the hideous water creature residing in the gloomy swamp surrounding the Great Tree. She resides in the middle of a desolate and misty landscape where only the bones of her victims are visible. Meg does not kill the fairy Screwball only because he is "foul tasting," and as soon as she sees Jack, she calls him a "juicy boy" and a "tender morsel," immediately declaring her will to eat him. Jack wisely uses his mouth (and its capacity for praise) to escape her by appealing to her feminine vanity and inviting her to "feast" on the beauty of her own reflection in his shield rather than on his body, thereby decapitating her, Medusa-like, while she is distracted.

Subsequently, the group of travelers also find themselves narrowly escaping a barbeque by cannibal executioners (actually the Dark Lord's cooks) who sleep on the kitchen table among the remains of their meals. The intruders even have to dig a still-alive "brother" out of a pie. Much of the discourse focuses, however, on Lili's being "sweet" and by extension, sexually palatable; even the Lord of Darkness (who is introduced in the first scene of the film while sitting at a prepared table) admits experiencing "desire" for her. He later asks her to join him at dinner, his eyes gazing at her hungrily as he plans his seduction through food.

Through his courtly behavior, the Dark Lord embodies the juxtaposition of opposite attitudes described by Plato in the *Phaedrus*. As with the internally conflicted Lecter, the Lord must balance his love for Princess Lili with his desire to physically possess her and probably consume her as a meal. His cooks, we should note, usually adorn his table with human and faerie meat. His love is quite uncharacteristic for a villain as unscrupulous and ruthless as he is, and it could be seen as probably ennobling despite his stereotypical guise as a force of evil. Indeed, for the majority of their encounter, the Dark Lord speaks softly, addresses her tenderly, and smiles. Were it not for his satanic appearance, he would probably appear to be a gentle and respectful character, a kind of proto-Lecter from another world.

On the other hand, the Lord of Darkness hardly restrains himself discursively when in front of Lili, immediately declaring his intention to share eternity with her. He is also prone to losing his temper, thereby revealing the cruel and authoritarian side of his character. Indeed, after her refusal to sit at the table, he angrily shouts his order—"Sit, damn you!"—scaring her all the more and hardly endearing himself to her. He later repeats the command while knocking over the dishes and glasses on the table. This monarch's will to immediately possess Lili's body and obtain her love surrenders to the unruliness of desire. We find herein a representation of *cupiditas* (greed), which is expressed through his fury, his verbal violence, and his bestial contortions and cries. Could we not argue that this also represents the concept of *erôs*? Could his fits of anger not be symbolic of the madness of his love for Lili and all that her "innocence" and "purity" entail?

The encounter between the Dark Lord and Lili is also a reference to the Greek myth of Persephone, who, after being abducted by Hades, is tricked into eating the food of the Underworld (specifically, a pomegranate seed), which plunges her into an eternal bond of undesired matrimony and obligation.[17] Lili manages to temporarily stall her dark captor by stating that it is her wish to kill the captured unicorn. She thus seduces him by appealing to his thirst for blood. She asks to be the executioner of the unicorn as a gift for their marriage and subsequently solemnizes such a union while she actually endeavors to free the remaining mare. She proclaims, "Let my offering be of flesh and blood," a triple reference to her murder of the sacred beast, her dreaded satiation of the Beast (the satanic husband-to-be), and perhaps a submerged allusion to the holy flesh and blood of the Eucharist. Perhaps this Dark Lord, in some ways, presages the more nuanced understanding and depiction of evil in *Hannibal*, whose villain offers Clarice the brain of Krendler as a sacrifice and as a fleshy "love poem" that doubles as dinner.

Hannibal and *Legend* are unique if thematically risky Ridley Scott films, both dealing with complex connections between *erôs*, madness, and food. Food is one means to conquer and seduce a partner and also a code word for the cannibalistic consumption of her organs and flesh (hardly, one might think, a reciprocal relationship). The villains of both films are divided between their serious and sincere love for the female protagonists and their desire to potentially eat these women's flesh as an expression of personal depravity. In both cases, the females refuse the (sexual) advances of these villains. This state of longing and incompletion begs the question of whether there exists any possibility of emotional redemption and physical satisfaction for their respective suitors. Also, we might ask, what of these women's own desires?

NOTES

1. Thomas Harris, *Red Dragon* (1981; London: Arrow Books, 1993), 64; Thomas Harris, *The Silence of the Lambs* (1988; London: Arrow Books, 2002), 13.

2. Thomas Harris, *Hannibal* (1999; London: Arrow Books, 2000), 309.

3. See also Antonio Sanna, "The Nostalgia of Hannibal Lecter: A Postmodern Reproduction of Dante Alighieri's Exile," *Kinema: A Journal for Film and Audiovisual Media* (Fall 2009): 68-69.

4. Jeffrey T. Schnapp, "Introduction to *Purgatorio*," in *The Cambridge Companion to Dante*, ed. Rachel Jacoff (Cambridge: Cambridge University Press, 1997), 203.

5. Clive Bloom, ed., "Introduction: Death's Own Backyard: The Nature of Modern Gothic and Horror Fiction," in *Gothic Horror: A Reader's Guide from Poe to King and Beyond* (Basingstoke: Macmillan, 1998), 13.

6. Ibid., 13.

7. Linda Mizejewski, "Stardom and Serial Fantasies: Thomas Harris's *Hannibal*," in *Keyframes: Popular Cinema and Cultural Studies*, ed. Matthew Tinkcom and Amy Villarejo (London: Routledge, 2001), 169.

8. Stephen M. Fuller, "Deposing an American Cultural Totem: Clarice Starling and Postmodern Heroism in Thomas Harris's *Red Dragon, The Silence of the Lambs*, and *Hannibal*," *The Journal of Popular Culture* 38, no. 5 (2005): 826.

9. Richard Davenport-Hines, *Gothic: 400 Years of Excess, Horror, Evil and Ruin* (London: Fourth Estate, 1998), 61.

10. Jerrold E. Hogle, ed., "Introduction: The Gothic in Western Culture," in *The Cambridge Companion to Gothic Fiction* (Cambridge: Cambridge University Press, 2002), 12.

11. Plato, *Phaedrus*, trans. Walter Hamilton (London: Penguin Books, 1973), 27.

12. Ibid., 36-37.

13. Ibid., 62.

14. Ibid., 63.

15. Plato, *The Symposium*, trans. Christopher Gill (New York: Penguin Classics, 2001), 35.

16. Ibid., 43.

17. See Apollodorus, *The Library of Greek Mythology*, trans. Robin Hard (Oxford: Oxford University Press, 1997), 33.

REFERENCES

Apollodorus. *The Library of Greek Mythology*. Translated by Robin Hard. Oxford: Oxford University Press, 1997.

Bloom, Clive. "Introduction: Death's Own Backyard: The Nature of Modern Gothic and Horror Fiction." In *Gothic Horror: A Reader's Guide from Poe to King and Beyond*, edited by Clive Bloom, 1-22. Basingstoke: Macmillan, 1998.

Davenport-Hines, Richard. *Gothic: 400 Years of Excess, Horror, Evil and Ruin*. London: Fourth Estate, 1998.

Fuller, Stephen M. "Deposing an American Cultural Totem: Clarice Starling and Postmodern Heroism in Thomas Harris's *Red Dragon, The Silence of the Lambs*, and *Hannibal*." *The Journal of Popular Culture* 38, no. 5 (2005): 819-833.

Hannibal. DVD. Directed by Ridley Scott. 2001; Beverly Hills, CA: MGM, 2001.

Harris, Thomas. *Hannibal*. 1999. Reprint, London, Harrow Books, 2000.

———. *Red Dragon*. 1981. Reprint, London: Arrow Books, 1993.

———. *The Silence of the Lambs*. 1988. Reprint, London: Arrow Books, 2002.

Hogle, Jerrold E. "Introduction: The Gothic in Western Culture." In *The Cambridge Companion to Gothic Fiction*, edited by Jerrold E. Hogle, 1-20. Cambridge: Cambridge University Press, 2002.

Legend. DVD. Directed by Ridley Scott. 1985; Universal City, CA: Universal Studios, 2011.

Mizejewski, Linda. "Stardom and Serial Fantasies: Thomas Harris's *Hannibal*." In *Keyframes: Popular Cinema and Cultural Studies*, edited by Matthew Tinkcom and Amy Villarejo, 159-170. London: Routledge, 2001.

Plato. *Phaedrus*. Translated by Walter Hamilton. London: Penguin Books, 1973.

———. *The Symposium*. Translated by Christopher Gill. London: Penguin Classics, 2000.

Red Dragon. DVD. Directed by Brett Ratner. 2002; Universal City, CA: Universal Studios, 2003.

Sanna, Antonio. "The Nostalgia of Hannibal Lecter: A Postmodern Reproduction of Dante Alighieri's Exile." *Kinema: A Journal for Film and Audiovisual Media* (Fall 2009): 61-70.

Schnapp, Jeffrey T. "Introduction to *Purgatorio*." In *The Cambridge Companion to Dante*, edited by Rachel Jacoff, 192-207. Cambridge: Cambridge University Press, 1997.

The Silence of the Lambs. DVD. Directed by Jonathan Demme. 1991; Beverly Hills, CA: 2004.

Chapter Nine

Detecting Puzzles and Patterns in *Numb3rs*: No One Escapes "Scott Free"

Janice Shaw

Detective fiction has an ambiguous presence: it is simultaneously a puzzle that challenges the reader and a narrative form with predictable generic characteristics. Even while being involved in a contest to find the solution to the crime before it is revealed by the fictional detective, the reader is still comfortably lulled by both the knowable conventions of the form and the sense of order these confer. A world is created in which crimes can be solved within the boundaries of the text, and in the case of television crime dramas, within the time frame of an episode. These qualities have lent detective fiction the reputation of being both escapist and unrelated to the real world. In the television series *Numb3rs,* producer Ridley Scott exploits both this presentation of crime as a solvable puzzle and the audience's desire for the program to divulge the motivations for the crime. If the detective and the viewers are able to construct a pattern and find a solution, then the crime becomes knowable; it is no longer an arbitrary (and thus frightening) event. To achieve this cathartic effect, Scott brings crime dramas to reality by embedding the solutions in real-world examples of mathematical patterns: that is, in "numb3rs." Furthermore, he uses computer-generated imagery (CGI) to present such patterning in highly visual terms, including graphs and data as they apply to observable and everyday human behaviors.

Scott and his late brother Tony Scott were both heads of the Scott Free production company that brought forth *Numb3rs* to public viewership. The series integrates crime drama and forensic science by following the exploits of two brothers, mathematician Charlie Eppes and Agent Don Eppes, who together solve crimes for the FBI. Charlie uses his scientific and analytical skills to help his brother solve the most difficult cases. Charlie the academic is able to apply principles of scientific rationalism and logical deduction to crimes, while in the process instructing both the FBI team and by extension the viewers in the application of complex mathematical models and formulae. The series uses a visual depiction of the way a mathematical principle applies by intercutting footage to show how the formula is used in everyday life. This application is then extrapolated to the case under investigation by the FBI, as Charlie instructs the agents in Don's team with his expertise. The process thus links scientific rationalism to the detective genre, combining the realm of abstract thinking with concrete applications. This strategy eliminates much of the mystery often ascribed to complex mathematics and by extension, critiques the narrow depiction of mathematicians in US literature, film, and popular culture. The escapism traditionally associated with detective fiction is challenged by the show's capacity to directly relate the process of solving crime to the actions of everyday life.

The ambivalent nature of the two sub-genres of detective fiction, classical and hard-boiled, is embodied by the two brothers in the series. Charlie is the intellectual problem-solver of classical detective fiction while Don is the experienced, worldly, and intuitive detective of hard-boiled detective fiction. In literary typologies such as the one constructed by John G. Cawelti, classical detective fiction is characterized by the detective being intellectual, logical, rational, scientific, and driven by rules.[1] The form, dominated by such British writers as Sir Arthur Conan Doyle and Agatha Christie, includes the famous detectives Sherlock Holmes and Hercule Poirot. These individuals seek patterns and quantifiable evidence to solve a crime, which they regard as a type of intellectual exercise as well as public service. These detectives are typically objective, dispassionate, removed from the world, and overly focused, therefore strongly relating to the depiction of Charlie as the stereotypical genius figure, able to relate to real-life practicalities only through his mathematical formulae.

In contrast, Don relates more to the way Cawelti categorizes the detective in hard-boiled detective fiction. The protagonists of works by American detective fiction writers of the 1950s (for instance, Raymond Chandler, Dashiell Hammett, and Mickey Spillane) come to mind. This detective is intuitive, seeks justice rather than blind adherence to the rule of law, and is subjective, involved, and caring. He or she (though mainly he) is the knight errant figure found in *film noir*. These figures are like Philip Marlowe or Sam Spade, world-weary but protective of those they consider it their duty to shield from the "mean streets." Both types of detective fiction use as their foundation the puzzle motif, or a contest of wits between the text and viewers or readers.

The televised storyline presents a challenge for the audience to solve the crime before the detective does at the conclusion of the program. The difference lies in the way each type of detective goes about doing his work: the classical detectives view crime as an intellectual puzzle to be approached with scientific detachment and objectivity whereas the hard-boiled detectives have a perspective that includes a sociological dimension. They employ strategies that incorporate personal experience and readings that assess the personality of both perpetrator and victim. Early critics and writers like R. Austin Freeman have voiced the ethos of classical detective fiction in such scientific terms as "an argument conducted under the guise of fiction" and presented its structure as a series of categories related to scientific enquiry, notably "the statement of the problem," "production of data," "discovery," and finally "proof of solution."[2]

As stated above, in *Numb3rs*, Scott extends this idea that detective fiction is based on scientific rationalism by structuring the plot of each episode on mathematical problem-solving and patterning. The ambivalent nature of detective fiction itself is represented by the two brothers: the FBI agent who is the traditional main character of police procedural fiction, allied with the hard-boiled detective and amateur Sherlock Holmes figure. The activity and physical presence of Don contrast the cerebral inclination of Charlie. The difference in approach between classical detective fiction and hard-boiled fiction lies in this philosophical contrast: whereas the classical form relies heavily on intellect and logic to solve the crime in a manner made famous by the Holmesian methods of deduction and Hercule Poirot's "little grey cells," hard-boiled detective fiction employs Philip Marlowe's knight errant approach and an instinctive knowledge of the crime scene to progress to the mystery's solution. In essence, where the former uses knowledge in the form of science and logical deduction, the latter employs instinctive and experiential knowledge of the milieu and its participants. This dichotomy both informs and affects the way the crime is solved. Scott uses the differing ends of the spectrum of detective fiction within *Numb3rs* to comment on both the use of scientific rationalism in contemporary crime drama, and also the current use of visual effects in popular television shows such as *CSI: Crime Scene Investigation* to reinforce this approach.

The Eppes brothers self-reflexively relate to the Scott brothers who produced the show, in keeping with the many references throughout the series both to Ridley Scott's oeuvre and its role in popular culture generally. This includes allusions to the older Scott's films, such as the comment in the episode titled "Hardball" where David and Colby, members of Don's FBI team, are walking through the Little Tokyo area of Los Angeles and Colby comments, "Do you know what this place kind of reminds me of?" David replies, "Let me guess: *Blade Runner*?" The exchange goes on to call attention to the almost surreal Asian-ness of their surroundings, in part reminiscent of the film's setting. Colby responds, "Yeah, exactly. Do you think Ridley Scott knew what the future was going to look like?" David answers, "No idea, but Darryl Hannah made one kick-ass cyborg." Playful, self-reflexive sections like this serve to emphasize the visual approach Scott has adopted in his films, as critics like William B. Parrill have pointed out.[3] His films are visually striking, with the *mise-en-scène* often dominating to the extent that it goes beyond simply establishing an atmosphere.

In *Numb3rs* the contrast between the academic perspective of Charlie and the practical approach of Don is symbolized by both material structures and artifacts in the problem-solving process. Charlie's traditional office at tranquil Calsci College, a fictional equivalent to Caltech, is cluttered with books, wooden tables, and arcane objects such as a sundial and an abacus, whereas the high-tech FBI areas, with their constant activity, are dominated by functionality. Here the *mise-en-scène* is glass and chrome, computer screens, and technical equipment. The difference in philosophy of the two men emerges in the decor: the traditional chalkboard used by Charlie in both his university environment and his workspace at his home contrasts with the modern glass boards at the FBI, through which we view Charlie's face inscribed by the formula he is writing. If one represents an older tradition of learning, the other represents the present and future.

In his role as producer, Scott is able to control the visual presentation and the philosophy of the series to a greater extent than in his role as director of feature films. Parrill compares the influence of the production team on a film with that of Scott's as director, concluding, "The way a film is made—that is, the aspects which are privileged by its maker, whether or not he always controls them—profoundly influences the finished product."[4] Furthermore, in an interview with Harlan Kennedy where he discusses *Blade Runner*, Scott characterized the producer as the "guiding mind" of the project. About his role as director, he states, "I find the process of filming very difficult—maybe this is why I want to be a producer—because it's like trying to write a book with many hands or paint a picture with many hands."[5] This has led Scott to have, as James Clarke observes, "an active role in the development of his films" so that in his later works "he has always, unofficially to start with, operated as producer."[6] In *Numb3rs*, this unofficial role is formalized so that Scott is able to invest the show with the primary characteristics he has displayed in his feature films: a focus on the visual and awareness of the conventions of genre.

In the feature films he has directed thus far, Scott is noted for what Parrill terms his "versatility in genre films" since "Generically, *Gladiator* is a sword-and-sandal epic, *Hannibal* is a horror film, and *Black Hawk Down* is a war film, mission subdivision." The critic adds that *Hannibal* also has "gothic elements."[7] This versatility means that Scott has utilized the formulaic, even stereotypical aspects of different genres in order to interrogate and extend their reach. As Clarke explains, Scott "has found ways to reinvigorate genre material to such an extent that it redefines a given genre for a whole generation of filmgoers."[8] He does this in what is considered a "crime trilogy" by Brian J. Robb: *Someone to Watch Over Me* (1987), *Black Rain* (1989), and *Thelma & Louise* (1991), since each film draws on the traditions of classical detective fiction while being crime dramas.[9] *Blade Runner* integrates multiple genres by combining hard-boiled detective fiction, *film noir* techniques, and science fiction through its origins in Philip K. Dick's work *Do Androids Dream of Electric Sheep?* This strategy re-emerges in *Numb3rs*, where Scott incorporates the conventions associated with classical and hard-boiled detective fiction into the visual and episodic form of a television series. To this he adds the scientific curiosity and public service premise of the police procedural drama.

In this way, as is typical of Scott's films, the visual elements dominate through exaggerated settings and stylized analogy sequences; these techniques relate the series to those made familiar by *CSI* and other forensic *cum* police procedural shows. In some respects, the visual analogies which cut into the episodes with an explanatory voice-over by Charlie are only too similar to what has become known as "the *CSI* shot," prompting reviewer Brian Lowry to refer to *Numb3rs* as an amalgamation of every other popular television crime show: "the same old crime scene investigating of cold cases left unsolved without a trace."[10] For Rowen Wilken, though, this "aestheticization of information" empowers the mathematician and mathematical discourse, first non-diegetically in the voice-over and the visual representations, and then diegetically in Charlie's explanation of how this process relates to the case. According to Sue Turnbull, the drama stresses that "crimes can be solved simply by looking at the evidence as revealed through science."[11] But the visual analogies also amplify the mathematical and scientifically rationalist aspects by relating them to the everyday experience of the viewer. They unite the two elements of the theoretical model, or Charlie's perspective, with that of Don's experience of the world, and so challenge the traditional notion of detective fiction as being escapist in nature, with little relevance outside its own fictional framework.

Charlie's analogies, presented through CGI, show the embeddedness of mathematical formulae in the real world, not as an escape from it. The analogies that he uses relate to the type of events and situations he refers to in his introductory voice-overs to the series. He claims, "We all use math every day to predict weather, to tell time, to handle money." He then deploys the Socratic Method, whereby the FBI agents supply the answers to his presentation based on their experience, and then they apply his method to the case in question. This procedure sets up a structure around a mathematical problem in which the viewer must follow a set of clues to find the solution. This scientific approach makes the television crime drama a contemporary analogue to detective fiction. It positions the forensic scientist in the role of the detective. By utilizing computer-generated images, graphs, and 3D models, the show presents "a visual model of the scientist's spoken explanation" of how science can be used to solve the crime. [12]

Charlie initially offers an interpretation couched in unfamiliar and mysterious terms (to the FBI agents especially), which are then translated through the medium of analogy and the CGI visuals to make them intelligible to the layperson viewers. This is in keeping with a current spate of film and television productions whereby the forensic scientist, mathematician, or academic translates hieroglyphics, symbols, codes, and even symptoms into a pattern that relates to the crime or mystery in question. Examples include *Stargate* (1994), *A Beautiful Mind* (2001), *The Da Vinci Code* (2006), and the television series *House* (2004-2012). In *A Beautiful Mind*, for example, the mathematician John Nash's belief in himself and his abilities is ironically presented as a form of delusion. His achievements are intimately related to the social and physical impediments caused by his mental disorder. Similarly, Charlie, as his early voice-overs indicate, believes that mathematics will solve "the biggest mysteries we know." However, the series presents his views as limited, favoring the intuitive and practical approaches of his brother. This bias is evident in "Thirteen," an episode where Charlie is confronted with the more speculative disciplines of religion and philosophy whose specialists he dismisses as "the bit of fluff." The series refers to the mysticism inherent in giving mathematical models and formulae obscure names by simplifying them and showing how they appear in real life. The Fibonacci Sequence thus becomes the pattern made by the petals of a flower, the Heisenberg Uncertainty Principle emerges in the well-known game Minesweeper, and the Socratic Method arrives at a logical conclusion through swift question-and-answer relays between two or more people. All of these academic constructs are now knowable and familiar; as Charlie (the ironic Pythagorean mystic here) explains, "Math is nature's language . . . its method of communicating directly with us. Everything is numbers."

That everything can be described as "numbers" supplies a metaphor for the way that, in Charlie's view, logic and deductive reasoning can *always* be used to solve mysteries such as crimes. In a sense, this is a reductive process which diminishes the complexity of human behavior to mathematical formulae. But it also offers the further metaphor that relates numbers to the wider mysteries of the universe because they constitute "nature's language." The search for justice exemplified by Philip Marlowe and Sam Spade becomes a search for meaning in human behavior. It offers a contrast to the recent extension of crime drama into scientific areas of forensic investigation in the manner of the *CSI* series, since this show's formula is based less upon the reason for the crime than the actions involved in its execution. Martha Gever argues, "*CSI* plots do not revolve around efforts to understand the motives of those who commit crimes" at all. [13] Further, because the main characters in these shows are scientists, "These protagonists care more about the application of scientific technologies to generate and organize knowledge than crime and punishment."[14] As a result, "the search for truth has been relocated . . . from reading minds to reading bodies."[15] Because *CSI*'s mantra is "The evidence doesn't lie," a clear emphasis lies on forensic methods and their assumed objectivity. As Wilken points out, "[S]cience and a (re)turn to and strong reinvestment in scientific rationalism (and its associated computational and representational technologies) is central to the resolution of crime" in shows such as *Numb3rs* and *CSI*.[16]

In a series such as *CSI* especially, the process of the crime is the focus instead of the meaning of or motive for it, such that E. B. Harrington considers the victim's importance to be lesser than that of the crime scene. His or her body "is read as a clue through scientific discourse that emphasizes the body as the object of enquiry."[17] This idea emerges in *Numb3rs* when Charlie becomes so immersed in the pattern of crime that he reduces it to a set of patterns and diminishes the human element. Don is able to present an intuitive solution based on his feelings about the criminal's response and behavior; thus, as a crime fighter who serves the people, he reinstates the humanity of the victim. Recalling the detective genre, he is the Watson who stands apart from pure scientific inquiry, unable to emulate Holmes in terms of deductive reasoning but able to see the human face of the crime and the criminal. According to the mathematician Paul J. Campbell, "The series intends to highlight different ways of thinking of the two brothers: 'highly ordered logical intuition' (FBI agent) vs. 'logic and evidence' (mathematician)."[18] In essence, Don Eppes, as the hard-boiled detective, is the hero who is, in Raymond Chandler's words, "a man of honor—by instinct, by inevitability, without thought of it, and certainly without saying it."[19] This is exemplified in the episode titled "Black Swan" when Don sends members of his team to interview a seemingly arbitrary bystander loitering near a crime scene. When, against all appearances, the man proves to be involved in the crime, David asks, "What tipped you off?" Don's reply of, "Don't know, something about him" emphasizes that intuition is knowledge based on experience or, as Larry Fleinhart suggests in an intercut scene, "Intuition is simply your rational mind finding a way of talking to you."

Again in contrast to his academic brother, Don is immersed in the practicalities of everyday life. In "Pandora's Box," an episode where the family home is robbed, Charlie devises a complex set of algorithms to recover the stolen goods, and while he is in the midst of this, Don arrives to return the items, having simply traced a missing laptop by means of the GPS tracker built into it. Ironically, while Charlie is similar to the Poirot character in Christie's fiction (dependent on his brain's "little grey cells"), Don is more like Miss Marple. This elderly detective, as Stephen Knight points out, bases her solution on her previous experiences, relating each fresh instance of crime to her knowledge of human behavior.[20] Like her, Don is attuned to the world around him; unlike Charlie, he is able to adjust to it and judge accordingly.

Don is practical, both in his sense of perspective toward the crimes and their solutions and his awareness that some aspects of life are inherently too complex to be summed up and resolved easily. As such, we learn that sometimes everything is *not* numbers; the knight errant has to walk away, not in accordance with the law, but in accordance with his personal code of honor and of justice. This is what we might call the law of the right, not the law of the land or of scientific rationalism. As a result of this choice, Don defies the laws of the FBI when they interfere with his personal code of ethics. In "Two Daughters," where a member of his team, Megan, has been kidnapped, Don allows the interrogation and torture of one of the members of the group who has taken her in order to gain information leading to her release. He does this by proxy: at no stage does the detective interact with the prisoner on this level, but he gives his permission for the abuse to occur. The succinct statement by the interrogating police officer—"If he knew anything, he would have told me"—is a damning admission to the off-screen torture Don has sanctioned in opposition to the FBI code of conduct. This episode is linked to the later "One Hour" in which Don reveals his feelings about his behavior as well as the motivations for it to a therapist. At this time, he divulges his awareness of complete responsibility for the team; emulating the hard-boiled detective's duty to his client, Don tries to protect all within his jurisdiction. The irony in this episode is that while Don is explaining to his therapist, "I don't have to trust *them*; it's their job to trust *me,*" the team is completing a complicated kidnapping case without him. His therapist points out that his responsibility is not to nurture and provide constant supervision of his team so much as ensure that they can operate efficiently on their own. His unwillingness to do this is due to his feelings of insecurity; as the therapist tells Don, "You're not worried that they can't get along without you: you're worried that they can."

As the series progresses, Scott does draw the divergent methodologies and perspectives of the two brothers closer so that Don becomes more intellectual in his approach. More tellingly, Charlie also becomes better attuned to human nature and less distanced from others. At the outset, even while Charlie explains how his models or formulae relate to the real world, it is all still theoretical. He emphasizes mathematical principles, expecting them to present an unvarying pattern; he discounts human behavior as variable and individual in nature. This deficiency is shown in "Uncertainty Principle" when Charlie confidently expects to predict the behavior of a group of bank robbers based on their previous *modus operandi*. According to his friend, the physicist Dr. Larry Fleinhart, he is confusing "the ability to predict with the ability to control." But beyond this, critic Kristen Miller feels that the episode is really demonstrating that "There are positives to using science, math and [Charlie's] problem-solving abilities . . . but it is arrogant to believe that he can really, accurately predict human behaviour."[21] Charlie's confidence is based on the accuracy of his application of the data to the model used and the reliability of the model itself. Unfortunately, he did not take into account other, more human variables, such as the effect the FBI intervention had on the previous robbery. First, in each non-violent case, there had been no police presence to hinder their actions; second, there were other, unseen accomplices at the robbery scene ready to become violent if necessary. This misreading had the effect of causing Don and fellow agents to become involved in a gun battle near the bank. One agent is killed and Don is injured. Charlie's lack of knowledge of these other influences is analogous to his lack of knowledge of human behavior generally.

Charlie's characterization is in keeping with media stereotypes of mathematicians and scientists—even academics generally—as divorced from the real world, knowing nothing of human nature, and narrowly immersed in their own fields of expertise. His reaction to the traumatic events he feels he has caused, or at least should have warned Don about, is to retreat into an area in which he feels comfortable: mathematics. He abandons the FBI case only to start work on a notoriously insoluble math problem, P versus NP, in the same manner (as the viewer learns) he worked on the problem during the last months of his mother's struggle with terminal cancer. Clearly, the program is sending the message that the intellectual is incapable of coping with reality, adopting instead the approach that if he can solve an insoluble problem in mathematics, he will be able to solve equally impossible problems in real life. Part of the charm of *Numb3rs*, then, is that the viewer is allowed access to what was previously viewed as unknowable or arcane knowledge through the visual analogies presented in each episode; they are also able to feel superior to the limited genius figure, depicted as lacking in real-life skills and caught within a sometimes helpless universe of complex but impractical knowledge.

Ironically, while mathematics and the sciences are depicted as having limitless potential to solve crimes and, by extension, the problems of humanity, the mathematicians who possess this knowledge emerge as flawed through their unquestioning faith in their respective disciplines. Charlie refuses to believe in any aspect of life not open to empirical testing; this bias is evident in the episode "Magic Show" which features the real-life illusionist Penn Gillette. The inclusion of this figure, one who crosses the boundaries of the real and fictional worlds, contributes to the self-referential aspect of the series. Television itself requires a willingness on the part of the viewer to see past a series of pixels on a screen and be receptive to its representation of reality. But in this episode, Charlie denies the legitimacy of illusion as an art form, seeing it only as a contrivance of strings and wires that conform to the laws of mathematics and physics. Even though the magic is not offered as anything but an illusion and a form of art, Charlie nevertheless is incapable of entering into that suspension of disbelief necessary to find appreciation and wonder in a magic act. He sees illusions as a degradation of mathematical and scientific principles and views only the physics used in the construction of the trick and the mathematics behind the act. The artistry of the performance itself is lost on him. His only acknowledgment of its essential beauty is by a smile at the conclusion of the episode when Amida, his fellow mathematician and girlfriend, re-creates the act as it was supposed to be performed with the words, "This is what I see in magic" as she is suspended mid-air in a fantasy atmosphere of billowing flower petals.

His inability to suspend disbelief and transcend the mechanics of science to appreciate magic as art again underscores the idea that geniuses are both distanced from the real world and incapable of operating within it; as a result, mathematical ability is often simplistically associated with autism, various other mental conditions, and the idiot savant figure. "Scan Man" depicts a character with a *Rain Man* type of autism displaying exceptional giftedness in mathematics, such as being able to count the number of paper clips up-ended on a table at a glance. In conjunction, the restrictions of this character in terms of everyday living are revealed through his inability to change or adapt to a new environment, even to the form and arrangement of his food. That Charlie's friend Larry Fleinhart displays similar traits as those associated in the public mind with Asperger's Syndrome (such as only eating white food) is indicative of the stereotypes commonly found in the literary presentation of those with above-normal mathematical abilities.

But while both characters display a set of behaviors made familiar by films such as *Rain Man* (1988), Charlie represents the mathematician staunchly in favor of scientific rationalism, while his colleague Larry regards knowledge of the physical cosmos as a complete worldview. *Numb3rs* is dominated by contrasts: between numbers and numerology, science and pseudo-science, scientific rationalism and non-scientific beliefs. But this is not to imply that non-scientific beliefs are reduced to the same questionable level as the divination tool of numerology and other practices deemed charlatanry and pseudo-science: through cosmologist Larry, the scientific and non-scientific beliefs are not shown to be mutually exclusive, and the series challenges the concept that scientific rationalism is inherently opposed to non-scientific beliefs. In "Magic Show," for example, Larry explains to Don, "My own quest for God has always been inextricably interlinked with my own work," and throughout the series, the former seeks a system of belief that encompasses both science and religion. This is displayed in the episode "Atomic No. 33," in which members of a church refuse to receive medical aid on religious grounds. Larry is initially incensed, feeling that they are refusing to accept the validity of science as being part of a divine pattern. He later realizes that because of his anger at their stance, he is equally denying the validity of their beliefs.

A similar inversion of perspectives occurs in the episode "Thirteen," where Charlie is positioned similarly to the FBI agents and viewers when he is given unfamiliar, arcane information by an expert in religion and philosophy. Ironically he scoffs at the same type of patterning process that he himself applies because it comes from what he considers a non-authentic source. When Al, the religion and philosophy expert, is consulted about the actions of a serial killer who chooses his victims by a mixture of Christian symbolism and numerology, Charlie is openly scornful, stating he cannot accept that "numbers are spiritual and magical and mystical." Larry points out, "Whatever system he is using obviously means something to him." In turn, Al challenges Charlie, since he is able to see meaning in a Fibonacci Sequence while still denying the validity of any other spiritual perspective. She states, "To understand why we're here takes more than scientific enquiry." Larry quotes the words of St. Augustine—"Numbers are the universal language offered by the deity to humans as confirmation of the truth" —as a cautionary statement meant to prevent Charlie from viewing mathematics and the sciences as higher-order knowledge that is beyond both the spiritual grasp and flawed reality of humanity.

In *Numb3rs*, Scott amalgamates the form of the police procedural with the crime drama to represent an on-screen equivalent of the detective genre: highly visual, based on scientific rationalism, and depicting science as yet another belief system that provides a comforting sense of security for the viewer. Rather than having the detective solve the case, a forensic scientist or mathematician provides the solution to the crime. In doing so, the characters' actions imply there is a pattern to the universe that only they are able to see and that they need to interpret for others. Here, the scientist functions in the same role as a priest or the police officer in more typical dramas of the genre. Ultimately, the scientific, rationalist view provides a comforting, escapist formula for the viewer, since it implies that there is a pattern to every event. Since all events can be qualified and formulated, they can also be predicted. Unlike the traditional view that detective fiction provides an escape by allowing the viewers or readers to immerse themselves in a fantasy world divorced from reality, this form relates strongly to everyday life. Yet it offers an equally escapist perspective that suggests science can solve all problems. Rarely is Charlie at a loss for a formula or model. This glibness brings forth the comforting—if unrealistic—idea that math and science must always have solutions to real world problems.

The opening credits of *Numb3rs* feature a voice-over by Charlie Eppes which exalts the capacity of mathematics to "solve the biggest mysteries we know." The paradoxical aspect of "mysteries" being based on knowledge rather than beliefs, and their being able to be solved by the application of scientific rationalism mirrors the contrasts presented throughout the series itself. This relationship between the classical detective story and rationalism is best described by John G. Cawelti in his typology of literary formulae: "Pursued as an end in itself the search for hidden secrets is primarily an intellectual, reasoning activity" and so "the actual narrative of a mystery involves the isolation of clues, the making of deductions from these clues, and the attempt to place the various clues in their rational place in a complete scheme of cause and effect."[22] Just as Ridley Scott has exemplified, parodied, and expanded such genres as *film noir* and historical epic in his films, the more prolonged expository potential of the television series allows him to interrogate the detective genre further, making its basis in contrasts, ambiguities, and the problematic dichotomy between beliefs and knowledge an ongoing platform for discussion and scrutiny.

NOTES

1. John G. Cawelti, *Adventure, Mystery, and Romance: Formula Stories as Art and Popular Culture* (Chicago: University of Chicago Press, 1976).

2. R. Austin Freeman, "The Art of the Detective Story," in *The Art of the Mystery Story: A Collection of Critical Essays*, ed. Howard Haycraft (New York: Simon and Schuster, 1946), 7-17.

3. William Parrill, *Ridley Scott: A Critical Filmography* (Jefferson, NC: McFarland, 2011).

4. Ibid., 5.

5. Harlan Kennedy, "21st Century Nervous Breakdown," *Film Comment* 8, no. 14 (July/August 1982): 68.

6. James Clarke, *Ridley Scott* (London: Virgin Books, 2002), 244.

7. Parrill, *Ridley Scott,* 15.

8. Clarke, *Ridley Scott,* 5.

9. Brian J. Robb, *Ridley Scott* (Harpenden, UK: Pocket Essentials, 2001).

10. Brian Lowry, "Cop Formula Gets Smart," *Variety* January 17, 2005, accessed July 21, 2012, http://go.galegroup.com.ezproxy.une.edu.au/ps/i.do?id=GALE%7CA127623476&v=2.1&u=dixson&it=r&p=PPFA&sw=w.

11. Rowen Wilken, "Fantasies of Control: *Numb3rs*, Scientific Rationalism, and the Management of Everyday Security Risks," *Continuum: Journal of Media and Cultural Studies* 25, no. 2 (April 2011): 207. Sue Turnbull, "The Hook and the Look: *CSI* and the Aesthetics of the Television Crime Series," in *Reading* CSI: *Crime TV Under the Microscope*, ed. Michael Allen (New York: I. B. Taurus, 2007), 32.

12. Elke Weismann and Karen Boyle, "Evidence of Things Unseen: The Pornographic Aesthetic and the Search for Truth in *CSI*," in *Reading* CSI: *Crime TV Under the Microscope*, ed. Michael Allen (New York: I. B. Taurus, 2007), 94.

13. Martha Gever, "The Spectacle of Crime, Digitized: *CSI: Crime Scene Investigation* and Social Anatomy," *European Journal of Cultural Studies* 8, no. 44 (2005): 454.

14. Ibid., 447.

15. Ibid., 455.

16. Wilken, "Fantasies of Control," 203.

17. E. B. Harrington, "Nation, Identity and the Fascination with Forensic Science in Sherlock Holmes and *CSI*," *International Journal of Cultural Studies* 10, no. 3 (2007): 373.

18. Paul J. Campbell, "Numb3rs," *Mathematics Magazine* 79, no.1 (February 2006): 75.

19. Raymond Chandler, "The Simple Art of Murder," *The Atlantic Monthly*, November 1945.

20. Stephen Knight, "Radical Thrillers," in *Watching the Detectives: Essays on Crime Fiction*, ed. Ian A. Bell and Graham Daldry (London: Macmillan, 1990), 176.

21. Kristen Miller, "From Fears of Entropy to Comfort in Chaos: *Arcadia, The Wasteland, Numb3rs* and Man's Relationship with Science," *Bulletin of Science, Technology and Society* 27, no.1 (February 2007): 90.

22. Cawelti, *Adventure, Mystery, and Romance,* 43.

REFERENCES

Allen, Michael, ed. *Reading CSI: Crime TV Under the Microscope.* New York: I. B. Taurus, 2007.

Bell, Ian A., and Graham Daldry, ed. *Watching the Detectives: Essays on Crime Fiction.* London: Macmillan, 1990.

Cawelti, John G. *Adventure, Mystery, and Romance: Formula Stories as Art and Popular Culture.* Chicago: University of Chicago Press, 1976.

Clarke, James. *Ridley Scott.* London: Virgin Books, 2002.

Freeman, R. Austin. "The Art of the Detective Story." In *The Art of the Mystery Story: A Collection of Critical Essays*, edited by Howard Haycraft, 7-17. New York: Simon and Schuster, 1946.

Gever, Martha. "The Spectacle of Crime, Digitized: *CSI: Crime Scene Investigation* and Social Anatomy." *European Journal of Cultural Studies* 8, no. 44 (2005): 445-463.

Harrington, E. B. "Nation, Identity and the Fascination with Forensic Science in Sherlock Holmes and *CSI.*" *International Journal of Cultural Studies* 10, no. 3 (2007): 365-382.

Haycraft, Howard, ed. *The Art of the Mystery Story: A Collection of Critical Essays.* New York: Simon and Schuster, 1946.

Kennedy, Harlan. "21st Century Nervous Breakdown." *Film Comment* 8, no.14 (July/August 1982): 64-68.

Knight, Stephen. "Radical Thrillers." In *Watching the Detectives: Essays on Crime Fiction*, edited by Ian A. Bell and Graham Daldry, 172-186. London: Macmillan, 1990.

Lowry, Brian. "Cop Formula Gets Smart." *Variety*, January 17, 2005, accessed July 21, 2012, http://go.galegroup.com.ezproxy.une.edu.au/ps/i.do?id=GALE%7CA127623476&v=2.1& u=dixson&it=r&p=PPFA&sw=w.

Miller, Kristen. "From Fears of Entropy to Comfort in Chaos: *Arcadia, The Waste Land, Numb3rs* and Man's Relationship with Science." *Bulletin of Science, Technology and Society* 27, no. 1 (February 2007): 81-94.

Parrill, William B. *Ridley Scott: A Critical Filmography.* Jefferson, NC: McFarland, 2011.

Robb, Brian J. *Ridley Scott.* Harpenden, UK: Pocket Essentials, 2001.

Sklar, Jessica K., and Elizabeth S. Sklar, ed. *Mathematics in Popular Culture: Essays on Appearances in Film, Fiction, Games, Television and Other Media.* Jefferson, NC: McFarland, 2012.

Turnbull, Sue. "The Hook and the Look: *CSI* and the Aesthetics of the Television Crime Series." In *Reading* CSI: *Crime TV Under the Microscope*, edited by Michael Allen, 15-32. New York: I. B. Taurus, 2007.

Weismann, Elke, and Karen Boyle. "Evidence of Things Unseen: The Pornographic Aesthetic and the Search for Truth in *CSI.*" In *Reading* CSI: *Crime TV Under the Microscope*, edited by Michael Allen, 90-102. New York: I. B. Taurus, 2007.

Wilken, Rowen. "Fantasies of Control: *Numb3rs*, Scientific Rationalism, and the Management of Everyday Security Risks." *Continuum: Journal of Media and Cultural Studies* 25, no. 2 (April 2011): 201-211.

Chapter Ten

Celebrating Historical Accuracy in *The Duellists*

Carl Sobocinski

The duel has been a common feature of action-adventure type films through-out motion picture history. They frequently accompany a fantastic plotline and are replete with exaggerated fight sequences. Scenes from *The Three Musketeers* and *The Mark of Zorro,* in their various cinematic incarnations since the first versions from the 1920s starring Douglas Fairbanks, invariably come to mind. In contrast to these standard and often unrealistic portrayals is the *The Duellists* (1977), Ridley Scott's first feature film. The plot is that of two officers of the French army who fight a protracted duel which lasts over fifteen years before it is finally resolved. Despite ongoing critical praise, *The Duellists* did not elicit much popular acclaim and is not well known. Para-doxically, its conscientious regard for accuracy may be a great reason for this, in that a proficient knowledge of the historical period is essential for understanding and appreciating this well-crafted film.

The Duellists's overall historic accuracy far outshines that of the block-buster *Gladiator* (2000), which, despite its exciting story and undeniable spectacle, is often weak historically. In *The Duellists,* scenes and costumes display a high degree of detail; as well, the film's setting (amidst specific events of the Napoleonic Wars), along with the characterization of actual historical individuals, correspond closely to fact. Furthermore, the duels themselves are grueling, gritty, and highly realistic. As such, the film is a welcome change from many period productions which too often present the facts and events incorrectly, or have their characters behaving in highly anachronistic ways.

The Duellists is set during the French Revolutionary and Napoleonic Wars, which occupied Europe from the early 1790s through Napoleon Bonaparte's final defeat in 1815. Napoleon, who rose from obscurity during the Revolutionary Wars of the 1790s, took advantage of the political and social disruptions of the times and managed to seize power in France by 1799. In 1804 he declared himself Emperor of the French, and following a series of stunning victories, came to dominate Western Europe by 1807. Peace was not at hand, however, for his restive conquests chafed under his often heavy-handed rule. Napoleon increasingly found himself at war to maintain his power. A disastrous invasion of Russia in 1812 irrevocably damaged his empire, and by 1814, he was defeated by a coalition of Prussians, Russians, Austrians, British, and sundry lesser powers. Forced into abdication and exile, Napoleon managed to return to France early in 1815, and for a period referred to as the "Hundred Days," attempted to rebuild his power before meeting defeat at the Battle of Waterloo. The Napoleonic Period ended with his final exile to the remote island of Saint Helena in the south Atlantic, and France returned to monarchy under the restored Bourbon king Louis XVIII.

The events of *The Duellists* are intimately connected to this historic setting. The narrative begins in 1800 by introducing its protagonists, Gabriel Florian Feraud (Harvey Keitel) and Armand D'Hubert (Keith Carradine), both cavalry officers in Napoleon's army. During one of the periodic lulls in warfare, they are assigned to garrison duty in the city of Strasbourg. Feraud has a far-reaching reputation as a hot-headed, easily offended Gascon who repeatedly initiates and fights duels despite an official prohibition.[1] After one such duel in which he seriously wounds the nephew of Strasbourg's mayor, his commanding general orders his arrest. By simple chance, this duty falls to D'Hubert. Finding Feraud at the *salon* of one of Strasbourg's leading ladies, D'Hubert quickly encounters the man's crescendo of anger and finds himself challenged to a duel on the spot. D'Hubert repeatedly and gently attempts to avoid conflict, but Feraud's belligerence and the embarrassing prospect of being chased down the street at the point of Feraud's sword induce D'Hubert to accept the duel as inevitable. The ensuing fight ends as a draw with both men injured and unable to continue.

The concept and rationale of dueling are probably reasons for *The Duellists*'s lack of popular appreciation. The concept of public honor in early-nineteenth-century Europe and the perceived need to fight to defend it are often lost on the modern audience, thus obscuring the essential theme of the film. Honor, in this context, was largely a matter of public image and reputation. In the twenty-first century, fighting for honor does persist in milieus such as criminal gangs or in clichéd romantic contexts. But, two centuries ago, it was an expected practice for men in public life, among them politicians and career soldiers. Insults, real or perceived, were often considered legitimate causes for a duel. The main point of the duel was to obtain "satisfaction," which did not necessarily mean the death of either combatant.

The process of dueling was sometimes detailed and protracted. A man would take offense at another's actions or words, resulting in the demand for an apology. If it was made and the offended party found it acceptable, the conflict would end there. If no apology was forthcoming, or the one given was found unacceptable, a challenge to fight ensued. The challenged party usually had the choice of weapons, generally pistols or swords. The challenger might announce that he had attained "satisfaction" by wounding his opponent, or by his opponent simply demonstrating his courage by a willingness to fight. In such cases, both men would emerge with their public honor intact. Failure to respond to a challenge or a demonstration of cowardice during the fight would ruin a man's reputation and would forever hinder his career aspirations. In serious cases, as with an impassioned and often irrational Feraud, death was the only means to attain satisfaction.

These procedures were prescriptions laid out in a body of regulations known as the "Dueling Code"; specifications varied between countries. It was often a body of oral traditions passed on from group to group, but in one famous instance, it was published in written form.[2] Elements of the Code appear throughout *The Duellists*, as D'Hubert attempts to avoid a fight while Feraud insists on pursuing it. After their initial confrontation ends in a draw, the beleaguered D'Hubert consults with fellow officers as to the details of the Code, endeavoring to avoid further conflict. He exploits such principles as the prohibition of duels between higher and lower military ranks, or during times of war when national conflict takes precedence over personal battles. Thus, as Feraud will accept no satisfaction other than D'Hubert's death, and as each duel ends with no clear resolution, the conflict extends over more than fifteen years, resumed whenever the protagonists are promoted to equal rank and no war demands their mutual attention.

The depiction of the various duels themselves is one of the notable features of this film. The settings are gritty and dirty, as befits nineteenth-century French army life. Feraud and D'Hubert confront each other cautiously, neither making any rash initial move which might make them vulnerable. The fencing postures and positions were based on actual nineteenth-century techniques and without the flamboyant choreographed fights of classic swashbuckler films. During one particular duel, Feraud and D'Hubert fail to injure each other seriously enough to end the fight. Instead, they continue until they collapse from exhaustion, leaving their seconds to intervene and declare the duel yet another draw.[3] No slashing at candles, no Gene Kelly leaping about effortlessly as if borne on wings,[4] this is just two men staggering to no resolution; there are no sounds other than the clashing of swords and the men rasping from fatigue.

Background sound effects and music provide more features which give *The Duellists* a high degree of realism. The musical score is frequently subdued, present only during moments with no dialogue in the service of creating transitions between scenes. More frequently, the film's background sounds are part of the scene itself, such as tavern musicians and bar-room clatter, rain and wind, or most striking, the howling winter storms during the French retreat from Russia. Almost all of the duels have no sounds other than what the participants themselves experience. One exception is a duel fought on horseback (as befits cavalry officers), during which the incidental music enhances D'Hubert's introspection of his and Feraud's intertwined fates as the adversaries once again fight to a draw. Such authentic sounds forge a stark contrast to traditional swashbuckler films where fights are frequently set to stirring music and few natural sounds are heard. If a viewer were expecting a more routine action-adventure film with the conventionally exaggerated fight scenes and dramatic background music, *The Duellists* might appear anomalous. This, along with the intricate historical setting, could make the film less appealing to viewers unfamiliar with such details.

While not strictly a historical film, the surrounding historical events further enhance *The Duellists*'s authenticity.[5] Specific events and places during the Napoleonic period are integral to the work, such as the garrison camps at Strasbourg and Lubeck, the disastrous retreat from Russia, Napoleon's exile to Elba (and his subsequent escape), and the restored Bourbon monarchy. Accurate references to these events and the film's characters' interactions during them provide yet another welcome contrast to the frequent blunders of many such period films. For instance, of particular importance to the conclusion of *The Duellists* are the events of 1814-1815. Following military defeat, Napoleon abdicated in 1814 and was exiled to the Mediterranean island of Elba. The younger brother of the executed Louis XVI became King Louis XVIII. But early in 1815, Napoleon escaped from Elba and returned to France to reclaim power. Quickly gaining the support of many of his former officers and staff, the former leader made a final desperate attempt to re-establish his empire, meeting defeat at Waterloo roughly one hundred days after his return. Without awareness of these developments, *The Duellists*'s conclusion may appear baffling or abrupt.

Feraud and D'Hubert became inextricably entangled in these events. Similar to many in France, D'Hubert has lost his revolutionary fervor and increasingly leans toward the restored monarchy. He refuses the call to rejoin Napoleon during the Hundred Days. In contrast, Feraud enthusiastically rallies after the former leader. After Waterloo, however, the restored monarchy faces the dilemma of how to deal with the ardent Bonapartists who remain in France. Feraud is proscribed and faces execution as an enemy of the state.

At this point Joseph Fouché appears, the only major historical figure portrayed in the film. Fouché's career ran the gamut of the French Revolution, from a seat on the Revolutionary Convention which sentenced Louis XVI and Marie Antoinette to death, to his personal actions suppressing counter-revolutionaries during the ensuing civil war in France, thence to Napoleon's own police force as its chief. In *The Duellists* Fouché appears as the chief of police under the Bourbon king Louis XVIII, a portrayal which is perfectly accurate in terms of actual historical record.

Learning of Feraud's proscription and having accepted a commission in the king's army, D'Hubert manages to meet with Fouché to obtain Feraud's parole, actions of which Feraud is unaware. D'Hubert thus returns to his new career as a royalist officer, while Feraud avoids prison and execution but remains under police surveillance. In this setting, the duel reaches its final phase when Feraud learns about D'Hubert's whereabouts and sends two seconds to reissue the challenge. D'Hubert's benevolence to Feraud may appear confusing. An innocent party through the entire story, D'Hubert bowed to social convention and persisted in the duel, however much he wanted to avoid it. But, as comrades-in-arms through many of Napoleon's campaigns, who at one point had fought side by side during the retreat from Russia, D'Hubert has come to feel some sympathy for his adversary. And, as unwelcome as he finds the duel's resumption, he refrains from demanding Feraud's arrest, which he could have easily done. This would not have impugned his public honor, as D'Hubert was a respected officer of the royal army and Feraud was legally a criminal who had narrowly escaped execution. But, as duels are considered private matters outside the jurisdiction of the state, the concept of honor which drove Feraud's actions through most of the Napoleonic wars has come to bind D'Hubert as well.

According to most accepted dueling codes, the challenged party has much control over the choice of weapons and the details of the duel. In some traditions, the duel could be fought in whatever manner to which the adversaries agreed. As such, D'Hubert prescribed two pistols for each duelist and expanded the field to a wooded area in which both men would stalk each other.[6] D'Hubert manages to trick Feraud into firing his two shots harmlessly. Thus having his long-time enemy at his mercy, D'Hubert refrains from killing him. Instead, he relates the story of how he has come to control Feraud's own destiny, from arranging his parole from Fouché's police to his domination of the final duel. Accepting D'Hubert's decisive victory, Feraud finally drops the cause and retires into obscurity as a wrecked Bonapartist indebted to his former enemy.

This seemingly inconclusive ending may be another reason for the film's dearth of public appeal. Accustomed to more predictable plots where the hero dispatches his rival in the final scene, a modern viewer may well emerge from the film baffled at why D'Hubert would spare the man who disrupted so much of his life for fifteen years (that is, if he or she is not already confused by D'Hubert's petition to Fouché to grant Feraud amnesty). Again, the answer lies in nineteenth-century codes of honor. Through various chances, their previous duels ended in draws. As such, Feraud never felt that he had received satisfaction, and thus continued his challenges. Despite their disagreement and personal dislike for each other, D'Hubert's victory in the final confrontation was so clear that Feraud could not dispute it. However unpleasant his personality was, Feraud found himself compelled to accept the results, pressured especially by his sense of honor. Thus the duel finally ends.

It would be easy to lay full blame on Feraud for the excessively protracted nature of their exchange, yet D'Hubert's own stake in the social values of public honor plays almost as great a part. He never seems to have considered other paths to avoid the fights. The duel first began after Feraud took personal insult when D'Hubert came to arrest him. Yet D'Hubert was not acting for himself; he was merely carrying out orders from his superior. If Feraud had resisted, D'Hubert would have been justified in using force, not to defend his honor but as a means of fulfilling his duty. Disputes of honor generally arose from personal interactions like insults, so D'Hubert's official duties might have shielded him from accepting Feraud's challenge. Later, D'Hubert's own commander orders him to refrain from dueling, yet he persists, fearing that he might be perceived as taking refuge behind his superior rather than facing his opponent.

D'Hubert never seriously considers any of these options. This is very much in keeping with the values of the times. Men frequently felt that they had the right to manage their own affairs even if it meant fighting to the death, regardless of whatever legal prohibitions were in place. Ironically, defiance of official edicts often enhanced a man's public image in that he regarded his personal honor as important enough to supersede the law. D'Hubert's own comments on his predicament illustrate the bind that codes of honor can bring. As he explained to his commanding officer, refusal to face Feraud might have tarnished his public image and could well have resulted in even more challenges from others. Practically speaking, he chose to fight one concrete duel instead of several hypothetical ones.

The characters Feraud and D'Hubert personify revolutionary and Napoleonic France in many ways. The film begins just after Napoleon has taken control of the revolution and had started to mold the environment to enhance his power. France was still officially a republic although Napoleon was the dominant leader. At this time, both men were officers of a republican army whose duty was to defend their country and preserve its revolutionary advances. As the revolutionary republic transformed into the Napoleonic Empire, Feraud transferred his political fervor to Napoleon's rising cult of personality, whereas D'Hubert remained more loyal to his duty than to the personhood of his leader. This was one point which Feraud later launched at D'Hubert as an accusation, that "he never loved the Emperor." By the end of the story when Napoleon has fallen, D'Hubert and many others in France readily transferred their loyalties to the returned Bourbon monarchy. Feraud, in contrast, represents the revolutionaries and Bonapartists who refused to adapt to the times; they instead nurtured their memories of past glory in desperate hope for a Napoleonic restoration.

Contrary as it may seem at first glance, the concept of dueling itself and its persistence through the remainder of the nineteenth century are evidence of changing social values in France. Dueling originated in medieval customs of trial by combat and the earlier tribal customs of families and individuals personally dealing with their affairs rather than relying on the jurisdiction of the state. As such, in earlier centuries, dueling was a custom only of the aristocratic classes; lower classes were considered too devoid of honor to appreciate the nuances of individual combat. But, as the French Revolution had eliminated hereditary social orders, any man thus felt himself capable of maintaining his honor by force of arms.[7] Although Feraud's and D'Hubert's respective social classes are not clearly explained, their ability to rise to high ranks in Napoleon's army was one result of greater social equality in post-revolutionary France. Earlier generations would have encountered many more restrictions based on social status.[8]

These concepts of social orders would have been familiar to the readers of Joseph Conrad, whose novella *The Duel* (1908) was the basis for Scott's film. Conrad, who is better known for his novels *Heart of Darkness* (1899) and *Lord Jim* (1900), published *The Duel* in a collection entitled *A Set of Six*. Early twentieth-century society, particularly Conrad's Britain, would have been very familiar with the principles of public honor which dominate the story, even though dueling itself barely persisted at that time. And, unlike the American audience of the 1970s, a British reader in 1908 would have found the Napoleonic Wars a very familiar and understandable setting. Napoleonic battles were common subjects in public school history, and many French and British army officers still perceived combat in terms of fixed bayonets and cavalry charges.

Scott's interpretation of Conrad's *The Duel* is highly faithful to the original. The film made very few alterations from the received plot, and the ones made are of little consequence. In one instance, the Conrad story has D'Hubert willing to rally himself in support of Napoleon during the Hundred Days but unable to mount his horse due to wounds suffered during Napoleon's earlier campaigns. The film version has him deliberately refuse the call to Napoleon and instead, he maintains his new allegiance to the restored monarchy. Another minor change is that in the film, D'Hubert was married and his young wife pregnant just as he met his final confrontation with Feraud; in the original story, D'Hubert was not married until after the duel was resolved. These changes are so minor that they warrant little criticism, although the latter scenario suggests that the stakes are higher given that a child might lose its father (and a wife her husband) if D'Hubert were to be vanquished once and for all.

One more fascinating detail in terms of adaptation is that Conrad's story may have been inspired by actual historic events experienced by an individual named François Fournier-Sarlovèze, a minor general during the Napoleonic Wars. In his biographical series on Napoleonic officers, retired French general Charles A. Thoumas recounted a story of Fournier-Sarlovèze having fought a protracted duel over nineteen years against another officer he refers to only as "Dupont." Similar to scenes in *The Duellists*, Fournier-Sarlovèze and Dupont fought several times, frequently wounding each other severely but with no resolution. Thoumas did not describe how the conflict was ever resolved and failed to give such stories much credence. During his military career, Thoumas could well have heard of such legends, as the romanticized image of the Napoleonic era was a common social theme of his time.[9] Thoumas published his biographical series more than a decade before the original text of *The Duel*. It is likely that Conrad learned of these stories and modified them to his own tastes.

Aside from the legend of a protracted and inconclusive duel, the potential historical foundations for *The Duellists* bear little resemblance to Thoumas's account. He condensed the tale of the duel to a single paragraph. Other accounts, purporting to be historically accurate, provide much more detail and resemble Conrad's narrative much more closely. For example, French writer Jean Delpech-Laborie in his book *Le général Fournier-Sarlovèze* recounts a story of a protracted duel with almost the same details as Conrad's tale. But, as it was published nearly sixty years after *The Duel* and contains no citations, its credibility is doubtful. Other popular accounts of the alleged historic duel such as Richy Craven's article "The Five Most Insane Duels Ever Fought" share the same weaknesses.[10]

Regardless of the verifiable historical details, *The Duellists* remains a stellar example of a nineteenth-century period film. The detailed costumes and setting are, of course, important, but the finishing touch was the way in which Ridley Scott captured the political ideologies and military values of the times. Without these ideals and values, the film might have been just another mundane swashbuckler. But by incorporating a fidelity to cultural context so effectively, Scott succeeded in creating a film which contains both exciting action sequences and historical accuracy, both too often absent from works of the same genre.

NOTES

1. The term "Gascon" refers to someone from Gascony in the southwestern region of France. Gascons were popularly seen as belligerent, reactive, and eager to fight. It is not coincidental that Alexandre Dumas made his character d'Artagnan in *The Three Musketeers* a Gascon.

2. This is the *Code Duello*, published in Ireland in 1777. Although there were many local variations, it set the standard for dueling in Europe and America. "Code Duello: Rules of

Dueling," *American Experience*, accessed July 2012, http://www.pbs.org/wgbh/amex/duel/sfeature/rulesofdueling.html.

3. "Seconds" refers to outside parties, often close friends of the duelists, who act as intermediaries and ensure that the duel is fought according to a recognized code.

4. This was demonstrated by the great dancer in the 1948 version of *The Three Musketeers*.

5. Rather, it is a fictional story set during a specific historical period. Very few actual historical figures are portrayed.

6. This was in the days before revolvers, so each pistol had only one shot.

7. Robert A. Nye, *Masculinity and Male Codes of Honor in Modern France* (Berkeley: University of California Press, 1993), 16-17, 42.

8. Napoleon's own career is evidence of this. Although he was born as a low-ranking aristocrat, social restrictions would have limited his military advancement had the revolution not disrupted the traditional French social order.

9. Charles A. Thoumas, *Les grands cavaliers du Premier Empire, Série II* (Paris: Berger-Levrault, 1892), 259.

10. Jean Delpech-Laborie, *Le général Fournier-Sarlovèze: le plus mauvais sujet de Napoléon* (Paris: Productions de Paris, 1967), 50-57; Richy Craven, "The Five Most Insane Duels Ever Fought," accessed July 2012, http://www.cracked.com/article_19709_the-5-most-insane-duels-ever-fought_p2.html.

REFERENCES

"Code Duello: Rules of Dueling." *American Experience*. Accessed July 2012. http://www.pbs.org/wgbh/amex/duel/sfeature/rulesofdueling.html.

Conrad, Joseph. *The Duel (The Point of Honor: A Military Tale)*. Accessed September 2011. http://www.readbookonline.net/readOnLine/2481/.

Craven, Richy. "The Five Most Insane Duels Ever Fought." Accessed July 2012. http://www.cracked.com/article_19709_the-5-most-insane-duels-ever-fought_p2.html.

Delpech-Laborie, Jean. *Le general Fournier-Sarlovèze: le plus mauvais sujet de Napoléon*. Paris: Productions de Paris, 1967.

The Duellists. DVD. Directed by Ridley Scott. 1977; Hollywood, CA: Paramount Pictures, 2002.

Nye, Robert. *Masculinity and Male Codes of Honor in Modern France*. Berkeley: University of California Press, 1993.

Thoumas, Charles A. *Les grands cavaliers du Premier Empire, Série II*. Paris: Berger-Levrault, 1982.

Chapter Eleven

Conceptions of Happiness in *Matchstick Men* and *A Good Year*

Basileios Kroustallis

At first glance, Ridley Scott may not be the director to look to when investigating cinematic depictions of happiness and the good life. His themes and plots are usually bleak visions of the future (*Blade Runner*, *Alien*), historical dramas that illuminate the abuses of authority (*Gladiator*, *Robin Hood*), or nightmarish present-day scenarios that challenge both the legal system and behavioral norms (*Hannibal*). So what can Scott teach us about happiness?[1]

Aristotle was one of the first intellectual authorities to propose that well-being is the highest goal in life. It can only be attained when an individual exercises his or her natural abilities to the fullest. He connects this capacity to moral virtue and only tangentially mentions the enjoyment individuals derive while advancing toward happiness. In *Enjoyment: The Moral Significance of Styles of Life*, the American philosopher John Kekes has a more liberal solution.[2] Like Aristotle, he argues against simply applying universal moral principles in an unqualified fashion, and strongly endorses a variety of life choices in the quest for happiness. A way of life, namely the specific way of doing things (less of a commercialized "lifestyle" burdened by public expectations than a "style of living") is more important for happiness than the particular activities pursued. Enjoyment of one's life is a key factor in detecting whether a person is on the right path to happiness and well-being, though "enjoyment" here is more comprehensive than the feeling associated with momentary or sensual pleasures.

Scott's dramas *Matchstick Men* (2003) and *A Good Year* (2006) present a counterexample to the additional claim made by Kekes that enjoyment of life needs to be measured on a scale of *admirable* versus *deficient* styles of life, even if these terms denote the individual's own reflections and not those of others. Kekes states forcefully that enjoyment of life cannot lead to complete happiness if it arises from deficient styles of life. Yet the successful con artist Roy Wallace (Nicolas Cage) in *Matchstick Men*, and the money-hungry investment broker Max Skinner (Russell Crowe) in *A Good Year* do not set forth examples of admirable lifestyles, even according to their own standards. Still, they clearly enjoy themselves when they are free to choose their paths and eventually change the tenor of their activities in a more positive direction.

TO BE HAPPY IS TO ENJOY ONESELF

The word "happiness" may simply describe an abstract psychological situation—that is, what it *feels* like to be "happy." However, happiness can also imply the individual's sense of well-being. A person may feel good and enjoy an activity that in the long run might not contribute to his or her well-being. Happiness, therefore, not only describes our fluctuating mental states, but also *prescribes* certain courses of action. It also has an evaluative angle: people should do some things and avoid others. More comprehensive theories of happiness as well-being promote factors such as sensory or intellectual pleasure, the satisfaction of specific desires (professional success or rewarding personal relationships), or, more generally, satisfaction with one's life as a whole.[3] These comprehensive theories point to a style of life that appears *worth* pursuing.

The concept of *eudaimonism*, for example, says that well-being is able to account for happiness in the psychological sense. As such, if we know that a person leads a good life then we should be able to know that a person exists in a happy state.[4] The individual achieves *eudaimonia* not when subjective desires or whole-life satisfaction is attained, but when he or she is able to exercise objective, natural capacities to the fullest degree. For instance, it is not enough for a person to be an eccentric film lover; if he or she perhaps has the talent to direct, that should be a future challenge and a goal (even if he or she does not feel like pursuing this challenge at that moment). Nevertheless, can individuals exercise their capacities and fail to lead a good life?

Kekes sidesteps the challenge by doing the reverse: instead of defining the prerequisites for leading a good life, he *extends* the meaning of enjoyment usually associated with happiness. Enjoyment does not denote mere pleasure, a positive attitude, or even a Pavlovian, non-reflective satisfaction with one's own life; it is much wider in scope. It entails a well-conceived plan executed over an extended amount of time (often a lifetime), which accommodates all personal psychological tendencies, beliefs, and desires into a scheme of things to be pursued. Therefore, eudaimonism, the appeal to happiness as well-being, can bridge both descriptive and evaluative senses of happiness. Enjoyment is not only an isolated psychological state, but also a continuous activity toward the right purpose—that is, personal well-being.

There are three main factors to consider when pursuing this kind of life. First, the individual needs to have a coherent, realistic, and durable plan. Individuals have to develop skills and competencies in all fields of life, as John Stuart Mill famously suggested[5]; they need to pursue these skills by means of an almost managerial approach. Second, a person's dominant activities should reflect that which she or he cares about the most; otherwise, the happiness project will not work. Third, it is important to reflect upon and evaluate one's own personal "style of life" and decide for oneself whether the path life takes is admirable (and so it stays) or deficient (and so it needs to be revised).[6]

The whole trio of requirements becomes a well-conceived and maximally conducive path to happiness. The problem is whether the enjoyment it envisions comes exclusively out of those ingredients. Kekes might answer that it works in some cases but not in others. This would be a false impression, though, since Kekes allows for pluralist conceptions of happiness. The new signification of enjoyment shows that it either has to apply to all cases examined or the new signification is false. *Matchstick Men* and *A Good Year* offer provocative case studies in this regard.

COHERENCE, REALISM AND DURABILITY

Kekes argues that happiness does not entail following a moral recipe which prescribes certain actions instead of others. What matters more is how a person does the specific actions he or she chooses.[7] It is a matter of style, not plain attitude (aesthetic or otherwise), even though there are unique concepts to pinpoint it. For instance, integrity as a style of life involves both commitment to moral values and critical reflection on the influences that have led to those commitments. Being faithful to this attitude renders the style of life admirable. On the other hand, morbidity is an intense fascination with pain and death (the sort that led the Japanese writer Yukio Mishima to his ritual suicide); if it is so powerful that it causes undue prudence and the subject's whole train of thought to succumb to its demands, then it constitutes a deficient, even destructive style of life. Therefore, an admirable style of life is a complex and thought-out plan that should successfully harmonize existing beliefs, emotions, and motivations. It would perpetuate life rather than seek to endanger or end it.

This managerial plan of living has three major pillars: consistency (which entails durability over time), coherence, and realism. We detect consistency when it is easy to predict actions that arise from a habitually practiced, individualized style of life; this ease reflects, in turn, the durability of the life to be led.[8] Consistency alone is not enough. Beliefs, emotions, and motivations of an individual all need to point in the same direction. If a person's dominant emotions are directed toward family life, yet his or her motives primarily involve considerations of how to earn more money, the person does not lead a consistent lifestyle. This, in turn, may result in a life full of frustration.[9] Realism is the third factor; it ensures that individuals acknowledge all available options while leading their lives, given their own capacities and the social context within which they operate through adequate thought and study.

Will "enjoyment of life," as Kekes understands the term, invariably emerge from this theoretical construction? *Matchstick Men* presents a character study of Roy Wallace (Nicolas Cage), a small-time con man suffering from obsessive-compulsive disorder.[10] Still, he seems to get along professionally with his exuberant partner in crime, Frank Mercer (Sam Rockwell). The arrival of Angela (Alison Lohman), his presumed daughter (since Roy has been divorced for over a decade), puts pressure on Roy to teach her his tricks. Reluctantly at first, but steadily afterwards, the troubled man apprentices her. But he soon learns a lesson about conning: he is not immune to the cons of his partners. The films ends with Roy abandoning his old job, finding a new one as a carpet salesperson, and making himself comfortable as a family man, reprioritizing his life-goals generally.

From one perspective, Roy's life in *Matchstick Men* is one of artistic experimentation. He is insecure and addled, yet he has his own way of becoming artistic with his *spaghetti all' olio* (a dish Angela is proud to detest), his retro vinyl records, and, of course, his way of conning people. After all, he states, "lying is creating a value for something that is not there." Is this not a way of describing art as well? Plato thought that art was an imitation of life, itself an imitation of the real world of Ideas; therefore, art was the product of a supremely fabricated world.[11] Yet despite his apparent talents, Roy has no managerial plan: what's more, his professional life is artificially (and not artistically) organized around the ordered disorder of his home life. His enjoyment only comes when he abandons the practice of conning; even then, he does not endorse a healthier means of organizing his life. His way of teaching Angela is to mock rules. "Never write anything down" is his first remark, followed by "90% of the trade is variable." Failing to demonstrate consistency and durability, no coherence can be found between Roy's beliefs, actions, and emotions; his plans and wishes regarding his professional life are hindered by the emotional troubles exacerbated by (and founded in) his health disorders. His sense of realism is not to be commended either: he is regrettably ignorant of Angela's character traits and motivations for connecting with him. Still, Roy enjoys all the moments he has with Angela, and enjoyment is not mere momentary pleasure, as Kekes warns against believing it to be.[12] He even starts to construct a way of living (but not a detailed or rule-based plan) that will secure his new role as a father. Enjoyment here is the *incentive* of a plan to lead a life, not the end result of it.

The successful British investment broker and womanizer Max Skinner of *A Good Life* has a well-organized business plan in gloomy but sophisticated London. His goals for success revolve invariably around money ("Winning isn't everything; it's the only thing"). His way of doing business determines his actions beyond that aspect of his life and they are reflected in his own self-assessments ("Greedy bastard day" and "me becoming an asshole" are Max's stock phrases). The question is whether Max enjoys this consistent and coherent plan in which personal affairs only receive a bare minimum of attention and must not distract from the money-making agenda. We would certainly think that he would continue on this path if the sudden death of his uncle, Henry (Albert Finney), in Provence, France, and the inheritance of the near-abandoned wine château did not make him reevaluate his priorities.

While in France, Max finds a new cousin (Abbie Cornish) and a semi-permanent love interest, the French waitress and café owner Fanny (Marion Cotillard). In his new home, he is able to say that the summers spent with his uncle as a little boy "saved his life" and that his memories from the period are not only good, but "grand." However, everything that Max plans goes awry. His plan to sell the house is unfulfilled. His intention to enter into a sexual relationship with his cousin (the Gallic mores are apparently in his favor) is suddenly abandoned when he meets Fanny. None of this would have been a problem beforehand, but now Max suddenly seems to have lost his timing and perspective on things—his jerky car movements when entering France only corroborate the effect of his disrupted life. Still, Max looks so much more at ease in France, we have to wonder what is transpiring.

Is all this the result of a laid-back attitude to life that Max has now adopted, one which allows him to enjoy himself? The man certainly seems to do so, but the contrast is not between his new, laid-back life and his former, fast-paced competitive one. He is as competitive about women and money in France as he was in England. This we witness up to the last scene when he decides to sell his London apartment. But living in France comes with an under-prepared, non-coherent life plan that makes him move along with the flow of daily experience. This suggests that enjoyment of life is not a pre-planned affair but one that emerges as a result of living in the moment.

DEEPEST CONCERN

Kekes argues that a single or central concern should justify why we enjoy our lives. Enjoyment happens because our dominant activities reflect what we most deeply care about. He contends, "Individuality follows if how we live and act reflects the central stream of what we feel indeed. That is what would make the activities that complete our nature enjoyable."[13] The only proviso is that we be cognizant at each point of our life of what constitutes our deepest concern. According to this theory of enjoyment, we should gladly accept a multiplicity of dominant activities corresponding to different lifestyles; after all, few—if any—individuals are the same. However, multiple activities which do not all correspond to a central deep concern are theoretically unaccounted for. Pluralism is valid only in interpersonal, not intra-personal contexts. If we feel otherwise, we have still not mastered the understanding of what constitutes our deepest concern.

Roy initially endorses that logic. He mistakenly thinks that only a single dominant concern, being a con man, is the thing he should most care about. He is troubled because he does not feel the enjoyment he thinks he should from the job. When he meets Angela, though, he feels pressed to admit that this singular life is morally and personally deficient. He proposes a life of familial love, devoid of any tricks, in order to make himself a responsible father. This proposal is not the result of previous experience or deference to convention. Roy *wants* to enter a father-daughter relationship and he is ready to devote himself to it. He even buys Angela an unrealistically huge tub of ice cream (contrary to his tuna fish diet) and arranges that more time be spent together. Yet, he simultaneously admits "We had the best time together" when they both planned and executed cons.

Laurence Raw notes that once Roy learns to trust those around him, he acquires a renewed strength of character, which then helps him to develop a new understanding of masculine roles.[14] But even if Roy gradually moves into a more admirable (if predictable) pattern of male behavior as a father and provider, his activities remain varied in scope. He would be wrong to follow a single pattern of activity instead of pursuing multiple ones. Roy is not a person that fares well in a dominant activity: his obsessive-compulsive behavior demonstrates an inability to concentrate on one task without being overwhelmed with anxieties. What he really enjoys the most is doing different things together (that is, multi-tasking).

A conjunction of two dominant activities may create a new dominant activity, a single combined thing that a person cares most about. There are two problems with this, though. First, this joint activity (fathering and conning) almost happened by chance, and its continuation is marred by the expressed possibility that either party might step out of it at any time. Second, no rules determine this joint activity. Creativity and adaptation, not careful planning, ensure success in the con business. As such, this case of combined concern does not fulfill the requirements for being a deepest concern, at least in line with Kekes's formulation.

Could Max in *A Good Year* actually fulfill Kekes's requirements? Perhaps the things Max in fact cares most deeply about—instead of what he *thinks* he cares most about—are the simple pleasures in life. A family life with a relatively anxiety-free occupation would be more gratifying than the money-hunting endeavors that consume his current existence. Granted, this line of reasoning again puts all the eggs in one basket. In *A Good Year*, it may be true that Max faces the dilemma, voiced by his lawyer, of deciding "The money or [his] life?" However, this is exactly the distinction between a single-handed interest, which parades as a deepest concern, and a cluster of other interests. Max gradually learns that the almost cynical behavior he used to exhibit does not suit all purposes. He may insult his cousin at a friendly dinner, asking for proof of her family's status, but he eventually fakes his uncle's signature to make her remain legal inheritor of the wine château. He initially describes his date with Fanny to his lawyer as an "obligatory cultural evening" but then manages to arrange his personal life as something that takes stock of his growing attraction to her. At the same time, he also does business on his own wine château. This range of different activities could fit under the umbrella term "simple pleasures," but their proper characterization is plural (instead of singular) activities. Each one needs to be evaluated independently, not classified in accordance with a dominant passion.

At the end of the film, Max abhors his former passions: his reaction to the Van Gogh painting his former boss has acquired is to protest by hiding it in the safe away from the enjoyment of viewers. He also does not embrace *all* of "life's simple pleasures" either: he is smart enough to admit that he will never be a good winemaker and leaves that to the others. He does not substitute a passion for a range of deepest concerns; he simply does not have any. Thus he admittedly enjoys himself.

RESPONSIBILITY AND ADMIRABLE STYLES OF LIFE

Kekes asks: "Does it not make a difference whether one's enjoyable dominant activity is collecting used matchsticks or teaching students to appreciate poetry? Is it true that, given equal enjoyment, it is a matter of indifference from what it is derived?"[15] He admits that individuals can set their own personal blueprint for life. Not all dominant activities count as admirable activities, though. Watching animated children's programs on television (the theorist's example) is not an admirable activity, while teaching about the Higgs Boson presumably is.[16] Yet, regardless of our agreement (or dissent) with the specific examples Kekes brings forward, the remedy he proposes for this ignorance is itself questionable and potentially limiting in terms of individual liberty: people who have "greater objectivity, deeper reflection, and more extensive experience" may dispute not only whether individual actions are right or wrong, but also whether individuals "should enjoy what [they] genuinely enjoy."[17]

Roy does not have an external guarding presence to correct his choices in life; he is even reluctant to unveil anything about his real profession to his psychiatrist, Harry Klein (Bruce Altman). However, his own internal watchman always tells him what is right for him and what is not; it tells him when he should enjoy something and when he should suffer through self-reproach. This metaphorical watchman carefully monitors his behavior, from his incessant tics to door-opening tactics. The expression of this voice is realized through conscientious responsibility. Roy suggests that Angela return the money she received from the con, a responsible thing for a father to suggest to a child. But Roy himself does not believe what his responsible inner voice tells him. When Angela ironically proposes that Roy give back the money they took from their joint con, Roy laughs. He never himself disputes whether enjoyment as a con artist is an enjoyable end in itself. It is only the watchman (conscience) that talks to him using the language of responsibility he is unable to digest (at least at first).

It is also ironic that when Roy utters the word "kindness," he is bound to put himself in danger. Being chased by his mark, Chuck Frechette (Bruce McGill), Roy wants to convince the female attendant of the parking space to keep the change for his parking ticket. She refuses to accept tips, and frightened of being caught, Roy utters anxiously, "It is an act of kindness." Interestingly enough, when Roy confronts Angela later in the carpet store, he suggests that he "gave" her the money she stole; he never uses the charged word "kindness" to describe his act. Kindness and responsibility as moral imperatives that lead to a different style of life are alien to Roy, even if they are generally admirable in theory.

Kekes posits that "External reasons take the form of others calling our attention to an aspect of our situation relevant to our sensitivity or vision, but one that we have missed."[18] Sometimes, external influences—namely people who know us—may contribute to enjoyment and happiness. In *A Good Year*, though, people close to Max attempt to influence him only in the context of the business framework. Their advice and comments are valid only if the person to whom they are addressed (that is, Max) acts comfortably within that style of life, not when he steps out of it. Even Kekes warns against this kind of interference; the problem is that no interference of the kind he envisions can be found in the film.[19]

Max's secretary, Gemma (Archie Panjabi), can give useful advice and will almost always act on his behalf, even in regard to Skinner's personal relationship issues. His lawyer, Charlie Willis (Tom Hollander) is shrewd enough to follow up on Max's wishes regarding financial settlements. Yet, when Max is in France, these aides both fail to make their advice relevant to him. They are unable to understand the widening of his scope of activities. The result is that they sound like grumpy, kvetching babysitters. Gemma uses irony when she asks Skinner, "Are you enjoying yourself, Max?" and

Charlie tells her that his adopted lifestyle will eventually be filled with boredom. They both make the assumption that enjoyment only accompanies a certain kind of activity that Max *used* to pursue. In that sense, they do not help him to define his own personal sense of enjoyment and happiness.

SELF-DEVELOPMENT AND ENJOYMENT

Aristotle was not blind to pluralism of attitudes, modes of behavior, and activities. He suggested that a life of virtue, honor, or simple pleasures can be justifiably pursued by different individuals in their search for happiness and well-being. Yet, instead of allowing multiple factors to jointly define well-being, Aristotle retreated to a single account of human nature. The claim that human beings, as a result of *their own nature*, move towards an endpoint makes it redundant to look for the nature of the endpoint itself (that is, happiness, virtue, or well-being as pleasure, among others). A person need only seek the means to that end through a life of virtuous activity (in Aristotelian terms); enjoyment would never fail to arise as a result. This is because such an activity would necessarily reflect one's own nature.[20]

Yet the self-development that is crucial to all aspects of the eudaimonist position, and which Kekes endorses with his systematic style of life plan, is not the only source of enjoyment of life. Russell Crowe admits in an interview that Max Skinner "learns that things that he was taught when he was a younger man have great value . . . [but] through his ambition, he has lost sight of the things that were really important and of the importance of the person who taught him those things."[21] Not all the film reviews agree with the above portrait of the protagonist. Anthony Quinn argues that "Crowe enters the story as an insufferably self-satisfied boor—and departs it unchanged."[22] Self-development may not imply a discernable endpoint, and enjoyment measured by that point is bound to lead to some wrong measurements. Max retains central aspects of his previous style of life throughout the film, but also learns to enjoy more things than he used to previously.

Perhaps it is the same unconscious complaint about a fake endpoint that seems to haunt criticism about the "happy" ending of *Matchstick Men*. One rewrite of the script left Roy both penniless and in search of a family.[23] Yet, the cosy family ending (coupled with an artistically prepared dinner) only shows that Roy has successfully developed a new style of life and derives enjoyment from many different things.

Worries about generic conventions also seem to reflect each character's motivations and end-purpose in life. William Parrill finds the "bright Southern California visuals" in *Matchstick Men* "inappropriate for such a dark story." He complains that a David Mamet–like script with sharp dialogue would have been more appropriate.[24] However, deviating from expected wittiness and over-the-top behavior only makes Roy and his partner bungling Everymen. They are troubled individuals who seek happiness, although in a rather small-scale way, not unlike the minor cons they manage to pull off. *Matchstick Men* is not a typical example of the con genre in which clever but morally depraved persons disrupt other people's lives to common disaster. The film reveals the need to pursue happiness, yet ensures that this endeavor is pursued in Roy's own way—that is, including his non-admirable actions— in order to secure a more believable sense of enjoyment on his part.

Does that imply that the enjoyment of life, which rests on morally admirable practices, will not bring happiness or that small-scale cons are necessary to attain what everyone wants? Both contentions may be true, but the way to find out is *not* to pursue the meaning of happiness using enjoyment as the main vehicle, as Kekes implies. We may not need universal moral principles to tell us how to be happy, but neither do we need a general, theoretical account of enjoyment that carefully maps our needs and desires according to our deepest concerns. At least, in their respective films, Roy Wallace and Max Skinner have no need for them.

NOTES

1. Fred Feldman, *What Is This Thing Called Happiness?* (Oxford: Oxford University Press, 2010).

2. John Kekes, *Enjoyment: The Moral Significance of Styles of Life* (Oxford: Clarendon Press, 2008).

3. For a whole life-based satisfaction theory, see Leonard Wayne Sumner, *Welfare, Happiness and Ethics* (New York: Oxford University Press, 1996).

4. See Feldman, *Happiness*, 181ff.

5. John Stuart Mill, *On Liberty* (Oxford : Oxford University Press, 2008).

6. Kekes, *Enjoyment*, 75.

7. Ibid., 8.

8. Ibid., 24.

9. Ibid., 34.

10. "Why would Ridley Scott, who usually works in the epic mode of *Gladiator* and *Black Hawk Down*, direct an intimate character piece about two LA con men?" Peter Travers, "Matchstick Men," *Rolling Stone*, September 8, 2003, accessed July 23, 2012, http://www.rollingstone.com/movies/reviews/matchstick-men-20030908.

11. Plato, *Republic,* trans. G. Grube and C. Reeve (Indianapolis, IN: Hackett, 1992).

12. Kekes, *Enjoyment*, 43.

13. Ibid., 63.

14. Laurence Raw, *The Ridley Scott Encyclopedia* (Lanham, MD: Scarecrow Press, 2009), 217.

15. Kekes, *Enjoyment*, 80.

16. See Daniel M. Haybron, *The Pursuit of Unhappiness: The Elusive Psychology of Well-Being* (Oxford: Oxford University Press, 2008).

17. Kekes, *Enjoyment*, 82.

18. Ibid., 86.

19. Ibid., 87.

20. See the first book of Aristotle, *Nicomachean Ethics,* trans. W. D. Ross (Oxford: Oxford University Press, 2009).

21. Raw, *Encyclopedia,* 83.

22. Anthony Quinn, review of "*A Good Year,*" *The Independent*, October 27, 2006, accessed July 24, 2012, http://www.independent.co.uk/arts-entertainment/films/reviews/a-good-year-12a--none-onestar-twostar-threestar-fourstar-421709.html.

23. Notably by Peter Bradshaw in *The Guardian.* Cited in Raw, *Encyclopedia*, 217.

24. William B. Parrill, "*Matchstick Men* (2003): Mean Street Men in Bright Colors," in *Ridley Scott: A Critical Filmography* (Jefferson, NC: McFarland, 2011), 127.

REFERENCES

Aristotle. *Nicomachean Ethics*. Translated by W. D. Ross. Oxford: Oxford University Press, 2009.

Feldman, Fred. *What Is This Thing Called Happiness?* Oxford: Oxford University Press, 2010.

A Good Year. DVD. Directed by Ridley Scott. 2006; Los Angeles, CA: Twentieth Century Fox, 2007.

Haybron, Daniel M. *The Pursuit of Unhappiness: The Elusive Psychology of Well-Being*. Oxford: Oxford University Press, 2008.

Kekes, John. *Enjoyment: The Moral Significance of Styles of Life*. Oxford: Clarendon Press, 2008.

Matchstick Men. DVD. Directed by Ridley Scott. 2003; Burbank, CA: Warner Home Video, 2009.

Mill, John S. *On Liberty*. Oxford: Oxford University Press, 2008.

Parrill, William B. "*Matchstick Men* (2003): Mean Street Men in Bright Colors." In *Ridley Scott: A Critical Filmography*, 125-128. Jefferson, NC: McFarland, 2011.

Plato. *Republic*. Translated by G. Grube. Indianapolis, IN: Hackett, 1992.

Quinn, Anthony. Review of "*A Good Year.*" *The Independent*, October 27, 2006. Accessed July 24, 2012. http://www.independent.co.uk/arts-entertainment/films/reviews/a-good-year-12a--none-onestar-twostar-threestar-fourstar-fivestar-421709.html.

Raw, Laurence. *The Ridley Scott Encyclopedia*. Lanham, MD: Scarecrow Press, 2009.

Sumner, Leonard W. *Welfare, Happiness and Ethics*. New York: Oxford University Press, 1996.

Travers, Peters. "Matchstick Men." *Rolling Stone*, September 8, 2003. Accessed July 23, 2012. http://www.rollingstone.com/movies/reviews/matchstick-men-20030908.

Chapter Twelve

Techno-Totalitarianism in *Alien*

Dan Dinello

The opening of Ridley Scott's *Alien* (1979) introduces the *Nostromo*—a rusted-out, factory-like spaceship travelling in space and functioning without people. Languorous interior pans and tracking shots present an exclusively technological environment: an autonomous, self-sustaining cybernetic organism that obviates the need for human control. Signifying its importance relative to human involvement, an apparently self-activated computer interface flashes to life and reflects in the glass surface of an empty space helmet. Lights blink on and a door slides open. Small and irrelevant, the human crew sleeps cocooned in tube-like compartments, demonstrating their helpless reliance on the technological system that operates the ship and regulates their life support. As early technology critic and sociologist Jacques Ellul stresses in *The Technological Society*, "The character of technique [whether a system or a machine] renders it *independent of man himself.*"[1]

Alien offers a pessimistic vision of humanity dominated by a technological empire. Programmed by an unethical corporation called the Company, technology emerges as a ubiquitous, insidious, and totalitarian force. The human victims of the technological system have been so conditioned to its rule that they perceive its stranglehold as the natural state of things, not even recognizing their enslavement. Reflecting the philosophy of techno-critics Ellul and political scientist Langdon Winner, *Alien* dramatizes the idea that "Technology is a source of domination that effectively rules all forms of modern thought and activity. Whether by an inherent property or by an incidental set of circumstances, technology looms as an oppressive force that poses a direct threat to human freedom."[2]

Ellul's *The Technological Society* and Winner's *Autonomous Technology* together express a comprehensive indictment of technology, both arguing extensively for its perilous and autonomous nature. Ellul defines technology

more broadly as "technique": machines, political organizations, and economic systems that value efficiency and order above all else. The technique of a
system or machine thus subjugates humans to the point where the demands
imposed by technical requirements stifle spontaneous, free behavior. Winner
expands Ellul's notion that "Technique cannot be otherwise than totalitarian.
Technique causes the state to become totalitarian, to absorb the citizen's life
completely."[3] To Ellul and Winner, humans are not the masters of technology, they are its slaves; this is a point made clear in *Alien* as the asymmetrical
relationship between humans and technology unfolds on the *Nostromo*.

MOTHER DEMANDS OBEDIENCE

Directing the ship and controlling its environment, the computer interrupts
the *Nostromo*'s journey home, awakening the crew and forcing them to risk
their lives investigating an alien signal on a nearby planet. The computer's
name, "Mother," reinforces the crew's childlike dependence on it and perpet-
uates the false image of technology as protective and nurturing. The computer's name also introduces the notion of perverse technological reproduction,
a fearful motif of numerous science fiction horror stories from Mary Shel-
ley's novel *Frankenstein* (1818) to Vincenzo Natali's film *Splice* (2009).
When awakened by Mother, the crew members emerge, nearly naked, from
their womb-like compartments as if they have been birthed. The opening of
Alien therefore suggests that the crew, as metaphorical children of a computer mother, are themselves quasi-technological entities, parts of a machine.

Realizing that Mother wants them to embark on a new mission rather than
go home, two crew members protest against investigating the unknown transmission. They argue that their contract does not obligate them to do so, a
claim quickly refuted by both science officer Ash and Captain Dallas who
reinforce Mother's investigative demands. In this regard, Captain Dallas—
earning a higher salary—sells out not only his crewmates but also himself as
he is later "rewarded" with death for serving as an instrument of corporate
ideology. Ash, quoting the contract's fine print, insists that failure to follow
orders will result in "no money."

Beyond the threat of not being paid, the crew has no choice in the matter:
the computer controls the ship, they do not. Quickly, the crew acquiesces to
Mother's demands. As it turns out, this supposedly protective mother (pro-
grammed by the Company) will betray her children and permit infanticide.
As such, Mother joins science fiction's roster of evil computers: Alpha 60 in
Jean-Luc Godard's *Alphaville* (1965), HAL in Stanley Kubrick's *2001: A
Space Odyssey* (1968), Colossus in Joseph Sargent's *Colossus the Forbin
Project* (1970), Proteus IV in Donald Cammell's *Demon Seed* (1974), and
AM in Harlan Ellison's novella *I Have No Mouth and I Must Scream* (1967).

Unlike Mother, these previous computers are gendered male, express arrogance, and act overtly to dominate humans. Mother, on the other hand, evokes female protectiveness, expresses stubbornness, and acts subversively. Like the other computers, Mother shares a disregard for human life but is unique in that her murderous actions stem directly from the exploitative intentions of the corporation that programmed her. As such, *Alien* links technological dominance to ruling-class power.

When Second-in-Command Ellen Ripley finally gains access to the computer following the death of the captain, she learns that the crew has been deemed "expendable" and that the Company's first priority is capturing the alien. The Company wants to use the creature as a component of a biological weapons system that will prove profitable. The unseen Company is the central monster of *Alien*: all the evil flows from its capitalistic and technological imperatives. A monolithic entity, the Company represents corporate totalitarianism: it deploys vast technological systems to enforce its interests while generating a bright aura of rationality and common sense to justify its designs. The crew members are so blind to their technologically enslaved states that none of them question the Company's right to make demands that jeopardize their lives. No one challenges the morality of the contract or tests the consequences of non-compliance. Their acquiescence persists, even as fellow crew members are killed off one by one for no known purpose other than to ensure the survival of the alien. Only at the end, when it is too late, do they offer any resistance to these extremes of technological authority.

All the humans must be transformed into technological components to suit the special needs and objectives of the corporate system (in this case, Mother and the *Nostromo*). As metaphorical children of a computer, the individuals operate as mere cogs in the machine. Anyone who does not function efficiently will be deemed "expendable." This instance of what Winner calls "technological politics" epitomizes how the corporate ruling class—through its control of technology—manipulates the decisions and needs of society to match its own interests. It deftly makes the whole arrangement appear rational, necessary, and free. Winner argues that "Human beings still have a nominal presence in the network, but they have lost their roles as active, directing agents. . . . They tend to obey uncritically the norms and requirements of the systems which they allegedly govern."[4] The importance of human beings emerges exclusively in relation to their capacity to serve assigned functions in the technological system whose demands, needs, and objectives assume paramount importance.

Obeying Mother's directive to investigate the planet, the crew discovers another monstrous mother: an alien ship that itself looks like two legs spread apart. Entering through a vagina-like opening, the investigative team finds that the biomorphic vessel is "pregnant" with alien eggs in a womb-like chamber. Crew member Kane foolishly takes a closer look at one of the pulsating eggs and a lecherous, crab-like being bursts out of it, clamping to his face, wrapping a tail around his neck, and inserting one end of its writhing body into the struggling man's mouth. It is a parody of rape. Still clinging to Kane's face, the alien "face-hugger" is transported inside the ship. While Ripley refuses Kane re-entry on the grounds of possible contamination, Ash overrides her order, first in the name of scientific research and then in the name of Company objectives.

KILLING MACHINE

Unbeknownst to the crew, Ash is an android; like Mother, he has been programmed by the Company to ensure capture of the alien at any cost. Significantly, it is Ash who explains to the protesting crew that their contract with the Company stipulates that they must investigate "any transmission indicating a possible intelligent origin." A technological extension of the Company, Ash becomes a robotic monster that sabotages the crew's welfare when it conflicts with Company interests. Utterly indifferent to human life, Ash uses the hapless, submissive humans as disposable instruments in his effort to capture and then protect the alien to secure profits for the Company's biological weapons division.[5] The ostensible human masters of technology are themselves mastered by it in the form of this robotic villain.

Designed to infiltrate and manipulate the crew undetected, Ash's technological composition remains unknown to the humans. His workspace is decorated with semi-pornographic pin-ups that reflect his misogynistic programming and disguise him as a typically macho male. Despite a supercilious attitude, he is trusted because he is so much like his colleagues. The robot's invisibility and unnoticed manipulations reflect modern technology's penetration into the world: technological systems have become so ubiquitous and so much a part of everyday life that they operate as part of the natural environment. For example, the evolving changes, disruptions, restrictions, and chilling effect of widespread surveillance technology—including networked cameras, data mining algorithms, electronic transponders, GPS-embedded cell phones, facial recognition software, biometric and personal information databases, and the arrival of domestic drones—have been mostly accepted as the price to be paid for security and convenience.

Ash tries to remove the face-hugger from Kane, not to save the human but to save the alien. But the crab-like life form tightens its tail around the victim's neck while dripping ship-destroying acid blood. Shortly thereafter, the alien disappears after surreptitiously dropping an egg into Kane where it gestates within his body. The man seems fine. He gets up and eats voraciously, and is to all appearances normal. But, like a uterus, Kane's body serves up to the alien parasite nutrients and protection from the environment. After a brief incubation, a penile creature with teeth is literally "born" by bursting out of the host's stomach. The creature quickly metamorphoses into a humanoid techno-surrealist killing machine. Android Ash aligns himself with the alien, inspired by its structural perfection, technological "purity," and unstoppable ruthlessness.

Ash's correspondence with the alien becomes even more direct when he attempts to defend it from Ripley's attack. In an echo of the quasi-rape of Kane (and since he presumably lacks a functional penis himself), Ash rolls up a pornographic magazine from his stash and forces it down Ripley's throat to suffocate her. Two crew members come to her defense and stop the oral assault, only to realize that Ash is a technological creature—not a man—after lopping off his artificial head. This kind of intervention is not, unfortunately, available on a larger scale.

TECHNOLOGICAL MONSTER

A projection of the techno-totalitarian ideal, the alien parasitizes humans, commandeers their organic machinery, and forces them to serve as its reproductive hosts. In this sense, the alien symbolizes the Company's capitalist voraciousness and its parasitic employment of the crew to serve the corporate agenda. A techno-organic hybrid, the alien also represents the horrors of the Company's weaponized technology and, more generally, exploits fears of perverse sexualities and non-standard reproduction. With its protruding mechanical teeth, battery-acid blood, reproductive resemblance to a virus, and metallic appearance that blends with the spaceship's pipes and wires, the alien evokes "futuristic machinery, skeletons, and verminous insects: a necrotechnological nightmare."[6]

Like a viral infection, technology evolves as an autonomous, invasive force that expands and fulfills its dangerous potential by reproducing and spreading through living creatures (in this case, the hosts are human). Voracious in its urge to possess and engulf, technology is a parasite that frequently undermines human integrity, invisibly infiltrating, controlling, and mutating its host to optimize its own survival and evolution. This view of technology as an independent, quasi-biological life form reduces humans to secondary status, as mere carriers of the techno-contagion. Like the alien, the technological virus uses humans as a breeding ground that combines and recombines existing structures to produce new mutations. These may—in the form of horrific weapons—ultimately result in the extinction of humanity. Winner observes, "Each generation extends the technical ensemble and passes it on to the next generation. . . . The mortality of human beings matters little, for technology is itself immortal and, therefore, the more significant part of the process."[7] Ellul draws similarly bleak conclusions about the role of humans in technological evolution: "Technique pursues its own course more and more independently of man. This means that man participates less and less actively in technical creation, which, by the automatic combination of prior elements becomes a kind of fate. Man is reduced to a catalyst."[8]

The technological virus undermines the human dream of control. With its vision of human-hating machine-monsters, *Alien* questions the notion that technology is neutral, simply a means to an end; it also refutes the assumption that technology invariably proves beneficial to human lives. Far from being neutral, technology reveals itself to be self-perpetuating and self-enhancing, growing and changing apart from (as opposed to alongside) human calculations and desires. Winner explains, "Human beings still have a nominal presence in the technological network but they have lost their roles as active, directing agents. They tend to obey uncritically the norms and requirements of the systems which they allegedly govern."[9] As such, the plague of technology, operating as a pervasive totalitarian force, thwarts human control and tends to modify then dominate the environment, psychology, motives, and behavior of society. "America is addicted to oil," claimed former President George W. Bush in his 2006 State of the Union address, at the height of the Iraq War. But, that is not quite right: our *machines* are addicted to oil. As such, society must be organized, to an extent, around the acquisition of oil whether through war, exploitation, or environmentally costly exploration. In this sense, humans become slaves to technology, even sacrificing their lives for its expansion.

TECHNOLOGY IN CONTROL

The technological systems of the *Nostromo* run independently of even the Company's control. At the end of the film, Ripley initiates the mechanism that will destroy the spaceship in ten minutes. The device is clearly marked with a fail-safe abort procedure for stopping the self-destruction. During the countdown to the *Nostromo*'s end, Ripley changes her mind. She fulfills the fail-safe system's requirements but the destruction mechanism continues anyway. Ripley curses Mother, blaming the computer for ignoring her desire to stop. The self-destruct system is so "efficient" once initiated that it cannot be reversed by human override even though destroying the *Nostromo* undermines the Company's interest. As Ellul puts it, "Man no longer possesses any means of bringing action to bear upon technique. He is unable to limit it or even to orient it. Technique is essentially independent of the human being who finds himself naked and disarmed before it."[10] Ellul's comment brings to mind the literal near-nakedness of the crew at the beginning of *Alien*, sleeping cryogenically under complete control of the *Nostromo*'s technological systems. We recall as well Ripley's near-nakedness at the end of *Alien* just prior to being attacked by the techno-monster in all its forms.

Despite her vulnerable state, the surviving crewmember rises up and defeats the last representative of techno-totalitarian force, the alien itself. In a final evocation of the film's reproductive motif, Ripley asserts sovereignty over her own body and, in an act of symbolic abortion, blasts the alien into space, even severing its umbilical cord. This conclusion seems to soften the techno-totalitarian theme of the film. Though the entire crew (save Ripley) has been killed, the Company's technology—the robot, the computer, the *Nostromo*, and the alien—have been destroyed. One of cinema's greatest monster fighters, Ripley appears to demonstrate that a tough, independent, resourceful human being can free herself from the forces of technological domination. But this interpretation is wrong: despite the temporary uplift, *Alien* ends on a deeply pessimistic note.

Ripley's victory over the monstrous embodiment of corporate technology—the alien—leaves the invisible techno-totalitarian system intact. She remains completely dependent upon the same Company technology that functioned to capture and protect the alien and that characterized her life as expendable. She anthropomorphizes the technology and subordinates her role in relation to it when she titles her last log entry "Final Report of the Starship *Nostromo*." She then returns to cryogenic sleep, putting her trust back into the techno-protection of the Company-controlled computer that operates the shuttle and regulates her life support system. Beyond that, she hopes to return to the Company, whose expensive robot and spaceship she has destroyed and whose profit-producing alien she has blasted into space. The Company will not be happy to see her; they would rather the alien were on board.

Alien paints a gloomy picture that depicts humans as the victims of ubiquitous, oppressive technological forces indicative of the moral flaws and authoritarian impulses of its corporate designers. Ripley has no choice but to once again place her faith in the Company's technological systems in order to survive. She and her now-dead crewmates put themselves in a position of extreme, even pathological dependence upon technology that is seemingly too complex to either understand or control. Though Ripley defeats the individual representatives of said technology, she remains at the mercy of the techno-tyrannical system that still dominates her.

NOTES

1. Jacques Ellul, *The Technological Society*, trans. George Wilkinson (1954 repr. New York: Knopf, 1964), 306.

2. Langdon Winner, *Autonomous Technology: Technics-out-of-Control as a Theme in Political Thought* (Cambridge, MA: MIT Press, 1977), 3.

3. Ellul, *The Technological Society*, 125, 284.

4. Winner, *Autonomous Technology*, 29.

5. In *Prometheus* (2012), Scott's disjointed and thematically confusing *Alien* prequel, android David plays a role generally similar to Ash's as an anti-human techno-monster programmed to serve corporate interests. David's puzzling behavior can only be explained by surmising that he views humans as experimental subjects for alien research. He infects one scientist, Holloway, with the black oil virus, killing him for no apparent reason other than possible contempt over belittling reminders of his non-human status. He cares nothing for scientist Shaw when she becomes impregnated with an alien fetus, even attempting to knock her out. Though it is not articulated clearly, David—like Ash—carries out a hidden corporate agenda that regards the human crew as expendable.

6. David Skal, *Screams of Reason: Mad Science and Modern Culture* (New York: W. W. Norton, 1998), 215.

7. Winner, *Autonomous Technology*, 59–60.

8. Ellul, *The Technological Society*, 134.

9. Winner, *Autonomous Technology*, 29.

10. Ellul, *The Technological Society*, 306.

REFERENCES

Alien. DVD. Directed by Ridley Scott. 1979. Los Angeles, CA: Twentieth Century Fox, 1999.

Ellul, Jacques. *The Technological Society*. Translated by George Wilkinson. 1954 Reprint. New York: Knopf, 1964.

Prometheus. Directed by Ridley Scott. Los Angeles, CA: Twentieth Century Fox, 2012.

Skal, David. *Screams of Reason: Mad Science and Modern Culture*. New York: W. W. Norton, 1998.

Winner, Langdon. *Autonomous Technology: Technics-out-of-Control as a Theme in Political Thought*. Cambridge, MA: MIT Press, 1977.

Part III

Gender, Identity, Selfhood

Chapter Thirteen

Through Space, Over a Cliff, and Into a Trench: The Shifting Feminist Ideologies of *Alien, Thelma & Louise,* and *G. I. Jane*

Aviva Dove-Viebahn

As a filmmaker who has consistently touted the importance of strong women in his films, Ridley Scott has directed some of the most highly contested (and painstakingly theorized) Hollywood productions relevant to both the popular and academic feminist imaginaries. There is little debate that Scott's *Alien* (1979) revolutionized the understanding of the role of women within the science fiction horror genre by featuring a protagonist, Ellen Ripley (Sigourney Weaver), who (mostly) avoids the traps of conventional cinematic femininity while simultaneously functioning within, in scholar Constance Penley's words, a "stunningly egalitarian" narrative framework.[1] Although their generic concerns are literally worlds away from Ripley's isolated-in-space mentality, Scott's later films *Thelma & Louise* (1991) and *G. I. Jane* (1997) are part of a lineage that extends from *Alien*. This is not only because of their explicit incorporation of and emphasis on the concerns of women characters, but also in their articulation of the political conundrums surrounding various contemporary feminist ideologies.

The premises of these films vary greatly, and yet they exhibit markedly similar themes. In *Alien*, a crew of seven on a routine space expedition to harvest mineral ore awakens from suspended animation in order to respond to a mysterious signal from a nearby planet. After a brief survey planet-side, one of the scientists is attacked by an alien life form. Bringing him back aboard for medical treatment (despite Ripley's vehement protests that he should remain in quarantine) invites the alien in as well. The crew spends the rest of the film fighting for and ultimately losing their lives—except Ripley, who "[r]ather than cry 'Eeek!' and freeze in the face of danger . . . becomes the dragon slayer who blows the beast into the vacuum of space."[2] Twelve years later, Thelma (Geena Davis) and Louise (Susan Sarandon) of Scott's eponymous film embark on a two-day fishing trip only to have their journey derailed by cowboy rapist Harlan. While Louise's murder of Thelma's would-be assailant and a flight from the law bring about the women's temporary empowerment and liberation from their oppressively sheltered lives, their adventure eventually spirals out of control when they decide to "keep going" over the edge of the Grand Canyon, choosing death over imprisonment. Finally, *G. I. Jane*'s Lieutenant Jordan O'Neil (Demi Moore) confronts the US Navy's entrenched sexism after being selected to be the first woman to take part in its brutal SEAL training program. She ultimately completes the program and proves herself to her male colleagues, but not before being subjected to political scheming and betrayal, false allegations of misconduct (a code word for lesbianism) under "Don't Ask, Don't Tell," the threat of sexual violence during a training mission, and "run-of-the-mill" sexism from virtually every soldier with whom she trains. Ripley, Thelma, Louise, and Jordan all find their journeys interrupted as the forces of institutional authority, patriarchal privilege, and a sexist status quo, respectively, compel them to take on the mantle of power and fight back against a relentless and, at times, seemingly insurmountable persecution.

Each of these films fits into a traditionally masculine genre, with Scott's cross-gender casting serving as the most obviously feminist element of his interventions into these genres.[3] Ripley is a sci-fi protagonist operating in the horror film mold; she remains strong in the face of the overbearing industrial complex for which she labors while vanquishing the otherworldly (ironically maternal) evil lurking in the dark recesses of her ship.[4] *Thelma & Louise*'s road trip functions as a backdrop for Scott's homage to women's freedom from the stereotypically feminine roles of submissive victims of both the patriarchal system of law enforcement and actual men. *G. I. Jane*'s military narrative, in a genre so often celebrating the personal sacrifice of male soldiers overcoming some larger-than-life conflict, frames the continuing controversy around American women in combat and the gender-specific dangers they face.

While Scott's twisting of generic codes to serve his women protagonists functions as valuable fodder for feminist identification, these narratives are not without their ideological problems, explored in dozens (or, in the case of *Thelma & Louise*, hundreds) of popular and academic critiques. My intent in this chapter is not to rehash previous assessments but rather to interrogate the progression of Scott's feminist approaches as they originate with *Alien* and evolve through to *Thelma & Louise* and *G. I. Jane*. Significantly, these were films released during the political debates around an anti-feminist "backlash," feminism's supposed "failure" and/or "death," and the emergence of "post-feminism" in the late 1980s and 1990s.[5] Several tensions emerge that invite further inquiry, particularly in light of Scott's trajectory through conventionally masculinized genres and his exploration of feminist philosophy within those frameworks: the visual and linguistic rhetoric of sexuality through the gendered bodies of the protagonists; sexual violence and feminine penetrability; and the feminist potential for resistance within the masculinist social order.

ON BECOMING WOMAN / AN (UN)BECOMING WOMAN

In *The Second Sex* (1949), French philosopher Simone de Beauvoir asks, "Are there women, really?" a question which leads her into an over 700-page analysis of the social, historical, cultural, and biological implications of gender divisions and roles.[6] This question, along with her famous assertion, "One is not born, but rather, becomes, a woman," foregrounds much of contemporary Western feminist thought about the distinction between sex and gender. For example, foundational feminist theorist Judith Butler considers Beauvoir's analysis a critical acknowledgment of gender's function as a social construction, further asserting in *Gender Trouble* that "Beauvoir contends that the female body is marked within masculinist discourse, whereby the masculine body, in its conflation with the universal, remains unmarked."[7] By asking "Are there women, really?" Beauvoir constructs a theory of gender which reveals both femininity and the conventional Western understanding of the gendered social order as masquerades, byproducts of the patriarchal imaginary.[8] In her philosophy and contemporary interpretations of it, we find the foundation upon which much of Scott's feminist inquiry about gender performance and conformity rests.

What does it mean to refuse the markers of femininity? Ripley begins *Alien* as a rather unremarkable mid-level officer who rises to heroic heights only after circumstances force her to take charge and either fight or die. Being a woman has nothing to do with her survival, nor is it an obvious aspect of her identity as a character, which is certainly part of what continues to make Ripley such a revolutionary feminist figure.[9] While, in a recent interview, Scott acknowledges that part of Ripley's strength as a character stems from the audience's thwarted expectations—"This rather pretty woman who everyone assumed in the first act was going to be one of the first ones to cop it gradually starts to take up the mantle, and the weapon"—he also admits that he did not initially intend to make a feminist statement through Ripley, nor did he recognize the gendered significance of her role as the film's star until Weaver had been cast.[10] In earlier interviews, the director frequently emphasizes that Ripley was originally meant to be a man, and admits that the film is far more interesting precisely because she is not: "She could easily have been a male character, but the pressure on that character would have been less because it would have been a familiar character."[11] Ripley is also not stereotypically feminine; for example, she wears minimal makeup and she does not become hysterical at the first sign of danger (here, she is a stark contrast to the other woman on board, Lambert). Still, she is recognizably a woman. Neither she nor the film stress or disavow her gender except, arguably, in her final confrontation with the alien, which finds her nearly naked and reveals her conventionally feminine body (pretty, slim, and vulnerable) to the spectatorship's gaze for the first (and only) time.[12]

In contrast to Ripley, Thelma, Louise, and Jordan all engage in a process of "unbecoming," of consciously discarding the signifiers of femininity which make them vulnerable to patriarchal limitations and/or attack.[13] At the beginning of the film, Thelma's stereotypically feminine helplessness leaves her wide open to Harlan's predation, and while Scott takes great pains to emphasize Thelma and Louise's difference from one another (Louise is organized and "uptight"; Thelma is chaotic and ditzy), he also reinforces their secure place as conventional feminine types. Louise fits the classic mold of the mature, cynical working-class woman with a commitment-phobic boyfriend, while Thelma is the beleaguered, under-appreciated housewife who, in Louise's words, "got what [she] settled for." Over the course of the film, both women literally, according to Christine Holmlund, "shed the accoutrements of femininity as they go. Louise trades her jewelry for a beat-up hat and throws her lipstick in the dust. Thelma switches from frilly blouses and bikinis to T-shirts with motorcycle insignia. . . . By the time the two stop their car in the Arizona desert they are as sweaty, dusty, nonchalant, and hardened as any pair of male outlaws would be."[14] But their appearance is not the only aspect that changes over the course of the film; Thelma and Louise's approach to the world, to the society that defines and confines them, shifts as they move further from their previous lives both in space and time.

In many ways, these two protagonists seem like ideal feminist archetypes. They take their lives into their own hands, find modes of empowerment that highlight their refusal to behave in accordance with feminine convention, and fight back against a system which oppresses them. And yet, the vehicle of their transformation is violent and angry, which makes them, for some, problematic feminist icons. Screenwriter Callie Khouri insists their resistance to patriarchal institutions should not be taken literally: "they were never intended as role models, for God's sake. I don't want anybody doing anything they saw in the movie." In his direction, however, Scott notably changed the emotional valence of Khouri's script, in which some of the men Thelma and Louise encounter were more sympathetic than their screen versions.[15] Scott also emphasizes the oppressive masculinity of the Southwestern landscape which the women must navigate.[16] In his oft-cited negative review, "Toxic

Feminism on the Big Screen," John Leo takes issue with the film's patriarchal metaphors and phallic symbolism, and though it is debatable whether the film's feminism is in any way "toxic," Leo's interpretation of Scott's *mise-en-scène* is not wrong: "Right from the start, they are hemmed in by and constantly intimidated by huge trucks, director Ridley Scott's symbol of suffocating male oppression. No movie has ever budgeted so many menacing trucks or so many hoses and spraying machines aimed at women—two or three hoses, two street sprinklers, an irrigation system or two, and one crop-dusting plane. (Calling Dr. Freud: What can all this male spraying represent?)"[17] By employing these symbols of phallic power, Scott opens up a space where Thelma and Louise's response to their physical and human environments feels, if not justified, then at least provoked.

The violence in the film, then, can be seen as a direct reaction to society's unrelenting insistence that the women *behave* (that is, act in a way that is acceptable to men). While a number of critics suggest that *Thelma & Louise*'s violence is excessive, Susan Sarandon argues that this indictment shows "what a straight, white male world movies traditionally occupy. This kind of scrutiny does not happen to *Raiders of the Lost Ark* or that Schwarzenegger thing [*Total Recall*] where he shoots a woman in the head and says, 'Consider that a divorce.'"[18] Sarandon's response calls attention to the double-standard inherent in the different ways spectators respond to violence enacted by men and women; yet to say that *Thelma & Louise*'s violent reaction to their circumstances has nothing to do with gender is specious. As with Scott's assertion that *Alien* is more interesting precisely because Ripley is a woman, the violence of *Thelma & Louise* is different and more noteworthy because of the characters who perpetrate it.

I do not mean to suggest that because we expect violence from men in action films that such violence is permissible whereas Thelma and Louise's is not; this is, however, an implication haunting some of the film's reviews.[19] In fact, repudiating or extolling the violence in the film is, in a way, beside the point. The violent behavior of the protagonists is different not because they are women but because their motives are explicitly gendered; arguably, threats of rape and other forms of sexual assault predicate most of the women's violent behavior toward men, an idea I will consider in greater depth below. Confronted by a world that is clearly out to get them, in fact and in form, Thelma and Louise gradually cast away feminine trappings, real and imagined, and engage in a violent resistance to victimization and objectification in order to reassert an agency that, the film suggests, is always already lost.

The progression we see taking place in *Thelma & Louise* occurs far more deliberately in *G. I. Jane*. Jordan does trade in her soft-spoken persona and slim, athletic build for an aggressive attitude and hard body in order to succeed in a masculine social order, but her violent behavior functions less as a defense against her own gendering and more as a side-effect of her becoming a model soldier, conditioned by the SEAL training program's imperative to fight fire with fire. While *G. I. Jane* cannot hold a candle to Scott's masterful negotiation of feminist tropes in *Thelma & Louise*, the film certainly is his most overtly (and aggressively, in several senses of the word) feminist film. Despite her assertion to her boyfriend early in the film that she is "not interested in being some poster girl for women's rights," Jordan "simultaneously insists on quite traditional feminist demands and claims," among them equal treatment with the men in her unit, integrated barracks, and combat experience.[20] Early in the film, the office of Senator Lillian DeHaven, who orchestrates the Naval integration program as part of a political power play, laughingly discards several candidates for training because they are too masculine ("Is this the face you want to see on the cover of *Newsweek*? She looks like the wife of a Russian beet farmer"; "[She's] perfect . . . if we do a chromosome check"). Jordan is selected because she seems capable while still remaining feminine enough in terms of appearance and talents (running triathlons and writing award-winning essays as opposed to power-lifting). She does not assault the older woman's perception of women both in the media and in terms of the general public's predicted response. And yet, the first thing Jordan does is begin to visibly and *intentionally* take on the trappings of masculinity.

In order to guarantee that her integration succeeds, she tries to align herself as closely as possible with her male comrades. Jordan's transformation from a bright, mild-mannered Navy intelligence officer to a brutal, no-nonsense warrior is complete and explicit, from her defiant head-shaving to Scott's training montages where the camera lingers over her muscular and capable body. She pushes herself through an increasingly difficult series of exercises: sit-ups, pull-ups, and, eventually, one-armed push-ups. The camera may objectify her in these moments (in much the same way the camera lingers on Ripley's scantily clad body in the final scene of *Alien*), but, as Amy Taubin argues, "This is woman as spectacle, but the spectacle is a gender bender that scrambles the iconography of top and bottom, butch and femme, exploding male and female identities in the process."[21] It is notable, however, that the first time after her transformation Jordan figuratively lets her hair down and socializes with other women, she is immediately accused of "conduct unbecoming an officer," military code for lesbianism. It is as if, having taken on the outward trappings of masculine strength and power, Jordan's sexuality also becomes suspect; if she "acts like a man," must she not also desire women? This accusation of misconduct, moreover, is not mere lip service to debates surrounding "Don't Ask, Don't Tell" in the mid-1990s, but also acknowledges the problematic nature of Jordan's gender performance. Lesbianism is the default position, according to heteronormative patriarchal "wisdom," for the woman who eschews femininity; reading the unfeminine woman as lesbian maintains a social order in which women dress and behave in accordance with the supposed wishes of men.[22]

Heteronormativity demands that men do not desire other men. Following this twisted logic, since men are presumed to desire feminine women (who are least like other men), women who are deemed unfeminine must have no interest in appealing to men. That Senator DeHaven makes certain Jordan is a "solvent heterosexual" before the latter's entry into the training program only to later attempt to orchestrate Jordan's dismissal through "Don't Ask, Don't Tell," starkly illustrates this elision of the difference between appearance, behavior, and identity.[23] Thelma and Louise similarly express a kind of socially-coded lesbian identification, not merely because of their final kiss, which has been interpreted as the culmination of a sub-textual lesbian romance, but because they repeatedly refuse to submit themselves as objects of exchange within the patriarchal sexual economy.[24] The homosocial relationship between the characters eventually becomes more important than their relationships with men, sexual or otherwise; that they put their faith in each other rather than give in to the entreaties of Louise's boyfriend, Jimmy (Michael Madsen), or the promises of leniency from the paternal detective, Hal Slocomb (Harvey Keitel), signals at the very least that Thelma and Louise's deep friendship puts them on what Adrienne Rich calls a "lesbian continuum."[25]

Responding to critics who myopically claim that his narratives are merely a "misogynistic exercise in 'turning women into men,'" Scott rejoins, "People who say that have just never met strong women."[26] This response is also limiting and somewhat disingenuous. The question remains as to where shedding the mantle of traditional femininity gets Scott's characters. In the process of unbecoming woman, what does one become instead? As Jordan's struggle illustrates, merely looking more like the men in her program does not actually protect her from the cultural burdens of being a woman nor does it allow her access to any sort of male privilege. Furthermore, Sharon Willis contends that while Thelma and Louise may escape certain feminine identifications, they are nevertheless still performing gender: "*Thelma & Louise*'s dramatic and exhilarating transformation of women's body language—posture, gesture, gait—does not read, however, as a revelation of the 'natural' body underneath the feminine masquerade of the housewife or service worker. . . . [The women] parade an interruption: where we expect them to exhibit the mark of sexuality for consumption, instead we see the body itself as masquerade."[27] Jordan, too, sheds her femininity only to reveal another layer of performance: that of the macho soldier and war hero. At no point in any of Scott's films is this transformation more explicit than when Jordan, in Taubin's words, "lays claim to the crucial male body part, neatly severing anatomy from destiny."[28]

"LOOK HOW I TURNED OUT": RAPE AND GENDER PERFORMANCE

When Master Chief Urgayle (Viggo Mortensen) takes a training exercise too far and makes motions to rape Jordan in front of the other soldiers, he claims to be demonstrating how women's ostensibly "natural" vulnerability to sexual assault renders the entire unit at risk. Thus, the film codes Jordan's subsequent triumph over him as a jubilant moment, the apogee of her becoming "more than" a woman in the eyes of her comrades.[29] Scott, who would go on in subsequent years to make films showcasing spectacular bloodbaths (*Gladiator*, 2000) and the gritty heartbreak of war (*Black Hawk Down*, 2002), does not shy away from the violence of this scene nor does he go easy on Jordan. While the training exercise is meant to simulate capture and interrogation, the acting moves dangerously close to a sadistic reality during Jordan's turn for questioning. When she refuses to provide any useful information, Urgayle drags her out of the interrogation hut and in front of the men. He holds Jordan's head under water, punches and kicks her until her face is broken and bloody, then forces her over a table, rips open her pants and begins to undo his belt. During this scene, he taunts the watching trainees: only if they give up their intel will he stop his assault. Jordan urges the other soldiers to stay silent and takes things into her own hands; she slams her head back, breaking Urgayle's nose and escaping his grasp. The caged soldiers cheer Jordan on as the two soldiers fight. Even though her ability to defend herself is significantly handicapped by her hands still bound behind her back, she gets in several bruising kicks, but is eventually knocked to the ground. While Urgayle attempts to explain himself to the trainees, who turn their back to him, Jordan struggles to rise: "Guys. I'm saving her life and yours. Her presence makes us all vulnerable, and I don't want you learning that inconvenient fact under fire." When he tells Jordan, now on her feet, blood dripping thickly from her face, to "seek life elsewhere," she responds with a line that both explicitly severs her ties with the constraints of gender normativity and acknowledges her understanding that her words are doubly damning because she is a woman: "Suck my dick." In response to her retort, the other trainees cheer and shout, rattling the bars of their pen and chanting "Suck my dick" in a refrain that crescendos until the cut. Scott does not reveal how the training exercise ends, but it is clear that, whatever the next step, Jordan has won. She proves that being a woman does not make her a liability, and shows how she can be an asset to her unit regardless of, rather than despite, her gender. Ironically, Jordan's ability to co-opt phallic power linguistically allows her momentary freedom from other people's expectations about her femininity while simultaneously emphasizing the power of her speech as a woman.

I read Jordan's victory not only as triumphant within the diegesis of *G. I. Jane*, but as a riposte extending outward into Scott's *oeuvre*, a poignant and subversive echo of Harlan's final line in *Thelma & Louise*. It is not his attempt to rape Thelma that results in his death, but his refusal to apologize and his catalytic imperative "Suck my cock," spoken to Louise, that drives her to shoot him. While her violent response muddies the water of her motives, it is no longer self-defense; Louise's belated action signifies her understanding of Harlan's utterance as a form of sexual aggression almost as vicious as his physical assault. According to Sarah Projansky, "[Louise's] action conveys the language-gaze-rape links directly. . . . By representing Harlan's actions as extensions of everyday forms of sexual harassment that includes visual and verbal assault . . . the film both acknowledges the pervasiveness of rape . . . and provides an image of a woman who fights back powerfully against both verbal and physical assaults—hence, against rape culture."[30] In fact, Scott's directorial choices and Khouri's screenplay continually remind spectators of the consequences of Harlan's attempted rape and the indistinct primal scene of Louise's past experience with sexual assault; while these moments may not *explain away* Louise's murder of Harlan, they do call attention to its origins in a patriarchal social order that repeatedly attempts to sexualize women and punishes them when they refuse to submit.[31]

Louise has little verbal recourse against Harlan; what can she say to take back his physical assault or forestall further verbal aggression? It is precisely because Louise cannot embody Harlan's position of power linguistically that she takes action physically. Michael A. Kaplan argues: "the irreducible *necessity* of [Louise's] response must not be missed. It is *because she cannot speak*, as it were, that she must shoot. Since the antagonism between them concerns the phallus, it concerns power as a prerogative of representation. . . . Unable to distinguish between Harlan and his discourse, she was in effect shooting his speech."[32] This kind of analysis does not excuse Louise's actions, as she and Thelma pay dearly for Harlan's death after all, but rather acknowledges that Harlan's power over the two women holds even after Louise has wrenched Thelma from his physical grasp. Harlan is a symbolic threat as much as he is a physical one. Throughout the film, Thelma and Louise must resist literal and symbolic threats on their autonomy and bodily integrity: denying the wishes and demands of their respective partners when these do not match up with their own; blowing up the rig of a trucker who persists in assaulting them with lewd gestures when they pass him several times on the road; and refusing to succumb to a justice system that does not acknowledge or respect the trauma of sexual assault. However, while Thelma and Louise enact their own rebellion against the patriarchal order in later moments of the film, neither of them possess the linguistic ability to disrupt or appropriate Harlan's privileged, gender-based access to hegemonic power.

Thelma and Louise also have no recourse to verbal retribution, but it is Jordan's interpolation into this ostensibly male linguistic prerogative in *G. I.*

Jane that allows her to silence her would-be attacker by speaking rather than shooting. Jordan's audience, too, is crucial. It is at the moment when she tells Urgayle to "Suck [her] dick," and that the other soldiers *accept and applaud her utterance*, that she truly becomes "one of the boys," no longer a liability as Urgayle prophesies, but an asset. Notably, Jordan's squad invites her out for drinks for the first time after this scene, a ritual of induction that she has earned. Jordan co-opts the masculine prerogative, marking her authority over Urgayle in that moment: "Liberated from a strict anatomical context, Moore's utterance suggests that we might all have enough of a dick to make it available for the purposes of insult: you do not necessarily have to actually *have* one to be able to tell someone what they can do with it. Yet to grasp the position from which 'dick' can be spoken and then, in words, to throw it back at your assailant makes the speaker the better endowed of both of them at this point in the film."[33] In claiming the phallus linguistically, Jordan destabilizes gender categories; she is "better endowed" in the role of brave, macho soldier than the toughest of the tough guys, Urgayle. However, it is immediately after this scene on the base that she becomes vulnerable to attack from outside it, by way of DeHaven's scheming and the Navy's false allegations of lesbianism. The more she conforms to the "masculine" performance required of her by SEAL training, the less she fits into a mainstream imaginary of the woman soldier. It is worth pointing out, though, that neither Jordan nor her boyfriend, Royce, seem the least bit disturbed by her new physique, her enhanced musculature, or her shaved head. In fact, Jordan revels in her newfound toughness when she threatens Senator DeHaven with exposure, insisting she be put back in the training program despite the politician's protests: "Don't tell me you wanted that kind of life. Squat-pissing in some third-world jungle with guys looking up your behind." Jordan's response, "I wanted the choice. That's how it's supposed to be," signifies her position as a feminist one and begs the question whether her transformation is really about masculinity after all.

While the woman action hero outwardly performs acts that seem to connote masculine gender expression—and Jordan serves here as an example *par excellence*—Jeffrey A. Brown posits that a feminist reading of these characters must acknowledge how they embody "the arbitrariness of gender . . . the popular press's perception of action heroines is not as much a recognition of gender as performative as it is a limiting of legitimate, alternative female identities."[34] Let us return, briefly, to *Alien*'s Ripley: interpreting her *lack* of overt feminine attributes as masculine, or even, for that matter, androgynous, is to automatically doom her to a hopeless compromise within a binary gender system. This is not to say that the fact that she is a woman does not matter, at least to spectators, but one could argue that as far as the diegesis is concerned, Ripley's gender is completely immaterial. Rather, the fact that we have no "feminine" categories to define a woman like Ripley (or

Thelma, Louise, and Jordan) leads to a specious reading of them as masculine. Along these lines, Willis posits that Thelma and Louise's "take-over" of cinematic roles that spectators have seen countless times enacted by men—the weary road warrior, the outlaw, the action hero—calls attention to precisely the kind of identification presumed "natural" between male spectators and male characters: "Within this framework, images of women raiding those nearly worn-out stories, trying on those clichéd postures, might have the effect of 'newness' and might challenge our readings of those postures themselves."[35] This posturing, taken as masculine, might acquire a special valence with women protagonists, but it does not necessarily follow that these women want to act or be like men.

In a decisive moment of her transformation from naïve housewife to adept outlaw, Thelma gestures toward the difference between her and Louise's gender(ed) performance, the roles occupied by men, and the male-dominated social order. When the women are pulled over by a cop, Thelma opts not to wait and see if he will discover the warrants out for their arrest; instead, much to Louise's astonishment, she holds him up at gun point and locks him in his trunk. To the cop's blubbering plea that he has a wife and kids, Thelma responds, "You do? Well, you're lucky. You be sweet to them, especially your wife. My husband wasn't sweet to me and look how I turned out." Thelma knows, as well as we do, that her husband, though emotionally abusive and self-serving, is not to blame for Harlan's attempted rape, nor is he the direct cause of her going on the lam with her best friend. Rather, Thelma's advice foregrounds her growing understanding that her husband's poor treatment of her shaped her sense of self, just as Louise's previous experience with sexual assault colors her relationships with men and her interpretation of their motives. While Thelma is responsible for her own choices, her freedom to make those choices has always been limited by the (patriarchal) world in which she lives and through which her husband frequently exerts power over her. An unlikely candidate for embodying a feminist outlook, *G. I. Jane*'s Urgayle nevertheless also theorizes that the obstacles Jordan faces are not really about her. When one of the instructors admonishes Urgayle for his behavior during the training exercise, "That was out of line in there. It ain't gonna happen again," he counters, "Yeah, it will. Maybe not with you or with these guys or with me. She's not the problem, we are." Even *G. I. Jane*'s most abusive character—although not, ironically, its most misogynist one—can see that the "problem" is not to be found in these characters *as* women, but lies rooted far deeper in cultural assumptions about men's right to power over women's autonomy and sexuality.

BODIES IN MOTION: A FEMINIST ESCAPE?

In her review of *G. I. Jane*, Phyllis Schlafly quips that Demi Moore as Jordan "proves she is a liberated woman by getting herself beaten to a bloody pulp, almost raped, and subjected to extreme bodily harassment. To the feminists, this is okay because her goal is to be treated just like men."[36] Although Schlafly's response represents her well-known anti-feminist viewpoint and disregard for nuance within feminist politics, she was not alone in her concern that Jordan, like many of Scott's women protagonists, takes up the mantle of supposed masculinity a bit too fiercely. Linda Ruth Williams, however, contends that "Critical confusion over whether Jordan is a man or woman means that across the spectrum of reception she/he is both: man enough to constitute a betrayal of feminism and femininity, but woman enough to be deemed hormone-driven, masochistic, and brutalized."[37] Counter to the paradox Williams identifies in the popular readings of Scott's films, I would like to consider, by way of conclusion, how *Thelma & Louise*'s highly contested ending acknowledges this conundrum of gender identity and problematizes the women's ability to challenge or escape its weight.

While the end of *Thelma & Louise* has their car freezing mid-flight over the cliff's edge, Scott's alternate ending of the film, in which Louise's Thunderbird continues its descent into the canyon, evokes an understanding of their imminent deaths as very real. This conception is further reflected in many critical responses to the film, indicting it for sacrificing its heroines right at the point when their empowerment is at its most profound. Khouri, however, sees Thelma and Louise's swan dive as more metaphorical than suicidal, asserting, "They flew away, out of this world and into the mass unconscious. Women who are completely free from all the shackles that restrain them have no place in this world. The world is not big enough to support them. They will be brought down if they stay here. They weren't going to be brought down. So let them go. I loved that ending and I loved the imagery. After all they went through I didn't want anybody to be able to touch them."[38] Khouri's view reads like a fairy tale with undercurrents of the utopia imagined by radical feminist separatism, even as she speaks to an understanding of the prevailing social order as a problem the film's protagonists ultimately fail to overcome.

Certainly, running away is no victory, unless it is escape (as in Ripley's case), although hers is brief given *Alien*'s preponderance of sequels. And although an alternate ending has Jordan gunned down during *G. I. Jane*'s final skirmish in Libya, the theatrical release's *dénouement* leaves her in typical Hollywood fashion: she has succeeded against all odds. If we choose to play dumb and buy into the hopeful tone of the film's final moments, we might believe that Jordan's post-training future is bright. More realistically, however, the future that awaits her will either be an unerring and interminable battle for respect, as she will need to prove herself to each new squad or unit she commands, or an utterly disappointing backpedal. Given the Navy's institutional resistance to gender integration (and the fact that the real-life SEALs are still men-only), the likeliest outcome of Jordan's labors is that she will be written off as an experiment and have some good stories to share as she sits back behind her desk in the Navy's intelligence office. In many ways, then, the ending of *Thelma & Louise* is both the most feminist and the most honest in its assertion that there are no easy answers. Instead of glossing over their challenge to and rebuke by a social order that will not accept alternative visions of women's gender expression, Thelma and Louise choose not to live in a world that does not want them. Their decision to "keep going" is a feminist disavowal of a world too small(-minded) to accept their freedom from the threat of sexual violence and from the bonds of gender conformity.

NOTES

1. Constance Penley, "Time Travel, Primal Scene, and the Critical Dystopia," *Camera Obscura* 5 (Fall 1986): 77.

2. Thomas Doherty, "Genre, Gender, and the *Aliens* Trilogy," in *The Dread of Difference: Gender and the Horror Film*, ed. Barry Keith Grant (Austin: University of Texas Press, 1996), 194.

3. For more on Scott's articulation of genre conventions in these films see Yvonne Tasker, *Spectacular Bodies: Gender, Genre and the Action Cinema* (London: Routledge, 1993).

4. Texts which famously address an understanding of *Alien* as a descendant of the horror film and, in the latter instance, its interrogation of birth and the maternal include Carol J. Clover, *Men, Women, and Chainsaws: Gender in the Modern Horror Film* (Princeton, NJ: Princeton University Press, 1992) and Barbara Creed, *The Monstrous Feminine* (London: Routledge, 1993).

5. See Susan Faludi, *Backlash: The Undeclared War Against American Women* (New York: Anchor Books, 1992).

6. Simone de Beauvoir, *The Second Sex* (New York: Vintage Books, 1989), ix.

7. Judith Butler, *Gender Trouble: Feminism and the Subversion of Identity* (New York: Routledge, 1999), 17.

8. See also Joan Rivière, "Womanliness as Masquerade," *International Journal of Psychoanalysis* 10 (1929): 303-313.

9. It is worth noting that Carol Clover considers Ripley an extension of horror film's "final girl," a character whose gender is "compromised from the outset by her masculine interests, her inevitable sexual reluctance, her apartness from other girls, sometimes her name. At the level of the cinematic apparatus, her unfemininity is signaled clearly by the exercise of the 'active investigating gaze' normally reserved for males and punished in females when they assume it themselves." Clover, *Men, Women, and Chainsaws*, 48. In an interview, however, Scott more or less counters this interpretation, distancing Ripley from horror's "final girl" narrative: "In *The Texas Chainsaw Massacre*, which was significantly frightening for me at that particular point cause I looked at it just prior to making *Alien*, that girl was still standing at the end covered in blood, but she'd survived rather than won. The difference with Ripley was that she had won *and* survived." Marlow Stern, "Ridley Scott Opens Up About 'Prometheus,' Kick-Ass Women, and 'Blade Runner 2,'" *The Daily Beast*, May 17, 2012, accessed July 25, 2012, http://www.thedailybeast.com/articles/2012/05/17/ridley-scott-opens-up-about-prometheus-kick-ass-women-and-blade-runner-2.html.

10. Stern, "Ridley Scott Opens Up."

11. Gary Dauphin, "Heroine Addiction," *The Village Voice*, August 26, 1997.

12. Yvonne Tasker argues that Ripley is marked by her gender in other ways, particularly as a foil to the woman in the film and in the way she is challenged by some of the men, although no particular mention is ever made about her being a woman: "In *Alien*, Sigourney Weaver's Ripley is defined against a series of other female types, such as Lambert, who is weak and hysterical and, at a more metaphorical level, the ship's computer Mother. . . . Yet, despite her rank, the narrative makes certain that Ripley should still be seen to struggle to establish her authority with Ash in *Alien*, a struggle that reprises an earlier scene, in which Parker and Brett drown out her words with steam. These hierarchical conflicts effectively position Ripley as an outside action heroine." Tasker, *Spectacular Bodies*, 148.

13. One could argue that Ripley sheds her androgyny (rather than her femininity) at the end of the film when she undresses, a moment Creed interprets as a brief respite from *Alien*'s relentlessly abject representation of femininity: "Compared to the horrific sight of the alien as fetish object of the monstrous archaic mother, Ripley's body is pleasurable and reassuring to look at. She signifies the 'acceptable' form and shape of woman. . . . The visually horrifying aspects of the Mother are offset through the display of woman as reassuring and pleasurable sign." Creed, *The Monstrous Feminine*, 23.

14. Christine Holmlund, "A Decade of Deadly Dolls: Hollywood and the Woman Killer," in *Moving Targets: Women, Murder and Representation*, ed. Helen Birch (Berkeley: University of California Press, 1993), 139-140.

15. Marita Sturken, *Thelma and Louise* (London: BFI Publishing, 2000), 65, 20.

16. Scott's challenge to the masculine imperative of the West is, on its own, an explicitly feminist statement. For further discussion see, for example, Sturken, *Thelma and Louise*, 37-39.

17. John Leo, "Toxic Feminism on the Big Screen," *U.S. News & World Report*, June 10, 1991.

18. Quoted in Richard Schickel, "Gender bender," *Time*, June 24, 1991.

19. Besides John Leo's piece, other examples of this kind of critique include Sheila Benson's "True or False: Thelma & Louise Just Good Ol' Boys?" *Los Angeles Times*, May 31, 1991.

20. Marysia Zalewski, "Tampons and Cigars: (No) Escaping Sexual Difference in *G. I. Jane*," *International Feminist Journal of Politics* 1, no. 3: 480.

21. Amy Taubin, "Dicks and Jane," *The Village Voice*, August 26, 1997.

22. See Judith Halberstam, *Female Masculinity* (Durham, NC: Duke University Press, 1998).

23. Senator DeHaven questions Jordan at the beginning of the film to make sure she is a "solvent heterosexual" so her experiment does not "blow up in [her] face," and yet it is through her machinations that these false allegations are made. After Jordan's integration proves too successful, DeHaven wants her ousted from the program, a plan which fails precisely because Jordan has gained newfound confidence and determination from her training. "I never expected you to do so damn well," DeHaven tells her. "I thought you'd ring out in two weeks. Bing, bang, it's over, and we're popular."

24. See Cathy Griggers, "Thelma and Louise and the Cultural Generation of the New Butch-Femme," in *Film Theory Goes to the Movies*, ed. Jim Collins, Hilary Radner, and Ava Preacher Collins (New York: Routledge, 1993), 129-141.

25. In her germinal essay "Compulsory Heterosexuality and Lesbian Existence," Rich contends that women who have significant and loving relationships with other women, whether sexual or platonic, fit on a "lesbian continuum." She asserts that a "pervasive cluster of forces" from the enforcement of feminine dress codes to the erasure of women's history strives to convince women that relationships with men are necessary and that heterosexuality is inevitable and "natural." *Signs* 5, no. 4 (Summer 1980): 648-649, 640.

26. Dennis Lim, "He's not a feminist, but . . ." *The Independent*, October 26, 1997.

27. Sharon Willis, *High Contrast: Race and Gender in Contemporary Hollywood Film* (Durham, NC: Duke University Press, 1997), 113.

28. Taubin, "Dicks and Jane," 73.

29. While this exact language is not used in the film, it is worth noting that the way the men understand Jordan after this moment mirrors Pino's famous declaration to Mookie in Spike Lee's 1989 film *Do The Right Thing* that his idols Magic Johnson and Prince are "more than black." We are to understand that what Pino means is that because these men have distinguished themselves, because they are popular and talented celebrities, they have risen, in his eyes, beyond the limitations of their race—the implication being that "normal" African Americans are fundamentally defined (and degraded) by their blackness in a way these men are not. A similar mechanism is at work for Jordan.

30. Sarah Projansky, *Watching Rape: Film and Television in Postfeminist Culture* (New York: New York University Press, 2001), 126-127.

31. Projansky, *Watching Rape*, 127.

32. Michael A. Kaplan, *Friendship Fictions: The Rhetoric of Citizenship in the Liberal Imaginary* (Tuscaloosa: University of Alabama Press, 2010), 96, 103.

33. Linda Ruth Williams, "Ready for Action: *G. I. Jane*, Demi Moore's Body and the Female Combat Movie," in *Action and Adventure Cinema*, ed. Yvonne Tasker (New York: Routledge, 2004), 180.

34. Jeffrey A. Brown, "Gender and the Action Heroine: Hardbodies and the *Point of No Return*," *Cinema Journal* 35, no. 3 (Spring 1996): 56.

35. Willis, *High Contrast*, 108.

36. Phyllis Schlafly, *Feminist Fantasies* (Dallas, TX: Spence, 2003), 81.

37. Williams, "Ready for Action," 179.

38. Sturken, *Thelma and Louise*, 73.

REFERENCES

Alien. DVD. Directed by Ridley Scott. 1979. Los Angeles, CA: Twentieth Century Fox, 1999.

Benson, Sheila. "True or False: Thelma & Louise Just Good Ol' Boys?" *Los Angeles Times*, May 31, 1991. Accessed August 26, 2012. http://articles.latimes.com/1991-05-31/entertainment/ca-2730_1_ridley-scott.

Brown, Jeffrey A. "Gender and the Action Heroine: Hardbodies and the *Point of No Return*." *Cinema Journal* 35, no. 3 (Spring 1996): 52-71.

Butler, Judith. *Gender Trouble: Feminism and the Subversion of Identity.* New York: Routledge, 1999.

Carlson, Margaret. "Is This What Feminism Is All About?" *Time*, June 24, 1991.

Clover, Carol J. *Men, Women, and Chainsaws: Gender in the Modern Horror Film.* Princeton, NJ: Princeton University Press, 1992.

Creed, Barbara. *The Monstrous Feminine.* London: Routledge, 1993.

Dauphin, Gary. "Heroine Addiction," *The Village Voice*, August 26, 1997.

De Beauvoir, Simone. *The Second Sex*. New York: Vintage Books, 1989.

Doherty, Thomas. "Genre, Gender, and the *Aliens* Trilogy." In *The Dread of Difference: Gender and the Horror Film*, edited by Barry Keith Grant, 181-199. Austin: University of Texas Press, 1996.

Faludi, Susan. *Backlash: The Undeclared War Against American Women.* New York: Anchor Books, 1992.

G. I. Jane. DVD. Directed by Ridley Scott. 1997; Burbank, CA: Hollywood Pictures Home Entertainment, 1998.

Griggers, Cathy. "Thelma and Louise and the Cultural Generation of the New Butch-Femme." In *Film Theory Goes to the Movies*, edited by Jim Collins, Hilary Radner, and Ava Preacher Collins, 129-141. New York: Routledge, 1993.

Halberstam, Judith. *Female Masculinity.* Durham, NC: Duke University Press, 1998.

Holmlund, Christine. "A Decade of Deadly Dolls: Hollywood and the Woman Killer." In *Moving Targets: Women, Murder and Representation*, edited by Helen Birch, 127-151. Berkeley: University of California Press, 1993.

Kaplan, Michael A. *Friendship Fictions: The Rhetoric of Citizenship in the Liberal Imaginary.* Tuscaloosa: University of Alabama Press, 2010.

Leo, John. "Toxic Feminism on the Big Screen," *U.S. News & World Report*, June 10, 1991.

Lim, Dennis. "He's not a feminist, but . . ." *The Independent* , October 26, 1997.

Modleski, Tania. *Feminism Without Women: Culture and Criticism in a "Postfeminist" Age.* New York: Routledge, 1991.

Penley, Constance. "Time Travel, Primal Scene, and the Critical Dystopia." *Camera Obscura* 5 (Fall 1986): 66-85.

Projansky, Sarah. *Watching Rape: Film and Television in Postfeminist Culture*. New York: New York University Press, 2001.

Rich, Adrienne. "Compulsory Heterosexuality and Lesbian Existence," *Signs* 5, no. 4 (Summer 1980): 631-660.

Rivière, Joan. "Womanliness as Masquerade." *International Journal of Psychoanalysis* 10 (1929): 303-313.

Rubin, Gayle. "The Traffic in Women: Notes on the 'Political Economy' of Sex." In *Deviations: A Gayle Rubin Reader*, 33-65. Durham, NC: Duke University Press, 2011.

Schickel, Richard. "Gender bender." *Time*, June 24, 1991.

Schlafly, Phyllis. *Feminist Fantasies.* Dallas, TX: Spence, 2003.

Shapiro, Laura. "Women Who Kill Too Much," *Newsweek*, June 16, 1991.

Stern, Marlow. "Ridley Scott Opens Up About 'Prometheus,' Kick-Ass Women, and 'Blade-Runner 2.'" *The Daily Beast*, May 17, 2012. Accessed July 25, 2012. http://www.thedailybeast.com/articles/2012/05/17/ridley-scott-opens-up-about-prometheus-kick-ass-women-and-blade-runner-2.html.

Sturken, Marita. *Thelma and Louise*. London: BFI Publishing, 2000.

Tasker, Yvonne. *Spectacular Bodies: Gender, Genre and the Action Cinema*. London: Routledge, 1993.

Taubin, Amy. "Dicks and Jane." *The Village Voice*, August 26, 1997.

Thelma & Louise . DVD. Directed by Ridley Scott. 1991; Beverly Hills, CA: MGM Video, 1997.

Tucker, Lauren and Alan Fried. "Do You Have a Permit for That?: The Gun as a Metaphor for the Transformation of G. I. Jane into G. I. Dick." In *Bang Bang, Shoot Shoot! Essays on Guns in Popular Culture*, edited by Murray Pomerance and John Sakeris, 165-174. Toronto, ON: Simon & Schuster, 1998.

Williams, Linda Ruth. "Ready for Action: *G. I. Jane*, Demi Moore's Body and the Female Combat Movie." In *Action and Adventure Cinema*, edited by Yvonne Tasker, 169-185. New York: Routledge, 2004.

Willis, Sharon. *High Contrast: Race and Gender in Contemporary Hollywood Film*. Durham, NC: Duke University Press, 1997.

Zalewski, Marysia. "Tampons and Cigars: (No) Escaping Sexual Difference in *G. I. Jane*." *International Feminist Journal of Politics* 1, no. 3: 479-481.

Chapter Fourteen

Why Doesn't Hannibal Kill Clarice? The Philosophy of a Monstrous Romantic in *Hannibal*

Matthew Freeman

The figure of Dr. Hannibal Lecter plays a prominent role in popular culture, his iconography and contradictory ideologies spawning both a series of novels devoted to the character as well as a film franchise that will soon expand once again to the arena of television. [1] While author Thomas Harris's creation has been at the epicenter of a small number of academic studies, many of which contrast the Lecter phenomenon with feminine gender roles or serial killer motifs, little attempt has been made to examine the philosophy of the character himself. Even fewer scholarly works have ventured into the world of Ridley Scott's *Hannibal* (2001), a film that offers a reinterpretation of the character as a moral monster of the Romantic Age.

This gap is particularly surprising given that the release of *Hannibal*, the long-awaited sequel to *The Silence of the Lambs* (1991), was caught up in a media flurry, as trailers for the film emerged even before production had begun. Philip L. Simpson notes that "audience expectations for the quality of the sequel were high, mostly because Anthony Hopkins had reprised his now-iconic role and because Ridley Scott was the director." [2] Indeed, *Hannibal* represented a rare beast: an *auteur*-quality horror film where audience's eagerness to see the film stemmed, as Simpson also points out, from their taste for "Lecter coming out of his cage." [3] Departing from the conventions of the police procedural thriller and the psychological horror film that characterized *The Silence of the Lambs*, *Hannibal* shifted the Lecter character to previously uncharted generic territory.

This chapter explores *Hannibal*'s engagement with such philosophical discourses as Romanticism (in particular, the Romantic hero), along with its more explicit references to Dante Alighieri, the famed Florentine poet of the thirteenth century. Dante's seminal influence on the Romantics and their meditations on monsters will position Lecter in this historical and cultural context. The chapter also explores the film's contrast of innocence and corruption in relation to cannibalism, thereby identifying Scott's compelling philosophical reinterpretation of this unique killer. The film's pronounced philosophical bases will finally be discussed in relation to the director's own ideological orientations, arguing that the film's portrayal of Lecter as a Romantic monster of the past occupying a modern world of even greater monstrosity should be understood in the broader context of Scott's cinematic oeuvre.

THE HONEY IN THE LION

The relish of seeing Lecter on the loose was not the only driving factor behind the film's popular appeal. The narrative of escape, resulting in challenges to an established order, characterizes a number of Ridley Scott films. *Alien* (1979) deals with the chaos caused by the sudden emergence of a deadly species; *Gladiator* (2000) is the story of one man who overthrows a corrupt empire; and *Blade Runner* (1982), a film that shares considerable narrative and thematic similarities with *Hannibal*, follows a determined detective's quest to stop an android fugitive in a society mired in moral flux. *Hannibal*, in many ways, operates against an entirely different generic backdrop from *The Silence of the Lambs*. While the latter film is a police procedural thriller, the former is a gothic romance; when genres shift, so too do the character types within them. Whereas *The Silence of the Lambs* presents Clarice Starling (Jodie Foster) as the free agent out to solve the case with Lecter (Anthony Hopkins) as an imprisoned mentor, *Hannibal* reverses that scenario: it is Lecter who serves as the narrative's free agent while Starling (this time portrayed by Julianne Moore) has since become trapped by her loyalties to the FBI. Her faith in the system cannibalizes her in a world inhabited by monsters of an altogether different kind—the scheming, administrative monsters not in straitjackets and prison cells but in suits and corporate offices.

In *The Silence of the Lambs*, Starling relies on her faith in the virtues of the FBI to help relinquish her inner demons. This fidelity to such systems of public "good" enables those awful memories of her past—about her father's murder and the haunting screaming of the slaughtered lambs—to be silenced. In *Hannibal*, however, that faith is under threat, those systems beginning to fail her. The FBI, the system of order to which Starling has devoted her entire life, begins to eat at her, cannibalizing her for upholding the very virtues that she once thought defined the institution. Such demoralization is reflected in

Scott's use of the color grey. The previous film's assured moral dichotomies between the law (good) and Lecter (evil) are thrust into a territory that is considerably "greyer." In striking contrast to the distinct greens she wears throughout *The Silence of the Lambs* (the color a symbol of the character's former sense of self-respect, balance, energy, even "freshness" as a young agent), Starling is costumed early on in *Hannibal* in a grey suit. This color-coding conveys her own growing ambivalence towards the system that formed her.

Chief Inspector Rinaldo Pazzi (Giancarlo Giannini) also wears grey, which reflects his own ambiguous moral code. Far from Starling's presence as a straight arrow, Pazzi is morally ambiguous to the point of being amoral. Working both within and outside the law in order to capture Lecter, a known killer and fugitive, Pazzi's motivations are born both out of justice and personal reward, the latter slowly devouring the former through corruption. Lecter, in contrast, is first introduced in the film wearing a clean, gleaming white suit—white being a heroic color traditionally associated with purity and innocence. Scott departs from the intimacy that defines both the aesthetic and the viewer's access into the world of *The Silence of the Lambs*, a stylistic reversal that many misinterpreted as a failure of Scott's film. In a review published on May 2, 2001, for example, *Variety*'s Todd McCarthy wrote, "Ridley Scott's opulent, impressionistic direction, while striking on its own terms, doesn't lend itself to the sort of sustained creepiness and complex character interplay delivered by Jonathan Demme's carefully tooled craftsmanship."[4] This review summarized many of the popular opinions at the time of *Hannibal*'s release, though such criticism ultimately fails to acknowledge that Scott's film is not concerned with "sustained creepiness" but instead with revealing the "creeps" that lurk across the entire social spectrum. Whereas *The Silence of the Lambs* consists largely of enclosed interiors, shot through shadowed corridors and with regular close-ups of increasingly disturbed faces in a way that allows access into the evil minds of those hidden away from society, Scott lends *Hannibal* an air of the grandiose, capturing its monstrous world in sweeping long-shots that accentuate the prevalence (even overabundance) of monsters in contemporary society.

Indeed, the film's canvas is broadened to such a degree that in this despicable world of corrupt chief inspectors, misogynistic government agents, and vengeful pedophiles—each defined by such traits as greed, amorality, and sadism—Lecter is perhaps the closest thing to a hero. Starling is a character that devotes her life to ridding the world of such evil, yet does so in a system that is similarly corrupt and broken. At one point she describes Lecter as a man who does almost the same thing as she does, fulfilling, in his eyes, a public service. Yet Lecter, unlike the disgraced agent, is free from an organization like the FBI. Framed alone in dark, empty spaces, regularly surrounded by cardboard boxes of old police evidence, Clarice is here represented as both immersed in her job and detached from the world outside of it. Lecter, meanwhile, is similarly detached and alone. Both characters are isolated, precise, and impeccably professional; each is grounded by a strict moral code, albeit with different aims. Looking back to Scott's *Blade Runner*, we might note that the replicants are quite similarly detached from their world as the film's protagonist, Rick Deckard (Harrison Ford). He, in turn, is not quite sure who or what he is. Lecter and Starling may not share Deckard's identity crisis, yet both occupy spaces of a forced or even voluntary detachment, isolated from society on account of an ever-growing distaste for that society. As such, each embodies an ontological crisis that defines a number of Scott's protagonists.

THE MONSTER AS ROMANTIC HERO

One version of the crisis emerges in the archetype of the Romantic hero. Lilian R. Furst argues that this figure—often used by scholars to illuminate the philosophies of European Romanticism around the end of the eighteenth century—in many ways prefigures the contemporary anti-hero. Lecter, or at least Scott's version of him in *Hannibal*, is not a modern anti-hero but a throwback to the figure of the Romantic hero, a representation that must be understood in the larger context of Scott's thematic interests as a filmmaker. The Romantic hero is regularly understood as a character that rejects a society that in turn rejects him. Furst writes that "in their preoccupation with heroism," the Romantics displayed both a devotion to and an unease with the idea of "the warrior's traditional heroism," a kind of "heroic ideal" that might be extended to personify moral incorruptibility and "human greatness."[5] I argue that Lecter has been constructed in *Hannibal* as an heir to the Romantic Age, devoted to preserving traditional heroism even if that devotion means, as the film puts it, "eating the rude." In turn, it is the old-fashioned heroism of a warrior—a rare thing in the mostly corrupt contemporary world of *Hannibal*—that Lecter sees in Starling.[6] Furst draws on the figure of Napoleon as the model of Romantic heroism, noting a similar incompatibility between the hero's chivalry and the savagery of the hero's world: "As for the living model of the [Romantic] hero, Napoleon, he soon proved a bitter disappointment to many. . . . Napoleon's ignominious end in exile, in glaring antithesis to his glorious rise, seemed to confirm the hollowness of heroism in the modern world."[7]

In this vein, Lecter, a throwback to the earlier century's vision, can indeed be understood as a Romantic hero who has essentially disassociated himself from a new world where few traditional heroes remain. His own acts of monstrosity (literally "eating the rude") thus altogether transcend villainy: his construction as a Romantic who rejects an amoral society that in turn rejects him creates a heroic villain, his monstrosity coinciding with his heroic ideals. Likewise, Starling *is* that heroic ideal, a figure of honor, devotion, and incorruptibility in a world where such ideals are not only unrewarded but vilified. In a film where more characters are corrupt than heroic, Starling is also something of a Romantic throwback, a character of such chivalry and heroism that she now seems out of place. In fact, the Lecter of *Hannibal* is only synonymous culturally with the villainous monster archetype as a result of his allusive relation to *The Silence of Lambs*, which serves to define his broader cultural affiliation with the serial killer tradition. As noted, while a number of critics described *Hannibal* as a failure because it did not correlate thematically with the serial killer archetype set out in *The Silence of the Lambs*, it is much more useful to point out that Scott's film is intended as a *subversion* of that archetype; it asks the audience, just as the director has done in such past works as *Blade Runner*, to reconsider the concept of monstrosity. As Furst explains,

> Almost inevitably [the Romantic hero] is a gentleman, a member of the leisured class at ease financially. Both his handsomeness and his freedom from mundane concerns raise him to the level of an idealised, glamorous figure sharply distinguished from the characteristic modern anti-hero with his petty subsistence-level anxieties, his frequent physical imperfections, his embroilment in the grotesque messiness of daily living. All this is alien to the Romantic hero, who exists . . . high above everyday reality.[8]

Many of these descriptions can be applied to the representation of Lecter in *Hannibal*, a character of gentlemanly stature, living a seemingly charmed and luxurious life in Florence even while a fugitive from the law. This city, one of the film's settings, has particular thematic significance: its associations with European Romantic literature inscribe a correlation between the settings portrayed in the film and the ones in literary history. While Anthony Hopkins describes *Hannibal* as being "like some great medieval drama,"[9] the film even shares structural characteristics with the Romantic heroes of European literature. As Furst notes, "the Romantic hero's dominance stems not from his activity, but from the interest in his psyche, since his heroic assertion is the egocentric one of his own personality."[10] This interest in his psyche, as Furst puts it, relates back to Philip L. Simpson's earlier observation in regard to *Hannibal*, which cites the broad appeal of the film as revolving around the audience's desires to learn more about Lecter's mind.

Such ancient philosophies are often inferred through the film's explicit references to Dante Alighieri, whose work is the subject of Lecter's scholarly lectures. These references are more than superficial. For Peter Manseau, *Hannibal* is "a film as much about Dante as serial murder."[11] In his cosmology, Dante examines the nature of the soul. Beatrice di Portinari is understood to be the primary inspiration for his *Vita Nuova* and serves as one of the writer's guides throughout his *Divine Comedy*. This was his epic allegorical meditation on the soul's journey through Hell, Purgatory, and Heaven. The work is divided into three parts reflecting this journey: *Inferno*, *Purgatorio*, and *Paradiso*. In *Inferno* Dante comes face to face with the Beast, sinking to the depths of depravity; in *Purgatorio* Beatrice guides Dante through Heaven; and in *Paradiso* he reveals himself to God at the pinnacle of love. Manseau argues that the philosophical meaning of Dante's work informs both the thematic underbelly and the narrative structure of Scott's film:

> Chasing Lecter, following him as Dante does Virgil, Starling is led downward; she is made an observer of ever darker levels of sin and its ever higher price. Meanwhile, chasing Starling (it is for her he returns from his exile in Florence), Hannibal is somehow elevated. Not purified, not rehabilitated, certainly not saved, and yet a transformation does somehow occur; something has begun. . . . If Hannibal can't be saved then neither can Starling. [12]

From monstrous fall to metaphysical ascent, Hannibal is a philosophical retelling of the *Divine Comedy*, reincarnated for twenty-first-century audiences. Just as Virgil leads Dante to the depths of Hell, so too does Lecter lead Starling, allowing her and viewers to once again reconsider precisely what we mean by our definition of "monster." As such, and despite the similarities between Starling and Lecter, there are also other notable differences that tie in with Furst's distinction between the Romantic hero and the traditional hero. This is a distinction that Scott complicates regularly. For example, Furst notes that "whereas the hero is often envisioned as the saviour, a redeemer . . . the Romantic hero all too frequently exerts a disruptive, indeed destructive force."[13] In *Hannibal*, it is Lecter who becomes the redeemer. Mason Verger (Gary Oldman), one of Lecter's former "victims," even describes his near-fatal encounter with the doctor as his moment of redemption, despite wishing to enact revenge for this very moment. In many ways, Lecter comprehends his own role as both that of the saviour (eradicating the rude and sinful to protect others) and that of the destroyer. For Lecter, the act of cannibalising the sinful is a redemptive act. Yet it is significant that *Hannibal* positions Lecter as a figure, much like the Romantic heroes of the past, who is content not to act on his loathing of the world. As Furst notes in relation to the Romantic hero, a point that similarly defines Lecter in Scott's film, "his antagonism to society takes the negative form of a withdrawal: in many instances it is a literal retreat into the remote backwoods. . . . Far from combating the social ills of his day . . . the Romantic hero chooses instead the path of evasion."[14] Indeed, in the case of Lecter, it is only the threat he witnesses to Starling that thrusts the man into action. He offers his hand in fighting to preserve her old-fashioned idealism despite the fact that such an act plunges him "more and deeply into solipsistic gloom."[15]

The theme of self-destruction certainly runs throughout *Hannibal*; this Romantic solipsism at Lecter's core is itself a means of self-devouring. The figure of the cannibal has regularly been used by critics to examine the collision and consumption of opposing worlds (namely, cannibalism implies the "eating" of one culture by another). The term itself is commonly associated with those who exist on societal margins, and writers have tended to group together multiple forms and iterations of the cannibal. It is important to identify how Scott differentiates between different types of cannibalism in relation to his philosophical agenda. It is thus useful to turn to the work of Frank Lestringant, author of "Cannibals: The Discovery and Representation of the Cannibal from Columbus to Jules Verne," who acknowledges two very distinct forms of cannibalism, both relevant to reading this film.

According to Lestringant, one of the earliest appearances of the cannibal motif was in the writings of the sixteenth-century French cosmographer André Thevet, who distinguishes between "good" cannibals who seek meaning and revenge through their tabooed act, and "bad" cannibals, who simply have a taste for flesh.[16] As well as correlating and in some ways reinforcing Furst's earlier distinction between the Romantic hero and the savagery of his world, Lestringant similarly points out that cannibalism also inherits a social function. He writes: "Far from being a meaningless practice . . . cannibalism is a symbolic action. . . . It is a mark of culture, a religious and social act that has a higher meaning and which, through contrast, reveals the senseless and base savagery of . . . life."[17]

Such impressions feed into the philosophy of *Hannibal*. Lecter is known in media circles as "Hannibal the Cannibal," as a serial killer previously incarcerated for killing and feasting on his victims. The cannibalism motif also extends beyond Lecter, used regularly in connection with Mason Verger, who, as is revealed in a flashback sequence, is convinced by Lecter to peel off his face with a shard of broken mirror while on drugs. Lecter watches the whole incident before feeding the flayed skin to Mason's dogs. For Lecter, such an act of brutality is entirely justified, since Mason is believed to have abused a number of children (cannibalizing them sexually), thus pairing the cannibalism motif with the theme of justice in a way that echoes Lestringant's distinction. Interestingly, the narrative itself mirrors this particular pairing with the flipside of justice—that is, revenge—as Mason seeks to capture and feed Lecter to a pack of man-eating boars. The story depicts the metaphorical cannibalism that lies at the rotting core of law enforcement in the United States and abroad as the honorably incorruptible Starling is "fed to the dogs," as it were, by her corrupt peers at the FBI. In this way, it is Lecter who emerges as the "good" cannibal in opposition to the likes of Verger, Paul Krendler (Ray Liotta), and Rinaldo Pazzi, each of whom embodies the traits of the "bad" cannibal. They crave only "flesh," so to speak, as each finds himself consumed by a desire for personal gain irrespective of the horror involved in achieving it.

It is precisely this moral ambiguity that Scott foregrounds against the Romantic love fomenting between a modern day Beauty and Beast. After all, Furst also acknowledges that a central concern faced by the Romantic hero is the realization that "the woman of his desires [is] beyond reach," while for Scott, *Hannibal* is an "impossible love story" whose underlying theme is "affection, and in some instances, you might even wonder, certainly from one direction, is it more than affection?"[18] The ending of the film revises the novel's unexpectedly surreal climax in which Starling is seduced by Lecter and they together enjoy a long life combining sex and art. The cinematic version altogether distorts such romantic leanings with a more tragically Romantic finale. Indeed, while Scott (re)introduces the character of Starling at the start of the film with a shot of her sleeping (thus evoking an allusion to the fairy tale of Sleeping Beauty), it is important to note that in Scott's story, unlike Harris's novel, the Beauty cannot be seduced by the allure of the Beast; there will be no "happily ever after." Whereas Harris perhaps envisioned *Hannibal* as a twisted, contemporary revision of the fairy tale, Scott instead distorts the tale's implications. While retaining the perverse romance of the novel, Scott's *Hannibal* is less a romantic fairy tale than a romantic tragedy (less "Beauty and the Beast," more *Romeo and Juliet*). As film critic Peter Travers notes in his review, *Hannibal* is "a freaky date movie for audiences who rooted for King Kong to get the girl."[19] Indeed, this dichotomy between the traditions of the fairy tale and tragedy is significant, since Scott's preference for the latter justifies his revised conclusion and altogether allows one to situate *Hannibal* in the context of the director's authorial prerogatives.

It is precisely Scott's decision to undermine Harris's conclusion that elevates Lecter to the plane of self-sacrificing Romantic hero. During the final encounter between Hannibal and Clarice, Scott demonstrates the moral immovability of Starling, whose undying incorruptibility is simultaneously what Lecter loves most about her and also what prevents her from ever letting him run free. In a scene devised by Scott and screenwriter Steven Zaillian, Lecter is handcuffed to Starling, her hair clamped to the inside of a refrigerator, thus preventing either from escaping. The sounds of police sirens surround the house. Lecter, reaching for the sharpest available kitchen knife, must choose to await arrest or to amputate his own hand or that of Starling. He chooses the latter, slicing himself at the wrist and thus ending the film with an affirmation of self-sacrifice. Lecter, a cannibal-monster who inflicts self-mutilation on the amoral and immoral, willingly self-harms in the name of protecting the beauty of this world (as embodied by Starling).

The endings of *The Silence of the Lambs* and *Hannibal* both have Lecter escape into oblivion. The earlier film leaves a sinking feeling of dread and disgust at the prospect of Lecter roaming free amongst us all, while the latter is quite the opposite: emotions of relief, joy, and even celebration are invited as the picturesque beauty of a firework display paints the sky following Lecter's narrow escape. As Scott asserts, "[I]t's rather perverse, but this person, this special criminal, this killer, is free, and [in *Hannibal*], I think that we're rather pleased that he is."[20] Thus when Scott's film reaches its climax and Starling sheds a tear of regret as her heroic incorruptibility presses her to deny Lecter his freedom even in a world of much greater sin, suddenly Lecter seems no more the villain of the story than does Starling. Even the grotesque prelude to Starling's final choice—where Lecter avenges the bribe-taking sins of Krendler by forcing the Justice Department official to devour parts of his own brain—serves only to amplify Lecter's complex status as a Romantic idealist. Both barbaric in content and elegant in form, the self-devouring of Krendler's brains is itself moral, at least according to Lecter's worldview. Krendler's prejudice towards Starling earlier in the narrative is monstrously unjust, causing her to be suspended from the FBI. Since her life is based on her work, he essentially cuts off her life. Therefore his comeuppance, no matter how monstrous, is entirely just. As Manseau eloquently concludes, "*Hannibal* is a necessary, modern elaboration on an ancient religious theme. When there no longer is an inferno to fear, no longer a paradise to pray for, we find ourselves in purgatorial times. Sin goes unpunished, virtue unrewarded; grace is hard to find. In such a landscape, what does it now mean to be saved? Who deserves to be?"[21]

Based on the dynamics of this film, Scott is best characterized as a Romantic filmmaker. He attests, "In some ways, I view *Hannibal* as a romantic tale. A dark and tragic one to be sure, but beneath its suspenseful, violent surface, I was always fascinated by its impossible love story."[22] Much of Scott's cinema can indeed be understood in light of its Romantic inflections, interested as it is in questioning and ultimately subverting assumptions about the state of the world and the people within it. This subversion of moral dichotomies, as in the subversive transformation of the replicants in *Blade Runner*, whose initial villainy is slowly revealed to be tragic if not infinitely heroic, has long been central to Romantic literature. As Furst points out, the texts of this period similarly "venture a radical reassessment of accepted assumptions."[23]

WE CAN ONLY LEARN SO MUCH AND LIVE

Hannibal can therefore be situated within the larger thematic context of Scott's oeuvre. Demme's *The Silence of the Lambs* is a film where Lecter unnerves audiences through disturbing contradictions: he is a paradox of intellectual charm and yet despicable monstrosity. The films of Scott mentioned earlier, however, often explore an even more complex search for humanity amongst a less rigidly defined monstrosity. *Blade Runner* is a story about beings who are not human striving for freedom in a world populated by a human race that is both the creator and the destroyer of their freedom. It is a film in which human beings seem less human and more monstrously destructive than the supposedly monstrous replicants that—in turn—long to be human.

Hannibal has much in common with *Blade Runner*: both examine "seeming" monsters who crave only freedom; both illustrate worlds populated with people who strive mostly to wrong one another. Once again, Scott is fascinated with examining a world that is more monstrous than the seeming monster at its core, a world where characters seem doomed by their own existence. Just as with *Blade Runner* and the case of replicant Roy Batty (Rutger Hauer), the "villain" of *Hannibal*, Lecter himself, similarly stands as the most morally righteous character besides Clarice. Lecter is the film's catalyst for posing philosophical questions that are pertinent to Scott's work: Who is the *real* monster of the story? Is Lecter the devil we remember from *The Silence of the Lambs*, or is the world of apparent order and civilization surrounding this devil perhaps the most devilish monster of them all?

Hannibal's Starling, much like *Blade Runner*'s Deckard, is a law enforcement officer uncompromisingly devoted to a cause. Both protagonists are constructed as virtuous heroes who are positioned as outsiders on account of such virtue. Both are devoted to stopping their respective "enemies" (the replicants in *Blade Runner*, the fugitive Lecter in *Hannibal*) even upon acknowledging that such enemies are perhaps less threatening and less sinful than the destructive modern world that created them. Both films even include an almost identical scene. During the rain-drenched *Blade Runner* finale, Deckard gazes upon the dying Batty who is just desperate to live; following Starling's final encounter with Lecter in *Hannibal*, both protagonists stare silently into the skies above. It is here that Deckard contemplates his devotion to the stopping of replicants whose greatest crime is their desire to be free, while Starling finally begins to question her devotion to the curtailing of a monster whose own eventual freedom in the face of a world of even greater monstrosity seems somehow morally triumphant.

Hannibal is simultaneously both a horror movie and a gothic romance inscribed by Romantic-era philosophies. Whether or not Dr. Lecter is ultimately placed on an ascendant path towards the paradise that Dante once described is questionable, yet Ridley Scott suggests that such an eventuality is at least possible as his Romantic hero flies off to a new land at the film's end. What is evident, however, is that where the Romantic hero of literature's past often "stands unhappily betwixt and between," distancing himself from as much of the world as possible, so must Scott's heroic villain.[24] His existential stability is left decidedly ambiguous even in the face of his own romanticism. In this way, Lecter verges on becoming a tragic, old-fashioned moral monster doomed by his own nature and yet admirable for it.

NOTES

1. *Hannibal*, an American television series, is being produced as of August 2012 by NBC; meanwhile, *Clarice*, a rival television series, is also being produced by MGM. Both are scheduled to be broadcast in 2013. For more on the legacy of Lecter, see Szumskyj (2008).

2. Philip L. Simpson, "The Horror 'Event' Movie: *The Mummy, Hannibal*, and *Signs*," in *Horror Film: Creating and Marketing Fear*, ed. Steffen Hantke (Jackson: University Press of Mississippi, 2009), 92.

3. Ibid., 93.

4. Todd McCarthy, "Hannibal," *Variety,* February 4, 2001.

5. Lilian R. Furst, *The Contours of European Romanticism* (London: Macmillan, 1979), 40.

6. Interestingly, in Thomas Harris's *Hannibal*, Lecter even refers to Starling directly as a "warrior." Thomas Harris, *Hannibal* (London: BCA, 1999), 32.

7. Furst, *The Contours of European Romanticism*, 41.

8. Ibid., 42.

9. Anthony Hopkins, "Breaking the Silence," *Hannibal*, directed by Ridley Scott (Universal City, CA: Universal Pictures/MGM, 2001), DVD.

10. Furst, *The Contours of European Romanticism*, 43.

11. Peter Manseau, "Hannibal Lecter's Harrowing of Hell," *Killing the Buddha*, accessed July 3, 2012, http://killingthebuddha.com/mag/exegesis/hannibal-lecters-harrowing-of-hell-2/.

12. Manseau, "Hannibal Lecter's Harrowing of Hell."

13. Furst, *The Contours of European Romanticism*, 44.

14. Ibid., 45.

15. Ibid.

16. Frank Lestringant, "Cannibals: The Discovery and Representation of the Cannibal from Columbus to Jules Verne," in *College Literature* 26, no. 1 (Winter 1999): 210.

17. Ibid., 210.

18. Ridley Scott, "Breaking the Silence," *Hannibal*, directed by Ridley Scott (Universal City, CA: Universal Pictures / MGM, 2001), DVD.

19. Peter Travers, "Hannibal," *Rolling Stone*, February 9, 2001, accessed July 4, 2012, http://www.rollingstone.com/movies/reviews/hannibal-20010209.

20. Ridley Scott, "Feature-Length Commentary," *Hannibal*, directed by Ridley Scott (Universal City, CA: Universal Pictures / MGM, 2001), DVD.

21. Manseau, "Hannibal Lecter's Harrowing of Hell."

22. Ridley Scott, promotional insert, *Hannibal*, directed by Ridley Scott (Universal Pictures, 2001), DVD.

23. Furst, *The Contours of European Romanticism*, 51.

24. Ibid., 53.

REFERENCES

Alien. DVD. Directed by Ridley Scott. 1979; Los Angeles: Twentieth Century Fox, 2000.

Blade Runner. DVD. Directed by Ridley Scott. 1982; Universal City, CA: Warner Bros. Pictures, 1999.

Furst, Lilian R. *The Contours of European Romanticism*. London: Macmillan, 1979.

Hannibal. DVD. Directed by Ridley Scott. 2001; Universal City, CA: Universal Pictures/ MGM, 2001.

Harris, Thomas. *Hannibal*. London: BCA, 1999.

Lestringant, Frank. "Cannibals: The Discovery and Representation of the Cannibal from Columbus to Jules Verne." *College Literature* 26, no. 1 (Winter 1999): 209-212.

Manseau, Peter. "Hannibal Lecter's Harrowing of Hell." *Killing the Buddha.* Accessed July 3, 2012. http://killingthebuddha.com/mag/exegesis/hannibal-lecters-harrowing-of-hell-2/.

McCarthy, Todd. "Hannibal." *Variety*, February 4, 2001.

The Silence of the Lambs. DVD. Directed by Jonathan Demme. 1991; Los Angeles: Orion Pictures, 2003.

Simpson, Philip L. "The Horror 'Event' Movie: *The Mummy, Hannibal*, and *Signs.*" In *Horror Film: Creating and Marketing Fear*, edited by Steffen Hantke, 85-98. Jackson: University Press of Mississippi, 2009.

Szumskyj, Benjamin, ed. *Dissecting Hannibal Lecter: Essays on the Novels of Thomas Harris.* Jefferson, NC: McFarland, 2008.

Travers, Peter. "Hannibal." *Rolling Stone*, February 9, 2001. Accessed July 4, 2012. http://www.rollingstone.com/movies/reviews/hannibal-20010209.

Chapter Fifteen

In the Guise of Character: Costumes, Narrative, and the Reality of Artifice in *Thelma & Louise*

Lorna Piatti-Farnell

Clothes are not simply pieces of fabric, carefully arranged to form a pattern. They also have social, cultural, and economic functions. Clothes and dress sense are representational in nature and can convey meaning within a given situation. When judged as "high quality," clothes can convey prestige and the wearer's relative social position. As objects affiliated with a particular cultural system or set of beliefs, clothes are, as Elizabeth Wilson argues, "images, communicating more subtly than most objects and commodities."[1] Clothes do not have a strictly material function, but also hold a symbolic one strongly connected to perceptions of the body wearing them. They are able to communicate meaning by virtue of their "intimate relationship with the body" and relate to the construction of both individual and group perceptions of self.[2] By this framework, items of dress may even partake in allegories that demonstrate how status, ideologies, and identities are played out across bodily surfaces. In filmmaking, costumes are essential to plot and characterization, providing seemingly solid ground for the construction of figurative systems on the cinematic canvas.

Until recent years, film studies scholarship has been reluctant to widely acknowledge the importance of costuming and design overall. In *Costume and Cinema*, Sarah Street points out how recent scholarship has finally acknowledged the importance and function of costumes in relation to film form (for instance, "the meaning of *mise-en-scène*") and how examples of dress chosen for a given film have an impact on conceptual representations.[3] Street also draws attention to how character representations, aided by specific costume choices, have an influence on how audiences understand everyday behaviors within a film. This understanding is essential for the successful suspension of disbelief which allows the film to function as a believable (depending, of course, on genre) narrative. Street concludes that film costuming "operates as a system . . . governed by complex influences" related to notions of "realism, performance, gender, [the] status quo and power."[4]

With costuming's semiotic function as a point of departure, this chapter unravels the multiple significances of apparel in Ridley Scott's *Thelma & Louise* (1991). The conceptual versatility of clothing allows the filmmaker to develop not only the individual characters and the construction of a believable reality, but also the implications of sartorial appearance in cinematography. Marking the distinction between "costumes" and "clothes"—and underlining their points of intersection—I will interpret garments as self-reflexive and pluralistic instruments which channel the representation of genre and gender systems within the film. I trace the changing apparel throughout the film as representations of the corresponding character's emotional and social status. Character passions are, directly or indirectly, often related to dress. In claiming such a communicative function for costumes—and their narrative understanding as clothes—the target is not to show that they can be used as the key to unveiling all the major conceptual secrets of the film. Rather, I focus on how an accurate analysis of Scott's use of costumes and accessories can illuminate the conceptual framework of the movie as text, highlighting its values, meanings, and symbolic patterns. Costumes, therefore, will be understood as a dynamic and noteworthy presence within *Thelma & Louise*.

This film was co-produced by Scott and written for the screen by Callie Khouri. It stars Geena Davis as Thelma and Susan Sarandon as Louise. Set in a small provincial town in Arkansas, the film tells the story of two friends—a submissive housewife and an unmarried waitress—who decide to take a vacation and drive to a cabin for a fishing weekend. From the very beginning, the women's jobs, personalities, and geographical location underscore the sense of entrapment they feel in their daily lives. Their journey, however, is not a straightforward one; on their way, they stop at a bar where, in the parking lot, Louise shoots the cowboy who attempts to rape Thelma. The incident initiates a series of events which lead the women to embrace a life of crime. The film ends with both—now considered dangerous outlaws—driving off a cliff into the Grand Canyon, claiming that they would rather "keep going" than be arrested by the authorities.

Upon release, the film was immediately successful with critics and audiences alike; for their refusal to submit to the patriarchal control of society, Thelma and Louise were hailed as "feminist icons."[5] Their iconic status was particularly emphasized by their distinctive clothing choices, which, by the end of the film, include cowboy hats, boots, and sullen (if triumphant) expressions to match. As a director, Scott had already captured attention for his unique uses of costumes in *Alien* (1979) and *Blade Runner* (1982), among others. Even after *Thelma & Louise*, Scott continued an effective relationship with meaningful costumes; several of his films—including *Gladiator* (2000) and *Kingdom of Heaven* (2005)—have either been nominated or won awards for costume design.[6]

Before discussing the garments in *Thelma & Louise*, however, a clear distinction must be made between "costumes" and "clothes." The first term refers to the dress items that are selected by directors and designing personnel for the actors to wear in a performance piece. Drake Stutesman suggests that the costume is "an object, a literal building that the actor enters, 'wears' or inhabits in order to perform."[7] Clothes, on the other hand, imply an agency on the wearer's part; although examples from scholarship, especially those centered around gender debates, such as Judith Butler's *Gender Trouble* (1989), will claim that all clothing is worn as part of a performance, the concept of costume maintains a performative quality which is imposed on characters by an outside force.[8] When it comes to film, clothes can only be understood as such within the specific plot, where characters (it is presumed) have made individual decisions about what to wear. Both costumes and clothes have an element of performance attributed to them, inasmuch as they work within parameters of cultural masquerade and can be used, as Annette Kuhn points out, to construct "the wearer's self."[9] The fundamental difference here is that acts of construction—in both contextual and psychological terms—can be seen as an "intra-narrative" when it comes to clothes and an "extra-narrative" when considering costumes.

From the extra-narrative perspective, the director uses costumes to serve the plot. This understanding of costume is connected to the construction of credible structures of reality. As Charlotte Gaines and Jane Marie Herzog argue, narrative realism "dictates that costume be curtailed by conventional dress codes."[10] This realistic use of costumes can be seen at work in other films by Scott. In *G. I. Jane* (1997), soldier Jordan O'Neil (Demi Moore) wears military garb that is traditionally gendered masculine in keeping with her placement in the Navy SEAL training camp. The use of the uniform here also functions as a homogenizing mechanism that aims to erase gender difference in both the character's and the audience's eyes. Conceptually, costumes are forms of artifice. All items of clothing unsettle the conceptual shift between what is natural and what is fictitious. In so doing, they are products of conventions within popular and period fashion. Clair Hughes points out that "being dressed never quite achieves the status of the natural."[11] Although this comment seems mundane in its simplicity, it highlights the importance of clothes in creating background narratives for characters and places them within socio-economic and socio-cultural categories.

In this context, French semiotician and literary theorist Roland Barthes confers a lot of attention to understanding how clothes function cinematically. In *The Fashion System*, he views clothes as "signs" and highlights the presence of costumes as an essential part within the system of cinematic reality. He sees the clothes the characters wear not as simple props, but as meaningful objects which have a strong representational function.[12] The construction of a sense of reality is a particular concern in Barthes's work, and he identifies clothes and dress as important pieces in the construction of the artificial world. "The reel garment" is the appellative that Barthes gives to film costumes, a category which becomes closely associated with his idea of how characters "communicate through clothes." Every specific item of clothing worn by characters, Barthes argues, cannot be understood simply as casual or accidental, but rather as part of "the general economy of clothing" which is unique to each film.[13] Reality is constructed not by ephemeral concepts but from very concrete forms of representation, so that the world of the film can find tangibility in its artifice thanks to the presence of these expertly arranged, even conceptually volatile, fabrics.

Within the reality agenda, the role of costumes in soliciting audience response is undeniable. Associations, both visual and conceptual, are made between characters and costumes, between emotional states and choice of outfits. A change in clothes—or, to be more precise, in style of clothes—on the character's part readily invites analysis. In terms of characterization and the act of constructing personality within the movie, clothes allow a clear (albeit temporary) delineation between the character's reality and the way in which it operates more broadly. Peter McNeil, Vicki Karaminas, and Catherine Cole argue that within a specific narrative context "clothes define, sustain and give voice to social momentum and stages."[14] Clothes provide a framework from which to maneuver and classify reality so that relationships and attitudes can be understood, processed, and catalogued. McNeil, Karaminas, and Cole contend that film audiences interpret "costumes avidly, their indicators and signs offering a visual subtext" to actions and structures within the work.[15]

Costumes lure the audience into trusting in their understanding of characters, since clothes in Western cultures tend to be regarded as expressions of personality and, as such, play an important role in social interaction and self-identification. In this sense, clothes can be understood as vehicles of material seduction operating at several levels. The term "seduction" here is reminiscent of the work of French sociologist and cultural theorist Jean Baudrillard on clothing and fashion. Baudrillard understands clothes as objects (or commodities) related to a communication based on seduction, a complicated concept which nonetheless highlights the connection between representation, pre-existing knowledge, and the construction of reality. In contemporary Western societies, seduction is the driving force for the ritual configuration of objects amongst which people live, which is inevitably connected to the concept of "image." Attachment to and recognition of objects by viewers remain essential for an understanding of the world and therefore, a working notion of reality. Seduction, according to Baudrillard, does not undermine, subvert, or transform existing social relations or institutions, but is merely a soft alternative, a play with appearances, and a game of provocations.[16] In Baudrillard's thinking, seduction is inevitably connected to simulation. "To simulate," he argues, "is to feign to have what one hasn't. But . . . to simulate is not simply to feign": it is also to instigate reactions and effects.[17] Thus, simulation threatens the difference between true and false, between real and imaginary.

If one translates seductive simulation from the socio-economic system of commodities to a filmmaking context, it is possible to see how costumes are employed in a similar manner. The simulator—understood here not as an individual but as a working group containing both animate and inanimate presences (such as costumes)—produces "true" symptoms; these symptoms are the belief that what one is watching is "real." The active seduction into representation in *Thelma & Louise*, therefore, is connected to pre-existing, procedural notions of garments and dress codes, which work in a ritualized manner with the viewer's previous knowledge. The choice of costumes worn by the characters simulates a sense of authenticity so accurately that the audience is seduced into believing both the responses from the actors and the contextual dynamics of the American Southwest are real.

In constructing the film's reality, costumes are essential in communicating impressions of Thelma and Louise as individuals. Hughes suggests that if one is to avoid the abstract reductivism that results when a viewer or critic only reads characters in relation to plot, then it is essential to understand that imprints of individuals within a film are comprised not only of their actions, but also of "visual, tactile and psychological" elements which are inevitably governed by "material facts."[18] Working in close relation with what is strictly visual, tactile here must be understood as the qualities of fabrics, colors, and shapes which the audience will be expected to recall and understand. Psychological delineation, in terms of costumes, goes beyond the narrative events which are on screen; although actions are often viewed as a consequence of emotional states in any given plot, garments give us an insight into dominant modes of psychological organization which go beyond initial events or impressions of character. Costumes, viewed as an unearthed expression of emotional response on the screen, often speak more loudly than events. Susan Kismaric and Eva Respini claim that each character's clothes actually function as alternative, "interrupted narratives," which "imbue the images with dramatic complexity" as well as "contribute to the aura of personal intimacy and authenticity."[19] When the plot stalls and no actual event takes place, items of clothing are able to tell the story and speak for characters in a way that narratives alone rarely can.

In order for costumes in *Thelma & Louise* to work organically with the audience's expectations, they must display a certain level of verisimilitude;

in short, they must conform to the contextual and generic codes to which the film itself relates. One must think here of examples such as the old gangster films, where hats and pinstripe suits were an essential part of defining not only the category to which the individual film belonged, but also the expectations in relation to characterization and plot. In *Thelma & Louise*, the extensive use of denim and boots is in keeping with the film's original setting in Arkansas. The presence of cowboy hats and boots in the film is not casual; it seemingly places the film within the specific parameters of genre—the Western, in this case—and builds the audience's expectations about what might appear on screen, including the use of grand-angle, panoramic shots and the treatment of themes such as isolation, travel, separation, and fighting for one's beliefs. [20]

Discussing the contextual role of visual imagery, Hughes argues that costumes are "visible aspect of history." [21] Within Scott's film, they are both contextual and conceptual agents. When Louise and Thelma enter the first bar on their trip, the place which initiates their downfall, clothes and accessories immediately communicate information to the viewers. Both the patrons and the staff are wearing what can be described as cowboy attire. Cowboy hats, boots, and checkered shirts abound; denim jeans and skirts are everywhere. The costumes here are not simply telling us that the venue is a cowboy bar; the costumes are communicating a whole system of organization and belief which goes hand in hand with so-called cowboy ideology. This is a man's world; men dictate the rules and women occupy an inferior or merely supportive position. Daniel Roche claims that while the fictional context of film can never coincide perfectly with a viewer's individual expectations, the contextual relationship to reality makes it possible to give clothes a social meaning. [22] The conceptual function of clothes is emphasized by the appearance of a Marlboro cigarette poster on the wall behind the bar. The Marlboro Man is an individual who embodies cowboy masculinity, presumably put into practice by patrons. This character and his clothes speak loudly to unveil how dress is "also language, part of a social system of signs." [23]

The symbolic role of the cowboy attire is observed by Louise upon surveying the bar; she claims she had not been in "a place like this since Texas." The comment encapsulates a number of issues, pointing in particular to an accepted system of gender relations. Texas, we later find out, was the place where Louise was presumably raped. "Texas" is not simply a geographical location here, but a traumatic reminder of where women can be treated as subordinate to men, even though this is defined only through one woman's experience and sites where such abuses occur are not exclusive to that state or the entire country for that matter. This delicate use of terminology is introduced and internalized for the viewers by the choice of costumes for the people in the bar, who wear the Texan cowboy image in more ways than one.

In *Thelma & Louise*, costumes do not just provide context for the scene, but as clothes, they act as "values made visible."[24]

By dressing the actors in believable and generically appropriate items, Scott makes a virtue of the role of costumes in providing the ever-important suspension of disbelief for the audience. The constant associations between situation and costume are the initiators of what Street calls "imagined embodiment," where the audience "imagines the characters [to exercise] a degree of individual agency when deciding what to wear."[25] Although that conscious process of decision-making is undoubtedly fictitious, the belief that both Thelma and Louise have exercised it as individual entities—and possess an "assumed" presence within the narrative—is an integral part of the audience's response to the characterization which will affect how the women and their actions are perceived. Inevitably, it is that perception of agency that allows costumes to reach another level of interpretation and transform the wearers into cultural icons.

Costumes also play an important role in the presentation of gender categories. Street points out that the director's choices of costume function as important vectors in setting up "codes and expectations" in relation to both behavior and attitude.[26] In *Thelma & Louise* the women's clothes construct their own psychological narrative. In a manner that is similar to the workings of dress in written fiction, clothes in film acquire emotional nuances; those nuances, of course, work on two different levels.[27] On the one hand, dress constructs a particular relationship with the character who wears it, highlighting the role of objects in demonstrated actions, whether covert or explicit; on the other hand, costumes command emotional responses from the audience. The very complex interaction between characters and clothes forms one of the key devices to the construction of the fictional world. In *Thelma & Louise*, costumes are used as a primary device in order to build what Peter Brooks calls the "semiotics of bodily adornment," where dress and personal accessories are an immediate way to develop plot and characterization.[28] Appropriate costumes, closely related to the initial and subsequent elements of characterization, aid the construction of a plausible reality for the plot. Hughes labels this definitive characteristic of costumes as "the reality effect," where clothes "lend tangibility and visibility to character and context," which are then generally simplified and naturalized within the structure of the film's "imagined world."[29]

If it is true that costumes help the viewers to define characters, then a change in each character's dress choice can be understood as an important part of altering perceptions and, to some extent, exposing the audience to a change in relationships and experience. As a result, clothes have the rare ability to immediately and materially communicate a shift in personalities, attitudes, and possible storylines; as Hughes suggests, they convey metamorphoses.[30] As it initially claims the audience's attention by aiding characterization, dress also unsettles them by proving to be confusing or treacherous when these signs are misread. Dress can also be highly revelatory. Choice, for one, cannot be seen as a simply functional concept; McNeil, Karaminas, and Cole remind us that "to adopt a style" is "to choose a socio-economic milieu."[31] The abundance of psychological development within the plot may necessitate a greater attention to use of fabric, colors, and shapes, so that the richness of feeling experienced by the characters can find a resonance in the richness of the costumes displayed.[32] In order to fully understand the emotional significance of dress in *Thelma & Louise*, it is necessary to step inside the narrative and evaluate items as they move from the external plane as costumes to their internal role as clothes. The focus on the relationship between choices in clothes and character emotion is an essential part of understanding how dress functions as the "complex signifier" for associated social and gender-related themes.[33]

Clothes become an important part of gender definition in the movie, validating Louise Wallenberg's claim that "dress is the primary object we use in our masquerading as sexually different individuals."[34] At the beginning of the film, Louise's look is pristine; her waitressing uniform is clean and tidy and compared to her co-workers at the diner, she seems controlled and in place. Later on, when she is getting ready to leave on her trip with Thelma, her appearance is again faultless; her clothes are carefully chosen to match. Her white shirt, jeans, and jacket work together in a structured ensemble. The structured nature of her appearance does not stop there: with her impeccably arranged hairstyle and observant use of lipstick, she is the embodiment of the 1960s housewife, who, when it comes to her appearance, travels through life with an immaculate attention to detail. Louise yearns for stability and marriage, priorities not shared by her long-term boyfriend, Jimmy. Her conceptual connection to the 1960s is maintained in the movie through her choice of car, the recognizable 1966 Thunderbird Convertible, an iconic model of the era. Louise's domestic habits possess a touch of a bygone era, when a woman's duties in the house were regarded as the central part of her life. Of course, this era was also that of social revolution. In this light, her choice of clothes and accessories is particularly relevant. She wears jeans, a headscarf, and large sunglasses, all iconic pieces reminiscent of that decade's popular fashion trends.

Thelma, on the other hand, sports a different look. She wears a robe and moves around nervously in her untidy home. When the audience first meets her, she looks as if she has just risen from bed and has not had time (or even the inclination) to get dressed. This sense of disorganization is emphasized even more when Thelma's controlling husband, Darryl, appears in the kitchen; he is clearly dressed for work in a suit and tie. His business-like appearance is juxtaposed with Thelma's housewife-like demeanor, and this divergence immediately communicates that he is the one in control, the breadwinner of the family who dictates the rules. Thelma thus holds a subservient position. His superior status is underscored by his derogatory comments to his wife. He reminds her, both in tone and in words, that he is a regional manager whereas she is a mere housewife. One can see here how clothes have aided the construction not only of hierarchical family dynamics, but also individual personalities. As Thelma gets ready to leave with Louise, her choice of clothes is starkly revelatory: she wears a long flowing skirt with a summer top and a little denim jacket. Her hair is "big" and her face heavily made-up. Thelma's look is traditionally feminine. It is noteworthy that before they embark on their journey, the women take a Polaroid picture of themselves, immortalizing their looks and, on a metaphorical level, themselves. The allegorical photograph will become significant at the end of the movie when, upon driving off the cliff, the image is blown away by the wind, signifying their deaths—if only at the physical level.

Functioning as both costume and clothes, dress in *Thelma & Louise* is complicit in reinforcing "the objectification of women's form via scopophilia."[35] Through dressing both characters in stereotypically traditional and evocative costumes, Scott highlights the women's function not only as objects of desire, but also as representations of the feminine ideals which can be dissected, deconstructed, and fetishized in relation to patriarchal expectations. From the inter-narrative perspective, both Thelma and Louise's choice of clothes at the beginning of the film mirrors their desire to conform to the roles that their social situations have imposed upon them: the overly-feminine, obedient, and seemingly unintelligent wife for Thelma, and the independent, unmarried, unfulfilled woman for Louise. The subtle irony here already emerges in our noticing that, as Thelma dresses in clothes that emphasize her spousal attachment and compliance, she is in fact escaping from her husband's control, even for what she believed was only a short period of time.

Working closely with the unraveling sequence of events, clothes are able to raise issues of identity politics.[36] With this concept in mind, any clothes-based transformation on the character's part cannot simply be attributed to contextual or spatial changes within the plot. After the attempted rape, Thelma's clothes are torn and disheveled, mirroring not only her emotional state, but also the first stages of her breaking away from her old self. After a stop at their first motel, Louise takes a shower, literally and symbolically washing away the events of the previous night. When she appears dressed and on the run, her attire is already visibly different from the unspoiled ensemble she showed in the first part of the movie. Her hair is loose and curly, rather than perfectly coiffed; the structured white blouse is exchanged for a loose, green top. Within the narrative, clothes have the ability to denote "startling make-over[s]" which often carry "a character from fledgling identity to full self-expression."[37] Indeed, as the film progresses, both women take on a different style and their clothing mirrors their emotional states. For instance, after a night of passion with the young outlaw J. D. (Brad Pitt), Thelma ditches her signature skirt for an all-denim outfit of shirt and jeans, emulating the clothes that J. D. himself was wearing when they met. It is difficult to determine whether this is an act of flirtatious imitation or symptomatic of the psychological awakening experienced by Thelma; she, too, will be an outlaw. In either case, the change in clothes signifies a behavioral shift that hinges on both gender and aesthetics.

By the time they are shooting at the truck in the desert to punish the driver who made overtly sexual comments and gestures at them, the women's attire has altered completely; they are both wearing jeans and loose, sleeveless, "masculine" tops. They no longer wear make-up and their hair is not combed. They are no longer subdued and express their feelings with a sense of possession and self-confidence which, in the typical Western, is often associated with strong male characters. Victoria Sturtevant claims that the film codes both Thelma and Louise's attire as "specifically masculine and performative."[38] It is particularly worth noting that both of them acquire many of their clothes and gestures from men.[39] Louise trades her jewelry for an old man's cowboy hat, while Thelma steals the trucker's hat. As they attain these items of male clothing, the women also take on more culturally-defined masculine qualities like resting their feet on the top edge of the car door and adding a swagger to their walks. These acts are an odd twist on Freudian introjection.

As they internalize their vision of the male experience by wearing male clothes, the women offer a highly dismorphic interpretation of masculinity, one that is not only performative in concept, but functions precisely "as a set of outrageous behaviors," working in connection with borrowed or stolen items.[40] In the end, Thelma and Louise reject the culturally dominant understanding of femininity that centers upon visual appearance through highly decorative clothing and accessories; simultaneously, however, they fail to achieve a sense of masculine power that can be sustained. At best, they can be seen as caricatures of the male ideal as portrayed in the Western genre. As both their behaviors and their attires undergo "dramatic transformations," they overturn the audience's perceptions of easy gender stereotypes.[41] They discard the femininity that defined them at the beginning of the film, and yet they challenge boundaries and classifications. By showing increased abilities to make decisions, including the one to "keep going" at the end of the film, the characters leave behind both their feminine clothes and the negative cultural associations leveled against female personalities as being laden with "hysteria, indecisiveness and talkativeness."[42] They are assertive in a way that, one might argue, attempts to defy gender. In highlighting points of difference and convergence between gender stereotypes and sartorial expectations, Scott gives us an outlook on the women which is clearly transgressive. Louise and Thelma's clothes, androgynous or unisex in their totality, are symptomatic of their refusal to conform to either one ideal or another.

Within the linear progression of Scott's film—and clearly within the emotional, conceptual, and cultural grid on which characters belong—changing clothes is never a simple act. It is a powerful statement, a vector for meaning, an avenue that reflects mental conversion. In the hands of characters, clothes are "dangerously protean."[43] They have the ability to change and adjust social positions and reveal emotional states. While concealing Thelma and Louise's bodies, clothes reveal the emotional underpinnings of a character's mind; they inspire, communicate, define, and disrupt. As they become the women's clothes within the film, costumes speak for characters in ways that transcend mere chronology. In that sense, clothes are a supplement to the main plot, a contrast to the predictable emotions which follow a linear narrative.

The clothes that Thelma and Louise wear speak in a way that their words very seldom could. Communication through clothes is immediate and not only open, but absolutely dependent on viewer interpretation. As they are transported into the reality of the film's narrative, clothes are codified.[44] That codification is visible throughout the critical history of *Thelma & Louise*, where costumes are essential in communicating a change in circumstances. Clothes-based transformations are revelatory and offer the distinct pleasure of grasping mutations and undercurrents which would not be fully registered by simply following the plot.[45] Costumes emerge in structuring and regulating the dynamics of the film, that highly cultural phenomenon which Scott, as director, specifically employs to "entertain and enlighten."[46]

NOTES

1. Elizabeth Wilson, *Adorned in Dreams: Fashion and Modernity* (London: I. B. Tauris, 2003), vii.

2. Ibid.

3. Sarah Street, *Costume and Cinema: Dress Code in Popular Film* (London: Wallflower Press, 2001), 1.

4. Ibid., 2.

5. Gladys Knight, *Female Action Heroes: A Guide to Women in Comics, Video Games, Film and Television* (Westport, CT: Greenwood Press, 2010), 293.

6. In 2000, *Gladiator* won an Academy Award for costume design; in 2005, *Kingdom of Heaven* was nominated for Outstanding Costume Design at the Satellite Awards.

7. Drake Stutesman, "Costume Design, or What Is Fashion in Film?" in *Fashion in Film*, ed. Adrianne Munich (Bloomington: Indiana University Press, 2011), 21.

8. Judith Butler, *Gender Trouble: Feminism and the Subversion of Identity* (London: Routledge, 1989).

9. Annette Kuhn, *Women's Pictures: Feminism and Cinema* (London: Verso, 1994), 52.

10. Charlotte Gaines and Jane Marie Cordelia Herzog, "The Fantasy of Authenticity in Western Costume," in *Back in the Saddle Again: New Essays on the Western*, ed. Edward Buscombe and Roberta E. Pearson (London: British Film Institute, 1998), 176.

11. Clair Hughes, *Dressed in Fiction* (London: Berg, 2005), 2.

12. Roland Barthes, *The Fashion System* (New York: Hill, 1983).

13. Ibid., 63.

14. Peter McNeil, Vicki Karaminas, and Catherine Cole, "Introduction," in *Fashion in Fiction: Text and Clothing in Literature, Film and Television,* ed. Peter McNeil, Vicki Karaminas, and Catherine Cole (London: Berg, 2009), 5.

15. Ibid.

16. Jean Baudrillard, *Seduction* (London: St. Martin's Press, 1991).

17. Jean Baudrillard, *Simulacra and Simulation* (Ann Arbor: University of Michigan Press, 1994), 3.

18. Hughes, *Dressed in Fiction*, 12.

19. Susan Kismaric and Eva Respini, *Fashioning Fiction Photography Since 1990* (New York: Museum of Modern Art, 2004), 12.

20. Stephen Neale, *Genre and Hollywood* (London: Routledge, 2000), 39.

21. Hughes, *Dressed in Fiction*, 2.

22. Daniel Roche, *The Culture of Clothing* (Cambridge: Cambridge University Press, 1996), 84.

23. Hughes, *Dressed in Fiction*, 2.

24. John Harvey, *Men in Black* (Chicago: University of Chicago Press, 1996), 17.

25. Street, *Costume and Cinema*, 7.

26. Ibid., 3.

27. Aileen Ribeiro, *Fashion and Fiction* (New Haven, CT: Yale University Press, 2005), 1.

28. Peter Brookes, *Body Work: Objects of Desire in Modern Narrative* (Cambridge, MA: Harvard University Press, 1993), 54.

29. Hughes, *Dressed in Fiction*, 2.

30. Ibid., 11.

31. McNeil, Karaminas, and Cole, "Introduction," 6.

32. Gaines and Herzog, "The Fantasy of Authenticity in Western Costume," 208.

33. Pam Cook, *Fashioning the Nation: Costume and Identity in British Cinema* (London: British Film Institute, 1996), 93.

34. Louise Wallenberg, "Foreword," in *Fashion in Fiction: Text and Clothing in Literature, Film and Television,* ed. Peter McNeil, Vicki Karaminas, and Catherine Cole (London: Berg, 2009), xvi.

35. Street, *Costume and Cinema*, 7.

36. McNeil, Karaminas, and Cole, "Introduction," 7.

37. Ibid., 6.

38. Victoria Sturtevant, "Getting Hysterical," in *Thelma & Louise Live! The Cultural Afterlife of an American Film*, ed. Bernie Cook (Austin: University of Texas Press, 2007), 57.

39. Ibid.

40. Ibid.

41. Knight, *Female Action Heroes,* 292.

42. Ibid., 300.

43. Hughes, *Dressed in Fiction*, 2.

44. Ibid.

45. Ibid., 11.

46. Ibid., 10.

REFERENCES

Barthes, Roland. *The Fashion System*. Translated by Matthew Ward and Richard Howard. New York: Hill, 1983.

Baudrillard, Jean. *Simulacra and Simulation*. Ann Arbor: University of Michigan Press, 1994.

———. *Seduction*. London: St. Martin Press, 1991.

Brookes, Peter. *Body Work: Objects of Desire in Modern Narrative*. Cambridge, MA: Harvard University Press, 1993.

Butler, Judith. *Gender Trouble: Feminism and the Subversion of Identity.* London: Routledge, 1989.

Cook, Pam. *Fashioning the Nation: Costume and Identity in British Cinema.* London: British Film Institute, 1996.

Gaines, Charlotte, and Jane Marie Cordelia Herzog. "The Fantasy of Authenticity in Western Costume." In *Back in the Saddle Again: New Essays on the Western,* edited by Edward Buscombe and Roberta E. Pearson, 172-181. London: British Film Institute, 1998.

Harvey, John. *Men in Black.* Chicago: University of Chicago Press, 1996.

Hughes, Clair. *Dressed in Fiction.* London: Berg, 2005.

Knight, Gladys. *Female Action Heroes: A Guide to Women in Comics, Video Games, Film and Television.* Westport, CT: Greenwood, 2010.

Kismaric, Susan, and Eva Respini. *Fashioning Fiction Photography Since 1990.* New York: Museum of Modern Art, 2004.

Kuhn, Annette. *Women's Pictures: Feminism and Cinema.* London: Verso, 1994.

McNeil, Peter, Vicki Karaminas, and Catherine Cole. "Introduction." In *Fashion in Fiction: Text and Clothing in Literature, Film and Television,* edited by Peter McNeil, Vicki Karaminas, and Catherine Cole, 1-10. London: Berg, 2009.

Neale, Stephen. *Genre and Hollywood.* London: Routledge, 2000.

Ribeiro, Aileen. *Fashion and Fiction.* New Haven, CT: Yale University Press, 2005.

Roche, Dennis. *The Culture of Clothing.* Cambridge: Cambridge University Press, 1996.

Street, Sarah. *Costume and Cinema: Dress Code in Popular Film.* London: Wallflower Press, 2001.

Sturtevant, Victoria. "Getting Hysterical." In *Thelma & Louise Live!: The Cultural Afterlife of an American Film,* edited by Bernie Cook, 43-64. Austin: University of Texas Press, 2007.

Stutesman, Drake. "Costume Design, or What Is Fashion in Film?" In *Fashion in Film,* edited by Adrianne Munich, 17-39. Bloomington: Indiana University Press, 2011.

Thelma & Louise. DVD. Directed by Ridley Scott. 1991; Beverly Hills, CA: MGM Video, 1997.

Wallenberg, Louise. "Foreword." In *Fashion in Fiction: Text and Clothing in Literature, Film and Television,* edited by Peter McNeil, Vicki Karaminas, and Catherine Cole, xv-xvii. London: Berg, 2009.

Wilson, Elizabeth B. *Adorned in Dreams: Fashion and Modernity.* London: I. B. Tauris, 2003.

Chapter Sixteen

Becoming Authentic in *Matchstick Men* Through the Ultimate Con

Elizabeth Abele

On the surface, Ridley Scott's *Matchstick Men* (2003) appears to be a combination of a clever grifter movie and a comic portrait of a genius with obsessive-compulsive disorder. The film opens by introducing Roy Waller (Nicolas Cage) as a con artist, or "matchstick man," who must complete a series of daily rituals before leaving his house to join his junior partner, Frank (Sam Rockwell). However, it is the addition of the third plot device of the film—Roy's transformation through his reunion with his daughter, a teenager named Angela (Alison Lohman)—that places the film firmly within conversations about American masculinity. This chapter examines how *Matchstick Men* presents a move from classic American masculinity to a more fluid American manhood. Such transformative journeys have been described by various cultural critics. In addition to bringing together multiple genres in a realistic plot, the film functions as an allegory of the mental illnesses of society variously diagnosed by such critics as Karl Marx, Jacques Lacan, Gilles Deleuze, and Erich Fromm. These illnesses accompany the sociopathic drive for success that exists in a capitalistic society like that of the United States.

Matchstick Men is a heightened version of the masculine-crisis film, as Roy experiences a more profound journey than the one found in Scott's *A Good Year* (2006) or films like *The Family Man* (2000) and *The Weather Man* (2005) that also feature Nicolas Cage as protagonist. In these works, as well as such related films such as *Regarding Henry* (1991), *City Slickers* (1991), *What Women Want* (2000), and *Up in the Air* (2009), professional middle-aged men at the top of their fields are forced by external events to recognize the emotional sterility of their lives; by the end of the respective films, they commit to a less goal-oriented and more emotionally connected life. What sets *Matchstick Men* apart is how Roy's illness—and his cure— dramatize various theories of social psychosis, presenting less an example of one man's crisis and more a parable for everyone.

As a criminal and a neurotic crippled by tics and compulsions, Roy may appear to have little in common with the glamorous and confident protagonists of these other masculine-crisis dramas. However, Roy's cons and neuroses function as exaggerated metaphors for "normal" behaviors. Waller mirrors the qualities of a typically successful man in capitalistic society: he defines himself through commitment to his profession; he aggressively sells fantasies by feeding on the fears and desires of others; he ignores the ramifications of his success; he lives alone in a modern and well-maintained abode; and his major comfort comes from the objects that he possesses and consumes. Not only is he the model of capitalistic success, his obsessive-compulsive behavior embodies Jacques Lacan's observation about the contemporary problem of the rigid ego. As part of Lacan's project to unify and formalize the field of Freudian psychoanalysis, he developed an anthropological account of the development of the psyche. He was particularly concerned with what he saw as the ego's increasing inability to move beyond narcissism to what he termed "truth," which he saw at the heart of "social psychosis." As Teresa Brennan summarizes in *History After Lacan*, this condition has increased progressively over time, with the rigidity of such self-identification at its worst in contemporary America.[1] However, she does not present this condition as being inescapable: "I assume that a living natural reality exists, and that knowledge of it is confused by a fantasmatic material overlay, just as the living reality of it becomes confused. . . . it does not follow that this is the only world possible."[2]

While Brennan's feminist work builds on Lacan's cultural diagnoses, her recommendations are echoed by mid-twentieth century American psychologists Erich Fromm and Abraham Maslow who advocate a move away from following social dictates toward self-actualization. Based on their observations of American men in response to cultural pressures, Fromm and Maslow theorized the self-destructive model of American success. They promoted instead a difficult journey toward a new level of existence, a more emotionally healthy life. Fromm wrote directly against a society focused on objects rather than feelings: "A society whose principles are acquisition, profit, and property produces a social character oriented around having, and once the dominant pattern is established, nobody wants to be an outsider, or indeed an outcast: in order to avoid this risk everybody adapts to the majority, who have in common only their mutual antagonism."[3] Roy's rigid commitments to acquisition of property, shored up by his OCD-driven behaviors, are challenged by a new therapist and the return of his long-lost daughter. Through this disruption of his routine, Roy learns to move out of his rigid self-identification toward self-actualization, finding a more authentic mode of person-hood.

The redemptive structure of the masculine-crisis film has been documented by Fred Pfeil and Susan Jeffords, with 1991 as a year when this type of narrative was particularly prevalent. These films feature a mid-life professional man who, after a disruptive crisis, becomes a "sensitive" family man. Jeffords notes in particular the artificiality of these men at the beginning of the film; each is "trying to do his job . . . in the way that it had been defined by a social-climbing, crime-conscious, techno-consumer society."[4] Similarly, in his essay "The Year of Living Sensitively," Pfeil documented the narrative structure of that year's masculine-crisis films from Hollywood, a narrative that has continued to surface into the early twenty-first century.

There is an important element that separates *Matchstick Men* from other masculine-crisis films, confirming its role as a parable beyond the particular case of Scott's protagonist. *Spoiler alert*: the crisis, the therapy, the reestablished family relationship—all common elements of the masculine-crisis film—are part of a long con. His "therapist" and "daughter" are merely players in a grift staged by Frank. Regardless, Roy's response to therapy and intimacy appear authentic, with the transformative results perhaps more convincing than the "happy" resolution that ties everything up so neatly in related films. *Matchstick Men* speaks to the value of fantasy in emotional healing and growth, particularly if the fantasy disrupts destructive patterns of behavior, allowing new patterns to take their place.

AMERICAN SUCCESS AS EMOTIONAL DEATH

Instead of Roy's obsessive compulsive disorder existing as an aberration, his dependence on objects and rituals operates merely as an exaggeration of materialistic behaviors by successful men in more socially acceptable professions. The less tangibly discernible their work, the more essential the grounding effect of these behaviors appears. In post-industrial America, many professional men are charged with selling fantasy; as *City Slickers*'s Mitch (Billy Crystal) admits, he "sells air." In *A Good Year*, Max Skinner (Russell Crowe) is a junk-bond trader who can make millions of profits by manipulating the price of a bond up, down, and up again—with no real change in the value of the bonds.

Roy's work is similarly concerned with hawking over-valued objects. He is running a scam with Frank where they sell a $50 water purifier for $700, with the false promise of both its high quality as well as its connection to a "guaranteed" dream prize (a trip, a diamond necklace, or a car). Frank's phone script demonstrates that what he and Roy are selling is a fantasy that is only remotely tied to a tangible object: "What's more important than family?

Then what can be more important than purifying the water that your family drinks? The Waterson 2000 offers you the cleanest filtration system available today." By this weak linking of the tangible filtration system's capacities to the immaterial value of family, they are selling a fantasy of purity and safety; the only difference between the matchstick men and advertising executives is the mark-up. Roy, like other successful executives, deals in over-valued objects, but he likewise only sees people as objects, as marks that only exist because of their assets. This makes it easy for him to ignore their humanity as well as his ethical responsibility to them as a businessman. Annalee Newitz observes a similar dynamic in horror films, which she sees as revealing people's fears of capitalism: "capitalism's monsters cannot tell the difference between commodities and people. They confuse living beings with inanimate objects."[5] Roy is a criminalized reflection of capitalistic "monsters," among them corporate attorneys, shock jocks, bond traders, and down-sizing consultants that populate other masculine-crisis films.

In tracing the implications of Lacan's critique of ego-psychology in contemporary society, Brennan notes the dangers of a global capitalism that promises the fulfillment of all consumer desires: "Before the advent of a Western technology capable of fulfilling the desires embodied in the foundational fantasy, it is contained. The advent of that technology is prompted by the fantasy and represents an acting out of it on an increasingly global scale, an enactment that reinforces the psychical power of the fantasy."[6] In this world of unlimited fantasies, the ego requires objects to keep it grounded: "construction of a commodity binds energy in the same way that it is bound in the repression of a hallucination."[7] Through such over-valuing of objects, this construction of commodities can be seen as a crutch for most people in contemporary society. This dependency may take on an even larger role with people whose egos, like Roy's, are unfettered by working with non-tangibles. As they simultaneously avoid intimate relationships with people, their fetishes are the only thing they have to convince themselves of their own reality.

Roy spins fantasies of desire that are only tentatively connected to reality; he is also dissociated from reality by operating outside of both the law and conventional morality. His OCD can be read as a compensation to balance the lack of limits on his ego, as he is overly attached to specific objects even more banal than a filtration system. He keeps his sparse house clean to the point of sterility, opening and closing each door three times to feel safe. For food, he only buys cans of tuna. Instead of a bank account, he keeps cash in a security deposit box and a ceramic dog. Recognizing the expansive potential of his ability to sell fantasy, Roy finds safety in overvaluing objects that lack any aesthetic, intrinsic, or human value. Perhaps tellingly, he says that he is an antique dealer: this is someone who deals with tangible objects whose surplus value is specifically tied to their craftsmanship and historical connections. These objects have connections to humanity that are documented and authenticated, and usually valued for generations, especially by families and collectors.

This reading of Roy's OCD as a corrective to his exploitive professional life is supported by another filmic portrayal of an OCD-plagued character: Melvin Udall (Jack Nicholson) in *As Good As It Gets* (1997). Like Roy, Melvin is at the top of his field, having written sixty-two romance novels, all of which feature moments of incredible intimacy. But as a cynical misanthrope, Melvin is arguably selling fantasies which he believes to be as unreal as the purity of the Waterson 2000. When asked by a fan how he writes women so well, he replies, "I imagine a man and then I take away reason and accountability." In this scene, he basically admits to a female reader, who believed he understood her heart, that he is a con man and even a misogynist. Instead of being an expert on intimacy and women, he lives in a spotless apartment wherein no being but himself ever enters. He turns his locks five times each to keep himself hermetically contained.

It could be argued that the protagonists of other masculine-crisis films equally depend on sterile, secure environments and overvalued objects to secure their insecure egos. Both *A Good Year*'s Max and *The Family Man*'s investment banker Jack Campbell (Nicolas Cage) live in exclusive, professionally decorated and cleaned condominiums, with doorman security and limited guests. These protagonists may dine on more than tuna, but the premium that they pay for their fancy meals, cigars, liquor, and high-end clothes is a socially-acceptable practice. They use over-valued objects to comfort themselves as they avoid human intimacy. Instead of celibacy, they hide from intimacy through superficial sexual encounters. It is not a coincidence that as part of Max and Jack's transformation, they are both forced to share less controlled houses with other people and to participate in more tangible business affairs than investments (respectively, a vineyard and tire sales).

Karl Marx noted this problem of objects being valued above their material and labor costs. He termed it *fetishization*. At the point that the societal value placed on an object becomes separated from its use-value, it "emerges as a commodity, it changes into a thing which transcends sensuousness."[8] The attachment to the object exceeds the physical pleasure that it provides, as the commodity gains power over the individual: "A commodity appears at first sight an extremely obvious, trivial thing. But analysis brings out that it is a very strange thing, abounding in metaphysical subtleties and theological niceties."[9] These separate objects become more dangerous as they form a system (in Fromm's terms) of "having"; as Rainer Funk elaborates: "orientation of existence toward having is marked by existential dependency upon the objects of having and has the quality of obsessive and narcissistic dependency. . . . The person oriented toward having is constantly threatened with the loss of his self: he stands under the threat of decompensating, of losing the ground under his feet, of falling into the abyss."[10] *Matchstick Men* dramatizes both this obsessive dependency and the danger of the loss of self into "the abyss."

Scott's production choices in *Matchstick Men* deliberately create a Los Angeles that is more interested in recycling or repackaging old ideas than producing anything new. The production design feels deliberately out-of-date, with clothing and interior sets that could as easily be from the 1960s as from today. Critics have particularly noted Roy's stark home as a retro LA throwback, but the same could be said of the offices, the bowling alley, the laundromat, and the airport terminal lounge. The soundtrack likewise features the jazzy classics of Frank Sinatra and Bobby Darin. These choices for décor and soundtrack serve several functions. Creating a sense of timelessness maintains the film's nature as a parable rather than being limited to a particular historical situation. This vision of LA establishes the sense that this environment offers nothing new to its inhabitants, that there is no vibrancy in their day-to-day existence. Lisa Schwarzbaum perceives a similar quality in *Matchstick Men*'s cinematography, for "the unsettlingly beautiful directorial study in geographical mood that it is. There's a certain kind of white, piercing, empty light to the Los Angeles sky at certain times of day—and gold, piercing emptiness at others—that can make a person want to commit suicide, or snort cocaine."[11] In Roy's case, it makes him want to scrub his house, eat tuna, and chain smoke. As Fromm reflects, "[W]e live in a vacuum and fill the gap with words, with abstract signs of values, with routine, which helps us out from the embarrassment."[12]

In his main body of work, Gilles Deleuze confirms the value of repetition as "necessary and justified conduct,"[13] but stresses that no repetition can truly be the same. It is in the differences between iterations that true experiences lies: "[Difference is] the only moment of presence and precision."[14] James Williams sees Deleuze as promoting a "search for completeness through chance-driven experimentation with new ways of expressing intensities."[15] Roy's problem lies less in his penchant for repetition and more in his deliberate ignoring of differences alongside his commitment to avoiding the intensity of chance. Deleuze recognizes that the most difficult thing is "to make chance an object of *affirmation*"[16] rather than see it as an occasion for possible loss.

Brennan confirms that though an ego may find externals to help balance its expansion and its resistance to truth, in the long run, this is a destructive path: "Of course if nature is endlessly consumed in the pursuit of a naturalizing course, then that course is dangerous for living; it constitutes a danger to one's own survival, as well as that of others. That, approximately, is the technical, legal definition of psychosis."[17] Like Brennan, Fromm also sees the end result of contemporary values to be mental illness: "Our society offers a picture of a low-grade chronic schizophrenia . . . with no emotions shown and often not felt, and certain separation between affective life and thought."[18] Both cultural theorists observe a mode of life that functions by creating activities to mask authentic connections, both to others and to the self.

This flattening of emotions and absence of emotional connections allow Roy and Frank, like other successful (if unscrupulous) executives, to view people only as a means to an end. Roy takes no responsibility for people "giving" him their money. But the money that he takes he fetishizes, alienating it from its use-value. It is significant that his nest egg is not an abstract account balance but physical cash, from which he derives no enjoyment. He does not go to Hawaii for a vacation or use his money to enjoy any sensual pleasures. Nor does it earn him interest or dividends. The paper bills exist purely to give him value, and to continue his habit of collecting more from his craft.

As the film opens, the fractures in Roy's complex coping mechanisms are apparent to him as well as to his partner, Frank. Minor triggers—like a mark opening a screen door to let in blinding sunlight—can disrupt Roy's performance. This can manifest as the eruption of tics in the middle of a con or an inability to leave his home altogether, resulting in him obsessively cleaning his cocoon and ignoring concerned calls from Frank. While Roy has the security of his nest egg and a house, Frank finds it challenging to manage on the income from their short cons—particularly when the irregularities of his mentor/senior partner can render Roy non-responsive and unproductive without notice. Frank has little choice but to intervene for his own stability.

Most protagonists in masculine-crisis films begin the narrative at least content within their "psychosis," if not downright smug. It is only after an external crisis—gunshots, metaphysical events, cancer, lost promotions—that these men change. Pfeil notes the incredible force required to change most of them: "For if white straight men cannot be changed short of shooting them, there is not much use pressing them to do so."[19] However, Roy does not need to be shot: the cracks in his armor are already apparent early in the film. His life may fall into Brennan's characterization of social psychosis as an "ego with a vested interest in flattening everything that exists into a grey mirror that reflects it."[20] It is clear that it takes a lot of effort to restrict his emotions; he consumes packs of Tareyton cigarettes (a 1960s brand) faster than he consumes tuna, and, at the dosage of medication required to control his tics, he's "lucky to be sitting up straight." He looks longingly at a grocery clerk Kathy (Sheila Kelly) but is unable to answer her friendly questions when he buys his tuna and cigarettes. With his lack of satisfaction in the defenses of his rigid ego, the only "crisis" required is for him to drop his medication down the garbage disposal unit. The loss of this one object is enough for him to admit new people into his life, to begin a journey toward emotional health, and feel moments of joy.

THE CON AS A RECUPERATIVE JOURNEY

Roy's crisis about his lost medication is compounded when he finds that his therapist has decamped. Desperate, he goes to see a new therapist recommended by Frank, who prescribes a different medication. Within a few weeks, Dr. Klein (Bruce Altman) reunites Roy with his 14-year-old daughter, eliminates his tics, and helps him to start letting go of repetitive behaviors. In addition, the patient chooses to retire as a con man, fully committing to the role of being a father to Angela. Roy and Angela celebrate not over tuna but with dinner (and dancing!) in a Mexican restaurant. By any measure, this is a remarkably successful therapeutic relationship.

However, the therapist, the daughter, and the medication are all fakes, part of a long con engineered by Frank to rob Roy of his million plus in cash. So can the therapeutic results be real if the process was a simulation, a virtual rather than an actual experience? There are similarities between the work of a therapist and the work of a con man. Both begin by establishing a relationship, where the patient/mark will feel comfortable enough to reveal his or her desires and weaknesses. By focusing on hidden desires and patiently working through any resistance, these professionals can move the patient/mark toward the goal of the relationship: mental health/a score.

Dr. Klein has several advantages over "actual" therapists. We can assume that he is fed information about Roy from his partners (Frank and Angela). Since Dr. Klein already knows what Roy is hiding, it is easier for him to diagnose this patient as well as to lead him to divulge his secrets. He and Angela also make an effective tag-team: Dr. Klein tells Roy that the secret with teenagers is to be honest and open with them, so that when Angela pushes him to be honest with her, Roy accepts that honesty is the right path.[21] Roy, in fact, does reveal more to Angela than he does to Dr. Klein. Not only is he quicker to reveal his criminal profession to her, he also admits that he feels sick about what the job entails. When she asks, "Then why do you do it?" he has no answer. Yet with Dr. Klein, he holds to his surface rationalization that his marks *give* him his money out of greed or weakness. Together, Dr. Klein and Angela move Roy away from his career as a matchstick man and toward a commitment to Angela—all part of Frank's long con against his partner.

Frank and his crew use Roy's fetishization of objects and other weaknesses to pull him in and manipulate him. To set up the long con, Frank continually asks about Roy's medication, reinforcing his dependence on it. The younger man thus accelerates his partner's need for more drugs and another therapist, whom Frank would supply as part of the plot. Initially, Roy is only interested in a relationship with Dr. Klein that involves a clear exchange, resisting any emotional relationship with him. Only to receive the experimental pill "Prefex" is he willing to talk to Dr. Klein at all. After admitting to curiosities about his ex-wife and potential child, he asks the psychiatrist to make the call for him—since predictably, he is unable to initiate the conversation. Dr. Klein now has a second object with which to lure Roy back into his office: "Angela" is presented in a way similar to the Waterson 2000 or Prefex (pre-fix?), with her name chosen so that Roy would think of her unconsciously as his angel. Later, when Frank's crew has manufactured a crisis to divide Roy and Angela, she gives him a dog-shaped ashtray. Not coincidentally, the ashtray features a cute animal with a halo: an angel from Angela. The long con against Roy strategically places objects along the path that the crew wishes Roy to follow.

For their first meeting, Angela arranges to meet Roy outside, which of course triggers his agoraphobia and keeps him unbalanced. He is doubly off-center since he is unused to responding to anyone on an emotional level and to emotional expressions from others. For instance, when she ends their meeting with "Nice to meet you, Dad," he idiotically parrots her with "Nice to meet you, Dad." She successfully turns her touching of him into a material act when she writes her phone number on his hand. Back in the office, he stares at the writing, caressing it as he might an object. This new fetish gives him the confidence and joy to agree to Frank's earlier suggestion of a long con, one that he had previously turned down as being too risky.

Another aspect that makes Roy vulnerable to a long con (and therapy) is his underlying ethical nature, despite his criminal profession. He not only refuses to swear but will not let Frank swear around him; Roy's preferred epithet is "pygmies." And though his livelihood is based on cheating people, he is deeply offended by people who do not tip, seeing a refusal to do so as a serious character flaw. These ethics could be seen as hypocritical, but they can also be symptoms that suggest he is unsuited for the life of a matchstick man (despite his talent for it). It takes very little prodding from Dr. Klein for Roy to reveal his deep regrets about the way he treated his pregnant wife when they divorced fourteen years ago. He admits that when he sees a school bus, he wonders what "Roy, Jr." would look like. Near the end of the film, the audience witnesses that his ex-wife uncannily resembles the clerk that he is attracted to, a sign that Roy has been unable to live with the credo that he taught Frank: to have no regrets for what they do.[22] He admits only to Angela that he often feels sick about taking money from people who do not deserve it, including "old people, lonely people, fat people." As much as grifter movies like *The Sting* (1973) or *Ocean's 11* (2001) present the joy of the con, Roy derives no lasting pleasure from his "art"; it has become merely a compulsive behavior that he is doomed to repeat.

While his OCD patterns pull him into Frank's con, it is Roy's underlying ethics and desires that allow this simulation of therapy to prove effective. His joy as he looks at Angela's phone number is the first moment of happiness that we witness. The sincerity of this connection will not allow him to refuse the girl when she shows up on this doorstep, expecting to move in with him for the weekend. She asks, imploringly, "It's OK, isn't it?" As much as everything in Roy's being wants to throw her out, he cannot deny her wide-eyed assumption that she is welcome after such a long absence on his part; this is especially since a refusal might kill this budding relationship and result in his rejection of her being repeated as well.

Though as far as the con is concerned, this vulnerability posed by Roy's guilty conscience allows "Angela" to case his house, it immediately forces him to change his patterns. At the grocery store, instead of buying tuna and cigarettes, he buys Ben & Jerry's ice cream and eggs, prompting Kathy to ask, "Big night planned?" For the first time, he responds to her comment, though he still bolts after her friendly follow-up question. Angela's presence disrupts the neatness of his house, bringing in new odors: "Everything smells like gum," he relates affectionately. But unlike before, disruptions do not cause him to hyperventilate or clean; instead he has become more open to direct experience. While Frank failed to compel Roy to try spicy calamari or enjoy their Thai food, he eats greasy pizza with Angela. After two more grocery trips, one with Angela, he actually introduces himself to Kathy and shakes her hand.

Overall, Roy's world gradually opens up as Angela disrupts his life, with Dr. Klein there to calm him down and keep him on course. These are both important steps for the therapy and the con. When he is concerned that Angela went out without notice, Roy forgets to take off his shoes before he walks on his carpet.[23] After an $80,000 sting goes awry, endangering Roy, Frank, and Angela, Roy tries to break connections with the girl. But he soon ends up in Dr. Klein's office in tears ("I've lost my little girl") with the full grief of the past fourteen years as well as this second separation. As Dr. Klein has already admitted that Prefex is just a hormonal replacement and an effective placebo, he is direct in his diagnosis that Roy's illness is all about his conscience.[24] Roy makes the commitment to change professions in exchange for a regular relationship with Angela, not for his own well-being alone, but for hers as well.

The final stage of Frank's long con places Roy in a position where he believes that Angela is in serious danger. Unable to get to her himself, he entrusts the passcode to his lockbox to Dr. Klein (as he had previously trusted Angela enough to put her signature on his account). Without regret about the loss of his cash, he sighs, "Angela's all right." Within a half hour, he slowly realizes that this final crisis was all staged, and that Dr. Klein was as real as Prefex. After he rushes to his ex-wife's home to find Angela, he learns from Heather (Melora Walters) that she had had a miscarriage—and thus he has no daughter. As he sobs on her stoop, Heather asks him compassionately if he is okay. He slowly admits that he is. Regardless of her failed reality, Angela has functioned for Roy as Deleuze's "problematic object" that "exceeds our representative capacities, but for the same reason provokes the exercise of all of our powers, creating a relay between sense, memory, imagination, and thought."[25] Through her, and supported by "therapy," Roy has become an integrated person. This "role-playing" succeeded in getting around the rigidity of his ego where talk-therapy had only limited success. As Lacan reflects, "The patient is held spellbound by his ego, to the exact degree that it causes his distress. It is this very fact that has led us to evolve a technique which substitutes the strange detours of free association for the sequence of the Dialogue."[26] The resolution of most masculine-crisis films immediately follows a secondary crisis like this. Pfeil describes these endings as the "shakily negotiated settlement"; as these men are altered rather than organically transformed, it remains "doubly impossible to imagine what might come after the ending."[27]

As cheerily as *A Good Year*'s Max seems to embrace his idyllic life in France, there is a question of how long he can enjoy this brief respite from who he was for so long. There is a difference with Roy. He rationally made the decision to give up his career and $40,000 before the staged crisis that then prompted him to give up the rest of his cash. After he tells Heather that he is okay, the screen fades to black until "One Year Later" bounces across it. In many ways, the Roy that we see from this point forward resembles the Roy at the start of the film. He still lives in the same house, shops at the same grocery store, and is in a sales-oriented job. However, he is less rigid in his habits. It is the differences in the repetitions that matter most. At the carpet store, he is not in charge; when his boss phones him with "Roy, we've got a live one," he responds by *serving* the customer rather than manipulating that person's weaknesses. He assists the man by suggesting a remnant rather than pushing him to buy more carpet than he needs. Even his reunion with "Angela" does not return him to his previously anxious patterns of behavior. Now dressed for her correct age (mid-20s), she enters the carpet store in the most stylish attire worn by anyone in the film. Though his first interactions with her are filled with contempt, he soon shifts to paternalistic concern. When she apologizes, he replies: "You didn't take anything from me; I gave it to you." Regardless of her duplicity, he maintains the sincerity of the relationship and deepens the integrity of his sacrifice with his maturity. As she leaves, she asks if he wants to know her real name. He affirms that he already knows it, to which she responds "I'll see you, Dad," waving to him from the car as her 14-year old alter-ego. Williams confirms the value in the mutual confirmation of this "felt" relationship: "True sensation and significance are a matter of incomparable events, movements that are uniquely significant to individuals."[28] While recognizing the irreversible changes brought about by their new knowledge, they choose to repeat the patterns of their previous relationship, one that both valued in their own ways.

While *Matchstick Men* opened ironically with the 1965 recording "The Good Life" sung by Bobby Darrin, Frank Sinatra's 1966 song "The Summer Wind" plays over the final scenes. But this time, the sweet, old-fashioned song matches Roy's outlook. At the grocery store, he says hello to the new (male) clerk. Among his array of grocery items, he buys the same ice cream that he first bought for Angela; this is another repetition with difference that confirms that he has moved forward without bitterness and without reverting to canned tuna. He walks into his house with a light, expectant step, without the ritual of shoe removal. The house is basically the same, with the addition of slight decorating touches that make the space warmer. Of course, the most significant change is the presence of Kathy, whom he tenderly surprises as she prepares a salad. As he stoops down to place his ear on her pregnant belly, his one eye closes—but this is a wink, not a tic. Roy has learned to appreciate difference. Writes Williams, "the marking of the same territory takes place against the background of variation in intensities. . . . It is these variations that give life . . . intensity and value, but also risk and error."[29] He has the courage of someone who has risked it all and lost, yet survived.

Los Angeles has not suddenly become contemporary and vibrant; old styles and music are still being recirculated. The difference lies in the sincerity of experience. Roy takes more pleasure in selling carpet remnants than he did in turning a cheap water purifier into a lucrative score. His house is no longer a fortress; with Kathy and his future child, it is a home. Pfeil notes that at the end of *Regarding Henry*, the protagonist "having given up nothing worth keeping . . . has now gained access to a corner of that world that is more beautiful, comfy, and life-affirming."[30] Roy's lockbox of cash was not worth keeping; his voluntary sacrifice for his fake daughter and his forgiveness of Angela made this actual child possible. Roger Ebert explains how this ending is more satisfying than related films' "tidy endings": "This is a scene that could have gone terribly wrong, spoiled by being too obvious, sentimental, angry or tricky. Ridley Scott and his players know just how to handle it; they depend on who these characters really are. If you consider what the characters have gone through and they meant to one another, then this scene has a kind of transcendence to it."[31] While the irony of the long con could complicate the neatness of the film's happy ending, it actually enriches it.

Roy could have gotten up from Heather's stoop and retreated to the comfortable familiarity of his OCD and his profession.[32] Over the past year, he has freely chosen a life that combined patterns that were genuinely his with an openness to the emotional attachment that his relationship with Kathy can offer. He has personified Fromm's advocacy and chosen a life of being over having: "The process of giving birth to himself leads to well-being and joy."[33] The reality of the journey is less important than the result.

LITTLE GLIMMERS

"Underneath the large noisy events," states Deleuze, "lie the small events of silence, just as under the natural light there are the little glimmers of the Idea."[34] Underneath the noisier events of Roy's OCD and the machinations of the long-con-within-a-long-con, the true focus of this film is on the "small events of silence" and "glimmer[ing] Ideas." Without the drama engineered by Frank, Roy would not have been able to benefit from the chance represented by Kathy, an opportunity that he could not see behind his carefully constructed and sheltered existence. This film opens by focusing on the paradoxically serene prison of Roy's existence, setting this closed environment as the problem to be addressed. By exaggerating the behaviors and objects that have created the barrier to "the good life," the film challenges its audience to beware of trading the comfort of rituals and commodities for self-actualization and the risky intensities of experience beyond them.

The only review that noted *Matchstick Men*'s potential to operate as an allegory for contemporary masculinity was negative: "a blah little exploitation picture that thinks it's a deep humanist parable."[35] Despite the careful construction of the film discussed throughout this chapter, Scott's production ultimately prefers to take itself lightly, carried out on a "summer wind." The constant potential in life for joy and surprise may be its most pressing message to an unhappy society. Though a modest message, it may be of value to those that remain vulnerable to the con-like idea that identity can be bought and secured through the capitalist marketplace.

NOTES

1. Teresa Brennan, *History After Lacan* (New York: Routledge, 1993), 31.
2. Ibid., 21.
3. Erich Fromm, *The Essential Fromm: Life Between Having and Being*, ed. Rainer Funk (New York: Continuum, 1998), 105.
4. Susan Jeffords, *Hard Bodies: Hollywood Masculinity in the Reagan Era* (New Brunswick, NJ: Rutgers University Press, 1994), 144.
5. Annalee Newitz, *Pretend We're Dead: Capitalist Monsters in American Popular Culture* (Durham, NC: Duke University Press, 2006), 2.
6. Brennan, *History*, 13.
7. Ibid., 118.
8. Karl Marx, *Capital: A Critique of Political Economy*, Vol. 1, trans. Ben Fowkes (New York: Penguin, 1990), 163.
9. Ibid.
10. Rainer Funk, "Editor's Foreword," in *The Essential Fromm: Life Between Having and Being*, by Erich Fromm (New York: Continuum, 1998), 12.
11. Lisa Schwarzbaum, "Movie Review: *Matchstick Men* (2003)," *Entertainment Weekly*, September 10, 2003, accessed August 6, 2012, http://www.ew.com/ew/article/0,,483992,00.html.
12. Fromm, *The Essential Fromm*, 31.

13. Gilles Deleuze, *Difference and Repetition*, trans. P. Patton (New York: Columbia University Press, 1994), 1.

14. Ibid., 28.

15. James Williams, *Gilles Deleuze's Difference and Repetition: A Critical Introduction and Guide* (Edinburgh: Edinburgh University Press, 2003), 22.

16. Deleuze, *Difference,* 198.

17. Brennan, *History*, 4.

18. Fromm, *The Essential Fromm*, 30.

19. Fred Pfeil, *White Guys: Studies in Postmodern Domination and Difference* (New York: Verso, 1995), 61.

20. Brennan, *History*, 23.

21. Dr. Klein connects honesty to Angela when he tells Roy of his phone call to Heather: "I'm a psychiatrist; I can't lie."

22. In the supplementary "Making of" documentary to the DVD, Scott noted his good fortune in finding actresses that so resembled each other to play the clerk Kathy (Sheila Kelley) and Roy's ex-wife Heather (Melora Walters).

23. There are similar moments in *As Good As It Gets* when Melvin forgets to lock his door and later accidentally steps on a crack because he is distracted by thoughts of Carol (Helen Hunt).

24. The fact that Prefex is in actuality a soy menopause supplement functions both as the crew's dig at Roy's manhood as the mark as well as the film's comment that his overtly masculine, aggressive behavior needs to be feminized (or at least sensitized).

25. Melissa McMahon, "Difference, Repetition," in *Gilles Deleuze: Key Concepts*, ed. Charles J. Stivale (Montreal, PQ: McGill-Queen's University Press, 2005), 47.

26. Quoted in Brennan, *History*, 30. Jacques Lacan, "Some Reflections on the Ego," *International Journal of Psycho-Analysis* 34 (1953), 12.

27. Pfeil, *White Guys*, 39.

28. Williams, *Gilles Deleuze's*, 8.

29. Ibid., 12.

30. Pfeil, *White Guys*, 40.

31. Roger Ebert, "*Matchstick Men.*" *Chicago Sun-Times*, September 10, 2003, accessed August 6, 2012, http://rogerebert.suntimes.com/apps/pbcs.dll/article?AID=/20030912/REVIEWS/309120303.

32. Perhaps it is significant that unlike the angry, bitter woman painted by Dr. Klein and Angela, Heather is compassionate and forgiving towards Roy. This resolution may have helped him to feel forgiveness toward Angela (and perhaps Frank).

33. Fromm, *The Essential Fromm*, 17.

34. Deleuze, *Difference*, 163.

35. David Edelstein, "Con Men: Two Duds from Robert Rodriguez and Ridley Scott," *Slate*, September 14, 2003, accessed August 6, 2012, http://www.slate.com/articles/arts/movies/2003/09/con_men.html.

REFERENCES

A Good Year. DVD. Directed by Ridley Scott. 2006; Los Angeles, CA: Twentieth Century Fox, 2007.

As Good As It Gets. DVD. Directed by James L. Brooks. 1997; Culver City, CA: Sony Pictures Home Entertainment, 1998.

Brennan, Teresa. *History After Lacan*. New York: Routledge, 1993.

City Slickers. DVD. Directed by Ron Underwood. 1991; Culver City, CA: Columbia Pictures, 2001.

Deleuze, Gilles. *Difference and Repetition*. Translated by Paul Patton. New York: Columbia University Press, 1994.

Ebert, Roger. "*Matchstick Men.*" *Chicago Sun-Times*, September 10, 2003. Accessed August 6, 2012.   http://rogerebert.suntimes.com/apps/pbcs.dll/article?AID=/20030912/REVIEWS/309120303.

Edelstein, David. "Con Men: Two Duds from Robert Rodriguez and Ridley Scott." *Slate.* September 14, 2003. Accessed August 6, 2012. http://www.slate.com/articles/arts/movies/2003/09/con_men.html.

The Family Man. DVD. Directed by Brett Ratner. 2000; Universal City, CA: Universal Studios, 2001.

Fromm, Erich. *The Essential Fromm: Life Between Having and Being*, edited by Rainer Funk. New York: Continuum, 1998.

Funk, Rainer. "Editor's Foreword," in *The Essential Fromm: Life Between Having and Being*, by Erich Fromm, 7-14. New York: Continuum, 1998.

Jeffords, Susan. *Hard Bodies: Hollywood Masculinity in the Reagan Era*. New Brunswick, NJ: Rutgers University Press, 1994.

Marx, Karl. *Capital: A Critique of Political Economy*. Vol. 1. Translated by Ben Fowkes. New York: Penguin, 1990.

Matchstick Men. DVD. Directed by Ridley Scott. 2003; Burbank, CA: Warner Home Video, 2004.

McMahon, Melissa. "Difference, Repetition." In *Gilles Deleuze: Key Concepts*, edited by Charles J. Stivale, 42-52. Montreal, PQ: McGill-Queen's University Press, 2005.

Newitz, Annalee. *Pretend We're Dead: Capitalist Monsters in American Popular Culture*. Durham, NC: Duke University Press, 2006.

Pfeil, Fred. *White Guys: Studies in Postmodern Domination and Difference*. New York: Verso, 1995.

Schwarzbaum, Lisa. "Movie Review: *Matchstick Men* (2003)." *Entertainment Weekly.* September 10, 2003. Accessed August 6, 2012. http://www.ew.com/ew/article/0,,483992,00.html.

Williams, James. *Gilles Deleuze's Difference and Repetition: A Critical Introduction and Guide*. Edinburgh: Edinburgh University Press, 2003.

Chapter Seventeen

Virginity in *Alien*: The Essence of Ripley's Survival

Sydney Palmer

"Ripley's unremitting drive to preserve her integrity," contends Stephen Mulhall, "is thus, in essence, an expression of her sense of alienation from life."[1] This insight fearlessly addresses the issue of integrity in Ridley Scott's *Alien* (1979) and at the same time, reduces it to the opposite of its true role. While I agree with Mulhall that Ripley's sense of integrity (and by extension, virginity) is the essence of her capacity to survive the alien encounter, I disagree with his assessment of it as "alienation from life." All evidence points to the contrary: the film consistently shows Ripley (Sigourney Weaver) to be the one crew member unafraid of genuine, shrewd, and honest interaction with her crewmates and her surroundings. Her defense of virginity, manifested most clearly in her protection of the ship and her crewmates, emerges from her deep attunement to life and to that which most threatens it.

I begin this chapter by discussing several points of agreement and disagreement with Mulhall's analysis of the alien's form and his definitions (and conflation) of celibacy, integrity, and virginity. Subsequently, I explore two scenes that reveal Ripley's capacity to analyze various situations effectively and her commensurate lack of fear when interacting with her crewmates. This strength directly emerges from her defense of virginity as a profound capacity to engage with, protect, and defend life itself. This leads into a discussion of her co-worker Ash's admiration for the alien as perfect and "pure." Finally I discuss Scott's contrast of virginity and purity as embodied by Ripley and the alien on the *Nostromo*.

MULHALL'S PHILOSOPHY OF *ALIEN*

Mulhall's interpretation fittingly grounds itself in the alien's form and its mode of reproduction, which he comes to see ultimately as a symbol for Ripley's rejection of human sexuality and her alienation from life through "resolute virginity."[2] I will follow two of Mulhall's key points—the meaning of the alien's form and Ripley's sense of virginity—both to deconstruct his profound insights but also to reorient them. They allow us to see Ripley not as resolutely closed, avenging the universe for sexuality itself, but as a woman so centered in a positive awareness of sexual difference that only she can defend herself and the rest of the crew.[3]

Mulhall analyzes the alien's physiology and mode of reproduction with notable astuteness, capturing why it embodies horror for us. Yet he makes one crucial error that has ramifications for his entire argument. He is absolutely right that the alien's reproductive cycle is a "nightmare vision of sexual intercourse, pregnancy and birth."[4] He misses commenting upon a profound confusion in the actual form, however, as it multiplies into other monstrous displacements involving a realignment of oral and genital images. The face-hugger slithers a tube down its host's throat in order to lay an egg. When Ash (Ian Holm) examines its corpse, he lifts and peels back labial layers from which the tube presumably extended. The "warrior" form (a metamorphic stage) of the alien has teeth within teeth, but it also includes a phallic, ramrod-like extendable mechanism, making the warrior's mouth something of a paradoxically phallic *vagina dentata* (a toothed vagina). In both cases, the alien's form conflates archetypal images for human sexual organs with exaggerated phallic and vaginal elements. This, if not horrific, is certainly disturbing because of the danger embodied within. But two other displacements occur here that cement our repulsion and horror.

These combinations of phallic and vaginal elements are actually less genital than oral. The face-hugger form has a flexible tube that descends down another organism's mouth to impregnate its host. Its mixed genitalia impregnate its host orally. The warrior's phallic vagina dentata does not impregnate, it rather kills. As far as we can tell from the film, the warrior form does not kill to eat but kills to avoid being killed. It is purely defensive and yet an undeniably efficacious weapon. But the second displacement common to both stages is that this disturbing mixture of human genital references with various oral foci is also the creature's way of seeing. Neither stage of the alien creature has eyes. Its way of navigating its surroundings in both cases is its masculine-feminine, genital-oral conflation. These stages view their world through a monstrous blurring of sexual symbols. Both forms can be understood as the "incarnation of masculinity, understood as penetrative sexual violence," one threat being that it turns humanity into a mere feminine receptacle.[5] Mulhall states, "The threat stalking the corridors and ducts of the

Nostromo is thus a vision of masculinity and femininity, hence of sexual difference as such, as monstrous."[6] The masculine emerges as pure penetrative violence, the feminine as pure disposable receptacle. But why does Mulhall assume and treat these horrific distortions as the essence of sexuality? Why does he assume that Ripley accepts this as her understanding of reality? It is the confusion in form (both masculine and feminine) and its polarization in act (exclusively masculine) that is monstrous. The alien's form and reproduction are not monstrous because they represent an (albeit extreme) version of human sexuality, but rather because they offer an astounding distortion of it through an unexpected combination of symbols. It is this distortion and the accompanying horror that Ripley fights against, not sexual difference or sexuality *per se.*

Mulhall's interpretation of the alien's predatory sexuality as essential masculinity then permeates and distorts his definition of virginity and integrity. He uses these terms—integrity, celibacy, and virginity—interchangeably. They all refer to Ripley's aptness for defeating the creature, whose very mode of reproduction is a "monstrous," parasitic version of human intercourse, which echoes Ripley's experience of sexuality.[7] Mulhall's reducing these concepts to Ripley's ostensible alienation from life makes these states literal, with celibacy implying something about Ripley's current sexual state/ stasis. However, we know nothing of this from the film itself. My focus is therefore not on Ripley's current and literal sexual involvements but on her intuition and comprehensive instinct to protect herself, the ship, and her crewmates from annihilation. Mulhall contends:

> She has always understood her body as a vessel whose integrity must at all costs be preserved. . . . [I]t is rather a confirmation of her basic view of the human world of sexual difference, and an opportunity for her to act upon her long-matured comprehension of how best to oppose its essential monstrosity— by doing whatever it might take to avoid the violation of heterosexual intercourse. . . Ripley's emergence as the human hero of this tale is empowered or underwritten by her implied celibacy; her refusal to submit to the alien's advances has been long-prepared by, is in a sense the apotheosis of, her resolute virginity.[8]

From this quotation, we can glean Mulhall's definition of virginity. Virginity, integrity, and celibacy are indicative of a desperate closedness, an understanding of all things male and masculine as, in essence, violative. Virginity is, above all, self-protective, less concerned with others and life and more disposed to barricading the self against any exchange, be it literally or figuratively sexual. This definition, while a pervasive stereotype in modern Western cultures, defies Scott's depiction of Ripley.

Virginity, integrity, and celibacy may be closely related but they are not interchangeable. On a denotative level, *virginity* implies that a person has never had sexual intercourse; *integrity* means a quality of being complete, whole, in "unimpaired condition," be it physical or moral; and *celibacy* refers to a person willfully abstaining from sexual intercourse. Mulhall's treatment of these three terms as synonyms muddies his basic insight. The greatest culprit here is the idea of celibacy. Aside from the fact that we know nothing about any of the crew's sexual behavior, it is the term that most dramatically restricts this insight at the literal level. Integrity is the most flexible of these terms, more clearly allowing for a physical and moral level. It is Ripley's moral level of integrity that ignites her physical protection of it most clearly in her attempt to safeguard the ship and eventually her crewmates. A literal interpretation of virginity is as restrictive and reductive as celibacy, but any character's actual sexual behavior in this film is irrelevant to the story.

Reading virginity through a Catholic theological lens is a far richer approach. Angelo Cardinal Scola defines it as "indissolubility" and "possession in detachment."[9] He claims that "virginity is the culmination of nuptiality—even for spouses."[10] While marriage is not at issue in *Alien* any more than literal sex is, this paradigm is helpful because it suggests that virginity is not something one has and then loses, but rather, at its deepest levels, it is something one becomes. It involves then a centeredness in oneself and true self-knowledge that allows a person to be fully open to another, not for one's own ends but for the other's own destiny (hence the "possession in detachment").[11] Destiny means both a way of being and a call to becoming. Virginity then is an absence of selfishness that fosters seeing others as they are meant to be in their own ways and on their own paths, not as one would wish them to be. Virginity, far from being "alienation from life," means such a profound inner integration with life and sense of one's indissoluble value that one can be open to life in others with an unmitigated freedom.

This model accords well with a literary perspective on virginity forwarded by Robert J. Sardello who opens his essay "The Landscape of Virginity" by saying, "Virginity . . . is a necessity of the soul . . . a transformation from instinctual bond to spiritual union."[12] The monster makes manifest a most distorted and inverted version of the instinctual bond that should exist between oneself and another by making the other merely a tool (in this case, an incubator). In her opposition to the alien, Ripley refuses to accept the instinctual bond as the summit of human life. In this particular case, Ripley's "spiritual union" is an interior integration of the many elements that her fellow crewmates possess in lopsided extremes (i.e. courage, discernment, a capacity to listen, reasoning in the face of death). Their extremes eventually lead to their deaths, while Ripley's balanced interior allows her to survive. Her own confidence and capacity to protect herself and others are such necessities of her soul that she never questions defending others, regardless of whether they choose to develop such capacities themselves. The alien, like Ash and Mother, reduces everything to biology, to the literal, natural level.

Ripley's intuition against this at every turn—from letting Kane (John Hurt) back onto the ship to interpreting Ash's infatuation with the face-hugger—reveals that there is more to life than the merely natural. John Layard writes, "The ultimate purpose of everything in life is always sacrifice, which means transformation, the transformation of something 'natural' into that which is 'supernatural,' that is to say not less but still more natural than biological nature because on a 'higher,' or as we should say 'deeper' level."[13]

Ripley understands the protection of the *Nostromo* and her crew not as an issue of brute survival (the alien's domain) but as the survival of the human community. They cannot relinquish this conviction without falling either to the level of the alien or to that of Ash and Mother (who have an equally brutal, if scientific, view of human expendability). One example of such sacrifice is Ripley's willingness to go into the ducts instead of Dallas (Tom Skerritt) to chase the creature. She understands that Dallas, as captain, is more important on a basic command level than she is, and so he should not be the one to search the ducts. His leadership is needed. Dallas overrides her attempt, but she does not shrink from seeing that she should be the one to go. She is not eager to do this, but she does not let a desire for self-preservation override what would be best for the community as a whole. Her virginity then allows her to see Dallas' call (or destiny, as discussed above) as essential for the crew. This would mean to act truly in accord with her assessment, even when a great sacrifice might be in order. It would be a sacrifice made as a deeper commitment to the community, not because of the mere fact that she is expendable.

Mulhall states that the ultimate extension of Ripley's fierce virginity is her need to sever all ties to fertility and maternity, although her rescue of Jones the cat is a vestigial trace of such concern.[14] Her fearless care burns itself into the viewer's imagination when she goes to check on Parker (Yaphet Kotto) and Lambert (Veronica Cartwright). Both the viewer and undoubtedly Ripley know that their screams coming over the intercom (while Ripley is alone on the bridge) mean that they will soon be dead. If Ripley's orientation were to protect herself at all costs, as Mulhall's definition of virginity suggests, she would not descend into the bowels of the ship to look for her crewmates. Instead, she risks her life in the faintest hope that they might be alive. If going to rescue Jones is a hint of maternal concern, this act on behalf of Parker and Lambert suggests that her maternal concern is as profoundly integrated with her approach to life as her virginity.

By portraying Ripley's tenacious belief in protecting as many lives as possible, Scott shows a comprehensive and contemplative understanding of virginity as the ultimate weapon against the alien's insidious symbolism. In the face of the creature's nightmarish conflation of sexual symbols, Ripley never casts male or female into negative roles, nor does she ever act as if "the human world of sexual difference . . . [is an] essential monstrosity."[15] Unlike

Lambert who has a more androgynous look yet acts like the quintessential female horror film victim, Ripley retains her femininity while also showing a fierce capacity to kill. She does not fall prey to victimhood. Lambert has profound reservations and fears, but instead of expressing them, she remains silent and passive-aggressive at best. Her victimhood culminates in her death when "she seems hypnotized by the alien, which is there given its most explicitly sexualized repertoire of gestures (its prehensile tail shown creeping between her legs)."[16] We know something of this already from hearing her and Parker's screams: Parker has a weapon and yells at Lambert to get out of the way. Lambert is frozen, unable to fight or even to move enough to allow Parker access to the alien. Ripley, on the other hand, fights with an unwavering conviction in the value of protecting life. The fact that she is portrayed at key moments alone on the bridge yet at ease descending into and conversing in the bowels of the ship visually suggests her higher level of integration. She reconciles the qualities that her crewmates have but in unequal measures: courage, insight, tenacity, protectiveness, instinct, and reason, all of which allow her to protect and to fight.[17] Nowhere is this more evident than in her descent to find Parker and Lambert, an act that defies common sense and self-protection, an act antithetical to all that the predatory alien represents.[18]

RIPLEY: WISE AS A SERPENT, INNOCENT AS A DOVE

The first scene where we see a surprising yet delightful picture of Ripley's shrewdness and capacity to engage in playful banter (and yet genuine exchange) is in the bowels of the drop ship. Ripley descends into the engine space to obtain Brett (Harry Dean Stanton) and Parker's assessment of the damage after landing.[19] Their conversation is barely audible and hardly even visible above the badly lit, clacking, hissing, steam-spouting equipment. To the uninitiated eye, it looks like the ship could blow up at any moment. Parker and Brett use this as an opportunity to press Ripley into better wage and bonus negotiations. Parker starts by asking if they will get a share of what is found. The tone of Ripley's first response says even more than her words: "Don't worry, Parker, yeah, you'll get whatever's coming to you." Ripley's words drip with double meaning: there is, of course, the face value of getting one's legal due, but she sees Parker's constant angling as the disgruntled manipulation that it is. The viewer, however, knows that there is another layer, the foreshadowing of the deadly events to come. As such, neither of these co-workers deserves what is actually coming to them. When Parker and Brett then begin a "What?" routine in response to all that Ripley says, she dishes out her saucy final retort: "If you have any trouble, I'll be on the bridge." Her tone reveals that she sees through all their bluster, both literal and metaphorical. Just to emphasize this point one more time, she

ducks under a blast of steam as she leaves. Since they have all been standing
in the midst of this internal storm, she need not have ducked. But doing so
highlights her skillful maneuvering around all the "hot air."

After she leaves, Parker flicks a switch and all the steam and noise abrupt-
ly stop. Only then do we realize how shrewd Ripley has been. If we were
confused by her apparent lack of concern about the ship, we now rest assured
at witnessing her capacity to discern the true gravity of a situation. While
everyone is rightly concerned about the vessel and the damage it has sustained, Ripley can tell the difference between hot air and a genuine crisis.
She fully engages with Parker and Brett, not just answering their questions
but also chatting with them, implicitly calling their bluff. While her sassy last
line, "If you have any trouble, I'll be on the bridge" could suggest that she
sees herself as superior to the engineers, it is more an invitation to engage
later in continued communication. She teases them, but she is never closed to
them, nor does she shame them. She implicitly challenges them to come up
to bridge level (her level) should they need something. It is not that the
bridge is devoid of games and manipulation either, but Ripley addresses
those in their turn as well. She "bridges" gaps and thus is not a woman
"alienated from life" whose understanding of sexuality and more comprehensive male-female interactions stems from an abhorrence of engagement and
social "intercourse." She challenges those who act at a level that is less than
direct and is so engaged that she gives the viewer nearly unmitigated confidence in her discernment of complex situations.

This trust comes into even starker relief when she is compared to Lambert. The preceding scene takes place on the bridge where Ash, Dallas, and
Kane discuss the planet's atmospheric and geological elements. What is particularly striking about this scene is that the majority of it is shot with the
camera focused on Lambert as she anxiously smokes a cigarette and listens
to the others discuss the "almost primordial" conditions outside. She barely
looks at them; she listens but says nothing, until at the very end when Dallas
tells her to suit up as she is joining him and Kane in the walk to the signal's
source. Even then she utters only one sarcastic, fear-laden word: "Swell." If
there is a female character that embodies a closed, resolute alienation from
life, it is Lambert. Her entire demeanor and lack of interaction are the exact
opposites of Ripley. She does not interact with any sense of confidence or
centeredness. She assumes her own voicelessness as she listens to the three
men discuss the surroundings. She faces neither her colleagues nor their
predicament and acts as a victim of both.[20]

During and after the scene between Ripley, Parker, and Brett, the expedition to the signal begins. Dallas, Kane, and Lambert head out into the howling, primordial world. In the initial shots, we hear the ripping wind and
experience the cloudy darkness despite the distant sunrise. Twice Lambert
says (or yells) in order to be heard over the wind, "I can't see a god-damned

thing!" The planet's atmosphere is, on one level, not unlike Parker's doc-
tored engine room: dark, loud, howling, and swirling with steam and gas.
The senses we normally rely on the most in a new or complicated situation,
sight and sound, are hampered in both cases. Ripley, however, does not let
the external noise interfere with her assessment of her surroundings and her
colleagues. If she can see through a situation, she will. Lambert, on the other
hand, willfully clouds her own vision. When she has the opportunity to
assess the outside even from the relative safety of the bridge, she refrains
from doing so. Once forced out into it, she refuses to engage with the world
around her. She defends herself by closing off as many avenues of exposure
as she can.

Lambert's resolute impermeability complicates our understanding of her
knowledge. One could say that she intuits danger, but by behaving passive-
aggressively and not engaging with her crewmates, she silences her own
voice. She chalks her own words up to mere griping, and so implicitly tells
her crewmates not even to bother listening to her. She tries to protect her own
integrity by closing up on every level: intellectual, emotional, physical. No
one could be more different from Ripley, who has confidence in her own
voice and a willingness to interact with her colleagues even when she thinks
they are behaving with juvenile abandon. This woman most definitely belongs on the bridge; she sees through storms.

THE MOMENT OF TRUTH: "OPEN THE HATCH!"

When Dallas and Lambert return to the ship carrying Kane, Ripley once
again reveals her strength and discernment, as well as trust in her own authority. The exchange begins on a note of reassurance between Ripley and
Dallas, with Ripley not just saying "I'm here" but "I'm right here." However,
she persistently questions him about what has happened to Kane. They go
back and forth about quarantine, with Dallas taking the compassionate view
towards Kane, who could die within twenty-four hours, and Ripley defending
the ultimate reason for the rule: if they do not follow it, they could all die.
Lambert's hysteria, while ostensibly about Kane, has more to do with her
own feeling of safety. Ripley hears her colleague's panic, but instead of
succumbing to it, she becomes increasingly centered. She begins to speak
more formally at this point, which appears to infuriate Dallas, who starts
yelling that he is *"ordering"* her to open the door. At this point Ripley
responds, "Yes. I read you. The answer is negative." Then Ash opens the
door, informing Ripley, "Inner hatch open."

Here lies the heart of Ripley's understanding of virginity in a comprehensive and contemplative sense. Her presence and openness to Dallas upon
return are clear. She is not just "here" but "right here." Ripley stresses her

availability and concern with that one "right." Her relief is contained but evident even despite her alertness to a possible complication with Kane. She does not push, rush, or panic. When she refuses to open the hatch, she is not following the rules merely for the sake of following them. Her refusal at first comes in the language of a friend and fellow crewmember, only transforming into formal speech when she realizes that she is not being heard. She understands why the quarantine rule exists: while it would be horrible to have a crewmember die, it is better that it be just one of them and not all. She has not wavered in her insistence on quarantine, but she is flexible and ready to reason. Quarantine is not arbitrary, and defending it in terms of the larger picture does not imply an antipathy to life.[21]

Ripley's refusal to open the hatch door and let her crewmates in happens while she is fully engaged and speaking with those outside. She is not coldly laying down the law. However, she is hampered on a certain level since she is on the bridge. Ash has outwitted her by positioning himself at the door and so is able to override her command. Ripley's reasoning, while emerging from deep within her own being, has limited effects. In all the various forms of terror and panic that erupt, no one listens to Ripley's wisdom. They are all speaking from lower parts of the ship; if we construe the ship as a bodily analogy, this position represents the instinctual reactions they all demonstrate. Lambert is in pure self-preservation and panic mode, while Dallas is the compassionate captain thinking along the lines of "leave no man behind." Once Kane is on board, Parker and Brett are willing to fix the ship as quickly as possible. Only Ripley understands the vessel as representative of them all, yet she remains alone on the bridge.

THE ALIEN AND PURITY

Ash's brief paean to the alien presages the horror of encountering the creature itself. The officer has been decapitated and unveiled as an android, but Ripley, Parker, and Lambert have hooked his head back up to see if he knows how to kill the monster.

> Ash: "You still don't know what you're dealing with, do you? A perfect organism. Its structural perfection is matched only by its hostility."
>
> Lambert: "You admire it."
>
> Ash: "I admire its purity. A survivor, unclouded by conscience, remorse, or delusions of morality."

Ash, executing the company's orders via Mother, is another kind of embodiment of dissociated masculinity, a counterpart to the alien's instinctual masculinity. Mulhall states, "For Ash . . . the alien symbolizes the true significance of the cosmic principle of life; it signifies the essential insignificance of human morality and culture. . . . Both Ash and his Mother [the ship's computer] identify themselves with life as such, not with human life and human concerns."[22] Mulhall's compelling analysis sees the alien's vicious reproductive cycle as the essence of life, irrespective of the costs to individuals within its milieu. The alien then represents not only masculinity but also life itself, so that the *Nostromo*'s crew is entirely expendable as a justification for its survival. On one level, Mulhall has a beautiful point: that there is a brutal aspect to life's relentless, amoral rhythm of propagation.[23] However, Ripley's resistance to this as the ultimate definition of life comes precisely from her clinging to the exact opposite set of values than those listed by Ash as the essence of the alien's purity. This signals not her rejection of life and all these qualities, but her defense of them in the face of Ash's and Mother's respective attempts to ignore them.

The qualities that make for purity according to Ash are structural perfection, hostility, and a life "unclouded by conscience, remorse, or delusions of morality." In terms of structural perfection, the defining feature of the alien's body (as explained above) is a monstrous amalgamation of male and female sexual symbols. For Ash, this conflation and confusion comprise perfection in the overriding of any value conferred to human sexual difference. It transforms this void of meaning into hostility towards all other life forms, which are instinctually interpreted as a threat. This ostensible freedom to treat all other life forms as a threat is made possible by its complete lack of any moral capacity. The alien is indeed all instinct and so consciousness as conscience is inconceivable. As Mulhall notes, it has no language, culture, reason, or capacity for play.[24] Its purity consists of the complete absence of any recognizably human qualities, especially those that symbolize vulnerability and need for one another (in everything from sex to showing remorse). Of course, it has the desire to reproduce, but this translates into a need for a living incubator, not the desire for a mutually loving relationship with another being. Purity, for the alien and according to an objectively scientific point of view, is the lack of vulnerability, a lack of need for another. In a sense, it is not unlike the definition earlier of virginity where a certain quality of centeredness in one's own being is essential. The critical difference is in the orientation of this centeredness. In the alien, it is pure, hostile self-protection. In humanity, and Ripley in particular, it is a capacity to see others clearly and then being able to do whatever is necessary to protect them as well as the self.[25]

PURITY VS. VIRGINITY: SURVIVAL ACCORDING TO SCOTT

Scott's negotiation of the relationship between purity and virginity focuses on an anthropocentric (human-centered) approach to sexual difference as being good, not overrun by any alien-like sexual confusion, conflation, or dissociated masculinity (be that of the alien's animal strain or Ash's robotic one). Purity in the world of the film is the complete absence of fundamental attitudes and attributes that make human culture what it is today. The decapitated and deracinated science officer Ash admires a creature whose very form and existence run counter to the vitality and vulnerability of humanity. This is science run amok, and the weapons to be used against it are those which act to affirm and sustain human culture.

Ripley's key moments of solitude on the bridge comprise the visual and narrative element that Scott uses to corroborate the threat of irresponsible science. She is alone when deciphering the signal and only she knows that it is probably a warning and not a request for help; later, she is alone when she refuses to break quarantine. She is again alone when she hears Parker and Lambert scream when the alien attacks. The bridge is, in essence, the head and command center of the ship. Scott shows Ripley being at ease on the bridge and willing to make the difficult decisions that such a position requires. She occupies this role with her whole being: she does not follow orders because the company insists upon it (unlike Dallas), and she understands the rules she tries to enforce. She does not impose them, at least initially, from on high but explains the reasons. Even though she acts from her privileged status on the bridge, she never abandons her humanity for a dissociated or metaphorically decapitated sense of scientific reason, nor for the ostensibly more humane reason of helping Kane. She alone senses that the signal could be decoded with more effort than Ash has put into it. Her intuition, calm demeanor, and protectiveness always make her aware of her surroundings.

Virginity, as established above, involves a continuous vigilance, but one that functions without anxiety. It is a discerning openness grounded in the values of protecting life, not even when faced with a creature whose ostensible purity consists of the absence of any moral values. Mulhall ends his chapter on *Alien* with a pithy discussion of Ripley's relation to Kane/Cain, the first character in the film to fall victim to the alien and whose name alludes to the first human murderer.[26] This rumination takes its cue from Ash's description of the creature newly burst from Kane's chest as "Kane's son." Mulhall suggests that this allusion makes Ripley Cain's daughter, lodging the drive to kill and murder within the very beginning of humanity itself. From a theological perspective, this is hardly surprising. We are all descendants of that first family, living out the ramifications of all its archetypal, primordial acts. While Ripley does certainly defend herself by relying on a capacity to kill, Mulhall has forgotten the other aspect of Cain's heritage: civilization.

The biblical Cain laments being condemned to wander, yet such sorrow begs the question: what happens when he leaves God's presence? He founds a city, the first larger-than-family human community.[27] From Cain's genealogical line comes, among other innovations, music and forgers of metal—in other words, the building blocks of culture. While the biblical genealogy of humanity passes through Seth and Noah, these foundational gifts from Cain and his progeny exist for the entirety of the Bible. They are such intrinsic realities in the text that we are apt to forget their origin in the first murderer, a person who transformed his punishment into life, fruitfulness, and places where human interaction and exchange abound. Ripley's violence, unlike Cain's, defends the human community and ultimately, herself. Her killing is not out of jealous wrath but hatred of that which destroys life and the community of which she is a part. She can survive because she intuitively places her maternal protectiveness and defense of virginity and integrity at the service of the *Nostromo*'s community.

In Ripley, the coexistence of virginity and maternity forms the bedrock for her vision of and approach to the world. Her openness grants her the ability to be discerning of others and of herself. She is not at the mercy of her wrath; unlike Cain, she controls and directs it. Her integration of the two extremes of Cain's legacy to humanity reveals that she is Cain's daughter in every figurative sense, not just in being able to use violence to effect major changes (in this case, ameliorative in spirit), but also in being able to value civilization. Ripley's greatest weapon against the alien is this comprehensive embodiment of virginity.

NOTES

1. Stephen Mulhall, *On Film* (New York: Routledge, 2002), 31.

2. Ibid., 25.

3. Ibid.

4. Ibid., 20. Mulhall does not discuss the element of mixed sexual imagery. It must be noted, however, that this topic touches on one of the few continuity issues in the film: when the face-hugger is dead, there is no sign of the tube that has been mentioned several times. Only in H. H. Giger's drawings, which director James Cameron then used in *Aliens,* do we see the vaginal opening with the retractable phallic tube on the face-hugger's underbelly.

5. Ibid.

6. Ibid., 20–21. Mulhall does note the alien's "intensely oral focus" in all its stages from face-hugger to chest-burster to warrior stage. He does not discuss the mix of sexual symbols in the context of this oral imagery, nor does he discuss it as the mode of "seeing."

7. Ibid., 19f.

8. Ibid., 24-25.

9. Angelo Cardinal Scola, *The Nuptial Mystery*, trans. Michelle K. Borras (Grand Rapids, MI: Eerdmans, 2005), 105–106, 256, 270, 274.

10. Ibid., 105.

11. Ibid., 105, 256, 271.

12. Robert, J. Sardello, "The Landscape of Virginity," in *Images of the Untouched,* ed. Joanne Stroud and Gail Thomas (Dallas, TX: Spring Publications, 1982), 39–40.

13. John Layard, "The Incest Taboo and the Virgin Archetype," in *Images of the Untouched,* ed. Joanne Stroud and Gail Thomas (Dallas, TX: Spring Publications, 1982), 152.

14. Mulhall, *Film,* 27.

15. Ibid., 24.

16. Ibid.

17. I should note that I am not using an essentialist dialectic that correlates instinct with the feminine and reason with the masculine. I have shown how the alien, in both its form and actions, is a horrific combination of sexual imagery that attacks the world through an instinctually masculine and aggressive modality. Instinct, therefore, cannot be correlated simply with femininity, but is an important and complex matter in its own right. The alien is a horrific combination of these elements, while Ripley is an integration of them.

18. Mulhall, *Film,* 27.

19. We know from *Aliens* that the planet is called LV 426. The planet in *Prometheus* (2012) is LV 223. In future projects, it is likely that Scott may reveal how the ship arrived on LV 426. Although whether the latter film is a prequel is a debatable premise, the plot continuities between the 1979 film and the 2012 are undeniable.

20. It should be noted that Veronica Cartwright played this closedness so superbly that she won the Academy Award that year for best supporting actress.

21. Scott revisits this theme in *Prometheus,* echoing this situation when Meredith Vickers (Charlize Theron) refuses to let an infected and dying Charlie Holloway (Logan Marshall-Green) return to the ship. Vickers more accurately displays a resolute antagonism to any engagement with life. Her icy demeanor chills the screen the instant she arrives on it, and her ruthless alienation from life has its manifestation on the ship itself. Her own quarters can be entirely self-sufficient if need be, even if they are separated from the main ship. If the crew is in danger, she ensures her own safety and integrity regardless of what happens to the others. Integrity for Vickers is purely about physical safety; she has no moral correlative. However, her willingness to kill Holloway at his insistence (and to Shaw's horror), displays some of Ripley's steel nerve in wanting to keep Kane out of the ship and in quarantine. Her focus never wavers from her *self*-protection, however. She, like Lambert, is resolute and closed. Vickers' flirtation and probable one-night stand with Captain Janek (Idris Elba) does not alter this interpretation. Given what the audience knows of her character, it fits with her desire and blatant willingness to use others for her satisfaction. She feels no hesitation in abandoning the ship when Janek and the remainder of the crew plan to ram the vessel into the Engineer's, since Shaw believes it is headed to destroy Earth. Vickers' willingness to use and then dispose of her crewmates when their actions endanger her personal safety again sounds far more like the "alienation from life" that Mulhall describes than does Ripley's behavior.

22. Mulhall, *Film,* 29.

23. Ibid., 26.

24. Ibid., 19.

25. Mulhall never addresses the significance of Ash's name. Ash, as a substance, is the remnant of fire and destruction; it symbolizes the absence of life. He, himself is unable to become ash but simply melts into a statue when Parker turns his flame-thrower on him, emphasizing his inorganic nature. He was never organic "life" to begin with. Ash, as the child of Mother in this story, then suggests that while they may be defending this certain version of "pure life," symbolized by the alien, the culmination of such an approach is ultimately death. The reason that Mother and Ash (and the alien, in a way) are trying to keep the alien alive is to use it as a life-destroying weapon. Granted, if Mother and Ash do so out of purely scientific interest and the alien does so out of instinct, their goals overlap. "Ash" may also allude to an image from antiquity, the phoenix. While its specific qualities vary by culture, the phoenix's basic myth is of a long-lived bird (between 500 and 1000 years) that, at the end of its life, builds a nest that ignites and reduces both the phoenix and its nest to ashes. A new phoenix arises from these ashes. The references to ash and to new life rising from it suggest that Ash's name might not symbolize death alone. In fact, once he is decapitated and decommissioned, Parker, Lambert, and Ripley do try to reanimate the head to find out if there is some way to kill

the creature. While his name and the sequence of his analogical death and decommissioning have resonance with the myth of the phoenix dying in flames and rising from its own ashes, the fact that his "resurrection" is only one part of his body emphasizes how completely removed from human life and culture Ash is, even in its mythological expressions of hope. Moreover, the phoenix dies so that new life might come from its ashes. Ash's work and goal have been to protect a creature that destroys life. He is the antithesis of the myth.

26. Mulhall, *Film*, 32.
27. Genesis 4:17ff.

REFERENCES

Alien. DVD. Directed by Ridley Scott. 1979. Los Angeles, CA: Twentieth Century Fox, 1999.

Bible. Revised Standard Version, Catholic Edition. San Francisco, CA: Ignatius Press, 2010.

Layard, John. "The Incest Taboo and the Virgin Archetype." In *Images of the Untouched*, edited by Joanne Stroud and Gail Thomas. Dallas, TX: Spring Publications, 1982.

Mulhall, Stephen. *On Film.* New York: Routledge, 2002.

Prometheus. Directed by Ridley Scott. Los Angeles, CA: Twentieth Century Fox, 2012.

Sardello, Robert J. "The Landscape of Virginity." In *Images of the Untouched*, edited by Joanne Stroud and Gail Thomas. Dallas, TX: Spring Publications, 1982.

Scola, Angelo Cardinal. *The Nuptial Mystery.* Translated by Michelle K. Borras. Grand Rapids, MI: Eerdmans, 2005.

Chapter Eighteen

Gladiator, Gender, and Marriage in Heaven: A Christian Exploration

Adam Barkman

Gladiator, Ridley Scott's most successful film—both in terms of awards and box office receipts—is one of those rare movies "liked as much by women as by men."[1] Traditional gender roles and themes, refreshingly played with a straight face, are a large part of this attraction. Men see in Russell Crowe's Maximus a man they would like to be, and "women see on the screen their dream man—a man who is very, very strong but very, very loving."[2] More-over, Scott brilliantly adds a transcendental element to all of this, transforming Maximus's journey to be with his wife and son from a mere physical one (as was the case in the first few drafts of the script) to a more profound metaphysical odyssey. Using the Christian language he was raised with, though correctly recognizing an enormous overlap between Roman polytheism and Christian monotheism, Scott says that "Heaven" (in the film, "Elysium") is the "central spiritual backbone to the movie."[3] What is satisfying for many here is the curious but ancient idea that we, as gendered beings, endure in the next life, and moreover, that many of our relationships (including some of our marriages) might also subsequently endure.

While many will find this suggestion satisfying as poetry, fewer will find it satisfying as philosophy. Atheists, for example, do not believe in Heaven; agnostics are not sure what is out there; Stoics, Vedantic Hindus, and most Buddhists do not think any personal identity—and thus, personal relationships—endure; and Taoists, along with followers of many shamanistic religions, see gender as a social construct. This paradigm posits that a gendered relation like marriage has no absolutely fixed meaning now or later; thus, Chinese philosopher Zhuangzi famously did not mourn his dead wife. Yet for many polytheistic religions of old, and still for Christian monotheism, the idea that one's gender and a gendered relationship like marriage might endure in "Heaven" is philosophically plausible.[4] True, Jesus said, "When the dead rise, they will neither marry nor be given in marriage; they will be like the angels,"[5] but what of this? Why think Jesus supposes angels—and spirits in general—to be *genderless* or marriages unable to *continue*? Since Roman polytheism is no longer practiced, and since Scott clearly invokes Christianity in his commentary on the movie, Christian philosophy seems to be the best basis from which to explore the director's vision of gender and marriage in Heaven. Just as Scott's ethereal vision sends the imagination far above the film, so will a careful Christian understanding of the relations between spirit and gender, body and sex, and masculinity and femininity take us far from the particulars of the film. Such flight will ultimately have the concrete purpose of convincing readers that Maximus was right when he tells Juba, "My wife and son are waiting for me."

GENDER AS AN ESSENTIAL PROPERTY OF THE SOUL

Many great philosophers—both in the East and West—have made the mistake of ridiculing as anthropomorphic or naïve the ancient idea that the gods (or God) have an essential gender. Marcus Aurelius, the Stoic philosopher and emperor we first encounter in *Gladiator*, would, in keeping with the word "great," correctly recognize that many of the ancient Greek and Roman myths about the gods are untrue, especially the ones that depict the chief god as a moral reprobate on par with the worst human beings. But why, in stripping the supreme god of moral imperfections and making him virtually synonymous with the Moral Good, does Marcus (following the Stoics, Plato, and the pre-Socratics before him) think that such a being should also be stripped of the attribute of Masculinity or the title of All-Father? Who is wiser in this respect: the sage emperor Marcus Aurelius, who denied that the supreme god literally had a gender, or the common man, Maximus, who without philosophical conceit, prays to the gendered spirit, "Blessed Father, watch over my wife and son . . ."?

Orthodox Christianity tends to side with Maximus, asserting, for the most part, that both the lesser gods—angels and demons, we might say—and the supreme God are gendered. I begin with the supreme God. Univocity means "in one voice" and those who think we can say some things univocally about God are also those who think that when we say "God is *Agape*," we attribute to Him precisely the characteristics of self-sacrifice and benevolence. We can, of course, make mistakes in our understanding of this and any other loaded word (misreading, for instance, the word "*agape*" for "a grape," and then wrongly imagining God to be purple and juicy). But in theory, we can understand that this word means and says something literally true of God.

Yes, most of our language about God tends to be analogy, metaphor, or simile, but, as medieval philosopher Duns Scotus pointed out, all analogy presupposes some univocity.[6] For instance, if we use the simile "God is like the sun," we do not mean God is literally a giant ball of burning gas, but we do mean, among other things, that God, like the sun, is life-sustaining.

The point is that most orthodox Christians and most ancient polytheists admit (consciously or unconsciously) that we can speak with some univocity in respect to God. For example, when we call God "Omnipotent," we mean He is literally so: He can do all that is logically possible. While many Christian feminists agree that we can speak about God univocally, most deny that gendered terms applied to God are literally true: Father, King, God, husband, she-bear, mother hen, and so on are metaphors, the literal truth behind them being something like "powerful," "leader-like," or "caring."

To make their case against God being gendered, Christian feminists typically argue thus:

All gendered words about God are social constructs.
"God," "King," and "Father" are gendered words used to describe God.
Therefore, "God," "King," and "Father" are social constructs.

Moreover, usually from a source that is not biblical (often a hybrid of Greek philosophy and neo-shamanism), Christian feminists typically assert that spirits are neuter and thus reason:

God is a spirit.
No spirit is gendered.
Therefore, God is not gendered.

But if, for a moment, one does not simply assume that all gendered terms must be metaphors, then the biblical language used to describe God becomes more complicated, some terms being best read as metaphors, to be sure, but others being best read as literal, univocal statements. John Cooper, for example, thinks that words like "Father," "King," and "God"—words depicting prime Masculinity—are "title-names"[7] or words literally true of God, while others like "husband" and "bridegroom" are metaphors based on God being literally masculine. C. S. Lewis has further argued that the biblical vision is one where "Gender is a more fundamental reality than sex."[8] If Lewis is right, then one could argue that since Father, King, and God are not clearly terms that can only, or primarily, be applied to sex and biological beings, there is no reason why we cannot imagine God to be, quite literally, the Prime Masculine or, in Platonic language, the "Original" Father whose "copies" are human fathers.

The metaphysics of this requires two things. First, Scripture (not to mention the arguments of the philosophers) makes it clear that God is a "Spirit," which, in Aristotelian language, is a (rational) soul, substance (as in, "Three persons in one substance"), or an indivisible whole with a number of essential properties (qualities or attributes that are *necessarily* part of that substance). Second, based on a number of fairly clear biblical claims, including God's own self-disclosure (such as in the Lord's Prayer), we have decent grounds to think that God has the essential property of "being masculine" (or, more precisely, "being Masculinity").

Let us say for the sake of argument that some agree; nevertheless, they might still ask, why imagine God limited to only one gender? Mary Daley, for example, implores us to use "bisexual imagery" for the "Father-Mother God,"[9] and there have been, of course, some religious traditions that portray their deities as bi-gendered. The Aztec Ometeotl and the Norse Loki are two such examples. Nevertheless, this notion seems to me incoherent. Without getting ahead of myself, if I were to define the masculine in terms of taking care of, providing for, and protecting the feminine, and the feminine as being receptive to these masculine gestures, then what would it mean for God to do this to Himself? For God to love Himself is one thing, given that we all understand what it means to love ourselves. But for God to demonstrate the dance of the genders within Himself and toward Himself seems implausible. I cannot imagine what this would look like and we certainly have no biblical evidence for this. Even in Trinitarian theology, the Father, Son, and Spirit are, individually and most consistently, spoken of in masculine terms[10] and the feminine terms used to describe God, such as "she-bear" or "mother-hen," are, unless we are to imagine God to have animal properties, certainly metaphors.[11]

Nonetheless, some will further object: if God made females, He must be the originator of this idea, and does this not suggest He is, if we must attribute gender to God at all, equally feminine? Not at all. To be sure, God is the originator of females and the feminine, but He is probably so not by "being" but by "possessing the idea of." In other words, while He would have the essential property "being Masculinity," He would have the essential property "possessing the idea of femininity." To clarify, we might say that while God has the essential properties of "possessing the idea of wings," "possessing the idea of rain," or even "possessing the idea of murder," He is neither a winged being or rain or a murderer. Thus, on this model, God is God—and not Goddess—but He, of course, made all things that are feminine from His eternal idea of femininity, which, I hasten to add, is a very beautiful idea indeed.

CREATED GENDERED SOULS

If God—the Spirit, Rational Soul, Person, or original Substance—is essentially masculine, then it seems possible, even probable, that those created in His image—other spirits, persons or rational souls—would also be essentially gendered. (I leave non-rational souls, such as animals, to the side.) Although the Bible does not say explicitly that angelic beings—polytheism's gods and goddesses—are made in His image, we can infer this through other essential properties they possess which seem to belong exclusively to spirits or rational souls. Among other things, angels have the ultimate capacity for free will (hence, Paul refers to the "elect angels"[12]), and they have the ultimate capacity for rationality (hence, Satan, Gabriel, and others challenge, calculate, argue, tempt, deliver messages, etc.). But do we have biblical evidence for created spirits—specifically, angels—being gendered? I think yes.

In addition to the (admittedly weak) testimony of modern people who underwent near-death experiences and actually saw gendered angels,[13] the Bible consistently speaks of the major angels or demons in masculine terms. Some have objected to this, however, saying that because there is no Hebrew neuter term, the masculine was used instead. But this is unconvincing for many reasons, none more than the fact that even though in Greek there is a neuter term, none of the proper names of angels are in the neuter.[14]

That angels are depicted as gendered is fairly clear. But are all angels *masculine*? Are there only "gods" and no "goddesses"? The Hebrew and Greek words for the general class "angel" always refer to them in the masculine, but this, in itself, is philosophically uninteresting. Human beings, when referred to collectively, have traditionally been classified in the masculine ("man"). Insofar as masculinity contains within itself the notions of representation or authority, it is quite proper to use the masculine to cover both the masculine and feminine. Moreover, even if the Bible did not mention any feminine angels, it would hardly follow that none exist. Nevertheless, I do think we have some concrete evidence for feminine angels, not only, again, from the testimony of people with near-death experiences, but also in the Bible itself. In Zechariah 5:9, we read, "Then I looked up—and there before me were two women with the wind in their wings!" Almost certainly this verse does not refer to human women since humans do not have wings. However, angels appear to possess them. Because it is not at all clear what these winged women would be metaphors for, it seems probable that this verse is depicting actual feminine angels. But, even if this reading were wrong, it seems very probable that angels, like God, are gendered spirits, and so we can say with relative confidence that whatever else Jesus means when He says we will "be like the angels" in Heaven, He is not denying us the privilege of gender.[15]

So, from the Uncreated Spirit (God) and the created angelic spirits (angels or "gods"), we finally arrive at created human spirits. Orthodoxy has usually maintained that the biblical understanding of a human being is that of a spirit, person, or rational soul which has a body.[16] We *are* souls and we *have* (most of the time) bodies. Of course, the connection between the soul and body is extremely tight, but for my purposes here, their distinction needs to be noted.

If God and angels—the two other spirit types that we know of—are essentially gendered, then it seems likely that humans would be as well. This argument can be further strengthened not only by some out-of-body experiences wherein the disembodied person recognizes himself or herself and other family members by their gendered qualities,[17] but also by biblical evidence, where those who appear after death, such as Samuel, Elijah, Moses, and Jesus, are recognizably gendered.[18] Moreover, since human bodies are distinguished by their sex (I leave difficult cases of sexual ambiguity to the side for the moment), it seems that human spirits are sandwiched between God and angels—gendered spirits—from above and sexed bodies from below. Very likely, then, we should think of ourselves, in our inner self, spirit, or soul, as being essentially gendered, either masculine or feminine.[19]

Indeed, this metaphysical speculation does seem supported by a lot of work in anthropology and psychology. Andrew Tolson, for example, thinks a "deep structure of masculinity"[20] can be observed. Thomas Gregor insists, after his study in the Amazon, that "there are continuities of masculinity that transcend cultural differences."[21] Walter Lonner believes culture "is only a thin veneer covering an essential universal" gender dimorphism.[22] John Williams and Deborah Best, in their study of thirty different cultures, say there is "substantial similarity" to be found "panculturally in the traits ascribed to men and women."[23] And David Gilmore, not at all dismissive of cultural anomalies, concludes: "[T]here is a recurring notion in world cultures that real manhood is different from simple anatomical maleness."[24]

WHAT GENDER IS TO SOUL, SEX IS TO BODY

Gender, as Scott envisions it in *Gladiator* and as I have argued using Christian philosophy, is an ontological fact: an essential property in the substance, soul, or spirit. Moreover, because a general principle in both the Bible and Nature seems to be that the higher guides, controls, or otherwise affects the lower, the human spirit (which is higher) would guide, control, or affect the lower aspect (the physical body). I read Thomas Aquinas's formulation of the soul-body interaction to be more or less the correct one here.[25]

In terms of gender and sex, what this means is that if your soul has the essential property "being masculine," then your soul, which guides the development of your body, would see to it that your body develops the corresponding sex, which is male. You are masculine and your body will likely reflect this insofar as you have male parts. Or again, if your soul has the essential property of being feminine, then your body will likely have female biology. You, then, would be feminine, and your body would be female. General biological differences, including general brain differences, then, are determined by the soul.[26]

This model fits fairly well with the latest research in biology. Physicians Gaya Arnaoff and Jennifer Bell of Columbia University posited recently, "There is increasing evidence to suggest that the brain is a sexual organ, that brain sex (i.e., the sex of the brain) is paramount in determining human gender identity."[27] Though I think they have it backwards—that gender determines sex rather than sex, gender—we may take their claim to be evidence that sexual biology is far from fluid. Even at birth, the sexual differences are present and significant, pace what some have imagined. As Leonard Sax succinctly explains:

> In men, many areas of the brain are rich in proteins that are coded directly by the Y chromosome. Those proteins are absent in women's brain tissue. Conversely, women's brain tissue is rich in material coded directly by the X chromosome; these particular transcripts of the X chromosome are absent from men's brain tissue. These sex differences, then, are *genetically programmed*, not mediated by hormonal differences. . . . They are present at birth.[28]

These programmed sex differences do result in many different concrete ways that boys and girls play and learn, even though, and this hardly needs to be said, *differences do not imply any kind of absolute superiority*. Quoting Sax again, "The bottom line is that the brain is just organized *differently* in females and males. The tired argument about which sex is more intelligent or which sex has the 'better' brain is about as meaningful as arguing about which utensil is 'better,' a knife or a spoon. The only correct answer to such a question is: 'Better for what?'"[29]

The pattern of gendered souls programming sexed bodies may be true of non-human rational souls as well.[30] Thus, in Genesis 6:1-8, the "sons of God"—which the Old Testament always refers to as angels[31]—appear to have taken on a biological form and have sex with "the daughters of men," producing the "nephilim" or giants. (Perhaps this is the basis for polytheism's stories about the philandering gods!) Even in the case of Spirit Himself, we can reason that if God is Masculinity, then it makes perfect sense that His incarnate body would be male. In other words, it is probably not at all accidental that Jesus was born a man and is, in the words of Robert Conant, "the supremely manly man."[32]

THE MEANING OF MASCULINITY AND FEMININITY

Theologian John Piper defines masculinity as "a sense of benevolent responsibility to lead, provide for and protect women in ways appropriate to a man's differing relationships," and femininity as "a freeing disposition to affirm, receive and nurture strength and leadership from worthy men in ways appropriate to a woman's differing relationships."[33] These definitions are worthwhile, but the trouble is that Piper takes an essential property that belongs to the soul and restricts it only to the human and biological realms. Thus, instead of saying that masculinity has within it the disposition to "protect women," we should rather say that it has within itself the disposition to "protect the feminine," and instead of saying that femininity seeks to strengthen "worthy men," we should say that it seeks to strengthen "the worthy masculine."

In respect to the angels, we do not know for certain that there are feminine ones, but if there are, then it seems likely that the masculine ones would generally feel inclined to protect them. Or again, God is the Eternal Masculine and so defines Himself partly through His eternal idea of the feminine. This literal truth is often expressed metaphorically when we talk about God's relation to Israel or the Church. God the Masculine protects the creation, which, metaphorically, is feminine in relation to Him (His "wife" or "bride"), but these, as I said earlier, are metaphors. God is essentially and literally masculine, but He is not literally a husband or bridegroom since the Christian idea of marriage is between one man (masculine) and one woman (feminine), and this would not at all work if God, the Prime Masculine, were to be cast as married to half a billion or so Christian men.[34] Thus, God is essentially and literally masculine; the creation is metaphorically feminine in relation to him. To speak personally, I am essentially and literally masculine and my wife is essentially and literally feminine, but we are metaphorically feminine in relation to God. These metaphors are valuable and do agree with my revised definition of Piper's reading of masculinity and femininity: that the masculine has a sense of benevolent authority over, and responsibility to protect that which is feminine, while the feminine has the sense of submission and the responsibility to strengthen and ennoble that which is masculine.

Because the ramifications of these gender distinctions both in general and in the human realm are too many to discuss here, I will restrict myself to a few loose comments about how masculine and feminine beings—in our case, incarnate human beings—should interact. Of course, I say "should" since, as with all things, a person can either treat gender justly ("treat it correctly or as God designed it") or unjustly ("treat it incorrectly or against God's design"). Thus, when a woman acts justly in respect to her femininity, she can be said to have acted "womanly" and to have started down the path of the feminine virtue of "womanliness" (for want of a better word), and when a man acts justly or correctly in respect to his masculinity, he can be said to have acted "manly" and to have started down the path of the masculine virtue of "manliness." This is probably what Gilmore means when he says all world cultures, save for those from Tahiti and Semai, see "masculinity as a prize to be grasped."[35]

Does this mean that if a man does not act masculine he is no longer a man? No; gender is an essential property not an accidental one, and neither of these are to be confused with virtue. Commodus is a *man* even though he enslaves and abuses women ("You *will* love me" he tells his sister). Commodus is a *man* but is a bad one for taking away a woman's freedom rather than preserving it ("I have been living in a prison of fear everyday because of him," his sister confesses). Commodus is a *man* but does not act in keeping with his true nature as a masculine spirit—not acting with the virtue of manliness—and so his father says ironically of him, "So much for the glory of Rome."

Thus, in general, and all things being equal (a key qualification in all moral deliberation), men can flourish as men insofar as they have a sense of benevolent responsibility toward women—whether women are present or not. A man, of course, does not have to be married to show chivalry to a woman: Maximus's five-year old son could hold the door open (if he could) for his mother, and thereby demonstrate his budding masculinity through his manly gesture; his (hypothetical) five-year old daughter, of course, could do the same, and it would be polite and nice, but it would have no effect on her *femininity* per se, which is to "nurture strength and leadership in men."

But let us consider the case of the married man Maximus. He has his wife's picture on his armor (which he wears everywhere); he prays for her protection; he knows precisely how long he has been away from her ("two years, two hundred and sixty four days and this morning"); he implores Quintus, "Promise me you'll look after my family"; and he has, in the words of Scott, a "spiritual premonition" that his wife and son are in danger and so starts to ride hard to them even when "a hundred miles off."[36] Now let us imagine an earlier, hypothetical time, when Maximus was walking with his wife down the street and they were attacked by a robber. We know Maximus would put himself between his wife and the robber and, in desiring to protect his wife, would flourish in his masculinity. He would act with manly virtue. But what if Maximus's wife were to put herself between Maximus and the robber? It goes without saying that she would flourish in respect to the virtues of courage and love, but I do not think she would flourish in respect to her *femininity* and womanly virtue. Of course, if Maximus had a war injury and could not fight and his wife were a skilled fighter, it might be better for her to *act*; yet even so, Maximus could, for the most part, still be manly insofar as he *wished* he could be the one to act, and his wife could still, for the most part, keep herself womanly insofar as she *wished* it were her husband acting.[37] This is to say that intention is at the root of all the virtues, including the virtues of manliness and womanliness.

Let us go further. Suppose it were two men or two women being robbed. In these cases, gender is not really a factor: a man can still demonstrate his masculinity and be manly by following or protecting other men, and a woman can still demonstrate her femininity and be womanly by strengthening or leading other women. Maximus would not necessarily be more manly if he were to refuse to follow Emperor Marcus Aurelius, for example. Sometimes we too hastily assume that "bravery" or "leadership in general" are equivalent to "manliness," but this is a serious mistake: bravery and leadership in general are not completely linked to one gender. The masculine and manly actions have to do with "protecting and leading the *feminine*" and femininity and womanly actions have to do with "nurturing strength and leadership in the *masculine*." Properly speaking, Maximus is not manly because he leads other men, but rather because he leads his wife and family. This type of distinction is, in my mind, part of what makes Scott such a brilliant director: he knows that strength, for instance, is not equivalent to manliness. Thus, he can both delight in the "strength" of Lucilla (who is strong for her son),[38] and yet have her say, when she is put in a position where she can receive genuine masculine protection—Maximus's—"I'm tired of being strong."

Healthy gender relationships, whether in everyday interactions, dating, marriage, and so on, depend on keeping an eye on how the masculine and feminine can flourish therein. In situations where a woman, for example, has *personal and direct authority over a man*, the woman *qua* woman and the man *qua* man will likely not flourish. Female drill sergeants are a case in point. Mothers, of course, will be in this dominant relationship with their young sons, but even there, a mother ought to take care to help her son flourish in his masculinity, perhaps by letting him open the door for her, for example. That being said, the types of jobs that males and females pursue as well as how they pursue these jobs are important considerations both in practice and in theory. Let us consider a final example. In one scene, Marcus Aurelius remarks that his daughter Lucilla would make "a fine Caesar" if she were a man. But would she? Well, obviously many good things could come from this: perhaps she would not waste as many lives on wars or gladiatorial games, for example, and she certainly would be in a better position to protect her son from her brother. On the other hand, since those *directly* below her authority—the senators—would all be men, neither she nor the senators would flourish in respect to their genders in that relationship. They could, of course, try to be chivalrous toward her in small things, and she, of course, would be feminine in receiving these gestures, but on the whole, this situation is not ideal in respect to gender. Nevertheless, what is ideal is not always what is possible, and on the whole, Lucilla would probably have made a much better emperor than Commodus.

MARRIAGE IN HEAVEN

Like *Gladiator*, this chapter's trajectory has been an epic odyssey, perhaps taking contemporary readers far from familiar or anticipated shores. But now it is time to come home. All the Christian philosophizing about gender and sex heretofore has been in service to the "spiritual backbone" or "the strong spiritual thread" Scott erected in *Gladiator*, namely the notion that some marriages, which are between gendered beings, continue in "Heaven."[39] This notion, as I stated earlier, is ridiculous to many, including a Stoic like the historical Marcus Aurelius, who in his *Meditations* remarks, "In a short time, you will no longer be anything or anywhere."[40] Indeed, in view of the living religions, it is a notion that is almost exclusively discussed by Christianity, whose language Scott appropriates in his commentary.

So where has Scott's vision and my argument taken us? To begin with, I argued that our souls may be essentially gendered, which is to say that we, "like the angels," will continue to be gendered in the afterlife. Connected with this supposition, I assumed that a husband and wife would recognize each other in Heaven since a person *is* his or her soul, which, as I have said, contains all the properties essential to personal identity. Additionally, Jesus's statement that "[the redeemed] will neither marry nor be given in marriage" is not an impediment since we can easily agree that while there might be no *new* marriages in Heaven (and is this for a short time or all-time?), He does not deny that some marriages might *continue* from this life to the next. To be sure, the biological aspect of the marriage relationship will be transformed (probably to a higher type of biology *qua* the new body), but I do not see why the rest would be so different.

Of course, some, like Danish philosopher Søren Kierkegaard, have suggested that in Heaven we will love all people equally and therefore all relationships of preference and intimacy will be done away with.[41] I find this dubious. A general moral principle that God, through nature, reveals to us is that all things being equal, we should prefer kin and those closest to ourselves over others. For example, if Maximus had only one indivisible unit of food and had two women in front of himself who were identical to each other in every way except that one had the property of "being his wife," then it would be *just* for him to give the food to his wife and *unjust* to give it to the other woman. And because *agape* love perfects justice rather than doing away with it, I conclude that every husband ought to think likewise. This would *not* be emotional weakness on Maximus's part but rather clear moral reasoning. Yet here is the point: since general moral principles are not arbitrary creations but rather flow from God's nature as the Righteous and Good (see Michael Garcia's chapter in this book), the moral principle that commands us to, all things being equal, prefer kin to others will almost certainly still be true in the next life.

All of this, coupled with the fact that we will almost certainly carry with us our memories of this life (purified by greater knowledge, to be sure) and the confidence that marriage is a good thing, makes my argument look something like this in summary:

We will likely be gendered in the next life.

If married, a person will likely remember the fact that he or she was married.

We will still have the moral duty to love those closest to ourselves in the next life.

Marriage is a good thing, since God designed it.

God would likely not do away with any good thing, but would rather redeem or perfect it.

Therefore, it seems likely that some marriages will continue to endure in the next life.

Of course, marriages that are legitimately dissolved here would also be so in Heaven (or, more precisely, the "New Earth"), and multiple marriages now would likely, as Jesus pointed out, make the continuation of these in the next life impossible. Perhaps this is why the Bible seems so harsh on divorce and only half-heartedly allows for remarriage. And perhaps something like this is at the root as to why both the ancient Romans praised Marcus Aurelius's mother as "faithful" for not remarrying after her husband died,[42] and the not-so-ancient Russell Crowe stated, somewhat curiously, that it would have been "immoral" for the widower Maximus to take Lucilla to his bed.[43]

And so I conclude with a poetic image from Roman polytheism: while a single man or woman might be like a single star in the heavens called God (alone, but never wholly alone), a married couple would be like a constellation therein. Truly, as Maximus puts it, "What we do in life echoes in eternity."

NOTES

1. Douglas Wick, "Documentary," *Gladiator: Extended Edition*, disc 2, directed by Ridley Scott (2000; Universal City, CA: Dreamworks, 2005), DVD.

2. William Nicholson, "Documentary," *Gladiator: Extended Edition*, disc 2, directed by Ridley Scott (2000; Universal City, CA: Dreamworks, 2005), DVD.

3. Ridley Scott, "Documentary," *Gladiator: Extended Edition*, disc 2, directed by Ridley Scott (2000; Universal City, CA: Dreamworks, 2005), DVD. Scott is no stranger to using Christian imagery to lend gravitas to his films. For example, in *Blade Runner*, he adds to Philip K. Dick's *Do Androids Dream of Electric Sheep?* the entire Christ-on-the-cross scene, where Roy Batty pierces his own hand with a nail, releases a white dove into the air, and, with his dying breath, saves Deckard's life. In *Prometheus*, protagonist Elizabeth Shaw insists on wearing her cross necklace, a symbol for faith that is compatible with science and a reminder of her late father, a missionary.

4. Of the major monotheistic religions, only Christianity really discusses the notion of marriage in Heaven. Judaism, for example, does not have any clear position on whether there is a Heaven or the nature of it if there were such a place. Islam, of course, is quite famous for the claim that its (male) martyrs will enjoy seventy-two virgins in Paradise, though I have never met an Islamic scholar who actually took this literally (if, for no other reason, than the fact that such a Paradise would likely be Hell for those virgins!).

5. Matthew 12:25.

6. Duns Scotus, *Ordinatio* pt. 1, d. 8, q. 4, n. 17.

7. John Cooper, *Our Father in Heaven: Christian Faith and Inclusive Language for God* (Grand Rapids, MI: Baker Books, 1998), 284.

8. C. S. Lewis, *Perelandra*, in *The Cosmic Trilogy* by C. S. Lewis, 145-348 (London: Pan Books, 1990), 327-328.

9. Mary Daly, "After the Death of God the Father: Women's Liberation and the Transformation of Christian Consciousness," in *Woman Spirit Rising: A Feminist Reader in Religion*, ed. Carol Christ and Judith Plaskow, 53-62 (San Francisco: HarperSanFrancisco, 1992), 59.

10. Cf. "Suppose the reformer stops saying that a good woman may be like God and begins saying that God is like a good woman. Suppose he says that we might just as well pray to 'Our Mother which art in Heaven' as to 'Our Father.' Suppose he suggests that the Incarnation might just as well have taken a female as a male form, and the Second Person of the Trinity be as well called the Daughter as the Son. Suppose, finally, that the mystical marriage were reversed, that the Church were the Bridegroom and Christ the Bride. Now it is surely the case that if all these supposals were ever carried into effect we should be embarked on a different religion. Goddesses have, of course, been worshipped: many religions have had priestesses. But they are religions quite different in character from Christianity. Common sense, disregarding the discomfort, or even the horror, which the idea of turning all our theological language into the feminine gender arouses in most Christians, will ask 'Why not?' Since God is in fact not a biological being and has no sex, what can it matter whether we say *He* or *She, Father* or *Mother, Son* or *Daughter*? But Christians think that God Himself has taught us how to speak of Him. To say that it does not matter is to say either that all the masculine imagery is not inspired, is merely human in origin, or else that, though inspired, it is quite arbitrary and unessential. And this is surely intolerable: or, if tolerable, it is an argument not in favour of Christian priestesses but against Christianity. It is also surely based on a shallow view of imagery." C. S. Lewis, "Priestesses in the Church?" in *C. S. Lewis: Essay Collection and Other Short Pieces*, ed. Lesley Walmsley, 399-402 (London: HarperCollins, 2000), 400-401.

11. In keeping with the spirit of *Gladiator*, it is worth pointing out that the Greco-Roman religions that depict Zeus and others as switching genders seem, upon close analysis, to insist that this "switching" is actually only "disguising," where disguises are to be abandoned once the undercover task (such as sneaking past Hera's careful eye) is accomplished. Certainly Zeus, despite his shape-shifting, has never been called, or sought the title "the King-Queen of the Gods." See Ovid *Metamorphoses* II. 405-531.

12. 1 Timothy 5:21.

13. Gary Habermas and J. P. Moreland, *Beyond Death: Exploring the Evidence for Immortality* (Eugene, OR: Wipf & Stock, 1998), 157.

14. This is just one example of many, but in Matthew 25:41 we read, "*hetoimasmenon to Diabolo kai tois angelois autou*" ("having prepared for the Devil and *his* angels"). The word "Devil" (*Diabolo*) is masculine in the Greek and so is the possessive pronoun "his" (*authou*). The chauvinistic attitudes of some in the Middle Ages prompted a few, like Michelangelo, to depict the Devil as feminine, and this tradition has trickled down to our modern age where we can still see, for example, Mel Gibson envisioning Satan in this way in his excellent (but imprecise) movie *The Passion of the Christ* (2004).

15. Many agree with me here, including John Frame, "Men and Women in the Image of God," in *Recovering Biblical Manhood and Woman*, ed. John Piper and Wayne Grudem, 225-232 (Wheaton, IL: Crossway, 1991), 232.

16. For a defense of this claim, see J. P. Moreland and Scott Rae, *Body & Soul: Human Nature & the Crisis in Ethics* (Downers Grove, IL: IVP Academic, 2000), 17-47.

17. Habermas and Moreland, *Beyond Death*, 162.

18. 1 Samuel 28:11-15, Matthew 17:1-13, John 20:25-27, and Revelation 11:1-12.

19. For support that our gender is an essential property or aspect of our enduring essence, see C. S. Lewis, *Miracles* (New York: Macmillan, 1947), 165-166; John Gilmore, *Probing Heaven* (Grand Rapids, MI: Baker, 1989), 80-90.

20. Andrew Tolson, *The Limits of Masculinity: Male Identity and the Liberated Woman* (New York: Harper and Row, 1977), 56.

21. Thomas Gregor, *Anxious Pleasures: The Sexual Life of an Amazonian People* (Chicago: University of Chicago Press, 1985), 209.

22. Walter Lonner, "The Search for Psychological Universals," in *Handbook of Cross-Cultural Psychology*, ed. Harry Triandis and William Lambert, 143-204 (Boston: Allyn and Bacon, 1980), 143.

23. John Williams and Deborah Best, *Measuring Sex Stereotypes: A Thirty-Nation Study* (Beverly Hills, CA: Sage, 1982), 30.

24. David Gilmore, *Manhood in the Making: Cultural Concepts of Masculinity* (New Haven: Yale University Press, 1990), 11.

25. Thomas Aquinas, *Summa Theologica* pt. 1, q. 76, art. 6-8.

26. What can we say about those with an ambiguous sex—the hermaphrodites, the transgendered, or those that appear both male and female? There are too many complexities to address any in depth here, but orthodox Christianity has always maintained that because of the falls (the angelic fall and the human fall), nature, including human bodies, has been damaged, though not all in the same way nor to the same degree. Diseases, disabilities, and physical death (to name a few) are probably effects of these falls. If this is so, why would we be surprised that occasionally there would be sexual irregularities? These would not be indicators that all is well, but rather that these human bodies are "broken" and need fixing, an evocative if problematic suggestion.

27. Gaya Aranoff and Jennifer Bell, "Endocrinology and Growth in Children and Adolescents," in *Principles of Gender-Specific Medicine*, ed. Marianne Legato (New York: Academic Press, 2004), 12.

28. Leonard Sax, *Why Gender Matters* (New York: Broadway, 2005), 14-15. See Arthur Arnold and Paul Burgoyne, "Are XX and XY Brain Cells Intrinsically Different?" *Trends in Endocrinology and Metabolism* 15 (2004): 6-11.

29. Sax, *Why Gender Matters*, 32.

30. I do not have room here to address the complexities of the animal kingdom, though typically Christianity agrees with many polytheistic and shamanistic systems in maintaining that animals have souls, albeit non-rational, mortal souls. If this is the case, then it seems possible that their souls or substance would contain the blueprints for determining the sex of their bodies as well.

31. Consider "Now there was a day when *the sons of God* came to present themselves before the Lord, Satan also came among them" (Job 1:6); "Again there was a day when *the sons of God* came to present themselves before the Lord, and Satan came among them to present himself before the Lord" (Job 2:1); and "Where were you when the morning stars sang together, and all *the sons of God* shouted for joy?" (Job 38:7). Emphasis added.

32. Robert Conant, *The Virility of Christ* (Chicago: n. p., 1915), 117.

33. John Piper, "A Vision of Biblical Complementarity," in *Recovering Biblical Manhood and Womanhood*, ed. John Piper and Wayne Grudem, 31-59 (Wheaton, IL: Crossway, 1991), 35-36.

34. For the sake of space and immediate relevance, I have left out any discussion of sexual orientation and, by extension, gay marriage, though I think these topics very important, and would have loved to say more about Proximo's "queer giraffes"!

35. Gilmore, *Manhood*, 14.

36. Scott, "Director Commentary."

37. Because neither the size nor the health of a man's muscles is essential to him being manly or not, it is worth noting some interesting new research. It has been shown that a man who is in an intimate physical relationship with a woman experiences a decrease in his testosterone. Does this make him less a man and thus contradict what I have just argued? Precisely the opposite. Masculinity is about protecting the feminine, not about who has got the largest sex drive. On the whole, women are better protected by a man whose sex drive has decreased

somewhat. Men with a slightly lower sex drive may be less likely to cheat on their wives, and thus may be more likely to remain faithful, protect, and provide. Of course, testosterone remains a biological factor and nothing more. A man with decreased testosterone might fail to act manly and vice versa. But dispositions do matter, and the ones that God has given us are for the purpose of upholding His good design (in this case, His good design for the sexes). Micah Toub, "Bye-bye, Dear Testosterone," *The Globe and Mail*, September 30, 2011.

38. Scott, "Director Commentary." Scott loves directing strong women who play strong roles; this, he says, goes back to his childhood, where his mother did not put up with any of his nonsense. See Ridley Scott, "Charlize Theron on Playing the Heavy," *Cineplex Magazine*, 13, no. 6 (June 2012): 42.

39. Scott, "Director Commentary."

40. Marcus Aurelius, *Meditations* VI.37.

41. Søren Kierkegaard, *Works of Love*, trans. Howard Hong and Edna Hong (Princeton, NJ: Princeton University Press, 1995), 53.

42. Anthony Birley, *Marcus Aurelius: A Biography* (New York: Routledge, 2001), 31.

43. Russell Crowe, "Director Commentary," *Gladiator: Extended Edition*, disc 2, directed by Ridley Scott (2000; Universal City, CA: Dreamworks, 2005), DVD.

REFERENCES

Aquinas, Thomas. *Summa Theologica*.

Aranoff, Gaya, and Jennifer Bell. "Endocrinology and Growth in Children and Adolescents." In *Principles of Gender-Specific Medicine*, edited by Marianne Legato. New York: Academic Press, 2004.

Arnold, Arthur, and Paul Burgoyne. "Are XX and XY Brain Cells Intrinsically Different?" *Trends in Endocrinology and Metabolism* 15 (2004): 6-11.

Aurelius, Marcus. *Meditations*.

Birley, Anthony. *Marcus Aurelius: A Biography*. New York: Routledge, 2001.

Conant, Robert. *The Virility of Christ*. Chicago: n.p., 1915.

Cooper, John. *Our Father in Heaven: Christian Faith and Inclusive Language for God*. Grand Rapids, MI: Baker Books, 1998.

Daly, Mary. "After the Death of God the Father: Women's Liberation and the Transformation of Christian Consciousness." In *Woman Spirit Rising: A Feminist Reader in Religion*, edited by Carol Christ and Judith Plaskow, 53-62. San Francisco: HarperSanFrancisco, 1992.

Frame, John. "Men and Women in the Image of God." In *Recovering Biblical Manhood and Woman*, edited by John Piper and Wayne Grudem, 225-232. Wheaton, IL: Crossway, 1991.

Gilmore, David. *Manhood in the Making: Cultural Concepts of Masculinity*. New Haven, CT: Yale University Press, 1990.

Gilmore, John. *Probing Heaven*. Grand Rapids, MI: Baker, 1989.

Gladiator: Extended Edition. DVD. Directed by Ridley Scott. 2000; Universal City, CA: Dreamworks, 2005.

Gregor, Thomas. *Anxious Pleasures: The Sexual Life of an Amazonian People*. Chicago: University of Chicago Press, 1985.

Habermas, Gary, and J. P. Moreland. *Beyond Death: Exploring the Evidence for Immortality*. Eugene, OR: Wipf & Stock, 1998.

Kierkegaard, Søren. *Works of Love*, translated by Howard Hong and Edna Hong. Princeton: Princeton University Press, 1995.

Lewis, C. S. *Miracles*. New York: Macmillan, 1947.

———. *Perelandra*. In *The Cosmic Trilogy* by C. S. Lewis, 145-348. London: Pan Books, 1990.

———. "Priestesses in the Church?" In *C. S. Lewis: Essay Collection & Other Short Pieces*, edited by Lesley Walmsley, 399-402. London: HarperCollins, 2000.

Lonner, Walter. "The Search for Psychological Universals." In *Handbook of Cross-Cultural Psychology*, edited by Harry Triandis and William Lambert, 143-204. Boston: Allyn and Bacon, 1980.

Moreland, J. P., and Scott Rae. *Body & Soul: Human Nature & the Crisis in Ethics*. Downers Grove, IL: IVP Academic, 2000.

Ovid. *Metamorphoses*.

Piper, John. "A Vision of Biblical Complementarity." In *Recovering Biblical Manhood and Womanhood*, edited by John Piper and Wayne Grudem, 31-59. Wheaton, IL: Crossway, 1991.

Sax, Leonard. *Why Gender Matters*. New York: Broadway, 2005.

Scott, Ridley. "Charlize Theron on Playing the Heavy." *Cineplex Magazine*, 13, no. 6 (June 2012).

Scotus, Duns. *Ordinatio*.

Tolson, Andrew. *The Limits of Masculinity: Male Identity and the Liberated Woman*. New York: Harper and Row, 1977.

Toub, Micah. "Bye-bye, Dear Testosterone." *The Globe and Mail*, September 30, 2011.

Williams, John, and Deborah Best. *Measuring Sex Stereotypes: A Thirty-Nation Study*. Beverly Hills, CA: Sage, 1982.

Index

About the Contributors

Elizabeth Abele is associate professor of English at SUNY Nassau Community College and Executive Director of the Northeast Modern Language Association (NEMLA). Her essays on American culture and masculinity have appeared in *Images, American Studies, Journal of American and Comparative Cultures, College Literature,* and *Scope,* and in the edited anthologies *Best American Movie Writing 1999* and *Critical Approaches to the Films of M. Night Shyamalan.*

Adam Barkman is associate professor of philosophy at Redeemer University College. He is the author of *C. S. Lewis and Philosophy as a Way of Life* (2009), *Through Common Things: Philosophical Reflections on Global Popular Culture* (2010), and *Above All Things: Essays on Christian Ethics and Popular Culture* (2011), and is the co-editor of *Manga and Philosophy* (2010) and *The Philosophy of Ang Lee* (2013).

Ashley Barkman is a part-time lecturer of philosophy and English at Redeemer University College and is the author of several articles on philosophy and pop culture including chapters in *30 Rock and Philosophy* (2010), *The Walking Dead and Philosophy* (2012), and *The Big Bang Theory and Philosophy* (2012).

Fernando Gabriel Pagnoni Berns is a graduate teaching assistant in Estética del Cine y Teorías Cinematográficas (Film Aesthetics and Cinema Theory) at Universidad de Buenos Aires, Facultad de Filosofía y Letras. He is a member of the research groups Investea (theatre) and ArtKiné (cinema) and has published articles on Argentinian and international cinema and drama in the following publications: *Imagofagia, Cinedocumental, Telóndefondo.org, Ol3media,* and *Anagnórisis: Theatrical Research Magazine.*

Dan Dinello is professor emeritus at Columbia College Chicago. He wrote two books while gestating an alien: *Technophobia! Science Fiction Visions of Posthuman Technology* (2007) and *Finding Fela: My Strange Journey to Meet the AfroBeat King* (2011). He also contributed chapters to *Anime and Philosophy* (2010) and *The Rolling Stones and Philosophy* (2011). A Directors Guild of America (DGA) member, Dan directed episodes of the television series *Strangers with Candy* and runs the website *shockproductions.com.*

Aviva Dove-Viebahn is an honors faculty fellow in the Barrett Honors College at Arizona State University, as well as the website content manager and an ex-officio member of the Board of Directors of the Society for Cinema and Media Studies. She has a PhD in Visual and Cultural Studies, and her dissertation explored the role of spectatorship and community formation at the intersection of art and television. She has published essays in the anthology *Queer Popular Culture* (2007) and the journals *Concentric: Literary and Cultural Studies*, *Invisible Culture*, and *Women's Studies: An Interdisciplinary Journal*. A co-editor for the journal *Invisible Culture*'s special issue "The Future of the Archive / The Archive of the Future," she has written articles on film, television, and new media for *Ms.* magazine and *The New Republic.*

Matthew Freeman is a doctoral candidate at the University of Nottingham. His thesis, "When Worlds Collide: Telling Tales of Superheroes across Comics, Film and Television," explores issues of narrative and adaptation across three distinct media formats. His past research includes an examination of the aesthetics of dreaming as a narrative and philosophical strategy in contemporary science fiction and horror cinema. His future projects include contributions to a forthcoming collection entitled *Being Lois*, which explores the figure of Lois Lane and her significance in popular culture.

Michael Nieto Garcia is assistant professor of literature at Clarkson University in Potsdam, New York. His scholarly work includes publications on Richard Rodriguez, Jorge Luis Borges, and Helena María Viramontes, as well as conference papers on Junot Díaz, Richard Wright, and Vladimir Nabokov. He is the translator of Indonesian author Djenar Maesa Ayu's celebrated collection of short stories, *They Say I'm a Monkey* (2005), and is currently working on a monograph titled *Narratives of the Ethnic Self in American Literature.*

Nancy Kang is assistant professor of multicultural and diaspora literatures at the University of Baltimore. She also served as postdoctoral Faculty Fellow in the Humanities at Syracuse University (2007–2011), affiliated with the Native Studies Program, the Asian & Asian American Studies Interdisciplinary Minor, and the Department of English. Her publications include current or forthcoming articles in *Canadian Literature*, *Women's Studies*, *The*

African American Review, *Callaloo*, *Essays on Canadian Writing*, and various chapters in edited collections.

Basileios Kroustallis is a teaching fellow at Hellenic Open University, Greece. His research focuses on philosophy of mind and perception, philosophy of film, and history of modern philosophy. His publications include essays appearing in *Journal of Mind and Behavior*, *History of Philosophy Quarterly*, *Philosophical Psychology*, *Film-Philosophy*, and *The Philosophy of Ang Lee* (2013).

Greg Littmann is assistant professor at Southern Illinois University, Edwardsville. Among his numerous published works include chapters in *Game of Thrones and Philosophy* (2010), *Sherlock Holmes and Philosophy* (2011), *The Walking Dead and Philosophy* (2012), *Breaking Bad and Philosophy* (2012), and *Doctor Who and Philosophy* (2010). Peer-reviewed articles have appeared in *Philosophical Papers* and *Acta Analytica*, as well as in collections like *The Law of Non-Contradiction: New Philosophical Essays* (republished 2010) and *Introducing Philosophy through Pop Culture: From Socrates to South Park, from Hume to House* (2010).

James Edwin Mahon is associate professor of philosophy and lecturer in philosophy and the law at Washington and Lee University. He is currently lecturer in the Program in Ethics, Politics, and Economics at Yale University, and a visiting researcher at Yale Law School. Forthcoming publications include "Lying for the Sake of the Truth: The Ethics of Deceptive Journalism," in *Contemporary Media Ethics*, "All's Fair in Love and War? Machiavelli and Ang Lee's *Ride With the Devil*," in *The Philosophy of Ang Lee*, and "MacIntyre and the Emotivists," in *What Happened In and To Moral Philosophy in the Twentieth-Century? Celebrating MacIntyre*. As an undergraduate at Trinity College Dublin, he wrote film reviews for *Trinity News* and the *Dublin Event Guide*, and he helped inaugurate the Galway Film Fleadh, the annual Irish film festival now in its twenty-fourth year.

Sydney Palmer is a theologian whose interests include literature, literary criticism, film criticism, depth psychology, and art. Though his publications specialize in theology and exegesis, he has also co-authored a chapter for *The Philosophy of Ang Lee* (2013). He attended Prague's PCFE Film School in August 2007 where he made his first short film, *Found & Lost*. His current research and writing projects include preparing his dissertation for publication, translating the French rabbi-philosopher Marc-Alain Ouaknin's book on the Ten Commandments into English, writing several articles offering close readings of Genesis 2–3, and writing a book that examines the positive and negative feminine elements in *Aliens* and *Star Trek: First Contact*.

Lorna Piatti-Farnell is a lecturer in creative industries in the School of Communication Studies at AUT University (Auckland). She is the author of two books, *Food and Culture in Contemporary American Fiction* (2011) and

Beef: A Global History (2012), and has written numerous articles on the philosophy of food.

Antonio Sanna's main research areas include Victorian literature and culture, Gothic literature, horror films, and postmodern culture. His publications include articles on Henry James's "The Turn of the Screw," Bram Stoker's *Dracula*, H.G. Wells's *The Island of Dr. Moreau*, Bret Sullivan's *Ginger Snaps: Unleashed*, Stephenie Meyer's *The Short Second Life of Bree Tanner*, and Ridley Scott's *Hannibal*, the *Alien* quadrilogy, and the *Harry Potter* films (in *Kinema: A Journal for Film and Audiovisual Media*). He has also contributed to *The Dictionary of Literary Characters* (2010) with entries on Thomas Harris's Hannibal Lecter novels and Edgar Allan Poe's short stories.

Janice Shaw is a contract academic in the School of Arts at the University of New England, Australia, where she lectures in film, media, and children's literature. She has a doctorate in Australian literature and her published articles are on detective fiction, film, and the short story, in particular on the work of Australian writers Frank Moorhouse and Beverley Farmer. She is currently writing on *The Big Bang Theory* and popular culture.

Carl Sobocinski is assistant professor of history in the East Asia International College at Yonsei University, Republic of Korea. His publications include "The Travails of Madagascar," published in *Distant Lands and Diverse Cultures* (2002), "Re-Staging World War II" in *Manga and Philosophy* (2010), and "Horace Allen and Ohio Connections to Early Modern Korea" in *Northwest Ohio Quarterly* (2011).

Silvio Torres-Saillant is professor of English at Syracuse University, where he completed two terms as Director of the Latino-Latin American Studies Program and served as William P. Tolley Distinguished Teaching Professor in the Humanities (2009–2011). He was the founder of the CUNY Dominican Studies Institute, an interdisciplinary research center located at City College, City University of New York. His publications include *An Intellectual History of the Caribbean* (2006), *An Introduction to Dominican Blackness* (1999), and *Caribbean Poetics: Toward an Aesthetic of West Indian Literature* (1997). He serves as associate editor of the journal *Latino Studies* and was one of the senior editors of *The Oxford Encyclopedia of Latinos and Latinas in the United States*.

David Zietsma is assistant professor of history at Redeemer University College. His interests include representations of American identity in film, the role of religion in US foreign relations, and the function of violence in personal and collective identity. He has published in *Diplomatic History*, *Rhetoric & Public Affairs* and in *The Philosophy of Ang Lee* (2013). In addition to courses on the history of the United States, he teaches seminars on film history and cinematic portrayals of the Vietnam War.